Jeffrey Merrick
Michael Sibalis
Editors

Homosexuality in French History and Culture

Homosexuality in French History and Culture has been co-published simultaneously as *Journal of Homosexuality*, Volume 41, Numbers 3/4 2001.

Pre-publication
REVIEWS,
COMMENTARIES,
EVALUATIONS . . .

"FASCINATING. . . . Merrick and Sibalis bring together historians, literary scholars, and political activists from both sides of the Atlantic to examine same-sex sexuality in the past and present."

Bryant T. Ragan, PhD
Associate Professor of History
Fordham University
New York City

More pre-publication
REVIEWS, COMMENTARIES, EVALUATIONS . . .

"A DAZZLING COLLECTION. . . . Nine historians, six literary scholars, and two journalists draw upon manuscript poems and arrest records, criminological treatises and novels, newspapers, and magazines. In a stunning series of interpretations, the bisexual pederasts of the seventeenth century, the effeminate men and the masculine women of the eighteenth and nineteenth centuries, and the late twentieth-century gays are all here."

Randolph Trumbach, PhD
Author, Sex and Gender Revolution
Professor of History, Baruch College and the Graduate Center
City University of New York

"AN INDISPENSIBLE TEXT IN THE HISTORY OF SEXUALITY IN MODERN FRANCE. Scholars and general readers alike will be shown a side of French culture and politics that has too long been hidden from view."

Robert A. Nye, PhD
Professor of History
Oregon State University

"This collection makes available an exciting range of information on French lesbian and gay studies from the sixteenth century to the present. SHOULD BE REQUIRED READING for anybody seeking to understand the varieties of French, and especially Parisian, LGBTQ lives!"

David Higgs, PhD
Professor of History
University of Toronto
Toronto, Ontario, Canada

Harrington Park Press

Homosexuality in French History and Culture

Homosexuality in French History and Culture has been co-published simultaneously as *Journal of Homosexuality,* Volume 41, Numbers 3/4 2001.

The *Journal of Homosexuality* Monographic "Separates"

Below is a list of "separates," which in serials librarianship means a special issue simultaneously published as a special journal issue or double-issue *and* as a "separate" hardbound monograph. (This is a format which we also call a "DocuSerial.")

"Separates" are published because specialized libraries or professionals may wish to purchase a specific thematic issue by itself in a format which can be separately cataloged and shelved, as opposed to purchasing the journal on an on-going basis. Faculty members may also more easily consider a "separate" for classroom adoption.

"Separates" are carefully classified separately with the major book jobbers so that the journal tie-in can be noted on new book order slips to avoid duplicate purchasing.

You may wish to visit Haworth's website at . . .

http://www.HaworthPress.com

. . . to search our online catalog for complete tables of contents of these separates and related publications.

You may also call 1-800-HAWORTH (outside US/Canada: 607-722-5857), or Fax 1-800-895-0582 (outside US/Canada: 607-771-0012), or e-mail at:

getinfo@haworthpressinc.com

Homosexuality in French History and Culture, edited by Jeffrey Merrick and Michael Sibalis (Vol. 41, No. 3/4, 2001). *"Fascinating. . . . Merrick and Sibalis bring together historians, literary scholars, and political activists from both sides of the Atlantic to examine same-sex sexuality in the past and present." (Bryant T. Ragan, PhD, Associate Professor of History, Fordham University, New York City)*

Gay and Lesbian Asia: Culture, Identity, Community, edited by Gerard Sullivan, PhD, and Peter A. Jackson, PhD (Vol. 40, No. 3/4, 2001). *"Superb. . . . Covers a happily wide range of styles . . . will appeal to both students and educated fans." (Gary Morris, Editor/Publisher, Bright Lights Film Journal)*

Queer Asian Cinema: Shadows in the Shade, edited by Andrew Grossman, MA (Vol. 39, No. 3/4, 2000). *"An extremely rich tapestry of detailed ethnographies and state-of-the-art theorizing. . . . Not only is this a landmark record of queer Asia, but it will certainly also be a seminal, contributive challenge to gender and sexuality studies in general." (Dédé Oetomo, PhD, Coordinator of the Indonesian organization GAYa NUSANTRA; Adjunct Reader in Linguistics and Anthropology, School of Social Sciences, Universitas Airlangga)*

Gay Community Survival in the New Millennium, edited by Michael R. Botnick, PhD (cand.) (Vol. 38, No. 4, 2000). *Examines the notion of community from several different perspectives focusing on the imagined, the structural, and the emotive. You will explore a theoretical overview and you will peek into the moral discourses that frame "gay community," the rift between HIV-positive and HIV-negative gay men, and how Israeli gays seek their place in the public sphere.*

***The Ideal Gay Man: The Story of* Der Kreis,** by Hubert Kennedy, PhD (Vol. 38, No. 1/2, 1999). *"Very Profound. . . . Excellent insight into the problems of the early fight for homosexual emancipation in Europe and in the USA. . . . The ideal gay man (high-mindedness, purity, cleanness), as he was imagined by the editor of* Der Kreis, *is delineated by the fascinating quotations out of the published erotic stories." (Wolfgang Breidert, PhD, Academic Director, Institute of Philosophy, University Karlsruhe, Germany)*

Multicultural Queer: Australian Narratives, edited by Peter A. Jackson, PhD, and Gerard Sullivan, PhD (Vol. 36, No. 3/4, 1999). *Shares the way that people from ethnic minorities in Australia (those who are not of Anglo-Celtic background) view homosexuality, their experiences as homosexual men and women, and their feelings about the lesbian and gay community.*

Scandinavian Homosexualities: Essays on Gay and Lesbian Studies, edited by Jan Löfström, PhD (Vol. 35, No. 3/4, 1998). *"Everybody interested in the formation of lesbian and gay identities and their interaction with the sociopolitical can find something to suit their taste in this volume." (Judith Schuyf, PhD, Assistant Professor of Lesbian and Gay Studies, Center for Gay and Lesbian Studies, Utrecht University, The Netherlands)*

Gay and Lesbian Literature Since World War II: History and Memory, edited by Sonya L. Jones, PhD (Vol. 34, No. 3/4, 1998). *"The authors of these essays manage to gracefully incorporate the latest insights of feminist, postmodernist, and queer theory into solidly grounded readings . . . challenging and moving, informed by the passion that prompts both readers and critics into deeper inquiry." (Diane Griffin Growder, PhD, Professor of French and Women's Studies, Cornell College, Mt. Vernon, Iowa)*

Reclaiming the Sacred: The Bible in Gay and Lesbian Culture, edited by Raymond-Jean Frontain, PhD (Vol. 33, No. 3/4, 1997). *"Finely wrought, sharply focused, daring, and always dignified . . . In chapter after chapter, the Bible is shown to be a more sympathetic and humane book in its attitudes toward homosexuality than usually thought and a challenge equally to the straight and gay moral imagination." (Joseph Wittreich, PhD, Distinguished Professor of English, The Graduate School, The City University of New York)*

Activism and Marginalization in the AIDS Crisis, edited by Michael A. Hallett, PhD (Vol. 32, No. 3/4, 1997). *Shows readers how the advent of HIV-disease has brought into question the utility of certain forms of "activism" as they relate to understanding and fighting the social impacts of disease.*

Gays, Lesbians, and Consumer Behavior: Theory, Practice, and Research Issues in Marketing, edited by Daniel L. Wardlow, PhD (Vol. 31, No. 1/2, 1996). *"For those scholars, market researchers, and marketing managers who are considering marketing to the gay and lesbian community, this book should be on required reading list." (Mississippi Voice)*

Gay Men and the Sexual History of the Political Left, edited by Gert Hekma, PhD, Harry Oosterhuis, PhD, and James Steakley, PhD (Vol. 29, No. 2/3/4, 1995). *"Contributors delve into the contours of a long-forgotten history, bringing to light new historical data and fresh insight . . . An excellent account of the tense historical relationship between the political left and gay liberation." (People's Voice)*

Sex, Cells, and Same-Sex Desire: The Biology of Sexual Preference, edited by John P. De Cecco, PhD, and David Allen Parker, MA (Vol. 28, No. 1/2/3/4, 1995). *"A stellar compilation of chapters examining the most important evidence underlying theories on the biological basis of human sexual orientation." (MGW)*

Gay Ethics: Controversies in Outing, Civil Rights, and Sexual Science, edited by Timothy F. Murphy, PhD (Vol. 27, No. 3/4, 1994). *"The contributors bring the traditional tools of ethics and political philosophy to bear in a clear and forceful way on issues surrounding the rights of homosexuals." (David L. Hull, Dressler Professor in the Humanities, Department of Philosophy, Northwestern University)*

Gay and Lesbian Studies in Art History, edited by Whitney Davis, PhD (Vol. 27, No. 1/2, 1994). *"Informed, challenging . . . never dull. . . . Contributors take risks and, within the restrictions of scholarly publishing, find new ways to use materials already available or examine topics never previously explored." (Lambda Book Report)*

Critical Essays: Gay and Lesbian Writers of Color, edited by Emmanuel S. Nelson, PhD (Vol. 26, No. 2/3, 1993). *"A much-needed book, sparkling with stirring perceptions and resonating with depth . . . The anthology not only breaks new ground, it also attempts to heal wounds inflicted by our oppressed pasts." (Lambda)*

Gay Studies from the French Cultures: Voices from France, Belgium, Brazil, Canada, and The Netherlands, edited by Rommel Mendès-Leite, PhD, and Pierre-Olivier de Busscher, PhD (Vol. 25, No. 1/2/3, 1993). *"The first book that allows an English-speaking world to have a comprehensive look at the principal trends in gay studies in France and French-speaking countries." (André Bèjin, PhD, Directeur, de Recherche au Centre National de la Recherche Scientifique (CNRS), Paris)*

If You Seduce a Straight Person, Can You Make Them Gay? Issues in Biological Essentialism versus Social Constructionism in Gay and Lesbian Identities, edited by John P. De Cecco, PhD, and John P. Elia, PhD (cand.) (Vol. 24, No. 3/4, 1993). *"You'll find this alternative view of the age old question to be one that will become the subject of many conversations to come. Thought-provoking to say the least!" (Prime Timers)*

Gay and Lesbian Studies: The Emergence of a Discipline, edited by Henry L. Minton, PhD (Vol. 24, No. 1/2, 1993). *"The volume's essays provide insight into the field's remarkable accomplishments and future goals." (Lambda Book Report)*

Homosexuality in Renaissance and Enlightenment England: Literary Representations in Historical Context, edited by Claude J. Summers, PhD (Vol. 23, No. 1/2, 1992). *"It is remarkable among studies in this field in its depth of scholarship and variety of approaches and is accessible." (Chronique)*

Coming Out of the Classroom Closet: Gay and Lesbian Students, Teachers, and Curricula, edited by Karen M. Harbeck, PhD, JD, Recipient of Lesbian and Gay Educators Award by the American Educational Research Association's Lesbian and Gay Studies Special Interest Group (AREA) (Vol. 22, No. 3/4, 1992). *"Presents recent research about gay and lesbian students and teachers and the school system in which they function." (Contemporary Psychology)*

Homosexuality and Male Bonding in Pre-Nazi Germany: The Youth Movement, the Gay Movement, and Male Bonding Before Hitler's Rise: Original Transcripts from Der Eigene, the First Gay Journal in the World, edited by Harry Oosterhuis, PhD, and Hubert Kennedy, PhD (Vol. 22, No. 1/2, 1992). *"Provide[s] insight into the early gay movement, particularly in its relation to the various political currents in pre-World War II Germany." (Lambda Book Report)*

Gay People, Sex, and the Media, edited by Michelle A. Wolf, PhD, and Alfred P. Kielwasser, MA (Vol. 21, No. 1/2, 1991). *"Altogether, the kind of research anthology which is useful to many disciplines in gay studies. Good stuff!" (Communique)*

Gay Midlife and Maturity: Crises, Opportunities, and Fulfillment, edited by John Alan Lee, PhD (Vol. 20, No. 3/4, 1991). *"The insight into gay aging is amazing, accurate, and much-needed. . . . A real contribution to the older gay community." (Prime Timers)*

Male Intergenerational Intimacy: Historical, Socio-Psychological, and Legal Perspectives, edited by Theo G. M. Sandfort, PhD, Edward Brongersma, JD, and A. X. van Naerssen, PhD (Vol. 20, No. 1/2, 1991). *"The most important book on the subject since Tom O'Carroll's 1980 Paedophilia: The Radical Case." (The North America Man/Boy Love Association Bulletin, May 1991)*

Love Letters Between a Certain Late Nobleman and the Famous Mr. Wilson, edited by Michael S. Kimmel, PhD (Vol. 19, No. 2, 1990). *"An intriguing book about homosexuality in 18th Century England. Many details of the period, such as meeting places, coded language, and 'camping' are all covered in the book. If you're a history buff, you'll enjoy this one." (Prime Timers)*

Homosexuality and Religion, edited by Richard Hasbany, PhD (Vol. 18, No. 3/4, 1990). *"A welcome resource that provides historical and contemporary views on many issues involving religious life and homosexuality." (Journal of Sex education and Therapy)*

Homosexuality and the Family, edited by Frederick W. Bozett, PhD (Vol. 18, No. 1/2, 1989). *"Enlightening and answers a host of questions about the effects of homosexuality upon family members and the family as a unit." (Ambush Magazine)*

Gay and Lesbian Youth, edited by Gilbert Herdt, PhD (Vol. 17, No. 1/2/3/4, 1989). *"Provides a much-needed compilation of research dealing with homosexuality and adolescents." (GLTF Newsletter)*

Lesbians Over 60 Speak for Themselves, edited by Monika Kehoe, PhD (Vol. 16, No. 3/4, 1989). *"A pioneering book examining the social, economical, physical, sexual, and emotional lives of aging lesbians." (Feminist Bookstore News)*

Monographs "Separates" list continued at the back

Homosexuality in French History and Culture

Jeffrey Merrick
Michael Sibalis
Editors

Homosexuality in French History and Culture has been co-published simultaneously as *Journal of Homosexuality*, Volume 41, Numbers 3/4 2001.

Harrington Park Press
An Imprint of
The Haworth Press, Inc.
New York • London • Oxford

Homosexuality in French History and Culture has been co-published simultaneously as *Journal of Homosexuality*, Volume 41, Numbers 3/4 2001.

Cover design by Marylouise Doyle.

Library of Congress Cataloging-in-Publication Data

Homosexuality in French history and culture / Jeffrey Merrick, Michael Sibalis, editors.

p. cm.

"Homosexuality in French history and culture has been co-published simultaneously as Journal of homosexuality, volume 41, numbers 3/4 2001."

Includes bibliographical references and index.

ISBN 1-56023-262-5 (alk. paper) – ISBN 1-56023-263-3 (alk. paper)

1. Homosexuality–France–History. 2. Homosexuality in literature–History. 3. French literature–History and criticism. I. Merrick, Jeffrey. II. Sibalis, Michael. III. Journal of homosexuality.

HQ76.3.F8 H647 2001
306.76′6′0944–dc21

2001039985

Indexing, Abstracting & Website/Internet Coverage

This section provides you with a list of major indexing & abstracting services. That is to say, each service began covering this periodical during the year noted in the right column. Most Websites which are listed below have indicated that they will either post, disseminate, compile, archive, cite or alert their own Website users with research-based content from this work. (This list is as current as the copyright date of this publication.)

Abstracting, Website/Indexing Coverage	Year When Coverage Began
• *Abstracts in Anthropology*	**2001**
• *Academic Abstracts/CD-ROM*	**1993**
• *Academic ASAP <www.galegroup.com>*	**2000**
• *Academic Search: Database of 2,000 selected academic serials, updated monthly*	**1995**
• *Academic Search Elite (EBSCO)*	**1996**
• *Alternative Press Index <www.nisc.com>*	**1996**
• *Applied Social Sciences Index & Abstracts (ASSIA) (Online: ASSI via Data-Star) (CD-Rom: ASSIA Plus) <www.bowker-saur.co.uk>*	**1987**
• *ATLA Religion Database (published by the American Theological Library Association) <ww.atla.com>*	**2001**
• *Book Review Index*	**1996**
• *BUBL Information Service, an Internet-based Information Service for the UK higher education community <http://bubl.ac.uk/>*	**1995**
• *Cambridge Scientific Abstracts <www.csa.com>*	**1993**

(continued)

- *CNPIEC Reference Guide: Chinese National Directory of Foreign Periodicals* 1995
- *Contemporary Women's Issues* 1998
- *Criminal Justice Abstracts* 1982
- *Current Contents/Social & Behavioral Sciences <www.isinet.com>* 1985
- *EMBASE/Excerpta Medica Secondary Publishing Division <www.elsevier.nl>* 1986
- *e-psyche, LLC <www.e-psyche.net>* 2001
- *Expanded Academic ASAP <www.galegroup.com>* 2000
- *Expanded Academic Index* 1992
- *Family & Society Studies Worldwide <www.nisc.com>* 1996
- *Family Violence & Sexual Assault Bulletin* 1992
- *FINDEX <www.publist.com>* 1999
- *Gay & Lesbian Abstracts <www.nisc.com>* 1999
- *GenderWatch <www.slinfo.com>* 1999
- *Higher Education Abstracts, providing the latest in research and theory in more than 140 major topics* 1997
- *HOMODOK/"Relevant" Bibliographic Database, Documentation Centre for Gay & Lesbian Studies, University of Amsterdam* 1995
- *IBZ International Bibliography of Periodical Literature* 1996
- *IGLSS Abstracts <www.iglss.org>* 2000
- *Index Guide to College Journal (core list compiled by integrating 48 indexes frequently used to support undergraduate programs in small to medium sized libraries)* 1999
- *Index Medicus* 1992
- *Index to Periodical Articles Related to Law* 1986
- *InfoTrac Custom <www.galegroup.com>* 2000
- *Leeds Medical Information* 1994
- *LEGAL TRAC on INFOTRAC web <www.galegroup.com>* 2000

(continued)

- *MasterFILE: Updated database from EBSCO Publishing* **1995**
- *MEDLINE (National Library of Medicine) <www.nlm.nih.gov>* **2001**
- *MLA International Bibliography (available in print, on CD-ROM, and the Internet) <www.mla.org>* **1995**
- *National Library of Medicine "Abstracts Section"* **1999**
- *OCLC Public Affairs Information Service <www.pais.org>* **1982**
- *OmniFile Full Text: Mega Edition (only available electronically) <www.hwwilson.com>* **2001**
- *PASCAL, c/o Institute de L'Information Scientifique et Technique <www.inist.fr>* **1986**
- *Periodical Abstracts, Research I (general and basic reference indexing and abstracting database from University Micro-films International (UMI))* **1993**
- *Periodical Abstracts, Research II (broad coverage indexing and abstracting database from University Microfilms International (UMI))* **1993**
- *PlanetOut "Internet site for key Gay/Lesbian Information" <www.planetout.com/>* **1999**
- *Psychology Today* **1999**
- *RESEARCH ALERT/ISI Alerting Services <www.isinet.com>* **1985**
- *Sage Family Studies Abstracts (SFSA)* **1986**
- *Social Sciences Abstracts & Social Sciences Full Text Indexes <www.hwwilson.com>* **2001**
- *Social Sciences Citation Index <www.isinet.com>* **1985**
- *Social Sciences Full Text (only available electronically) <www.hwwwilson.com>* **2001**
- *Social Sciences Index (from Volume 1 and continuing) <www.hwwilson.com>* **1991**
- *Social Science Source: Coverage of 400 journals in the social sciences area; updated monthly* **1995**
- *Social Scisearch <www.isinet.com>* **1985**
- *Social Services Abstracts <www.csa.com>* **1982**
- *Social Work Abstracts* **1994**
- *Sociological Abstracts (SA) <www.csa.com>* **1982**
- *Studies on Women Abstracts* **1987**
- *Violence and Abuse Abstracts: A Review of Current Literature on Interpersonal Violence (VAA)* **1995**

Special Bibliographic Notes related to special journal issues (separates) and indexing/abstracting:

- indexing/abstracting services in this list will also cover material in any "separate" that is co-published simultaneously with Haworth's special thematic journal issue or DocuSerial. Indexing/abstracting usually covers material at the article/chapter level.
- monographic co-editions are intended for either non-subscribers or libraries which intend to purchase a second copy for their circulating collections.
- monographic co-editions are reported to all jobbers/wholesalers/approval plans. The source journal is listed as the "series" to assist the prevention of duplicate purchasing in the same manner utilized for books-in-series.
- to facilitate user/access services all indexing/abstracting services are encouraged to utilize the co-indexing entry note indicated at the bottom of the first page of each article/chapter/contribution.
- this is intended to assist a library user of any reference tool (whether print, electronic, online, or CD-ROM) to locate the monographic version if the library has purchased this version but not a subscription to the source journal.
- individual articles/chapters in any Haworth publication are also available through the Haworth Document Delivery Service (HDDS).

Homosexuality in French History and Culture

CONTENTS

ABOUT THE EDITORS

Jeffrey Merrick, PhD, is Professor of History at the University of Wisconsin at Milwaukee. He has published articles about same-sex relations in eighteenth-century France and co-edited (with Bryant T. Ragan, Jr.) *Homosexuality in Early Modern France: A Documentary Collection.* He has served as coordinator of the Committee on Lesbian and Gay History, affiliated with the American Historical Association, and as coordinator of the Lesbian, Gay, Bisexual, and Transgender Studies certificate program at UWM.

Michael Sibalis, PhD, teaches modern European and French history at Wilfrid Laurier University in Waterloo, Ontario, Canada. He has published articles and essays on the French labor movement in the early nineteenth century, the police state of Napoleon I (1799-1815), and the history of French homosexuality. He is currently working on a book on the gay male community of Paris since 1700.

∞ ALL HARRINGTON PARK PRESS BOOKS
AND JOURNALS ARE PRINTED
ON CERTIFIED ACID-FREE PAPER

In memory of Pierre Hahn (1936-1981) and Michel Rey (1953-1993),
pioneers in the study of gay history in France

Introduction

Jeffrey Merrick
Michael Sibalis

In an interview published in 1997, the French journalist Didier Eribon declared that "the history of French homosexuality . . . has not yet been studied." He should have known (and indeed did know) better, but, as is so often true in France, an apparently objective and authoritative statement (which Eribon, to his credit, later revised) had a political rather than a strictly scholarly purpose.[1] On the eve of a colloquium on gay and lesbian studies at the Centre Pompidou in Paris, Eribon wanted to stress the originality of what the invited speakers would say. And so, without much ado, he dismissed the work of a generation of French researchers: Marie-Jo Bonnet, Claude Courouve, "Marc Daniel" (pseudonym of a well-known archivist), Jacques Girard, Christian Gury, Pierre Hahn, Claudie Lesellier, Maurice Lever, Frédéric Martel, and Michel Rey, to say nothing of the many "Anglo-Saxons" (as the French call anyone whose native language is English) then laboring in the field of French lesbian and gay history. Their articles and books are cited extensively in this collection, which constitutes both a tribute to and continuation of their pioneering work.

And yet Eribon did have a point. With very few exceptions, professional historians in France have avoided the subject of homosexuality. The French academic world is notoriously conservative, and young scholars have feared, with reason, that any interest in gay and lesbian issues might prove damaging to their careers. Two of the first professionally trained historians who began working in lesbian and gay history more than two decades ago–Marie-Jo Bonnet (b. 1949) and Michel Rey (1953-93)–did so for profoundly personal reasons. Bonnet, one of the founders of the Homosexual Front for Revolutionary Action and the Red Dykes (both in 1971), wrote a thesis on lesbianism in

[Haworth co-indexing entry note]: "Introduction." Merrick, Jeffrey, and Michael Sibalis. Co-published simultaneously in *Journal of Homosexuality* (Harrington Park Press, an imprint of The Haworth Press, Inc.) Vol. 41, No. 3/4, 2001, pp. 1-4; and: *Homosexuality in French History and Culture* (ed: Jeffrey Merrick, and Michael Sibalis) Harrington Park Press, an imprint of The Haworth Press, Inc., 2001, pp. 1-4. Single or multiple copies of this article are available for a fee from The Haworth Document Delivery Service [1-800-342-9678, 9:00 a.m. - 5:00 p.m. (EST). E-mail address: getinfo@haworthpressinc.com].

France since the sixteenth century that appeared as a book in 1981. As she explained at the time, "I needed to reflect on love between women. It was a way of prolonging and deepening my militancy as a feminist and a lesbian."[2] Rey, who wrote his master's thesis on eighteenth-century Parisian sodomites, remarked, "The fact that I was more or less involved in the homosexual movement was not irrelevant to my undertaking." And he added, "I think that it is time that homosexuals take their history in hand. . . . I feel a complicity with those people" (whom he was studying).[3] Bonnet has never been able to get a permanent academic position in France and remains a part-time teacher and independent scholar. Rey, who died of AIDS in 1993, enjoyed more success in the academic world, but he shifted his primary research interest to the less controversial subject of friendship in the Renaissance.

That is not to say that only homosexuals have written about homosexuality in history or, even less, that they alone should do so. But it is hardly surprising that such work, in France as elsewhere, initially emerged out of the gay liberation movement of the 1970s. Gays and lesbians have increasingly conceived of themselves as a minority along the lines of social, ethnic, and racial minorities, and, like these minorities, they have sought to retrieve their history. The development of lesbian and gay history thus parallelled attempts to write histories of working people, immigrants, slaves, and other neglected groups. It was the natural consequence of the much maligned "identity politics." But gay and lesbian history has by now outgrown its militant childhood and entered the academic mainstream in many countries, although not in France, or at least not until very recently.

There are at last some encouraging signs that this situation may have started to change. Florence Tamagne's recent doctoral dissertation on European homosexuality in the 1920s and 1930s, submitted to the Institut des Sciences Politiques, found its way into print (and in a prestigious series) less than two years after the defense, and she has embarked on an academic career at the University of Lille.[4] To the extent that "gay and lesbian studies" have begun to develop in France, however, it is not historians but sociologists (like Rommel Mendès-Leite), legal scholars (like Daniel Borillo), or journalists (like Didier Eribon) who are leading the way. Eribon in particular has done a remarkable job of promoting the field through his columns and book reviews in the prestigious weekly magazine *Le Nouvel Observateur* and through his many books, including the recent *Reflections on the Gay Question*.[5] Several French institutions of higher learning now offer seminars treating various aspects of homosexuality and homosexual culture, but only tangentially gay and lesbian history.

Nor so far has there been much of a concerted effort to preserve the precious documents needed by present and future historians. The private papers of gay militants have regularly been discarded after the deaths (often of AIDS) of their owners, and those who have sought to entrust their collections to public institutions have been turned down by archives and libraries. The publishers who own the papers and library of *Gai Pied* (the country's leading homosexual periodical from 1979 to 1991), important sources that researchers could consult with profit until a few years ago, have consigned them to cartons in a basement, where they risk damage and destruction. Despite much talk and some efforts, the lesbian and gay community has not as yet managed to mount an effective campaign to preserve the records of its past. A few individuals, however, are attempting to overcome this indifference. Patrick Cardon, a teacher who lives in Lille and runs his own publishing house (Gai-Kitsch-Camp), which reprints historical texts dealing with homosexuality, has recently received a government grant to establish a research center there. In Paris, both Jacques Girard and Olivier Jablonski run websites that make sources available online (http://www.multimania.com/jgir/ and http://semgai.free.fr).

As the essays in this volume demonstrate, a wealth of documentation is available to anyone who wants to search it out and investigate France's queer past. The contributors have used different kinds of sources, and they have approached their material in different ways. Some have analyzed unknown or canonical literary texts and found in them meanings that eluded or offended previous scholars. Others have studied guidebooks, newspapers, memoirs and autobiographies, medical literature, police reports and judicial records, or artistic and journalistic images for insights into urban homosexual subcultures. Several have used gay and lesbian periodicals, interviews, or their personal recollections of their own participation in the gay and lesbian movement.

A number of themes run through many of the essays. Implicitly erotic and explicitly sexual relations between members of the same sex have been stigmatized in religious, legal, and medical discourse as forms of sin, crime, and disease. Associated with urban problems and foreign peoples, they have been identified in no uncertain terms as a threat to social order and national integrity. But same-sex relations have also been represented in less negative or even more positive ways through the language of friendship and marriage and through imaginative indulgence in forbidden desires. As gay and lesbian subcultures have become more visible and, eventually, more vocal, the rhetoric of condemnation has coexisted with the reality of toleration. Sporadic and selective prosecutions, as well as debates within the subcultures, have highlighted stereotypes and anxieties about separatism, class and age differences, and gendered roles. Several essays address the ways in which sociability and consciousness have operated differently for men and women.

For all they tell us about lesbians and gays in the past and the present, the essays also remind us that there is much more work to be done. We know more about Paris than about other cities, not to mention remote villages, more about the educated elite than about the anonymous masses, and more about men than about women. In this regard, as in so many others, we must continue working for parity between the sexes.

The editors conceived this volume as part of an ongoing international and interdisciplinary campaign to promote the study of the French lesbian and gay past. They are happy that so many contributors responded to the invitation to participate in the project, and they are pleased to have included essays by French contributors, independent scholars, and members of both history and literature departments. Michael Sibalis gratefully acknowledges financial support for this project from a grant funded partly by Wilfrid Laurier University operating funds and partly by the SSHRC General Research Grant awarded to the University.

EDITORS' COMMENTS

The editors have translated five essays by French contributors. The other authors are responsible for the translations of the quotations included in their essays unless noted otherwise. Limitations on space have made it impossible to include the original French in the texts or the notes.

The following abbreviations are used in notes: AN for Archives Nationales; APP for Archives de la Préfecture de Police; BHVP for Bibliothèque Historique de la Ville de Paris; and BN for Bibliothèque Nationale.

NOTES

1. "Alternatives intelligentes," *Têtu* 15 (June 1997): 44. In a revised statement in the introduction to the papers presented at the Center, Eribon spoke of the "quasi-absence of work in the form of books" and mentioned the recently published *Homosexuality in Modern France*, ed. Jeffrey Merrick and Bryant T. Ragan, Jr. (New York, 1996). "Introduction," in *Les Etudes gay et lesbiennes: Colloque du Centre Georges Pompidou, 23 et 27 juin 1997*, ed. Didier Eribon (Paris, 1998), 17.

2 Interview in *Homophonies* 8/9 (1981).

3. http://www.multimania.com/jgir/rey.htm.

4. Florence Tamagne, *Histoire de l'homosexualité en Europe: Berlin, Londres, Paris 1919-1939* (Paris, 2000).

5. Didier Eribon, *Réflexions sur la question gay* (Paris, 1999). An English translation is forthcoming from Duke University Press.

"That Friendship Which Possesses the Soul": Montaigne Loves La Boétie

Marc D. Schachter

> Friendship is a sacred name, it is a holy thing . . . that has its true sustenance in equality.[1]

> Pardon, Love, pardon: o lord, I vow to you
> The rest of my years, my voice and my writings. . . .[2]

> But love is similar to a disturbing emotion, friendship to a fixed disposition, since love is no less bestowed to those things that are inanimate, whereas men befriend each other in measure with the judgment of the soul, which arises from a fixed disposition.[3]

This article addresses what is perhaps the most celebrated friendship in all of French letters, the perfect union that Michel de Montaigne records having shared with Étienne de La Boétie before his friend's untimely death. I begin with a discussion of the curious textual relationship between La Boétie's *Voluntary Servitude* and Montaigne's *Essays*. I then consider more specifically Montaigne's description of the relationship he shared with La Boétie. My de-

---

Marc D. Schachter would like to thank the many interlocutors who have provided him with criticism, suggestions, and encouragement as he worked on this project. The members of the Pre- and Early Modern Studies research group at the University of California–Santa Cruz, and in particular Carla Freccero and Deanna Shemek, have provided invaluable assistance through the years. Rob Halpern has offered provocative discussion on the natures of friendship.

[Haworth co-indexing entry note]: " 'That Friendship Which Possesses the Soul': Montaigne Loves La Boétie." Schachter, Marc D. Co-published simultaneously in *Journal of Homosexuality* (Harrington Park Press, an imprint of The Haworth Press, Inc.) Vol. 41, No. 3/4, 2001, pp. 5-21; and: *Homosexuality in French History and Culture* (ed: Jeffrey Merrick, and Michael Sibalis) Harrington Park Press, an imprint of The Haworth Press, Inc., 2001, pp. 5-21. Single or multiple copies of this article are available for a fee from The Haworth Document Delivery Service [1-800-342-9678, 9:00 a.m. - 5:00 p.m. (EST). E-mail address: getinfo@haworthpressinc.com].

liberations center on the chapter "Of Friendship" in the *Essays*, which I read in light of the classical male friendship tradition and Renaissance attitudes towards love and women. I suggest that Montaigne's "Of Friendship" highlights the limits that misogyny and "homophobia" imposed on friendship in Renaissance France and argue that, rather then being a paradigmatic example of male friendship, the relationship Montaigne describes having shared with La Boétie is characterized by incommensurable elements of the early modern discourses of love and male friendship. Whereas male friendship was distinguished by reason and deliberation, love, at least in its unsublimated forms, was often considered irrational and tyrannical. In describing the relationship he shared with La Boétie as a kind of hybrid of love and friendship, Montaigne may have sought to redress an absence in the spectrum of conceivable relationships between men, a spectrum in which friendship occupied a privileged but highly circumscribed position. As I will show, this hybrid relationship remained deeply imbricated with misogyny.[4]

Montaigne's melancholic celebration of his friendship with La Boétie finds its most obvious elaboration in the chapter "Of Friendship," which famously opens with the author's proclamation of his intention to publish his friend's *Voluntary Servitude* in the *Essays*. By analogy to the work of a painter in his hire, Montaigne asserts that his own chapters are but "*(a)*grotesques and monstrous bodies, pieced together of diverse members, without definite shape" (I: xxviii, 135), fit only to showcase La Boétie's masterpiece.[5] His friend's treatise, on the other hand, is "*(a)*as full as can be" (I: xxviii, 135). The chapters composing the first book of the *Essays* are thus presented (or re-presented, as "Of Friendship," the twenty-eighth chapter, is located almost at the mid-point of the book, which contains fifty-seven chapters) as a frame for La Boétie's *Voluntary Servitude*, which was written, Montaigne tells us, "*(a)*in honor of liberty against tyrants" (I: xxviii, 135). By the end of the chapter on friendship, however, the reader must view this opening passage in a different light, for the *Voluntary Servitude* does not appear in the *Essays*. At the conclusion of "Of Friendship," after lamenting that others have published La Boétie's treatise "*(a)*with evil intent" (I: xxviii, 144), Montaigne withdraws his pledge to produce the work as the central chapter of his book, offering in its place La Boétie's *Twenty-Nine Sonnets*, which occupy the central (that is to say, the twenty-ninth) chapter of the first book of the *Essays*. Although La Boétie's poems are present in all editions of the *Essays* published during Montaigne's lifetime, they too are ultimately absent. In the *exemplaire de Bordeaux*, a copy of the 1588 edition of the *Essays* in which Montaigne, until his death in 1592, was making corrections and additions for a subsequent edition, the sonnets are literally crossed out and replaced with the words, "*(c)*These verses may be seen elsewhere" (I: xxix,

145). So, finally, at the center of the 1595 posthumous edition of the *Essays* (and in modern editions), the reader finds a void.[6]

Skeptical of Montaigne's own account of his motives for these editorial decisions, numerous critics have read his dual suppression of La Boétie's texts (first the *Voluntary Servitude* and then the *Sonnets*) as a response to an anxiety of influence, or an anxiety about a position of subordination he ostensibly occupied in his relationship with La Boétie. For example, Barry Weller posits that Montaigne sought to redress a prior passivity by actively suppressing his friend's text and by seeking out prospective new friends among his readers. Drawing on the Hegelian concept of the master-slave dialectic, Anthony Wilden writes in a similar vein that the *Essays* enables Montaigne to work through his feelings of inadequacy *vis-à-vis* an introjected, idealized La Boétie. François Rigolot, in turn, argues that Montaigne works to reverse a father-son dynamic through the course of writing the *Essays*, while for Beryl Schlossman it is a teacher-student relationship. And, finally, Floyd Grey describes a process whereby Montaigne's writing enables a reversal of the negative attributes of the *Essays* and the positive attributes of the *Voluntary Servitude*.[7]

While this eclectic set of readings includes some of the most perspicacious accounts of the evolution of Montaigne's authorial subjectivity, the emphasis on the absence of the *Voluntary Servitude* and the *Sonnets* from the *Essays* results in a lack of attention to the possibility that Montaigne might have undertaken, in "Of Friendship," a sustained engagement with La Boétie's absent writings. Indeed, a reading of the chapter looking for possible allusions to the *Voluntary Servitude* and the *Sonnets* suggests that these texts remain central to it. In a classic study, Michel Butor suggested that the *Essays* constituted a textual architectonic edifice to the deceased friend, one in which the humanist conversations about freedom and servitude so central to their relationship could continue.[8] More recently, Patrick Henry has argued that the first book of the *Essays*, especially essays twenty-three to thirty-two, which, he suggests, engage themes of particular importance to the friends, constitutes a sort of literary tomb for La Boétie.[9] My observations here are in part inspired by these earlier efforts and seek to shift the terms in which Montaigne's relationship (textual and otherwise) with La Boétie is understood. Moreover, what I see as Montaigne's subtle but significant engagement with the politically volatile *Voluntary Servitude* may have implications for our understanding of the essayist's politics. I will only be able to touch on this topic briefly here. As for the present absence of the *Sonnets*, it evokes in particular the question of homoeroticism in the *Essays*, a question that is more germane to this volume and which has largely been rejected or ignored in a scholarly tradition that describes Montaigne's textual relationship with La Boétie in terms of son and father, slave and master, student and teacher, negative and positive, passive and active, but never, for example, beloved and lover.[10]

Although critics have astutely remarked some ambivalence in Montaigne's characterization of La Boétie and his writings, it is in Montaigne's deployment of the concept of friendship that this ambivalence is most profound.[11] A comparison of the respective roles of friendship in the *Voluntary Servitude* and in "Of Friendship" shows that on numerous accounts Montaigne avails himself of language used by La Boétie to characterize friendship's political role but reconfigures it to apply to the dyadic relationship of an ideal, apolitical friendship (the sort of friendship he claims to have shared with La Boétie). Importantly, there is no concept of ideal friendship in the *Voluntary Servitude*. Rather, La Boétie writes of a universal fraternity originating with nature, requiring mutual aid and guaranteeing freedom:

> Nature, minister of God and governor of men, made us all in the same form, indeed it seems from the same mold, so that we might all know each other as companions, or even as brothers. And if in dividing the presents that she made for us, she gave more of her goodness, be it in the body or in the mind, to some more than to others . . . it must be believed that in thus making greater parts for some, and for others lesser ones, she wanted to make place for fraternal affection, so that it would have a place for use, some having the strength to give aid, and others needing to receive it . . . and if she gave us all this great gift of the voice and the word so that we might become acquainted with one another and fraternize more, and make by the common and mutual declaration of our thoughts a communion of our wills; and if she has attempted by all means to narrow and tighten so strongly the knot of our alliance and society; if she has shown us in all things that she does not want so much to make us all unified as all one: it must not be doubted that we are all naturally free, since we are all companions, and it must not come to be understood by any person that nature, having put us all in company, has put any of us in servitude.[12]

Montaigne may most proximately derive his definition of the terms of friendship as a "[(a)]harmony of wills" (I: xxviii; 186; 137) from this passage, along with numerous other choices of metaphor and lexicon in "Of Friendship," some of which appear in passages I cite below.[13] These borrowings, however, occur alongside radical redeployments of La Boétie's concepts. Whereas for La Boétie, friendship should unify all men in mutual aid, for Montaigne its bond closes the couple off from outside intercourse: "[(a)]For this perfect friendship I speak of is indivisible: each one gives himself so wholly to his friend that he has nothing left to distribute elsewhere . . ." (I: xxviii, 141).

Moreover, Montaigne would seem to see what La Boétie figures as man's natural obligation to help his brothers as an imposition on the freedom that is essential to friendship:

> [a]And then, the more they are friendships which law and natural obligation impose on us, the less of our choice and free will there is in them. And our free will has no product more properly its own than affection and friendship. (I: xxiii, 185; 137)

In this passage, Montaigne proposes his most radical revision of the *Voluntary Servitude*, amending the title of his friend's treatise in coining the phrase *liberté volontaire*. This term is often translated, as in Donald Frame's rendering quoted here, as "free will," but this wording misses the significance of Montaigne's phrase, and not only by switching the noun and the adjective. In French, "free will" would normally be *libre arbitre*, literally "free judgment," derived from the Latin *liberum arbitrium*. In the titles of both Erasmus's 1524 *De libero arbitrio* (*On Free Will* or *On Free Judgment*) and Luther's 1525 refutation, the *De servo arbitrio* (*On Enslaved Will* or *On Enslaved Judgment*), it is the noun *arbitrium* that is modified. The same is true in the case of St. Augustine's *De libero arbitrio voluntatis* (*On Free Choice of the Will*). A more literal, and, I would argue, a better, translation of *liberté volontaire* would therefore be "voluntary liberty," or perhaps even "willed freedom."[14]

Montaigne's term "voluntary liberty" is thus both novel and significant, at once revising La Boétie's politically inflected concept of voluntary servitude and distinguishing itself from the traditional Latin and French theological terms for free will. Rather than viewing free will as a capacity that should be disciplined, *a priori*, by law and natural obligation (let alone by adherence to God's will), Montaigne describes a voluntary liberty that functions more or less independently of such restraints. He makes the relative autonomy of voluntary liberty clear in a passage found in "Of the affection of fathers for their children":

> [a]Since it pleased God to endow us with some capacity of reason, so that we would not be slavishly subjected to common laws as beasts are, but rather apply ourselves with judgment and voluntary liberty, we should indeed borrow a bit from the simple authority of nature, but not allow ourselves to follow her tyrannically. Reason alone should be the guide of our desires.[15]

Montaigne here emphasizes the place of deliberation in the exercise of the will. The concept of voluntary liberty suggests that freedom is not something natural and pre-lapsarian that is then corrupted through man's misuse, as La

Boétie's treatise or theological discourse would often have it, but rather something that must not only be willed or desired, but imagined, thought, actively sought through critical reflection. If, amidst his charged invective, La Boétie addresses with some precision the causes of voluntary servitude, he is not at all concerned to interrogate the mechanism of the will to freedom. He writes, "Be resolved to serve no more, and behold! you are free."[16] For Montaigne, writing in a different time and genre, the matter of freedom would seem not quite so simple. Perhaps the essayist's oft-remarked conservatism reflected less his comfort with the status quo than his sense that evolving political realities required newly envisioned forms of resistance in the pursuit of a not yet imaginable liberty.

Rather than reading Montaigne's ambivalent comments about the *Voluntary Servitude* and his revision of La Boétie's text in terms of an anxiety of influence, we might see in them a critical exercise in freedom. When Montaigne coins "voluntary liberty" from La Boétie's "voluntary servitude," he takes a politically dangerous concept used to characterize and condemn a people's willing embrace of their own subjection and redeploys it to describe a closed relationship between two individuals: "And our free will has no product more properly its own than affection and friendship." Montaigne thus distinguishes his perfect friendship from, for example, the relationship between a father and a son or between two brothers, which are not chosen, and marriage, about which he observes, "(*a*)it is a bargain to which only the entrance is free–its continuance being constrained and forced, depending otherwise than on our will" (I: xxviii, 137). And yet the concept of voluntary liberty may do other work as well. Montaigne singles out the *Voluntary Servitude* as the origin of his friendship with La Boétie, which would seem to emphasize a particularly political sympathy between the two men, and perhaps suggests a political inflection to his "voluntary liberty." Moreover, Montaigne's restriction of "voluntary liberty" to a pair of private friends is itself ambivalent, in that at least within the terms of the friendship tradition, it is precisely the citizen-couple that champions liberty and proves itself dangerous to tyranny. As Jacques Derrida remarks, "[the] tension between politicism and apoliticism is all the more paradoxical since the model of the fraternal couple for such comparisons is regularly engaged in an extremely politicized scene."[17] In fact, Montaigne mentions two such couples prominently in "Of Friendship": the Athenian lovers Aristogiton and Harmodious and the Roman friends Tiberius Gracchus and Caius Blossius. For my purposes in this essay, it is the Greek couple that is important.[18]

The passage in "Of Friendship" discussing Aristogiton and Harmodius first appeared in a long manuscript addition, or *alongeail* (to use Montaigne's word), in the *exemplaire de Bordeaux*. After listing several other benefits to be had, according to the "Academy," from a pederasty nobly pursued, Montaigne writes:

> [(c)]From that general community, the greatest and most worthy part of it exercising its offices and predominating, the Academy said that there came from it very useful fruit both in public and in private, and that it was the strength of the countries that received its use, and the principal defense of equity and liberty: witness the salutary loves of Harmodius and Aristogiton. Thus they named it sacred and divine. And there is nothing, in their account, except the violence of tyrants and the cowardliness of the people that are adverse to it. (I: xxviii, 138)

This description, which summarizes various positions expressed in Plato's *Symposium*, is in part remarkable because of its almost celebratory nature, following as it does Montaigne's assertion (present since the first edition of the *Essays*) that "[(a)]that other Grecian license is justly abhorred by our mores."[19] Of course, his enumeration of the virtues of pederasty, including in particular its role in guaranteeing political liberty, is a paraphrase of the opinion of the "Academy," implicitly contrasted with "our mores," and thus not necessarily his own view. Nonetheless, Montaigne's portrayal of Aristogiton and Harmodius avoids an easy association with sodomy, that paradigmatic sin against nature.[20] Sodomy was punishable by death in early modern France, and accusations of its practice proliferated in the *ad hominem* rhetoric of political tracts and satirical poems during the last decades of the sixteenth century.[21] Indeed, in 1610, only two decades after Montaigne penned this addition, the Greek lovers would be associated with sodomy in a pamphlet written in the wake of the assassination of Henri IV: "Greek history teaches us that Aristogiton was a sodomite who had Harmodius for his catamite. . . ."[22] The anonymous author of this pamphlet interprets the story of the classical Athenian lovers in terms of the contemporary pejorative concept of sodomy and condemns them as regicides; Montaigne, on the other hand, reports a celebratory reading of Aristogiton and Harmodius that implicitly valorizes their traditional association with tyrannicide. Montaigne's discussion may be particularly salient given that it was most likely added to "Of Friendship" after the assassination of Henri III in 1589, when regicide was no longer only a hypothetical question in France.[23]

If this discussion of the Greek lovers seems salutary, at the beginning of the *alongeail* Montaigne rejects the adequation of the "Grecian license" to ideal friendship. In the 1595 edition of the *Essays*, the sentence on the Grecian license is immediately succeeded by the following elaboration:

> [c]Since it involved, moreover, according to their practice, such a necessary disparity in age and such a difference in the lovers' functions, it did not correspond closely enough with the perfect union and harmony that we require here. . . . (I: xxviii, 138)

Montaigne has just rejected the "Grecian license" on account of "our mores"; here he offers another reason, namely the constitutive inequality between the lovers in what would seem to be Athenian pederasty (the antecedent for "it" is the "Grecian license"). Significantly, however, Montaigne treats the "Grecian license" much as he does other, less august human relationships.[24] It is inadequate to the demands of perfect friendship, to be sure, but inadequate in ways analogous to, say, the relationship between a father and a son, about which Montaigne writes, "[a]From children towards fathers, it is rather respect. Friendship feeds on communication, which cannot exist between them because of their too great inequality" (I: xxviii, 136).

Although Montaigne's discussion of the relationship between a father and a son provides one analogue to his remarks on the "Grecian license," perhaps the more salient comparison would be with the "friendship" between a man and a woman. Indeed, although contemporary editorial practices obscure this fact, the rejection of the "Grecian license" occurs in the context of the rejection of what I might hazard to call "heterosexuality." This is particularly clear in editions of the *Essays* published during Montaigne's lifetime. After presenting a long discussion of the incommensurability of relationships between men and women with ideal friendship, Montaigne wrote, in the 1580 (and first) edition of the *Essays*:

> In addition, to speak the truth, the ordinary capacity of women is not sufficient to respond to this conference and communication, nurse of this holy seam, nor does their soul seem to be firm enough to sustain the grip of a knot so tight and so strong. And certainly without that, if it would be possible to establish such an acquaintance, free and voluntary, where not only the souls would have this entire pleasure, but where the bodies as well would take part in the alliance, it is reasonable that the friendship on this account would be fuller and more complete. *But no example of this sex has yet been able to achieve it, and that other Grecian license is justly abhorred by our mores.*[25]

In the editions of the *Essays* published during Montaigne's lifetime, the punctuation of this passage changed slightly, but no text was added. In a move not authorized by sixteenth-century editions, many modern editors separate with a paragraph break Montaigne's discussion of "heterosexuality" from the subsequent discussion of the Grecian license. The ideological nature of this division becomes apparent if we trace it to its origin. It does not appear in any of the sixteenth- or seventeenth-century editions of the *Essays*. Pierre Coste's 1724 edition would seem to introduce the practice. In a marginal note opposite the paragraph break, Coste opines, "*Friendship against Nature, very common in the Greeks: what Montaigne thinks about it.*"[26] Coste's editorial intervention would thus not only quarantine the discussion of pederasty by separating it from the discussion of a possible "fuller and more complete" friendship but also neutralize a conspicuous innovation in Montaigne's text by referring to "that other Grecian license" as "against nature," when Montaigne in fact says "abhorred by our mores" or "customs."[27]

The paragraph break encourages misreading of the passage and, in particular, obfuscates Montaigne's immediate point: if it were possible to have a friendship in which both the body and the soul could be involved, then perfect friendship would be even *more* perfect. Women are, however, at least as of yet, inadequate to the demands of friendship, Montaigne tells us, and "that other Grecian license is justly abhorred by our mores."[28] We see here how the borders of perfect friendship are policed by both misogyny and homophobia. By implication, it would seem that even Montaigne's perfect friendship with La Boétie is missing something, the possibility of physical union. As Montaigne's subsequent elaboration of the mention of the Grecian license makes clear, however, he is rejecting pederasty, and not an egalitarian, sexual relationship between men, a concept that his discussion suggests was not available to him, even as he may seem to desire it and strive eloquently to describe it.[29]

Attention to Montaigne's dual rejection of "heterosexuality" and pederasty may help to tease out the implications of each. Significantly, the goal of the corporeal and spiritual union desired by Montaigne is "full pleasure," and not reproduction. In the 1580 edition of the *Essays*, Montaigne notes that "reproduction" is one of the utilitarian purposes served by marriage that make it inappropriate for his ideal, non-utilitarian friendship.[30] In the 1595 edition, Montaigne enigmatically associates pederasty both with the "*(c)*false image of corporeal reproduction" that attracts the lover to the beloved and, in a curious misreading of Plato, with a "*(c)*spiritual conception" that ideally occurs in the beloved, who is inspired by the spiritual beauty of his lover.[31] These attitudes may help us understand how some versions of ideal friendship exclude women even as they depend upon the metaphoric appropriation of such female capabilities as biological reproduction.[32] Indeed, we find that Montaigne has almost nothing positive to say about women at all in "Of Friendship," even though some of his ancient sources, including Aristotle, do. On the other hand, his discussion of the possibility of erotic relations between men is ambivalent. Leaving aside for want of space the problematic category of "mores" in Montaigne's work and a possible equivocation on the meaning of the word "license" in sixteenth-century French, Montaigne's discussion of pederasty, while bracketed by rejections, remains strikingly positive, and strikingly political. Elsewhere in "Of Friendship," Montaigne denies the political utility of ideal friendship, whereas here, albeit not addressing ideal friendship, he remarks the association of pederasty, as a form of friendship, with political liberty, and observes that it is precisely on account of this association that it was called by the Academy "sacred and divine," language used by both Montaigne and La Boétie to describe friendship. Might Montaigne seek to salvage something from the exemplary ruins of Greek love?[33]

Curiously, while evoking a classical Greek association of pederasty with political liberty, Montaigne's account of ideal friendship's autonomy and freedom employs the very language of servitude that his coinage of the term "voluntary liberty" would seem to want to avoid: "*(a)*Common friendships can be divided up . . . but this friendship that possesses the soul and rules it with absolute sovereignty cannot possibly be double" (I: xxviii, 141). Montaigne here revises a standard figure in love poetry that depicts the relationship between the lover and the god of love (or, alternatively, between the lover and his beloved) in terms of the feudal relationship between a vassal and his lord. Montaigne's revision consists in installing friendship rather than love as that which reigns over the soul "with absolute sovereignty." A paradox emerges: if ideal friendship is based on voluntary liberty, then how can a friend's soul be possessed and ruled? Is this the same paradox inherent in the concept of voluntary servitude itself, in the willful alienation of liberty and the desired submission to servitude that it signifies?

The *topos* of servitude, perhaps voluntary, to the God of Love is precisely the tradition that informs the opening lines of La Boétie's *Sonnets* in which the lexical field of feudalism is used to describe the lover's enslavement:

> Pardon, Love, pardon: o lord, I vow to you
> The rest of my years, my voice and my writings,
> My sobs, my sighs, my tears and my cries:
> Nothing, from anyone but you I promise to take nothing.[34]

If "love" were changed to "friendship" in this quatrain, it could almost be Montaigne speaking of his dedication to his deceased friend. The distinction between the voluntary servitude of love and the voluntary liberty of friendship–which would seem so crucial to Montaigne's discussion of his relationship with La Boétie–may become difficult to maintain. In fact, Montaigne's ideal friendship is emphatically beyond the bounds of understanding and indeed of choice. His account of the desire he and La Boétie felt for one another before they had even met emphasizes the inability of reason to account for their affection:

> [c]We sought each other before we met because of the reports we heard of each other, which had more effect on our affection than such reports would reasonably have; I think it was by some ordinance from heaven. We embraced each other by our names. (I: xxviii, 139)

Their relationship developed not in keeping with judgment. Rather, their "affection" was moved unreasonably, as if "by some ordinance from heaven." Divine intervention? Perhaps. Choice? No.

Montaigne is aware of the extent to which this account of the development of his friendship violates the traditional strictures of ideal friendship. Indeed, he presents an apology of sorts for the haste with which their friendship reached "its perfection":

> [c]Having so little time to last, and having begun so late, for we were both grown men, and he a few years older than I, it could not lose time and conform to the pattern of mild and regular friendships, which need so many precautions in the form of long preliminary association. (I: xxviii, 139)[35]

Particularly striking in this passage is an inversion that Montaigne works on the classical friendship tradition. In Aristotle and Cicero, it is in large part the "many precautions in the form of long preliminary association" that distinguish perfect friendship from more mundane kinds. For example, in a sixteenth-century Latin translation of the *Nicomachean Ethics*, we find the following admonition:

> Truly, those who too quickly bring about between themselves all those things which pertain to friendship desire to be friends indeed to each other, but nonetheless they are not, unless they are worthy of friendship and truly reciprocally examine each other. Quick indeed is born the desire to bring about friendship, but not likewise friendship.[36]

Montaigne's friendship with La Boétie, the essayist would seem to be saying, is as far above such classical perfect friendships as it is above quotidian friendship, so far above, in fact, that it can dispense with the very requirements of traditional perfect friendship, and indeed characterize such friendships pejoratively as "mild" and "regular."[37]

In "Of Friendship," Montaigne strives to recuperate an irrational sentiment. He seems to struggle against the restrictions of the discourse of perfect friendship itself and not only to glorify further his own relationship. The love tradition, which does allow for passion and the loss of reason, is clearly inappropriate for his friendship because of the laws and cultural prejudices against sodomy and conventional attitudes towards masculinity, but also, and perhaps more importantly, because love in the Renaissance, whether heterosexual or pederastic, was founded on a constitutive inequality. The discourse of friendship, which does emphasize reciprocity and equality, and thus in this respect fulfills Montaigne's requirements, describes relationships that seem moderate and overly rational when compared to the intensity of Montaigne's passionate commitment to La Boétie. Neither is adequate to the friendship he describes having shared with his lost friend.

The tension between the expression of an ineffable and irrational desire and the need to figure an egalitarian relationship with the friend manifests itself in the textual evolution of what is perhaps the most erotic and mystical passage in the *Essays*. In 1580, the passage in question read as follows:

> If one were to press me to say why I loved him, I feel that this cannot be expressed; it seems to me that there is, beyond all my discourse and all that I can say about it, I know not what divine and fatal force, mediatrix of this union. It is not one special consideration, nor two, nor three, nor four, nor a thousand. It is I know not what quintessence of all this mixture which, having seized all my will, led it to plunge and lose itself in his. I say lose in truth, leaving it nothing that was its or its own.[38]

Beyond his ken, Montaigne's union with La Boétie is mediated by an inexplicable and fateful force. Here, there is no mention of a voluntary liberty. Instead, Montaigne speaks of his will as being seized by some quintessence and led to plunge itself into the will of the other. This description of a force beyond reason that seizes the will resonates with a description of the power of love found in a poem from La Boétie's *Sonnets* that begins, significantly, "It is done, my heart, let us give up freedom":

> If we must give ourselves up, the season is come
> when reason is no longer with us.
> I see that love, when I do not merit it,
>
> without any right, has come to seize me;
> and I see that yet, even when he is wrong,
> to this great king must reason serve.[39]

Both Montaigne's friendship and La Boétie's erotic love are characterized by the abdication of reason and the submission to a superior force. How then to distinguish between the two? Comparing men's sexual desire for women with friendship, Montaigne writes:

> [a]Its ardor . . . is more active, more scorching, and more intense. But it is an impetuous and fickle flame, undulating and variable, a fever flame, subject to fits and lulls, that holds us only by one corner. In friendship it is a general and universal warmth, all gentleness and smoothness, with nothing bitter and stinging about it. (I: xxviii, 137)

Heterosexual desire is powerful, but bitter, inconstant, and as Montaigne goes on to note, subject to satiety. This in large part conforms to the description of love in the *Sonnets* as something fickle, disruptive, and enslaving. Friendship, on the other hand, is perhaps less intense but more pleasant and "*(a)*enjoyed according as it is desired" (I: xxviii, 137). Nonetheless, we might begin to wonder if, in recounting the relationship he shared with La Boétie, Montaigne is describing perfect friendship or perfect love.

In later editions of the *Essays*, Montaigne made several additions and lexical changes to his account of his fateful desire for La Boétie. To his observation, "If one were to press me to say why I loved him, I feel that this cannot be expressed," he added perhaps the single best-known phrase in the *Essays* "*(c)*except by responding, 'Because it was he; because it was I.' "[40] A perfect alexandrine, with symmetrical hemistiches separated by the requisite medial caesura, this sentence expresses stylistically a relationship of equality.[41] Also striking is a modification to the image of the penetrating will, which Montaigne renders reciprocal. In the 1595 edition, the text reads as follows:

> It is not one special consideration, nor two, nor three, nor four, nor a thousand; it is I know not what quintessence of all this mixture which, having seized all my will, led it to plunge and lose itself in his; which having seized all his will, led it to plunge and lose itself in mine, with equal hunger and rivalry.[42]

Whereas in the earlier editions of the text, Montaigne's will penetrated and lost itself in La Boétie's, the wills now interpenetrate, circumventing the gendered hierarchy of penetrator and penetrated, "active" and "passive." These additions and revisions evince the equality and reciprocity so important to Montaigne's notion of ideal friendship even as they are used to undermine the centrality of voluntary liberty to it. The wills come together "with equal hunger and rivalry," but they are still seized by an inexplicable "quintessence of all this mixture." This image of the interpenetrating souls, perhaps an elaboration of the "harmony of the wills" mentioned earlier in the chapter, thus describes an erotics of reciprocity impossible in pederasty or (normative) heterosexuality, because these are dependent not so much on the different or the "hetero" as on constitutive inequality.

The individual exclusions that structure ideal friendship in "Of Friendship" do not all function identically. Montaigne's rejection of friendship's political utility might be a strategic dissimulation enabling him to engage in a potentially volatile conversation about political liberty. The rejection of the political is also implicated in Montaigne's ambivalent disavowal of "that other Grecian license," because it is under the sign of this disavowal that the most extensive discussion of the relationship between friendship and political liberty takes place. I write "ambivalent" because the homoeroticism disavowed under the sign of pederasty returns in Montaigne's characterization of his friendship with La Boétie, where we find proliferating the very erotic connotations of voluntary servitude that Montaigne would seem to want to banish from the realm of ideal friendship. What is striking in this regard is the extent to which the development of ideal friendship in Montaigne depends on an economy of appropriation whereby attributes ascribed to women or to "heterosexuality" are transfigured and reapplied in the context of a relationship between two nominally equal men. Thus, a spiritual conception, for which women are held inappropriate, can be celebrated in the *Essays* while biological reproduction, for which women are necessary, is scorned. And the return of the erotic to Montaigne's ideal friendship operates in part through the appropriation of the language of desire, be it "heterosexual" or pederastic, to describe a relationship between men, while the heteroerotic itself, and in particular women, remain outside the bounds of ideal friendship. Let me suggest in conclusion that these dynamics continue to inform, in complicated and sometimes conflicting ways, the modern discursive fields of homosexuality and heterosexuality. Attention to sexuality's early modern patrimony, and I use this word advisedly, may help us better understand and more successfully resist not only homophobia, but also the manifold imbrications of contemporary homosexuality and misogyny.

NOTES

1. Étienne de La Boétie, *Discours de la servitude volontaire*, in *Oeuvres complètes* ed. Louis Desgraves, 2 vols. (Bordeaux, 1991), 1: 94-5.

2. La Boétie, *Vingt neuf sonnetz*, in *Oeuvres* 1: 1-2.

3. Aristotle, *Aristotelis ad nicomachvm filivm de moribvs, quæ Ethica nominantur* (Paris, 1548), 202 (VIII.v.5 in modern editions).

4. By focusing my attention on discursive systems rather than questions of who did what with whom and what that might have meant, I seek to sidestep the debates between "essentialists" and "constructionists" that continue to shape explorations of homosexuality and its histories. I would argue that whether or not "homosexuals," "homosexuality," or even "sexuality" have a place in early modernity, the consolidation of modern and contemporary discourses of homosexuality and heterosexuality

draws on pre-existing discursive traditions; modern discourses rely in part on earlier traditions for their intelligibility (at the same time that they inherit some of their incoherency from them) and their efficacy. Attention to salient elements in relevant pre- and early modern discourses and the conditions of continuities and ruptures between "archaic" or declining discourses and the modern discourses of homosexuality might offer insights into the organization of homosexuality and heterosexuality, insights that might otherwise be occluded by sexuality's contemporary hegemony.

5. Michel de Montaigne, *Complete Works*, ed. Donald Frame (Stanford, 1957). Unless otherwise noted, English translations from Montaigne are drawn from this volume. Parenthetical references include the numbers of the book, essay, and page. Text following the symbol [(a)] first appeared in the 1580 or 1582 edition of the *Essays*; following the symbol [(b)] first appeared in the 1588 edition; and following the symbol [(c)] appears only in the *exemplaire de Bordeaux* and/or in the posthumous 1595 edition.

6. Or almost a void: Montaigne's dedication of the *Sonnets* to Madame de Grammont remains.

7. Barry Weller, "The Rhetoric of Friendship in Montaigne's *Essais*," *New Literary History* 9 (1978): 503-24; Anthony Wilden, "Par divers moyens on arrive a pareille fin: A Reading of Montaigne," *Modern Language Notes* 83 (1968): 577-97; François Rigolot, "Montaigne's Purloined Letters," *Yale French Studies* 64 (1983): 145-66; Beryl Schlossman, "From La Boétie to Montaigne: The Place of the Text," *Modern Language Notes* 98 (1983): 891-909; and Floyd Gray, *La Balance de Montaigne: Exagium/Essai* (Paris, 1982). See also Maurice Merleau- Ponty, *Signes* (Paris, 1960), 261-2.

8. Michel Butor, *Essais sur les Essais* (Paris, 1968).

9. Patrick Henry, *Montaigne in Dialogue: Censorship and Defensive Writing, Architecture and Friendship, The Self and the Other* (Saratoga, 1982), 73-100.

10. On the question of Montaigne and homosexuality, see William J. Beck, "Montaigne face à l'homosexualité," *Bulletin de la Société des Amis de Montaigne* 9 (1982): 41-50, and "The Obscure Montaigne: The Quotation, the Addition, and the Footnote," *College Language Association Journal* 34 (1990): 228-52; as well as Marc Schachter, "Montaigne," in *Gay Histories and Cultures: An Encyclopedia*, ed. George Haggerty (New York, 2000), 608-9.

11. Although numerous critics have suggested that Montaigne's implicit differences of opinion with La Boétie undermine his assertion that the friend was "a second self" (I: xxviii, 143), the giving and receiving of criticism is in fact an essential part of the classical male friendship tradition in which the metaphor of the second self plays such a prominent role.

12. *Servitude volontaire* 73-4.

13. "Most proximately" because Aristotle and Cicero also describe friendship in strikingly similar terms.

14. For a more extensive discussion of "voluntary liberty," see my " 'Voluntary Servitude' and the Politics of Friendship: Plato, Ariosto, La Boétie, Montaigne" (PhD dissertation, University of California-Santa Cruz, 2000), chapter 3.

15. My translation from *Essais*, ed. Pierre Vilar; reed. V. L. Saulnier (Paris, 1965; 1992) (II: viii, 387).

16. *Servitude volontaire*, 73.

17. Jacques Derrida, *Politics of Friendship*, trans. George Collins (New York, 1997), 182.

18. For a discussion of the Romans, see my "Voluntary Servitude," chapter 3.

19. My translation from *Essais*, I: xxviii, 187. Aristigiton and Harmodius are discussed in Plato's *Symposium*, 182b-d.

20. See Jacques Chiffoleau, "Dire l'indicible: Remarques sur la catégorie du *nefandum* du XIe au XVe siècle," *Annales* 45 (1990): 275-96.

21. See Guy Poirier, *L'Homosexualité dans l'imaginaire de la Renaissance* (Paris, 1996), 45-59.

22. *Les Remercîments des beurrières de Paris, au sieur de Courbouzon Montgomery* (n.p., 1610), 13.

23. It is impossible to know exactly when Montaigne made the additions that appear on the *exemplaire de Bordeaux*, but in any case they were written after the publication of the 1588 edition. François Rigolot has also addressed the figures of Aristogiton and Harmodius in Montaigne, drawing intriguing conclusions that differ in many ways from my own. See his "Montaigne et la 'Servitude Volontaire': Pour une interpretation platonicienne," *Le Lecteur, l'auteur et l'écrivain: Montaigne 1492-1592-1992*, ed. Ilana Zinguer (Paris, 1994): 85-103 and "Reviving Harmodius and Aristogiton in the Renaissance: Friendship and Tyranny as Voluntary Servitude," *Montaigne Studies* 11 (1999): 107-20.

24. In this Montaigne follows Aristotle, whose discussion of friendship in books eight and nine of the *Nicomachean Ethics* compares *teleia philia* or perfect friendship, with other forms of friendship, including pederasty.

25. My emphasis. Montaigne, *Essais: Reproduction Photographique de l'édition originale de 1580*, ed. Daniel Martin (Geneva, 1976), 206. Note the resonances between this passage and the long quotation reproduced above from La Boétie's *Voluntary Servitude.*

26. *Les Essais de Michel Seigneur de Montaigne*, ed. Pierre Coste, 3 vols. (London, 1724), I: 184.

27. Montaigne, of course, is famous for troubling the relationship between nature and custom.

28. On the question of woman and friendship, see in particular Donald Stone, "Women and Friendship," *Montaigne Studies* 8 (1996): 23-34; Jacques Derrida, "The Politics of Friendship," *Journal of Philosophy* 85 (1988): 632-44; and Carla Freccero, "Cannibalism, Homophobia, Women," *Women, "Race," and Writing in the Early Modern Period*, ed. Patricia Parker and Margo Hendricks (New York, 1992), 73-83.

29. Numerous critics have argued that there was no model for egalitarian same-sex sexual relations in the Renaissance. The seminal work on the topic as it relates to friendship is Alan Bray, *Homosexuality in Renaissance England* (London, 1982), which has been much contested. See also Michael Rocke, *Forbidden Friendships: Homosexuality and Male Culture in Renaissance Florence* (Oxford, 1996); and David Halperin, "How to do the History of Male Homosexuality," *GLQ* 6 (2000): 87-124. For a different opinion, see Bruce Smith, *Homosexual Desire in Shakespeare's England* (Chicago, 1991).

30. Montaigne, *Essais 1580*, 259.

31. My translations from *Essais*, I: xxviii, 187. I suggest that Montaigne misconstrues Plato on this point because, in the *Symposium*, at least in Diotima's speech, it is the lover and not the beloved who conceives spiritually.

32. Particularly interesting considerations of the relationship between "heterosexuality" and pederasty in Montaigne are offered by Stone, "Women and Friendship"; and Constance Jordan, "Sexuality and Volition in 'Sur des vers de Virgile,' " *Montaigne Studies* 8 (1996): 65-80.

33. On Montaigne's strategies for exploring potentially dangerous topics in the *Essays*, see Henry, *Montaigne in Dialogue*, 23-5.

34. *Sonnetz*, I: 1-4.

35. See also La Boétie's poem, "Ad Michaëlem Montanum," in *Oeuvres*, 2: 71-9; and James Hirstein, "La Boétie et la justification difficile d'une amitié précoce: Le Début (vers 1-32) de la 'Satyre latine' (*Poemata* XX) et le *Laelius* de Cicéron," *Montaigne Studies* 11 (1999): 121-36.

36. Aristotle, *Aristotelis ad nicomachvm filivm de moribvs*, 199.

37. On the gendered implications of this language, see Patricia Parker, "Virile Style," in *Premodern Sexualities*, ed. Louise Fradenburg and Carla Freccero (New York, 1996), 201-22.

38. Montaigne, *Essais 1580*, 261-2. The antecedent for the indirect object pronouns and the possessive pronoun in the last sentence is unclear; this ambiguity is certainly telling, dissolving as it does the boundaries between Montaigne, La Boétie, and their respective wills. Halperin, "Male Homosexuality," 100-1, discusses this passage as it appears in modern editions but does not attend to the passage's textual history, which would complicate some of the claims of his argument.

39. *Sonnetz*, 2: 143-4.

40. My translation from *Essais*, I: xxviii, 186-7.

41. Jean Starobinski, *Montaigne en mouvement* (Paris, 1982), 55.

42. Montaigne, *Les Essais de Michel Seigneur de Montaigne*, ed. Mademoiselle de Gournay (Paris, 1595), 109. This passage deserves more attention than I can give it here.

Female Friendship as the Foundation of Love in Madeleine de Scudéry's "Histoire de Sapho"

Leonard Hinds

In her "Histoire de Sapho," Madeleine de Scudéry depicts a feminocentric world where friendship between women serves as the basis for all kinds of relationships between men and women. To this end, she casts female friendship in terms of intimacy, inseparability, devotion, and passion. She superimposes the terms of female emotional attachment on relations between the sexes and, in fact, privileges such bonds as the only ones through which the *précieuse* could form enduring relations with a person of either sex. A certain sexual ambiguity pervades homosocial and heterosocial relations that involve a strong emotional component. Lillian Faderman has alluded to the fine, if not imperceptible, line between the erotic and the homosocial in Renaissance English writing and women's letters in seventeenth-century France.[1] According to Eve Kosofsky Sedgwick, female homosocial desire is not as radically crosscut as male homosocial relations are by the distinction between the sexual and the nonsexual and by the social imperative of the marital exchange of women as commodities.[2] In fact, as we shall see, Scudéry obviates all the pitfalls of marriage in her female character's dealings with males and other females.

To understand better the continuum of female homosocial relations and its role in fashioning bonds between men and women in Scudéry's text, it would be best to pose a series of questions. First, why has Scudéry chosen Sappho,

[Haworth co-indexing entry note]: "Female Friendship as the Foundation of Love in Madeleine de Scudéry's 'Histoire de Sapho.' " Hinds, Leonard. Co-published simultaneously in *Journal of Homosexuality* (Harrington Park Press, an imprint of The Haworth Press, Inc.) Vol. 41, No. 3/4, 2001, pp. 23-35; and: *Homosexuality in French History and Culture* (ed: Jeffrey Merrick, and Michael Sibalis) Harrington Park Press, an imprint of The Haworth Press, Inc., 2001, pp. 23-35. Single or multiple copies of this article are available for a fee from The Haworth Document Delivery Service [1-800-342-9678, 9:00 a.m. - 5:00 p.m. (EST). E-mail address: getinfo@haworthpressinc.com].

the sixth- to fifth-century B.C.E. Greek poet, as a vehicle for the depiction of these social relations? Second, how did French Renaissance and early seventeenth-century writers conceive of the original Sappho? How was she represented in the translations of her poetry, in medical treatises, and in legal discourse? The answer to the second set of questions will elucidate the interdictions against female homosexual and homosocial relations and will inventory the legendary material Scudéry uses and transforms in her text. Third, how does Scudéry adapt this figure to represent the French salon of preciosity and especially the ideal of social relations born from that historical context? Fourth, and most importantly, what aspects of Sappho's sapphism, namely her sexual proclivities, influence Scudéry's picture of female friendship and opposite-sex love?

Joan DeJean has provided a comprehensive answer to the first question. Scudéry appropriates Sappho to inaugurate an image of the female writer of the heroic novel, a literary genre on the rise during the first two-thirds of the seventeenth century in France. According to DeJean, Scudéry rewrites the narrative presented by Ovid in his *Heroides*, one in which the abandoned Sappho pines over her separation from her male lover, Phaon, and promises to refrain from social and sexual relations with women. In the "Histoire de Sapho," DeJean finds most successful the depiction of the woman writer offering a new genre to the public. Just as successful is the feminist treatment of marriage, which the *précieuses* consider "a long slavery" (*Art.*, 10: 343).[3] Scudéry's Sapho prefers social and affectionate bonds with men, or specifically with one man, outside the confines of marriage. For DeJean, Scudéry manages to construct a utopic space or sanctuary where the professional female writer can thrive and where she sets the terms of her relationship with a man.[4] However, DeJean points out that although the ideological ends of Sapho's story are clear, the representations of sexuality and gender identity are fraught with ambiguity.[5] It is the purpose of this study to examine more closely these ambiguities as they appear in the formation of various social relations.

SAPPHO IN THE FRENCH IMAGINARY IN THE SIXTEENTH AND EARLY SEVENTEENTH CENTURIES

How was Sappho represented in literary, legal, and medical discourses in the sixteenth and early seventeenth centuries? What legacy in the social imaginary did translators, poets, physicians, and magistrates leave to Madeleine de Scudéry? I prefer to focus on texts in French because Scudéry knew no classical languages and because such documents bear witness to the dissemination of knowledge and judgments of Sappho. While Scudéry did read Italian and

Spanish, she had no training in classical languages and probably resorted to published translations in French or had friends translate for her.[6] To write her heroic novel, *Artamène, or the Great Cyrus*, she probably resorted to French translations of Xenophon's *Cyropaedia*, Herodotus's *Histories*, and Philostratus's *Life of Apollonius of Tyana*. In addition, Sappho's poetic corpus was also available in the original Greek and in Latin and French translations.

Sappho expresses same-sex desire most clearly in her fragment 31, later titled "Ode to a Female Beloved" in French translation. Already made available in a Greek edition and translated into Latin by Henri Estienne in 1556, fragment 31 immediately became a source text for translators and poets. Rémi Belleau provides a precious adaptation that nevertheless remains faithful to the sapphic love triangle:

No one seems better to equal
The lofty gods
Than he who face to face
Hears you speak and sees the grace
Of your gracious smile,

Which goes to the center
Of my senses
To pillage the mind that wanders,
For seeing your rare beauty
I feel my voice failing.

My tongue becomes dull
And there comes to me
A small flame that runs
Under my tender skin
So captive am I of your beauty.

Nothing more do I see by mine eye
Close to you
Mine ear is always ringing.
A cold and heavy sweat
Suddenly flows in me.

I am hunted by horror,
By fear,
I am more pale, more white
Than the blade of grass
Wilted by the heat.

Already Death is about to
Carry me

> Aboard his small boat
> And suddenly one sees me
> Exhaling my half-dead soul.[7]

Belleau presents a female speaker marked by feminine modifiers who addresses a woman being charmed by a man comparable to the gods. It is clear that the speaker focuses attention on the female object of desire, for she admires her rare beauty. Belleau thus preserves the sapphic love triangle for the French reader: a woman feels desire for a woman cajoled by a man. Such a relationship suggests two exceptions to the rules of the classic love triangle presented by René Girard. In Sappho's fragment 31, the mediator whose desire the speaker imitates is a man, but his presence does not inspire her to hate him. Moreover, the rival does not constitute a father figure serving as an obstacle to the desiring male; instead, he is like a divinity depriving an amorous female of access to her beloved.[8] Only when fragment 31 will be adapted by the likes of Ronsard, du Bellay, and de Baïf will the Girardian triangle be completed by a male lover substituted for the desirous, female speaker.[9]

Furthermore, while some sixteenth-century French poets and translators allow Sappho to speak her desire for the same sex, they soon add moral qualifications in line with religious and legal prohibitions of their time. In later sixteenth-century adaptations, poets introduce a moralizing voice to judge Sappho's desire. For instance, in 1567 de Baïf adds a loose translation of Catullus's poem to the end of his version of Sappho's ode to warn her against an idleness that gives birth to pernicious desires:

> Pleasure preoccupies you too much, delicate Sappho
> Pleasure will destroy great kings and towns
> Pleasure will make you perish.[10]

By the second half of the sixteenth century, Sappho appears in a pejorative light as a female enslaved to sensual pleasures.

In legal discourse, French magistrates subsumed lesbianism under the term of sodomy along with other non-reproductive sexual acts, such as masturbation, bestiality, the use of phallic substitutions, and oral and anal sex between men, between women, and between members of the two sexes. When it came to tribadism as a form of sodomy, they regularly used Sappho as a case in point.[11] In 1565, Jean Papon clearly states that "two women corrupting one another together without a male are punishable unto death."[12] It is an interesting coincidence that a second edition of Papon was published in 1648, the year Scudéry began writing *Artamène*, the heroic novel that contains the "Histoire de Sapho." In fact, this edition of Papon names Sappho as the classic tribade.[13]

Claude Le Brun de La Rochette follows Papon's original statement, and he too mentions Sappho as a classic example:

> As for women who corrupt one another, whom the Ancients used to call Tribades (in whose ranks are placed Sapho [sic] and Bassa . . . whom Tertullian calls "frictrices") there isn't a shadow of a doubt that they are committing among themselves a kind of sodomy . . . And that is a crime worthy of death.[14]

These documents attest to the qualifications that accrued around the figure of Sappho in legal discourse. In addition to poetic adaptations in which she was seen as a woman given to licentiousness, in legal discourse she became a classic reference of tribadism and specifically of female "sodomy." Both legal practice and medical treatises suggest that female same-sex relations threatened male sexual prerogatives. David Greenberg points out that judicial proscriptions against male same-sex activity were sometimes extended to the other sex in order to prosecute females in Western Europe during the Renaissance.[15] Although Guy Poirier documents only one execution of a woman for same-sex activity between 1565 and 1648, Louis Crompton finds evidence of at least two cases of capital punishment and two of torture of female sexual partners in Renaissance France.[16] Despite infrequent and inconsistent application of these practices to women, cases were public enough to draw the attention of late sixteenth-century writers such as Michel de Montaigne, who reports one such incident involving female to male cross-dressing.[17] It is precisely the usurpation of male prerogatives that Sappho comes to represent in legal and medical treatises. In 1647 the physician Thomas Bartholin classifies Sappho with "some women [who] misuse the clitoris instead of the virile member and couple together, and whom the Greeks call tribades."[18] Sappho thus becomes the cultural emblem of phallic substitutions and the exclusion of the male from affective and sexual relations between females.

This is not to say that writers and translators did not try to recover her as a literary icon of the female writer. At the dawn of the seventeenth century, Ovid's depiction of Sappho took hold of the French literary imaginary. Pierre de Déimier, Jean de Lingendes, and the sieur de Bachet published a series of translations of Ovid's *Heroides* from 1612 to 1626. Writers such as Scudéry were then familiar with the legend recounted in Ovid's fifteenth epistle: Sappho turns from her many female loves to woo back her male suitor, Phaon, who has abandoned her.[19] This letter relates a conversion story in which lesbian affection is overcome by heterosexual love. The text itself reminds the French readership of the "wrongdoing or blame" of Sappho's female loves, and this qualification echoes the cautions of sixteenth- and seventeenth-century poets, magistrates, and physicians.[20] In contrast, Scudéry will not present the conversion of Sappho from homosexuality to heterosexuality; instead, she will pattern Sappho's relationship with Phaon after female homosocial bonding.

MADELINE DE SCUDÉRY'S SAPHO

Scudéry's "Histoire de Sapho" promotes female friendship as a basis for love of the opposite sex. This statement in itself points to the ambiguity of gender roles in the French Sapho's world (her name from now on will be spelled as Scudéry spelled it). Writing through Sapho in an effort to paint the ideal portrait of the new woman writer of the seventeenth century, Scudéry rearranges the markers of her characters' genders to offer a utopic representation of friendship and love between women as well as between man and woman.[21] By extension, Scudéry herself claimed the name Sapho in her literary circle, and literary criticism concerning her *Artamène* has presented the "Histoire de Sapho" as an autobiographical account of her creative life and her salon.[22]

As a writer reflecting the values of her literary society, Scudéry inflects the depiction of friendship and love with concerns for propriety and decency. According to Roger Lathuillère, the refinement of language and comportment were inherent to the very origins of preciosity in seventeenth-century France.[23] Scudéry's representation of Sapho is not as radically polarized as Ovid's, namely a woman torn between love for other women and love for a man. In one of the discussions in the "Histoire de Sapho," Scudéry addresses the issue of propriety in the presentation of love and desire: "Since the act of propriety is not satisfied by forbidding criminal loves, and since it forbids even the most innocent ones, one must follow it and not expose oneself in the slightest to scandal" (*Art.*, 10: 411). The reader should, therefore, not expect to see a narrative of genital, sexual relations; instead, relations between members of the same sex and between members of different sexes are situated on the level of affect and sentiment.

It is also important to note that the traditional marks of gender appear mixed, that is, shared by both sexes in the depiction of their origins and their personalities. For instance, as DeJean has perceived, Sapho's origin is of an androgynous nature.[24] Scudéry changes Sapho's father's name from Scamandronymus to Scamandrogine, which contains the two Greek words for man and woman (*Art.*, 10: 330). In line with this mixed origin are the mixed gender traits present in Sapho's portrait. As Tisandre, one of her suitors, tells her: "You are the only woman in the world, who has discovered the art of uniting all the virtues and all the good qualities of the two sexes in one person . . ."

(*Art.*, 10: 344). By being a writer and an esteemed mind in her circle of male and female friends, Sapho assumes some masculine roles as they existed in seventeenth-century France. While presumably remaining female and feminine, Scudéry's Sapho is a psychological and social androgyne, as her father's name would suggest.

Scudéry also offers an equivocal portrait of Sapho's male beloved, Phaon, who physically incorporates traits of both sexes:

> He is without a doubt extremely handsome, however due to a beauty that does not resemble that of Ladies: and he conserves all the good appearance of his Sex, with all the beauty of theirs. He has a beautiful and noble height, although he is not very tall: very brown hair, black and beautiful eyes, an agreeable shape of the face, beautiful teeth, a well-proportioned nose, and a high expression. Moreover, he has beautiful hands for a man. . . . (*Art.*, 10: 372)

Scudéry's portrait of Phaon is indeed contradictory, but its contradictions are what make him so interesting to Sapho. Although he does not resemble a woman (that would be too close to overt effeminacy), he possesses a certain degree of female beauty, in fact, "all the beauty" of women. Scudéry depicts him in terms that are more frequent in objectifying portraits of women; his hands are almost too beautiful to be those of a man. Scudéry begins to paint the psychological portrait of Phaon when she describes his eyes: "He has a certain passionate quality in his eyes, although they are devoid of all affectation" (*Art.*, 10: 372). What ignites Phaon's passion? Phaon finds that there is an indescribable quality in Sapho's gaze that inspires passion in others, and he is continually searching for expressions of love in her glances (*Art.*, 10: 419). Their looks constitute intersubjective exchanges between Sapho, the psychological and social androgyne, and Phaon, the physical androgyne, a male gifted with feminine beauty.

The growing affection between Sapho and Phaon will pose a problem for the heroine, for she is strongly opposed to marriage with a man who would exchange the role of a slave to her for that of a tyrant over her (*Art.*, 10: 343-5). As DeJean argues, Sapho asserts the primacy of female friendships, and she places her relationships with men in a subordinate position to those with women. During most of the narrative, she surrounds herself with female friends, principally Amithone, Erinne, Athys, and Cydnon. Indeed, Cydnon is described as her first friend in life, and she has her most intimate conversations with her (*Art.*, 10: 338). In their discussion of Platonic love, a love that transcends the dissoluteness of carnal passion, Sapho and Cydnon trace the definitions of ideal friendship and pure love. The one definitive characteristic that friendship with women and a rarified love with men share is the free exchange of thoughts between, on the one hand, friends, and on the other, lovers:

> There are a thousand completely pure and completely innocent sweet things in a mutual affection [says Sapho]. Indeed, this agreeable exchange of thoughts, and of secret thoughts that takes place between two people who love one another is an inconceivable pleasure: and to judge love by the measure of friendship, I assure you, my dear Cydnon, that presently I have more joy telling you without dissimulation what I think than I have when we are together at the most magnificent festivals. But to have this entire pleasure, replied Cydnon with laughter, so tell me, I beg you, your most secret thoughts. (*Art.*, 10: 415)

Sapho here articulates the tie between love and friendship, and it will be along this continuum of originally female homosocial relations that her affection for Phaon will progress. It is also important to note that this exchange of secret thoughts already exists between Sapho and Cydnon, who asks her immediately after the exposition of intense friendship to share her thoughts with her. Sapho continues to say that she seeks a love that "has the solidity of friendship" and that she prefers a lover who provides this affection to a husband who would be incapable of doing so (*Art.*, 10: 415). Sapho manages to realize this ideal with Phaon in a scene of reconciliation. Once she avows her love to him, they effect "an exchange so sincere of their most secret thoughts that one could say that everything that was in Sapho's mind passed into that of Phaon, and that everything that was in Phaon's passed into that of Sapho" (*Art.*, 10: 503). Sapho has succeeded in superimposing her requirements for Platonic friendship on relations with a man. Phaon now plays the role that Cydnon played earlier in the narrative, and he thus conforms to the criteria of the solid friendship that subtends relations between women. Furthermore, Sapho realizes her ideal of finding a lover who would follow the code of female friendship.

Female friendship provides yet another basis for love between Sapho and Phaon in the episode of the lover's quest to confirm the passion of his beloved. Phaon is so set on determining whether Sapho really loves him that he would like her to write verses in which "his passion would be depicted" (*Art.*, 10: 420). Of course, Phaon is passionate to learn whom Sapho loves. Before he hears her avowal, he yearns to find out whether she is capable of passionate love and whether she has ever really loved anyone. Without fearing that Phaon would learn anything compromising about her, she is willing to share some of her verses with him. Phaon reads some of her poetry addressed to Cydnon, and he is able to confirm that Sapho is capable not only of affection but of extreme passion: "She admirably depicted the sweetness of glances, the beating of hearts that an agreeable surprise gives one, the emotion in the face, the agitation of the mind, and all the movements of a passionate soul" (*Art.*, 10: 456). Phaon reads in her verses addressed to Cydnon "the happiness of two Persons who love one another" and the greatest expression of "the most delicate love" (*Art.*, 10: 457). Without considering for a moment that Sapho really feels intense love for a woman, Phaon reads her passionate verses to Cydnon as an exaggerated expression of female friendship. Nonetheless, he is convinced that Sapho loves someone, for without knowledge of true love and passion, she would not be capable of writing such verse. Since lesbian love per se could not be represented in a heroic novel conforming to rules of propriety, the male suitor conceives a "jealousy without an object," namely jealousy without an explicit mediator to inspire it in the Girardian sense (*Art.*, 10: 458). For Phaon, Sapho's female friends cannot serve as obvious mediators for his passion; however, he does wish desperately that Sapho direct the passion expressed in her verses to him. Phaon is, therefore, not jealous of her female friends; instead, he is jealous of the intense feelings Sapho has for them.

Having seen the proof of Sapho's ability to love, and convinced that she could not express such affection without having experienced it with a man, Phaon embarks on a second quest to find the male rival. Yet Phaon is shortsighted, as we shall see, because Sapho has never loved a man; instead, she has cultivated intense friendships with women. Phaon resorts to stealing some poems that Sapho is too modest to show him. In one, he reads a stanza in which a blank space, marked with asterisks, indicates where the name of the male suitor should be:

> Seeing ***** my soul is satisfied,
> And not seeing him sorrow is in my heart:
> I am still unaware of my defeat,
> But perhaps he is my conqueror. (*Art.*, 10: 472-3)

While Sapho herself is free from jealousies at this point, Phaon practically needs a rival to make reason of his own passion. In other words, he needs a mediator whose desire he could imitate. Not once does he imagine that it could be his name that would scan so perfectly in the verse written by Sapho. Here, Scudéry examines the blind patterns of love triangles that men unconsciously form to justify their desires. She also underscores men's inability to perceive the intense, competitive force of female friendship. Only when Phaon hears Sapho's avowal of love is he finally convinced that the purloined verses were written about him. His jealousy dissipates when he learns that he was his own rival. Scudéry depicts an admittedly heterosexual world; however, this world is ordered according to female homosocial bonds. In fact, it is precisely the solidity of these bonds that she asks of Phaon in the end.

After the avowal scene, Sapho imagines for Phaon and herself a utopic situation: the two can remain inseparable lovers as long as Phaon never marries her (*Art.*, 10: 511-2). Soon Sapho hears of the perfect utopia where she may maintain such a bond with Phaon: the Land of the New Sauromates. Scudéry borrows here from the Forth Book of Herodotus's *Histories*, in which he describes a land where the native Scythians mate with the Amazons and establish an autonomous state surrounded by a great wilderness.[25] Scudéry rewrites the history to present a Greek state surrounded by vast deserts to protect the people and to create an enclave where the arts and letters may flourish (*Art.*, 10: 569-70). A young queen reigns and maintains a regime under which laws prescribe the behavior of lovers so they remain faithful to their beloved (*Art.*, 10: 573-4, 597). The passage of couples in and out of the main city is controlled by the Prince, who has all candidates for residence in the utopia interviewed to see if they qualify in character and faithfulness to one another (*Art.*, 10: 572). While Phaon vows to accompany Sapho to the Land of the New Sauromates, she makes him promise that he will remain faithful to her and never mention marriage (*Art.*, 10: 595, 600). By refusing the bond of marriage, Sapho paradoxically tries to assure that she and her lover will remain inseparable. In this instance, she applies another criterion of female homosocial bonding in the heterosexual relationship: inseparability. In the very opening of the narrative, Scudéry describes Sapho and her friends as "inseparable" (*Art.*, 10: 340). Phaon, upon proposing to Sapho that they enter this self-imposed exile, vows to make their fortunes indivisible: "That is why in order to put you at peace, and to make me happy, keep me always in your sight, and let's make, if you please, our destiny inseparable" (*Art.*, 10: 597). Once in the Land of the New Sauromates, outside the bonds of marriage, they live "in the sweetest peace," and the queen forbids any foreigners to enter her realm for a period of ten years so that no one may trouble the peace of mind of the two lovers (*Art.*, 10: 607-8). For Sapho and Phaon, a passionate love resembling female friendship replaces marriage and assures them tranquility in their undisturbed exile.

It would seem here that Scudéry sacrifices female homosocial bonding for a heterosexual relationship. One may even think that Scudéry has struck a compromise with the Ovidian narrative that presents the conversion of Sapho from criminal love with women to complete devotion to a man. However, she stages a significant transformation of opposite-sex relations by inscribing within them the qualities inherent to Sapho's ideal of Platonic love, which she shares with men as well as with women. The Platonic relationships with friends and lovers are based on the unhindered exchange of secret thoughts, on passionate attachment expressed in poetry, and on the imperative of inseparability. The homosocial continuum involves a wish to frequent others and to derive pleasure from such familiarity.

CONCLUSIONS

Madeleine de Scudéry's "Histoire de Sapho" provides ample evidence of the importance of female homosocial relations in fashioning a utopian vision of a heterosexual world. Of course, the judicial statements concerning female lovers, the pejorative representation of Sappho in medical and literary discourses, and especially the literary values of propriety, or *les bienséances*, probably discouraged Scudéry from exploring the full range of female relationships along the homosocial spectrum. These factors did not discourage her, however, from maintaining close and transparent relations with women of her time. During her sojourn in Marseille with her brother Georges, Scudéry kept up a regular correspondence with Mademoiselle Paulet, another *précieuse* who frequented the same circles as she, most notably the "blue room" of Madame de Rambouillet, Catherine de Vivonne. In one letter, Scudéry quotes for Mademoiselle Paulet some of François Malherbe's love poetry and pines over their geographic separation:

> But, after all, in the midst of this Paradise of Turks, I said to myself, while musing about you, a verse that Malherbe once pronounced, in speaking of Madame d'Auchy:
>
> Where Caliste is not, there is my hell.[26]
>
> Really, Mademoiselle, I have not caught my mind in the least moment of tranquil pleasure since I have been out of your presence.[27]

Just as in her descriptions of Sapho's relations with female friends, the terms of love, passion, and attachment apply to the continuum of women's homosocial relations. While men exchange women to form alliances and marriages in their forging of homosocial bonds, women exchange missives and poems depicting their affection for one another.

It is clear that in the first half of her "Histoire de Sapho," Madeleine de Scudéry pits networks of homosocial relations against one another. Following Phaon's approach, if a male admirer wishes to enter the continuum of female relations, he must intercept the poem or epistle in search of the inscription of his desire. Phaon desires that Sapho be conquered by her passion for him, and he is finally satisfied to learn that he is the "conqueror," as she puts it. However, he pays the price of sacrificing all his other social relations by agreeing to exile himself with Sapho. In the conclusion of the story, this mutual agreement ends the cycle of Phaon's victory over his beloved and her subordination, for they enter the Land of the New Sauromates as willing equals. Sapho and Phaon are both saved from the potentially destructive, subordinating effects of passion. Furthermore, Scudéry's Sapho triumphs over social constraints, since she extricates herself from the male homosocial traffic in women by refusing the contract of marriage. The woman writer sets the terms for her relationship with her lover and retreats with him to a utopian space to realize those terms. In her self-imposed exile, Sapho succeeds in obviating the requirements of propriety, whose representatives take umbrage at even the most innocent of relations between members of opposite sex, especially in the absence of marriage. Yet it is interesting to note that female homosocial relations appear quite innocent at this time. While it is never a question of genital sexual activity between women in Scudéry's narrative, these characters enjoy a great amount of emotional freedom and intellectual pleasure. Scudéry endows her characters with a mental androgyny that permits them to perceive and analyze both kinds of homosocial relations so they may fashion their utopias of love and affection.

NOTES

1. Lillian Faderman, *Surpassing the Love of Men: Romantic Friendship and Love Between Women from the Renaissance to the Present*, 2nd ed. (New York, 1988), 66, 68.
2. Eve Kosofsky Sedgwick, *Between Men: English Literature and Male Homosocial Desire* (New York, 1985), 2-3, 23.
3. Madeleine de Scudéry, *Artamène, ou le Grand Cyrus* (1656; reprint, Geneva, 1972), cited in the text.
4. Joan DeJean, *Fictions of Sappho: 1546-1937* (Chicago, 1989), 60-78, 103-10. DeJean also sees the ideological import of Scudéry's space as a response to the end of the Fronde. See her *Tender Geographies: Women and the Origins of the Novel in France* (New York, 1991), 48-50.
5. DeJean, *Fictions*, 105.
6. Edme Jacques Benoît Rathery and Boutron, *Mademoiselle de Scudéry, sa vie et sa correspondance avec un choix de ses poésies* (Paris, 1873), 6; and Nicole Aronson, *Mademoiselle de Scudéry, ou Le Voyage au pays de Tendre* (Paris, 1986), 57-8, 86-7. See also DeJean, *Fictions*, 104.
7. Quoted in Robert Aulotte, "Sur quelques traductions d'une ode de Sappho au XVIe siècle," *Bulletin de l'Association Guillaume Budé, Supplément, Lettres d'humanité* 17 (1958): 110.
8. René Girard, *Mensonge romantique et vérité romanesque* (Paris, 1961), 15-67.
9. Aulotte, "Sur quelques traductions," 111-4; and DeJean, *Fictions*, 32-3, 35.
10. Quoted in Aulotte, "Sur quelques traductions," 117. Compare with Catullus's poem 51, in *Catullus: The Poems*, 2nd ed., ed. Kenneth Quinn (London, 1973), 30.
11. Marie-Jo Bonnet, *Un Choix sans équivoque: Recherches historiques sur les relations amoureuses entre les femmes, XVIe-XXe siècle* (Paris, 1981), 21-67.
12. Jean Papon, *Recueil d'arrêts notables des cours souveraines de France* (1565), quoted in Guy Poirier, *L'Homosexualité dans l'imaginaire de la Renaissance* (Paris, 1996), 46.

13. Ibid., 47.
14. Claude Lebrun de la Rochette, *Les Procès civil et criminel divisé en cinq livres* (1611), quoted in ibid., 53.
15. David F. Greenberg, *The Construction of Homosexuality* (Chicago, 1988), 302-3.
16. Poirier, *Homosexualité*, 48; and Louis Crompton, "The Myth of Lesbian Impunity: Capital Laws from 1270 to 1791," *Journal of Homosexuality* 6 (1980-1): 17. Maurice Lever, *Les Bûchers de Sodome: Histoire des "infâmes"* (Paris, 1985), 87-94, confirms these statistics.
17. Crompton, "Myth," 17.
18. Thomas Bartholin, *Institutions anatomiques* (1647), quoted in Bonnet, *Choix*, 30.
19. DeJean, *Fictions*, 65-96.
20. Ovid, *Héroïdes*, ed. Henri Bornecque (Paris, 1928), 91, 92.
21. DeJean, *Fictions*, 104.
22. Victor Cousin, *La Société française au XVIIe siècle d'après Le Grand Cyrus de Mlle de Scudéry*, 2 vols. (Paris, 1858), 2: 120-305.
23. Roger Lathuillère, *La Préciosité: Etude historique et linguistique*, vol. 1: *La Position du problème* (Geneva, 1966), 638-52.
24. DeJean, *Fictions*, 105, 338.
25. Herodotus, *The Histories*, ed. Aubrey de Sélincourt (London, 1996), 249-51.
26. "Sonnet: Quel astre malheureux ma fortune a bâtie?" in François Malherbe, *Oeuvres*, ed. Antoine Adam (Paris, 1971), 83.
27. Rathery and Boutron, *Mademoiselle de Scudéry*, 162, quoted by Faderman, *Surpassing the Love*, 68, 426.

Masculinity and Satires of "Sodomites" in France, 1660-1715

Lewis C. Seifert

Throughout Ancien Régime France, charges of sodomy were a recurrent feature in satires of public figures. In the larger scheme of things, to be sure, such charges were far outnumbered by allusions to the heterosexual transgressions of cultural, ecclesiastical, and political personages during the same period. And yet, accusations of sodomy gained particular prominence in two of the most turbulent moments of the Ancien Régime. At the end of the Wars of Religion, Henri III was the object of virulent pamphlets, many of which put sodomy high on the list of his "crimes."[1] Later, during the Fronde, charges of sodomy surfaced in a number of the *mazarinades* that targeted Anne of Austria's Italian minister, Jules Mazarin.[2] Given that the satires of Henri III and Mazarin appeared at times of severe political turmoil, it is hardly surprising that they invoked the widespread early-modern understanding of sodomy as a symptom of cosmic and/or cultural disorder.[3] That is, the term "sodomy," which during this period *denoted* a wide range of sex acts over and beyond sex between men, *connoted* charges of heresy, tyranny, graft, and gluttony, and even responsibility for natural disasters, such as earthquakes, storms, and the like.[4] For satirists of Henri III and Mazarin, then, the charge that their victims engaged in sodomy with other men was shorthand for expounding upon their (perceived) threat to the divinely ordered body politic.

In satires from the second half of the seventeenth century, by contrast, accusations of sodomy assumed different meanings. The volumes of the manuscript *Chansonnier Maurepas* for the period 1660 to 1715 contain no fewer than seventy texts that connect prominent men to sodomitical acts or inclina-

[Haworth co-indexing entry note]: "Masculinity and Satires of 'Sodomites' in France, 1660-1715." Seifert, Lewis C. Co-published simultaneously in *Journal of Homosexuality* (Harrington Park Press, an imprint of The Haworth Press, Inc.) Vol. 41, No. 3/4, 2001, pp. 37-52; and: *Homosexuality in French History and Culture* (ed: Jeffrey Merrick, and Michael Sibalis) Harrington Park Press, an imprint of The Haworth Press, Inc., 2001, pp. 37-52. Single or multiple copies of this article are available for a fee from The Haworth Document Delivery Service [1-800-342-9678, 9:00 a.m. - 5:00 p.m. (EST). E-mail address: getinfo@haworthpressinc.com].

tions. Ranging from drinking songs and parodies of operatic libretti to epigrams and other poems not set to music, these manuscript texts are considerably lighter in tone than the pamphlets published during the Wars of Religion and the Fronde. Even more significant, they, unlike the political pamphlets that preceded them, make little or no effort to conflate sodomy with cosmic and/or cultural disorder. In this respect, they employ the type of satirical discourse that was probably a ubiquitous feature of early modern court gossip. Late sixteenth- and early seventeenth-century manuscript satires of sodomy in such sources as the *Registres-Journaux* of Pierre de l'Estoile and the *Historiettes* of Tallemant des Réaux do bear resemblance to those of the *Chansonnier Maurepas*, although they are far less numerous.[5] But even if they continued a long-standing tradition, the manuscript satires composed between 1660 and 1715 constituted the dominant satirical discourse of sodomy for this period. During Louis XIV's reign, then, there were not two parallel types of satire about sodomy, as there had been in the late sixteenth and early seventeenth centuries, but one.

Now at first glance, it might be tempting to concur with the critics of generations past that these satirical texts are useful for little more than anecdotal biographies of members of the high nobility and royal family, military officers, cultural personalities, judges, and Church officials.[6] To adopt such a dismissive attitude, though, would be a mistake. Like all satires, these poems and songs reveal the phantasmic fears of at least a certain section of the public of their time. Using (satirical) humor, they are also an imaginary response to these fears. From this perspective, satires reveal less about the satirized than they do about the satirists and their public. In this essay, I will work from the presupposition that what is being satirized becomes a means of identifying some of the cultural anxieties of a particular period. The satires of "sodomites" discussed in the following pages reveal not only anxieties about sodomy during the second half of the seventeenth century but also anxieties about masculinity in general.[7] For, not only did these satires appear during a period of intense "gender trouble" (as evidenced, among other things, by the numerous outbreaks of the centuries-old *querelle des femmes*), they were also contemporaneous with a burgeoning discourse on sexuality that took the form of pornographic novels and medical treatises. As we will see, the satires of "sodomites" in the pages of the *Chansonnier Maurepas* suggest that late seventeenth-century France was preoccupied not only with (re)defining femininity and heterosexual desire, but also with masculinity and male same-sex desire.

* * *

It is extremely difficult to reconstruct in any detail the historical contexts of production and reception of the late seventeenth-century satires of "sodomites." Most of them remain anonymous, and it is difficult to ascertain either the extent or the nature of their circulation. This said, we can glean a few clues from the collection in which they are found: the multi-volume *Chansonnier Maurepas* at the Bibliothèque Nationale de France. Compiled, organized chronologically, carefully annotated, and bound in volumes by Pierre Clairambault (1651-1740), these songs and poems were then recopied in elegant script and supplemented with later (eighteenth-century) texts under the supervision of Jean-Frédéric Phélypeaux, comte de Maurepas (1701-1781). From all indications, this *Chansonnier*, one of many compiled in the eighteenth century, was created to satisfy its owner's historical and anecdotal interests rather than to serve as a genuine songbook.[8] About the composition and reception of the songs themselves, we have less precise information. We do know that these *Chansonniers* include texts penned by members of court (even by two of Louis XIV's illegitimate daughters, the princess de Conti and the duchess de Bourbon) and that some of them circulated there as well. But we also know that these collections contain poems by the famous Pont-Neuf bards known as the Savoyard and the Cocher de Monsieur de Verthamont; that satirical songs are said to have been written and sung in cabarets of the neighborhood of the Temple by the likes of Boileau, La Fontaine, and Racine; and further, that the lieutenants general of police, La Reynie and d'Argenson, made note in their bulletins, from which Clairambault is said to have taken many texts, of potentially subversive songs sung in the streets of Paris.[9] All of this seems to indicate that these satires were composed and circulated both at Court and in the City. It is possible, then, that satires of "sodomites" circulated in both venues as well.

In the absence of more precise information about their composition and reception, we are forced to turn our focus to the songs and poems themselves. Fortunately, the historical events and persons satirized in most of the texts included in the *Chansonniers* have been identified (often amply so) by Clairambault, although their authors remain for the most part anonymous. Accordingly, the allusions and plays on words in these manuscript texts are often far less mysterious for us than many of those in the earlier printed political pamphlets. Even without the benefit of Clairambault's erudition, the manuscript satires, beyond the reach of censorship, eschew the types of intentionally enigmatic turns of phrase employed, of necessity, by the pamphlets.

Beyond this, the manuscript satires also differ from the earlier printed ones in terms of motivation, content, and humor. While the *libelles* against Henri III and Mazarin emanated from readily identifiable political factions, such was not nearly as often the case for songs and poems about late seventeenth-century "sodomites." In these later satires, as I have already mentioned, sodomy is not implicated either in cosmic and cultural disorder or in political instability. Of course, one explanation of this fact would be that the second half of the seventeenth century was a period of relative cultural and political stability, corresponding as it did to the reign of Louis XIV. Satirists lacked the explicit political motivation to invoke sodomy as part of any particular crisis. In comparison with the printed pamphlets from the Wars of Religion and the Fronde, these songs and poems seem to present satire for satire's sake. More precisely, their satire is akin to the perennial gossip about public figures during the Ancien Régime. This is not to say, however, that these satires were without political meaning or ramifications. Like the secret histories of (mostly fictional) sexual liaisons at court published in the Netherlands beginning in the 1680s and smuggled into France, the satirical songs and poems about "sodomites" were part of an emerging "literary underground" (to use Robert Darnton's phrase) that, in the eighteenth century, would play such an important role in undermining the philosophical foundations of the Ancien Régime. To be sure, these brief satires are hardly the extended sexual/political biographies of members of Louis XIV's court found in historical novellas (*nouvelles historiques*) and manuscript newspapers (*nouvelles à la main*). And yet, like them, they provide the elite political class with the opportunity to laugh at itself or its favorite victims from within its own ranks.[10] Occupying an intermediary position between the attack on individual reputation that characterized the Renaissance style of politics and attacks on the regime that appeared during the Enlightenment, the satires of "sodomites" contribute in their own way to the faultlines in the representational system of Louis Quatorzean absolutism. That is, they are part of what Peter Burke has termed a "crisis of representations."[11]

Now if it is true that one of the most salient aspects of the "crisis of representations" during the reign of Louis XIV is a preference for empiricism over mysticism and literalism over metaphor and analogy, then the poems and songs about "sodomites" are most certainly symptomatic of that crisis.[12] On the whole, explicit descriptions of male same-sex desire and sex acts are preferred to euphemisms and vague allusions. There are, nonetheless, important differences among these texts. On the basis of rhetoric and thematics, these satires can be sorted into five different categories. By far the most common are texts that make an accusation of sodomy in a third-person voice and that refer to historical events. Thus, one satire, which takes the form of an extended parody of a popular song, mockingly recounts the aftermath of Louis XIV's discovery of the so-called "confraternity" of "sodomites" at court in 1682 and specifically names seven individuals implicated in this scandal.[13] However, the vast majority of these satires concern incidents involving just one individual. For instance, to mark the death of Philippe d'Orléans, brother of Louis

XIV, in 1701, one poem purports to rectify the official account and to reveal a "secret" truth that goes against accepted wisdom.

> Philippe died with a bottle in his hand;
> The proverb is far from certain
> That says that man dies as he usually lives;
> He shows us quite the contrary;
> For, if he had died as he had lived,
> He would have died with his cock up an ass.[14]

Besides Philippe (who was a favorite target of the satirists), Jean-Baptiste Lully, the famous seventeenth-century composer and Superintendent of the King's Music, was satirized almost as frequently for "offenses" ranging from his responsibility for a botched fireworks display to his relationship with a musician at court. Other personalities targeted include Jacques Chausson, Achilles de Harlay, Auguste Servien, Charles-Belgique-Hollande de la Trimouille, Henri de Turenne, Louis-Joseph de Vendôme, and Louis de Vermandois.[15]

A smaller number of satires employ rhetorical and thematic strategies other than the third-person accusation. These include:

a. Link between anal intercourse and venereal disease. A piece entitled "Verses to put under the portrait of the duke de Vendôme," for instance, equates his siege of Barcelona with his syphilis.

> This hero whom you see represented here,
> Favorite of Venus, favorite of Bellona,
> Got syphilis and took Barcelona
> Both from the wrong side. [*Maurepas*, 5: 180]

b. Phantasmic punishment for sodomy. One frequently quoted song (dated 1674) suggests that people make up for their disappointment at Lully's failed fireworks by watching him burn at the stake alongside Chausson, who was indeed executed for sodomy in 1661 and whose case gained notoriety at the time.

> Apologies, Sirs, if Baptiste
> Prepared so lugubrious, so sad a fire for you,
> And served you so ill for your *demis louis* [coins paid to watch the fireworks],
> Chausson's trial continues; if it ends
> It will soon show you another [fire] in the Grève [site of executions],
> With which you will be more pleased. [FF 12619, folio 101]

c. Mock confession or request in the first person. In one song, Chausson, at the stake, cries out for Tarnaut, who was tried and punished with him.

> Chausson cried out loudly:
> Where is Tarnaut?
> Ah! Sir Lieutenant,
> Before you burn me,
> Permit me to fuck him in the ass
> And I will die happy. [*Maurepas*, 4: 318]

d. Mock imperative. In this group, the poet invites readers and/or the target(s) to engage in anal intercourse. One song, dated 1668, enjoins:

> Friends, let us imitate those great personages,
> The glory of their ages,
> Who preferred to the cunt
> The ass of a beautiful boy. . . . [*Maurepas*, 1: 131]

The poem then lists "sodomites" from ancient Greece and Rome and sixteenth- and early seventeenth-century France before mentioning contemporaries from the entourage of Philippe d'Orléans.

No matter which rhetorical or thematic strategy they employ, the songs and poems about "sodomites" in the *Chansonnier Maurepas* highlight a fundamental ambiguity. According to its classic definition, satire constitutes a form of aggression whose target is made responsible for corrupting an ideal order. By depicting this corruption, satire is said to enact a symbolic punishment and to express the desire for return to the lost ideal. Now it is certainly possible and, indeed, legitimate to use this definition to interpret the satires of "sodomites" from the reign of Louis XIV. It goes without saying that all of these satires display a hostility toward the "sodomite(s)" they portray. Yet this hostility is made explicit to widely varying degrees. On one end of the spectrum is a small subset of satires in which hostility not only is explicit, but takes the form of phantasmic violence. Thus, one song (dated 1661) laments the unequal treatment given to two "sodomites" of different social backgrounds (Chausson, a bourgeois, and Guitaut de Comminges, an aristocrat) and implies that both deserved to die at the stake.

> Good gods! Where is your justice?
> Chausson is going to die at the stake,
> And Guitaut through the same vice,
> Earned the *cordon bleu* [of the Order of the Holy Spirit]! [*Maurepas*, 4: 245]

In many other satires, though, hostility is made explicit through insults, as in the following song about the playwright Campistron (dated 1686) that plays on the word "bardash" (the pejorative term frequently used until the end of the eighteenth century to designate the passive partner in anal sex).[16]

> Who would believe that Campistron
> In the ass, like an infamous one
> Fucks the ugliest woman
> Just like the handsomest boy?
> Without fearing hair nor moustaches,
> Pimps nor whores,
> Keep clear, little bardashes,
> Of the most bardash of humans. [*Maurepas*, 5: 52]

At the other end of the spectrum are satires in which hostility is implicit, if indeed it can be detected at all. Perhaps the most extreme example is a song (dated 1677) in which la Trimouille, a peer of France, admits his pleasure at the thought of oral sex.

> Ah! how the nose tickles me![17]
> Said the good la Trimouille;
> What pleasure when it wets me
> And when it does that to me!
> I love the juice from the balls
> And often I cover myself with it;
> A cock never comes out unsatisfied
>
> When it's put there, there, there, there, there
> A hard cock
> Is so charming
> And whoever says otherwise
> Lies, lies, lies, lies, lies. [*Maurepas*, 1: 272]

To be sure, this song is not quite devoid of satire. La Trimouille admits to being the passive partner, a role routinely stigmatized in this period and, moreover, deemed all the more unworthy for those of elevated social status.[18] Ridicule is also apparent in the two monosyllabic series, which are elements of the song that is parodied. Beyond this, though, the text does not allude to any form of punishment nor does it explicitly insult Trimouille. And ultimately, a homoerotic reading, or singing, of the song is entirely conceivable.

Whether they are more or less explicitly hostile, the satires of "sodomites" as a whole display a humor that is considerably lighter in tone than what is found in the pamphlets about Henri III and Mazarin, and this lighter tone generally softens allusions to sodomy. In the pamphlets from the Wars of Religion and the Fronde, humor serves above all to underscore the disorder purportedly created by the "sodomite" who becomes "abject," that is, the embodiment of an alterity that both defines and threatens order.[19] In Paul Scarron's "The Mazarinade," for instance, the repetition of the word "bugger" in one passage stretches semantic reference far beyond ordinary usage. With a flourish typical of the mid-seventeenth-century *burlesque* aesthetic, Scarron uses "bugger" to refer to sex acts (bestiality, pederasty, masturbation, anal intercourse) but also, and especially, to tyranny. Mazarin is portrayed as a "Bugger sodomizing the State."[20] In the end, the relentless repetition of the word "bugger" and the multiple referents applied to it make Mazarin abject, as it does the synecdochical category of sodomy itself, which covers a wide range of vices and crimes.

As a whole, the satires produced during the reign of Louis XIV also render "sodomites" and sodomy abject. And yet, over and beyond the comparatively lighthearted humor, at least three features of these songs and poems combine to alter the nature of the disgust that the satirical "sodomite" is supposed to inspire. First, in the satires from the period 1660 to 1715, the referents for sodomy are considerably fewer than in the pamphlets about Henri III and Mazarin. Indeed, sodomical acts among men are the primary focus, and such descriptions are not nearly as frequently linked to political, social, and religious disorder. Second, these satires frequently employ ironic approval of sodomy, a stance that is only rarely found in the earlier pamphlets. Third, and related to this irony, the songs and poems from the *Chansonnier Maurepas* occasionally express mock admiration for their very targets. Thus, the marquis de Créquy is addressed as "handsome Crequy" [FF 12620, folio 89], and, in one distinctly ambivalent song, Vendôme is called the "best bugger in the world" [*Maurepas*, 2: 229]. The combined effect of these features is to humanize, in a relative sense, the "sodomites" targeted by the manuscript satires. This is obviously not to say that satirists from the second half of the seventeenth century express anything approaching sympathy for their victims, but rather that the "sodomites" ridiculed are less frightening and less caricatural than the subjects of the earlier pamphlets.

This different satirical approach makes it possible to understand these songs and poems as an example of what Peter Stallybrass and Allon White have termed "phobic enchantment." In this type of fantasy, "repugnance and fascination are the twin poles of [a] process in which a *political* imperative to reject and eliminate the debasing 'low' conflicts powerfully and unpredictably with a desire for this Other."[21] Now I do not mean to imply that the notion of "phobic enchantment" could not be applied to the attacks on Henri III and Mazarin. Yet, precisely because their tone is lighter and their satire less dehumanizing, the satires from the *Chansonnier Maurepas* seem to be a better illustration of this notion, or at the very least of a "phobic enchantment" in which fascination with the debased Other is expressed more openly and explicitly. Of course, it is not only the Others, the "sodomites," who are the object of fascination, but sodomy itself. This is all the more significant in view of the fact that sodomy is not primarily functional, not first and foremost a means to the end of attacking the actions, beliefs, or policies of the men who are satirized. Allusions to their actions, beliefs, and/or policies do appear in these songs and poems; however, it is questionable whether many of them would have been targeted by satirists at all had it not been for their reputations as "sodomites."[22] In any event, sodomitical reputations and, especially, sodomitical acts are the central focus of the songs and poems from the *Chansonnier Maurepas*. This centrality thus raises the question of how we are to understand satirists' predilection for the motif of sodomy during the years 1660-1715.

* * *

Maurice Lever has described the second half of the seventeenth century in France as "homophobic," in contrast with what he considers to be the decidedly more "homophilic" first half.[23] Part of Lever's argument is based on literary sources: During the first half of the century, as he shows, several poets incorporated homoerotic themes into their verse, whereas the second half of the century witnessed the flourishing of the satires I have been discussing here. Beyond the properly historical problems with Lever's thesis, the literary sources he cites cannot be so easily reduced to the homophilic-homophobic opposition he tries to establish.[24] In particular, as I have already suggested, the satires constitute more than a verbal repression of or an expression of hostility toward sodomy. Rather, as I have already argued, they might be seen as an example of "phobic enchantment," in which repugnance and fascination are conjoined. Reading them in this way would encourage us to reevaluate the complexity of attitudes toward sodomy during the reign of Louis XIV. This is hardly to deny that this period was marked by repression of sodomites. On the contrary, the executions of Jacques Chausson, Jacques Paulmier, Claude Le Petit, and Philippe Bouvet de la Contamine and the disbanding of the infamous "confraternity" at court in 1682, to cite but a few examples, demonstrate the very real consequences of this repression. At the same time, this repression contributes in many cases to a fascination with the "sodomite" and sodomy, a fascination that is amply expressed in the songs and poems of the *Chansonnier Maurepas*.

To understand this fascination and its consequences, it is crucial to recognize the complexity and, specifically, the ambivalence of attitudes toward sodomy during the reign of Louis XIV. Indeed, the fascination-*cum*-repression that characterizes the production of satires about "sodomites" is part of a broader fascination with sexualities and gender differences in this period. It is now well known that the second half of the seventeenth century was a period of intense "gender trouble," a period during which the discourses of sexual difference addressed the roles of women in society. From the proto-feminist treatises of François Poullain de la Barre (*On the Equality of the Two Sexes* and *On the Education of Ladies*) to the latter-day *querelle des femmes* between Nicolas Boileau ("Satire X: Against Women") and Charles Perrault ("The Apology of Women") and including the substantial writing, both fiction and nonfiction, by women, the reign of Louis XIV was marked by fierce debates about the definitions of femininity. During the same period, as is increasingly well known, discourses of sexuality were also flourishing in the form of pornographic novels and marriage treatises. As Jean Mainil in particular has shown, novels, such as *The School of Girls*, *Lust or Modesty Undone*, *Venus in the Cloister*, and *The Academy of Ladies*, and treatises, such as Nicolas Venette's *Portrait of Love Considered in the State of Marriage*, were part of a broad epistemological attempt to define women as radically "other," fundamentally different from men. Although they give detailed descriptions of the sexualized female body, texts such as these, nonetheless, never quite accord women a complete ontological autonomy, nor do they articulate their submission to patriarchal dominance. What they ultimately serve to do, according to Mainil, is to define that which is *not* male, that which gives consistency to the male and the masculine.[25]

At first glance, the satires of "sodomites" that circulated during the second half of the seventeenth century would also seem to define that which is *not* male, all the better to reaffirm, by contrast, what normative masculinity *should* be. In this way, sodomites would seem to fulfill a role similar to that of women in the pornographic novels and the medical treatises. They are one of the means by which an emerging heterosexual masculine norm can be defined. In this sense, they resemble the sodomites and, more precisely, the "mollies" of early eighteenth-century London studied by Randolph Trumbach.[26]

This, however, is only part of the story, for women are not entirely absent from this corpus. A number of the satirical songs and poems from the *Chansonnier Maurepas* juxtapose male-female and male-male sex acts and desires. The king and his brother offered satirists obvious material for such a juxtaposition. According to one poet:

> Love in different ways
> Ignited two brothers with its flames.
> One sighed for the Ladies;
> The other loved only boys. . . . [FF 12643, folio 222]

Usually, however, the juxtapositions of heterosexual and sodomitical acts concern the same person. For instance, one of several songs devoted to Lully's leaving Mademoiselle Certain for the musician Brunet has the composer confess, in the first person:

> The old Certain is angry
> That Brunet is my minion
> She is an old cow
> He is a pretty bardash
> Her cunt is wide and deep
> His asshole is small and round. [FF 12688, folio 258]

Granted, satires such as these exploit a motif already present in early seventeenth-century libertine poetry. Still, the fact that this motif reappears later in the century, at a time when women's social and sexual roles were of central interest, suggests that the satires of "sodomites" are themselves a recognition that sexualities and gender differences are inextricably intertwined. Moreover, by satirizing sodomy, these songs and poems not only delineate the contours of heterosexual masculinity, they also sketch out a hierarchy of relations among sexual and gendered identities, a hierarchy that aims to reestablish a sense of order and propriety, the ultimate goals of all satire. But precisely what sort of hierarchy do these particular songs and poems endorse?

Most obvious and most central is the fact that sodomitical desire is usually portrayed as subordinate and inferior to different-sex desire. In a song about Louis XIV and Philippe d'Orléans, the "backside" is rejected by the king and is hierarchically inferior to the object of his own pleasure.

> When Louis took the front,
> He left the backside;
> He abandoned that part
> To the lot of Monsieur
> His brother, his brother, his brother. [*Maurepas* 5: 75])

It is worth noting that sodomy, however subordinate and inferior, is not made overtly abject by the comparison with different-sex desire and/or sex acts. Nor is it in any of the satires that juxtapose male-female and male-male inclinations or acts. Indeed, in some of the songs and poems, heterosexual and sodomitical inclinations are interchangeable. One song, for instance, declares that the marquis de Breauté "does not know which one to choose, / Between Venus and Ganymede" [FF 12619, folio 219]. More important, though, is the fluidity and instability of the male-female and male-male desires that are portrayed by this sub-group of satires about sodomy. In one song, Lully states that the beauty of the duchess de la Ferté enchanted him so much that "I who am Florentine, I've changed sides" [*Maurepas* 1: 256]. Like Lully, the "sodomites" targeted by late seventeenth-century satirists may have a predisposition for same-sex desire; but such a predisposition does not signify an immutable and unidirectional "sexual orientation."[27] Rather, they suggest that different-sex and sodomitical desires and acts are fluid and unstable. These particular satires would seem to confirm Thomas Laqueur's conclusion, based on early modern medical thought, that "the male body . . . seemed equally capable of responding erotically to the sight of women as to attractive young men. . . ."[28] More generally, in many of these satires, sodomy is not, and seemingly cannot be, cordoned off from different-sex desires and acts. At a time before the modern oppositional construction of heterosexuality and homosexuality, these songs and poems seem to illustrate Trumbach's assertion that, in Northern Europe of the seventeenth century, "persons who engaged in sexual relations with their own gender were presumed to be attracted to the other gender as well."[29]

By relegating sodomy to the subordinate position, then, these satires counteract the fluidity between hetero- and homoerotic desire. Many of them also do so by linking sodomy and misogyny. In extreme cases, "sodomites" are accused of rejecting women altogether. Thus, one song devoted to the "confraternity" of 1682 depicts its members as "anti-cuntists" who leave the women at court disconsolate (*Maurepas* 5: 37-39). More often, however, women appear as the less desirable of two erotic objects available to the "sodomite." Such is certainly the case of another song (dated 1681) about Lully's rejection of Certain for Brunet, a song that recalls depictions of the grotesque female body common in early seventeenth-century libertine poetry.

> Leave your Certain there, button up your doublet;
> Believe me, my dear Lully, go on to other things;
> See her old ma, over there in a corner,
> Who scratches her cunt into which a beam would fit!
> Leave all those cunts that don't fuck you:
> Take the cock of Brunet who's going to fuck you. [*Maurepas* 2: 28-9]

Through its ironic imperatives, this song of course targets the "sodomites" Lully and Brunet. Yet it establishes a causal link between the ironic endorsement of sodomy and the degrading portrait of Certain's mother. The final imperative, because it mockingly approves Lully's passivity as a bardash, is obviously ironic. However, this irony is made all the more blatant by the reference to what is an anatomical impossibility ("cunts that don't fuck") but also an assimilation of Lully and the "old ma." Even as Lully is enjoined to reject the two female erotic objects, he resembles them, paradoxically, because he is a bardash and, at least implicitly, effeminate.[30] By degrading the "old ma," then, this satire simultaneously degrades the "sodomite" Lully all the more forcefully. And ultimately, Lully is the "feminized" sodomite, but he is also, by association, a misogynist. In the seventeenth century, mocking women was an outright rejection of the good taste and refined manners of which they were the supreme arbiters. As a "sodomite" and a misogynist, according to this song, Lully is presumed to be a double social outcast.

Of course, the implicit causal link this satire attempts to make between sodomy and misogyny cannot cover up the fact that it is the ironic third-person songster who *explicitly* casts Certain's mother as the grotesque "old ma." In a twist of the very irony directed at Lully, this satire reveals that it is actually the songster who is responsible for misogyny. This (seemingly unintentional) admission is hardly insignificant, and this for two reasons. First of all, it is indicative of a broader strategy on the part of the satirists whose work is preserved in the *Chansonnier Maurepas*. Throughout this songbook, misogyny is rampant, not only in satires of "sodomites" but also in the (far more numerous) songs and poems about the heterosexual liaisons of various well-known figures. If all of these satires, sodomitical and heterosexual, are considered as a whole, the implicit causal link between "sodomites" and misogyny may offer a means for songsters, poets, and listeners to defend themselves against charges of hostility toward women and to preserve sociable respectability. Misogyny, they might claim, is ultimately the fault of the "sodomites" they deride in so many of their songs and poems. It is as if misogyny is, in effect, a phenomenon propagated by a marginal few, like the "anti-cuntists" of the "confraternity" disbanded in 1682.[31]

More generally, though, the unwitting admission by the songster in the poem about Lully reveals just how central, and how linked, the epistemological problems of Woman and the sodomite are in this period. At a time when heterosexual masculinity was in the process of being constituted on various discursive fronts, it was imperative to establish conceptual boundaries against which this norm could be defined. By intervening so directly in the song about Lully, the songster reveals the sleight of hand that is at work in *all* of the satires I have been discussing here. In an important sense, the "sodomites" in the *Chansonnier Maurepas* are indeed creations both *by* and *for* satirical songsters and poets during the reign of Louis XIV. These "sodomites" are proof of just how concerted the efforts were to give solidity, through (satirical) repression, to an emerging heterosexual masculine norm.

No matter how satirical, these "sodomites" might also provide useful suggestions for defining future research into the history and representations of sodomy and the sodomite in the France of Louis XIV. For instance, even a cursory glance at the satires in the *Chansonnier Maurepas* suggests that Randolph

Trumbach's seminal account of the sodomite in late seventeenth-century and early eighteenth-century England does not apply completely to the sodomite in France of the same period. If, according to Trumbach, the seventeenth-century English sodomite was thought to be attracted to both women and boys, in France he could desire women and boys, women and men, or exclusively boys and/or men. While the English sodomite changed from being a rake in the seventeenth century to being an effeminate molly in the early eighteenth century, the French sodomite of these same periods came in many different guises– rake, effeminate man, warrior, among others–and, arguably, did not transform from one type into another. Finally, Trumbach's argument that the late seventeenth- and early eighteenth-century English sodomite was used to distinguish between men and women at a time when this difference was increasingly blurred is very useful for understanding the function of the French sodomite, but not for the same reasons. Whereas in England the rise of the "egalitarian family" would seem to have been the culprit, in France it was perhaps much more the widely acclaimed, but no less angst-provoking, cultural and civilizing authority of women.

These and no doubt other features of sodomy in the France of Louis XIV deserve to be investigated further. Reading through satires such as the songs and poems about "sodomites" in the *Chansonnier Maurepas* gives us a glimpse not only into a period before heterosexuality had been "invented," but also into a period when elite masculinity was just beginning to oppose itself radically to male same-sex desire. Attempting as they did to marginalize and stigmatize sodomy through laughter, satirists during the reign of Louis XIV paradoxically revealed just how central it was to evolving conceptions of the self, gender differences, and sexuality. Of course, a similar paradox endures in the homophobic jokes and representations that pervade our own culture. But analyzing that paradox and its history is surely an essential step in the struggle against the satirists, and the repression, of our own time.

NOTES

1. Guy Poirier, *L'Homosexualité dans l'imaginaire de la Renaissance* (Paris, 1996); Donald Stone, "The Sexual Outlaw in France, 1602," *Journal of the History of Sexuality* 2 (1992): 597-608; David Teasley, "The Charge of Sodomy as a Political Weapon in Early Modern France: The Case of Henry III in Catholic League Polemic, 1585-1589," *The Maryland Historian* 18 (1987): 17-30; and Rebecca Zorach, "The Matter of Italy: Sodomy and the Scandal of Style in Sixteenth-Century France," *Journal of Medieval and Early Modern Studies* 28 (1998): 581-609. The author is grateful to Catherine Gordon-Seifert, George Hoffmann, and Gretchen Schultz for their many insightful comments on earlier versions of this essay.

2. Jeffrey Merrick, "The Cardinal and the Queen: Sexual and Political Disorders in the Mazarinades," *French Historical Studies* 18 (1994): 667-99; and Lewis C. Seifert,

"Eroticizing the Fronde: Sexual Deviance and Political Disorder in the *Mazarinades*," *L'Esprit Créateur* 35 (1995): 22-36.

3. On the early modern understanding of sodomy as both cosmic and cultural disorder, see Alan Bray, *Homosexuality in Renaissance England* (London, 1982); and, especially, Cameron McFarlane, *The Sodomite in Fiction and Satire, 1660-1750* (New York, 1997).

4. These included, among other things, heterosexual anal intercourse, pederasty, bestiality, clerical concubine-keeping, abuse of a young girl by an adult man, sexual intercourse between Christians and Jews, masturbation, and coitus interruptus. This multireferentiality notwithstanding, sodomy increasingly denotes male-male sex acts throughout the seventeenth and, especially, eighteenth centuries. McFarlane, *Sodomite*, 2-3.

5. Of course, it is entirely possible that just as many satirical songs and poems circulated before 1660. But it is impossible to know if the greater number of satires in the *Chansonnier Maurepas* is due to a quantitative increase in production or to more systematic and thorough preservation.

6. For instance, the anonymous editor of an extremely rare nineteenth-century edition of selections from the *Chansonnier Maurepas* cites a vague "historical interest" among the "upper classes and enlightened men" to justify publication. *Recueil dit de Maurepas: Pièces libres, chansons, épigrammes, et autres vers satiriques sur divers personnages des siècles de Louis XIV et Louis XV*, 6 vols. (Leyden, 1865), 1: xi. Ultimately, historical interest may have been a cover for other motivations. The elegant format, printing, and binding of this edition liken it to numerous editions of historical erotica published during the nineteenth century. Twentieth-century biographers and historians of homosexuality have often cited texts from the *Chansonnier Maurepas*, although usually without extended commentary. A notable exception is Marc Daniel, *Hommes du Grand Siècle: Etudes sur l'homosexualité sous les règnes de Louis XIII et de Louis XIV* (Paris, 1957).

7. Throughout this essay, I use the term "sodomite" in quotation marks so as to bracket the often undecidable question as to whether the men satirized in the songs and poems I study could indeed be categorized as such.

8. Annette Keilhauer, *Das französische Chanson im späten Ancien Régime: Strukturen, Verbreitungswege und gesellschaftliche Praxis einer populären Literaturform* (Hildesheim, 1998), 162.

9. Paul d'Estrée, "Les Origines du Chansonnier de Maurepas," *Revue d'histoire littéraire de la France* (1896): 334; Keilhauer, *Französische Chanson*, 162; and "Préface," in *Chansonnier historique du XVIIIe siècle*, ed. Emile Raunié, 10 vols. (Paris, 1879), 1: xxxiv-xl.

10. This is precisely the type of reader response that Robert Darnton concludes was possible among elite readers during the Ancien Régime. *The Forbidden Best-Sellers of Pre-Revolutionary France* (New York, 1995), 193. The consequence of this type of response, according to Darnton, is that "a political system may be most endangered when its most favored elite ceases to believe in its legitimacy."

11. On this "crisis," albeit from different perspectives, see Peter Burke, *The Fabrication of Louis XIV* (New Haven, 1992), 125-33; Darnton, *Forbidden Best-Sellers*, 181-216; and Kathryn Hoffmann, *Society of Pleasures: Interdisciplinary Readings in Pleasure and Power During the Reign of Louis XIV* (New York, 1997), 149-58.

12. Burke, *Fabrication*, 125-33.

13. *Maurepas* 5: 37-8. Further citations from this nineteenth-century edition of selections from the *Chansonnier Maurepas* are given in the text. On the "confraternity"

disbanded in 1682, see *Homosexuality in Early Modern France: A Documentary Collection*, ed. Jeffrey Merrick and Bryant T. Ragan, Jr. (New York, 2001), 118-24.

14. BN, Ms, Fonds Français 12643, folio 197. Further citations from the *Chansonnier Maurepas* are given in the text.

15. Jacques Chausson was burned at the stake for sodomy in 1661. Achilles de Harlay, First President of the parlement of Paris. Abbé Auguste Servien. Charles-Belgique-Hollande de la Trimouille, member of a well-known family of the high nobility. Henri de Turenne and Louis-Joseph de Vendôme, famous military officers. Louis de Vermandois, illegitimate son of Louis XIV, implicated in the "confraternity" scandal of 1682.

16. On "bardash," see Claude Courouve, *Vocabulaire de l'homosexualité masculine* (Paris, 1985), 61. Courouve cites this song as evidence that the term could sometimes be used to refer to "all male homosexuality." Such a conclusion seems questionable since the primary meaning of passivity dominates this song.

17. "Nose" is often a euphemism for penis in the seventeenth century. Although the nineteenth-century edition of the *Chansonnier Maurepas* gives only "nose" here, the original manuscript provides the variant "cock" (*vit*). BN, Ms, FF 12619, folio 395.

18. For a discussion of the transgressive connotations attached to such a role, see Michel Rey, "1700-1750, Les Sodomites créent un mode de vie," *Cahiers Gai-Kitsch-Camp* 24 (1994): xix-xx.

19. I borrow this definition of the "abject" from Julia Kristeva, *Pouvoirs de l'horreur* (Paris, 1980).

20. Paul Scarron, *Poésies diverses*, ed. Maurice Cauchie, 2 vols. (Paris, 1960), 2: 32. For more of the text in English, see *Homosexuality in Early Modern France*, 109-10.

21. Peter Stallybrass and Allon White, *The Politics and Poetics of Transgression* (Ithaca, 1986), 4-5. I am indebted here to McFarlane's treatment of Stallybrass and White, especially *Sodomite*, 108, 121-2.

22. Although several figures identified as "sodomites" are attacked in other satires for reasons other than sodomy, Philippe d'Orléans and Lully, the most popular targets, are exclusively satirized for sodomy.

23. Maurice Lever, *Les Bûchers de Sodome: Histoire des "infâmes"* (Paris, 1985).

24. There are, of course, numerous examples of repression of sodomy during the first half of the century, as Lever himself acknowledges. *Bûchers*, 99-142.

25. Jean Mainil, *Dans les règles du plaisir: Théorie de la différence dans le discours obscène, romanesque, et médical de l'Ancien Régime* (Paris, 1996), 38.

26. Randolph Trumbach, *Sex and the Gender Revolution*, vol. 1: *Heterosexuality and the Third Gender in Enlightenment London* (Chicago, 1998), 9.

27. Lully's Italian origins were presumed to give him just such a predisposition. Throughout the early modern period, French satirists regularly portrayed sodomy as being far more widespread in Italy than in France.

28. Thomas Laqueur, *Making Sex: Body and Gender from the Greeks to Freud* (Cambridge, MA, 1990), 52.

29. Trumbach, *Heterosexuality*, 8.

30. In seventeenth-century France, effeminacy was not necessarily linked to sodomy, nor were sodomites necessarily thought to be effeminate. Seifert, "L'Homme de ruelle chez les dames: Civility and Masculinity in the Salon," in *Actes de New Orleans*, Biblio 17 (Tübingen, forthcoming).

31. McFarlane, *Sodomite*, 68, makes a similar observation about satirical representations of sodomy in early modern England.

The Abominable Madame de Murat

David Michael Robinson

I

Several of the early eighteenth-century reports of the Parisian lieutenant general of police, René d'Argenson, recount the scandalous behavior of a noblewoman who flaunted, among other shocking practices and beliefs, her lesbianism.[1] Under the heading "Disorders of Madame de Murat" (otherwise known as Henriette de Castelnau, countess de Murat), d'Argenson writes:

> 6 December 1699. I have the honor to send you the memoir that it pleased you to ask of me, concerning Madame de Murat; it is not easy to express in detail all the disorders of her conduct, without wounding the rules of decency, and the public is pained to see a lady of this birth in such shameful and such flaunted dissoluteness.
>
> 24 February 1700. The crimes that are imputed to Madame de Murat are not of a kind that can be easily proven by means of information, since it has to do with domestic impieties and a monstrous attachment to persons of her sex. However, I would like very much to know what she would respond to the following facts:
>
> A portrait pierced with several knife cuts, by the jealousy of a woman whom she loved and whom she left, several months ago, to attach herself to Madame de Nantiat, another woman of the utmost dissoluteness, less known for the fines levied against her because of gaming, than for the disorder of her morals. This woman, lodged at her home, is the object of her continuous adoration, in the presence even of valets and some pawnbrokers.
>
> The execrable oaths proffered while gaming and the infamous discussions over the dining table, to which Monsieur the count de Roussilon, now on bad terms with Madame de Murat, was witness.

[Haworth co-indexing entry note]: "The Abominable Madame de Murat." Robinson, David Michael. Co-published simultaneously in *Journal of Homosexuality* (Harrington Park Press, an imprint of The Haworth Press, Inc.) Vol. 41, No. 3/4, 2001, pp. 53-67; and: *Homosexuality in French History and Culture* (ed: Jeffrey Merrick, and Michael Sibalis) Harrington Park Press, an imprint of The Haworth Press, Inc., 2001, pp. 53-67. Single or multiple copies of this article are available for a fee from The Haworth Document Delivery Service [1-800-342-9678, 9:00 a.m. - 5:00 p.m. (EST). E-mail address: getinfo@haworthpressinc.com].

> Dissolute songs sung during the night and at all hours.
>
> The insolence to piss out the window, after a long debauch.
>
> Her impudent conversation with Monsieur the vicar of Saint-Cosme, equally removed from both modesty and religion.
>
> 1 December 1701. I will add, in regard to Madame de Murat of whom this memoir makes mention, that she has returned to Paris after an absence of eight days, that she has reconciled with Madame de Nantiat, and that the horrors and abominations of their reciprocal friendship justly horrify all their neighbors.
>
> 4 December 1701. I take the liberty of sending you a letter that I received, this morning, concerning the abominable conduct of Mesdames de Murat and de Nantiat, who create new public scenes every day. The writing of this letter appears constrained, and one can easily suspect that the reconciliation of these two women has excited sentiments of jealousy or vengeance in the heart of a third, who reigned previously over that of Madame de Murat; but the blasphemies, the obscenities, and the drunkenness with which they are reproached are not less true for that. Thus, I hope that the King will very much want to use his authority to expel them from Paris or even to imprison them, if one cannot do otherwise.[2]

By the time these reports were written, the author was able to draw upon a longstanding antilesbian rhetorical tradition, one that offered a variety of tones, motifs, structures, and strategies for confronting the troubling notion that women could not only love but also have sex with other women and that some women indeed preferred such same-sex relationships and activities to love and sex with men.[3] Here, the chief antilesbian rhetorical strategy is demonization; d'Argenson depicts lesbianism as something that, as Claude Courouve puts it, "inspires terror and repulsion," referring to it as "a monstrous attachment for persons of her sex," and speaking of "the horrors and abominations of their reciprocal friendship [that] justly horrify all their neighbors," and of "the abominable conduct of Mesdames de Murat and de Nantiat." The police chief combines the tried-and-true idea of lesbians as monsters with traditional religious condemnation of homosexuality.[4]

II

Most early twenty-first-century readers would not be surprised at d'Argenson's horrified moralizing. While still very much current today, it is what one expects to encounter in a text (particularly a police report) written three hundred years ago. Of course, anyone familiar with late seventeenth-century libertine and pornographic writings, such as Nicolas Chorier's *Académie des dames* or the anonymous *Ecole des filles*, or with gossip and scandal novels of the period, such as Delarivier Manley's *The New Atalantis* or Antoine Hamilton's *Memoirs of the Count de Gramont*, has encountered a markedly different antilesbian tone: the amused condescension of the man (or in some cases woman) of the world, an amusement that, as I argue elsewhere, masks a good deal of anxiety.[5] Indeed, both *The New Atalantis* and *Memoirs of the Count de Gramont* provide masterful examples of the antilesbian rhetorical strategy that, drawing upon Eve Kosofsky Sedgwick's essay "Privilege of Unknowing," I call mock-unknowing: a tongue-in-cheek ignorance, an arch pretense of innocence that depends upon a shared knowingness between author and intended readers.[6] When a character like Manley's Lady Intelligence exclaims, "Two beautiful ladies joined in an excess of amity . . . innocently embrace! For how can they be guilty? They vow eternal tenderness, they exclude the men, and condition that they will always do so. What irregularity can there be in this?", her pose of *unknowing*, of innocent and ignorant questioning, merely underscores the *knowingness* of everyone involved.[7] Simultaneously mocking lesbians on the one hand, and hysterical, prudish, overreactive lesbophobes on the other, author and reader in such texts as these congratulate themselves and each other on their sophistication and superiority.

The period saw other approaches to the discussion and representation of lesbianism, however. In contrast to d'Argenson's horrified moralism and Manley's arch-but-anxious worldliness, Madame de Villedieu, in her bestselling novel *Memoirs of the Life of Henriette-Sylvie de Molière* (1672), evinces an untroubled neutrality on the subject. In this novel, the countess d'Englesac, enemy of the heroine, Henriette-Sylvie, attempts to turn the queen mother and the entire court against the young woman. But Henriette-Sylvie receives protection from an interesting quarter:

> the good & virtuous Madame . . . was still on my side. She loved passionately, said she, beautiful women, & the desire [for] the vermilion of my lips had made her come to be one of my friends, in order to be able to kiss me to her heart's content sometimes; (what will your Highness say about this effect of my beauty?) this desire, I say, having attached to my interests a person like that; it was impossible for the countess d'Englesac to succeed further in her initial designs. . . .[8]

As Michel Cuénin, editor of the modern reprint of the novel, points out, the lady portrayed here as having lesbian tendencies is associated with *les dévotes*, a pious crowd at court overlapping with, although not identical to, the learned, literary women disparagingly dubbed *les précieuses*. Yet whereas most such ascriptions of lesbian desire and/or practices to *les précieuses* occur in satirical, anti-*précieuse* contexts, this passage is not hostile toward the lesbian it portrays.[9] Although there is *some* amusement in the narrator's voice (particularly when she asks the woman to whom her memoirs are addressed, "what will Your Highness say about this effect of my beauty?"), or at least an implicit suggestion that Madame . . . 's desire is unusual, neither the text nor any of its characters denigrate the lesbian. At worst, this "good & virtuous" woman might seem somewhat shallow, since her favorable disposition toward Henriette-Sylvie springs from a response to the latter's beauty. But unlike several of the young woman's male protectors, whose concern for the heroine is also prompted by her beauty, Madame . . . is never shown attempting to take sexual advantage of Henriette-Sylvie's vulnerable position. What is more, other characters' *bad* opinion of the young woman, as opposed to Madame . . . 's *good* one, is at least equally ill-founded. All in all, then, since Madame . . . comes to the aid of Henriette-Sylvie, for whom readerly sympathies have already been engaged, it is quite likely that at least some readers would have responded positively to this female character who voices same-sex desires.

But if such slightly amused tolerance would challenge the assumption of many readers today that past societies have been uniformly antigay and antilesbian, it would merely confirm others in the competing belief, particularly popular among some historians and literary critics, that lesbianism simply did not signify, did not matter, in the past. Because it did not involve a penis (as male homosexuality did) and because it could not result in pregnancy (as heterosexual fornication and adultery did), it simply would not have been threatening to pre-twentieth-century men.[10]

III

Yet if moralistic condemnation, libertine mockery, and amused tolerance all, therefore, seem believable or predictable late seventeenth-century responses to lesbianism, what most readers today would *not* expect to find in a turn-of-the-eighteenth-century text is a prolesbian rejoinder to antilesbian thinking, writing, or action. At least one such lesbian-affirmative text has been identified: Aphra Behn's poem "To The Fair Clarinda Who Made Love To Me, Imagin'd More Than Woman. By Mrs. B." (1688), a work that amusingly and daringly manipulates antilesbian ideology, turning it against itself in order to justify and celebrate love between women.[11] In fact, it is the closest thing (so far as I am aware) to a clearly sexual, lesbian-affirmative text written by a woman for public circulation in seventeenth- or eighteenth-century England or France. As other critics have noted, in this poem Behn seems playfully to exploit phallocentric definitions of sex as necessarily involving a penis, definitions according to which sex between two women is a contradiction in terms, "innocent" because insignificant (both in the sense of unimportant and meaningless).[12] Behn appropriates this antilesbian thinking for her own lighthearted, pleasurable, prolesbian ends.

The poem thus begins by registering the problematic nature of its own undertaking:

> Fair lovely Maid, or if that Title be
> Too weak, too Feminine for Nobler thee,
> Permit a Name that more Approaches Truth:
> And let me call thee, Lovely Charming Youth.
> This last will justifie my soft complaint,
> While that may serve to lessen my constraint;
> And without Blushes I the Youth persue,
> When so much beauteous Woman is in view.

A "soft complaint," an amorous address, from one woman to another requires justification. Behn is responding to lesbian love's forbiddenness, or else to its supposed impossibility, the unknowing of it by the conventional assertion that a sex-changing metamorphosis is required to set things right, an assertion most famously dramatized in Ovid's tale of Iphis and Ianthe in Book IX of *The Metamorphoses*. But rather than contest such thinking directly, Behn playfully embraces it. With a wave of her magic pen, she transforms her beloved Clarinda from a "Fair lovely Maid" into a "Lovely Charming Youth."

Behn's appropriation of antilesbian rhetoric becomes even more explicit when the poem's speaker declares,

> In pity to our Sex sure thou wert sent,
> That we might Love, and yet be Innocent:
> For sure no Crime with thee we can commit;
> Or if we shou'd–thy Form excuses it.

Behn here reveals the potential of the stock antilesbian tropes of innocence and crime, ignorance and knowledge, to offer a convenient, safeguarding cloak or excuse for lesbian sex and love. In asserting that "sure no Crime" could be committed between women, she employs the unknowing refusal to believe in the possibility of lesbian sex. In adding that even if such acts *should* be committed, Clarinda's "Form excuses it," she manipulates two additional antilesbian arguments. If one reads "thy Form" as referring to Clarinda's female body, then the line parrots the belittling dismissal of lesbianism as unimportant and unthreatening. If one reads "thy Form" as referring to Clarinda's masculinity, then the line explains away lesbian desire by revealing it actually to be heterosexual. It is natural and thus excusable for women to respond to masculine attractions. In all three cases, Behn converts antilesbian ideology into carte blanche for women to do as they please with one another.

The poem ends by once more calling to mind Ovid's *Metamorphoses*, this time even more clearly, when "Mrs. B." writes,

> Thou beauteous Wonder of a different kind,
> Soft *Cloris* with the dear *Alexis* join'd;
> When e'r the Manly part of thee, wou'd plead
> Thou tempts us with the Image of the Maid,
> While we the noblest Passions do extend
> The Love to *Hermes, Aphrodite* the Friend.

Once again reproducing phallocentric ideology, Behn appears to endorse the notion that male-female relationships offer romantic and sexual love while female-female relationships offer ideal friendship. But she subverts this logic by depicting her relationship with Clarinda as offering both types of feelings, a state of affairs she justifies by converting Clarinda into a hermaphrodite, the male part her lover and the female part her friend. While pretending to accept antilesbian ideology, Behn implicitly asserts the superiority of her lesbian love to heterosexual love. The former includes everything the latter has to offer and more. And given that Clarinda's hermaphroditism is imaginary–the poem's title is, after all, "To The Fair Clarinda . . . *Imagin'd* More Than Woman"–the text subversively mines yet another stock antilesbian notion: lesbianism as "merely" imagination or fantasy, in comparison to "real," "solid" heterosexual sex.[13] From start to finish, Behn's poem thus exemplifies dissident prolesbian writing, hijacking antilesbian rhetoric and turning it against itself, so that strategies intended to erase or contain lesbianism encourage it instead.[14]

IV

Behn's poem brings me back, at long last, to the abominable, or admirable, Madame de Murat. For it is my contention that she authors another prolesbian text of the period, or rather, a prolesbian textual moment, a brief swipe at antilesbian crusaders that culminates in what I believe is a subtle, even coded, but nonetheless amusing lesbian joke. Her novel, *The Memoirs of Madame the Countess de M**** (1697), which Joan DeJean describes as an "allegedly autobiographical work by a notorious woman," purports to be the first-person heroine's attempt to preserve or restore her reputation, sullied by accusations of sexual misconduct.[15] While virtually all of this suspected misconduct is heterosexual, at one point the heroine and the female friend with whom she is living are accused of maintaining a lesbian relationship:

> The absence of Saint-Albe left his wife at full liberty to exercise her hatred against me; nothing gave her so much pleasure as to hear my conduct ill-spoken of; her friends who knew her sentiments nourished her malignity by complaisance, finally she resolved to work to ruin me entirely, & to succeed in that she took it into her head to compose some Letters herself, in which she said horrible things of Mademoiselle Laval and me; these Letters were put into the hands of the [Spiritual] Director of whom I have already spoken, who imagining that the glory of God demanded that he revenge himself for the little store I set by his counsels, with a hypocritical circumspection had them shown to Mademoiselle Laval's Husband, then to my Mother & Husband; he didn't rest there, he found means to have the Queen informed of my bad conduct, & to beg her to interpose her authority, to remedy the disorders about which he groaned & of which it would have taken him nothing to see the falsity, if he had wanted to take the trouble to examine by whom these Letters had been given to him, but Prudence & Charity are virtues that false zeal does not know. . . .
>
> When reputation is torn apart by the indiscreet zeal of false devout people, it is an evil without remedy. The Letters of which I have spoken caused a great stir; Madame de Châtillon warned me that even the Queen had heard tell of them, & that an order was solicited from that Princess to imprison us, Mademoiselle Laval and me. All that was done, as I have already said, through the pious efforts of the Director of whom I have spoken. I do not doubt at all that our enemies would have obtained what they wished, if Madame de Châtillon, had not had the goodness to disabuse the Queen, but she justified me, in such a manner that the Director could not harm us.
>
> Nevertheless Madame de Châtillon counseled us to go live in a Community, until my husband and Mademoiselle Laval's had been obliged to render us justice, we followed this counsel, & I can say that we followed it without repugnance.[16]

Although lesbianism is referred to as "horrible things"–the strongest words the narrator has so far used to describe any of the many slanderous accusations and stories that have been leveled at and told about her, and a term that will be echoed in d'Argenson's reference to "the horrors" of Murat's relationship with Nantiat–the passage's antipathy is leveled squarely, and dead seriously (notwithstanding the irony of such phrases as "the pious efforts of the Director"), at people who try to ruin women by accusing them of lesbianism, people who even attempt to incite royal punishment of lesbian behavior, as in real life d'Argenson would do a few years later. Eventually, Murat and Nantiat were placed under house arrest in separate chateaux.

This approach to the subject (skewering antilesbian crusaders while barely pausing to condemn lesbianism itself), combined with what we know of Murat's subsequent reported behavior a few years later, might lead us to question whether she really endorses her heroine's characterization of such behavior as "horrible things." So might the fact that the heroine and her friend are advised to move into an all-female community in order to *prevent* further accusations of lesbianism. As Christopher Rivers explains, in ancien régime France the convent was a paradoxical place, "both part of . . . society and removed from it, a commonplace and an enigma, simultaneously quotidian and exotic to those outside its walls."[17] The convent offered both freedom and imprisonment. Some women sought refuge there from abusive husbands; others were confined there by husbands wanting their wayward spouses kept under surveillance. In both cases, the desirability of a convent was predicated upon the assumption that it guaranteed its inhabitants' "virtue"; by excluding men it excluded sexuality. And yet, it was precisely in its relationship to sexuality that the paradoxical nature of the convent was most evident. In his study of libertine convent novels, Rivers makes this point particularly well. "The convent novels," he writes, "often articulate the notions that interdiction serves to heighten, not diminish, sexual desire and that the true secret of the cloister is the fact that it shuts sexuality in as well as out."[18] In other words, while readers of Murat's novel knew that having recourse to a convent in order to safeguard a woman's reputation was a routine practice, they also knew about "what goes on in convents": that they were not a sanctuary for virtue but a site of license, especially lesbian license.

Might not, then, Madame de Châtillon's counsel, and the two women's following it "without repugnance," be a surreptitious joke aimed at lesbian or prolesbian readers? Another d'Argenson entry about the abominable Murat strengthens this suspicion. He writes:

> 11 February 1702. Madame de Murat continues to distinguish herself by her ardors and by the disorder of her morals. She knows that the King is informed of them; but she counts on there not being found a single religious community bold enough to receive her. I do not think, actually, that there is one, and I could not have a good opinion of those that would want to run the risks: thus, what other course could one take, in regard to a woman of this character, than to lock her up in a distant château, where [a sum of] 100 écus will suffice for her subsistence and for that of the oldest female servant one could choose?[19]

I cannot help but have the same suspicions about the community that accepts Murat's heroine and her friend. Or, to be more precise, noticing that Murat's text unknows the by then well-known association (both real and imagined) between nunneries and lesbianism, and seeing that several years later Murat is reported to be well able to conceive of the suspicions that might be aroused by such a female religious community taking in a woman accused of lesbianism, I consider it quite probable that she is having some covert prolesbian fun, treating her allegedly autobiographical heroine and that heroine's female friend to a sojourn in an all-female community, as if rewarding them for having weathered a bout of antilesbian persecution.

V

"So what?" you may ask. What does this fleeting moment in an otherwise heterosexually focused text matter?

If one is firmly committed to the creation of strong rather than weak theory–terms recently borrowed from systems theory, via psychologist Silvan Tomkins, by Eve Sedgwick in her enormously important essay "Paranoid Reading and Reparative Reading"–the answer is, "It doesn't."[20] If one is more or less satisfied with revising Foucault's claims about the history of (homo) sexuality, if one is content with, and convinced by, formulations that posit the "invention" of homosexuality in the late nineteenth (or early eighteenth or late seventeenth) century, or the "insignificance" of lesbianism prior to the mid-eighteenth (or late nineteenth or early twentieth) century, one can simply dismiss this textual moment as an exception. But if one is dissatisfied with these particular strong theories, if one believes (as I do) that their acceptance is premature, if one regards them as hypotheses not borne out by the evidence available to us, evidence too often dismissed as merely exceptional because it contradicts the theory being proposed, then this fleeting fictional moment might seem quite significant, quite suggestive, indeed.[21]

It might suggest, for instance, that a great deal more primary research remains to be done before we can make broad generalizations about the history of (homo)sexuality that are adequately grounded historically as well as theoretically. One might be struck, as I am, by the potential for isolated moments in little-known texts otherwise unconcerned with same-sex eroticism to trouble the grand historical narratives that have gained ascendancy in our field, narratives based on material with which many of us are by now quite familiar.

Murat's possible prolesbian joke might also suggest that it is time to reexamine the currently unfashionable notion of closeted lesbian and gay writing. In fact, such a reexamination has already been carried out, in James Creech's *Closet Writing/Gay Reading*.[22] With theoretical sophistication to spare, Creech made the case for the legitimacy, even the necessity, of reading for closeted gay texts. Yet his book sank without a trace. It merits reconsideration, as do the reading practices it champions.

Calling a text "closeted" is, of course, an act of *projection*, an interpretive practice with which many, perhaps most, academically trained theorists and critics today are profoundly uncomfortable. The same goes for its close companion *identification*. For all the current distrust of positivist, Enlightenment ideals of science, objectivity, rationalism, and the like, most of us are still trained to believe we should approach texts dispassionately. We should *read* texts, but not *read into* them.

In contrast, I would like to join Creech in reminding fellow practitioners of lesbian and gay studies and/or queer theory that if there are as yet undiscovered closeted texts out there, the only way to receive the partially concealed messages they were meant to convey to certain readers is to engage in what Creech calls "wild surmise" about their authors' sexual desires and/or identities, to commit oneself rashly to speculation about these authors' intentions, even though one's speculations may turn out to be fallacious.[23] Indeed, in many cases (such as Murat's possible joke), the validity or falsity of such speculations will prove unresolvable. Nonetheless, the speculation is fruitful, even necessary, for a greater appreciation of dissident lesbian and gay authorial, readerly, and textual possibilities.

Yet surely some readers will object that the cost of such speculation, of such projection and identification, is too high, the benefit too small. Why not, they might ask, express your conclusion about Murat's text without focusing upon her (always uncertain) intentions? For I might just as easily have written the following: "For readers familiar with the by then well-known association (both real and imagined) between nunneries and lesbianism, readers able, like d'Argenson, to conceive of the suspicions that might be aroused by such a female religious community's taking in a woman accused of lesbianism, but, unlike d'Argenson, sympathetic toward lesbians, or at least hostile toward antilesbian zealots, the text may have induced some prolesbian laughter." What is wrong with such a non-intentionalist approach? If critics can make compelling arguments about the lesbian/gay/queer workings of texts while avoiding the notorious pitfalls of authorial intention and literary biography, what is the problem?

The problem is that such avoidance is a deformation of lesbian and gay criticism, a defensive reaction to heterosexual hostility that falsifies and diminishes lesbian and gay history and culture. Our avoidance of speculation about authorial intention has not been freely chosen. Not that we have not developed powerful alternative investigative and interpretational methodologies: Barthes's semiotics and Foucault's discourse-analysis. Both, I would argue, significantly shaped (but by no means, therefore, invalidated) by their mostly closeted lives, come immediately to mind. Recent attention to dissident queer reading possibilities has a great deal to offer, as well.[24]

But notwithstanding the strengths of these and other non- or anti-intentionalist approaches, I cannot accept them as the whole story. The Death of the Author seems a lot less harmless to me, and a *lot* less liberating, when it is a potentially lesbian, gay, or bisexual author being killed off. Given the frequency with which heterosexual and/or normatively gendered people have enforced invisibility on gay and/or non-normatively gendered people; have misrepresented, dismissed, silenced, and even exterminated us; and have done their best to erase the traces of this misrepresentation, dismissal, silencing, and extermination, I cannot accept the contention that a question such as "Was Author X a lesbian? Was she a woman erotically oriented toward other women?" is unimportant, irrelevant, or uninteresting, unworthy of being asked. Such a question may be *unresolvable*. Yet "unresolvable" does not mean "false," and it does not mean "unimportant." We may not be able to *prove* that Author X was lesbian or that a particular text of hers is a closeted lesbian text. But the perspective that makes visible only the probable unresolvability of such questions is the one to which we should be saying, "So what?" Instead, we have allowed the typical homophobic rejoinders to such speculation to constrain, even dictate, our critical practice.[25]

Rather than capitulate to such homophobic dismissal, I suggest we head in the opposite direction. Creech modestly states that he "do[es] not want to suggest . . . that we should avoid speculating about anachronistic concepts such as coming out . . . relative to [figures] who wrote most of [their] work before the invention of homosexuality and the panoply of concepts–like the closet–which develop from it." I would go further: I would say that we *must not* avoid such speculation. For, as Creech himself argues, "such speculation may eventually reveal that our current problem with these terms has been that our conceptual arsenal contains instruments still too unrefined to catch the nuances of attitude and behavior . . . which, mutatis mutandis, might be profitably considered the functional equivalents of that complex of self-knowledge or behavior which we call 'coming out.' "[26] If Creech is correct, and the moment from Murat's novel that I believe (but can never conclusively prove) to be a covert prolesbian joke suggests that he is, we have prematurely abandoned the hunt for traces of closeted lesbian and gay lives and closeted lesbian and gay writings. If we learn to look and listen more sensitively–practicing especially the kind of "unhurried, undefensive, theoretically galvanized . . . close reading" that Sedgwick advocates and that I have attempted (successfully, I hope) in this article–we are likely to find that other, less obviously abominable authors than Madame de Murat are hailing us, even cruising us, in ways and from places we never suspected.[27] Without projecting ourselves out on that critical limb, we will never know.

NOTES

1. Despite the risk of anachronism, I use the terms "lesbian" and "lesbianism" partly for the sake of convenience (to avoid the awkwardness of constructions such as "female same-sex eroticism") but mostly because of my belief that Lesbian, Gay, and Queer Studies of the past decade have overprivileged discontinuity and difference in the history of sexuality, to the detriment of our ability to perceive continuity and similarity. I intend to highlight some of these continuities and similarities by using "lesbian" as Emma Donoghue does in *Passions Between Women: British Lesbian Culture 1668-1801* (London, 1993), 7: "as comprehensible shorthand ... an umbrella term for seventeenth- and eighteenth-century concepts" such as tribades, fricatrices, and other women characterized by "unnatural" affections for their own sex. I do not mean to imply that seventeenth- and eighteenth-century conceptions of lesbianism are identical to late twentieth-century ones, much less to imply a transhistorical or transcultural lesbian identity. But the recognition of historical and cultural differences in the meanings attached to love, sex, and sexual desire between women is not an insurmountable barrier to a transhistorical or transcultural use of the term "lesbian." As Richard Mohr argues regarding the word "homosexual," "we can and typically do disambiguate senses of a term even when its multiple senses are applied correctly to the same object. . . . [W]e can disambiguate the [modern] sense of 'homosexual' from its possible minimal or core sense, 'the desire for sexual relations with members of one's own biological sex,' and use the core sense in perfectly respectable, culturally neutral ways." *Gay Ideas: Outing and Other Controversies* (Boston, 1992), 240-1. Likewise, using the term "lesbian" to refer to women characterized by a predominant or exclusive sexual attraction to other women does not automatically entail anachronism. As Bernadette J. Brooten observes in *Love Between Women: Early Christian Responses to Female Homoeroticism* (Chicago, 1996), 18, "The historical discontinuities are . . . no greater than with such other terms as 'slavery,' 'marriage,' or 'family,' and yet we have no qualms about applying these terms to historical and cross-cultural phenomena, even though, for example, a 'family' can include slaves or not, multiple wives or not, or the legal power of a man to kill family members or not." Like Brooten, 18, I thus consider "the material I present here as part of lesbian history, which is as variegated and diverse as any other history."

2. *Rapports inédits du lieutenant de police René d'Argenson (1697-1715) publiés d'après les manuscrits conservés a la Bibliothèque Nationale*, ed. Paul Cottin (Paris, 1891), 10-1, 87-8, 88-9. For some further discussion of this material, as well as of Murat's life and work, see Elizabeth Wahl, *Invisible Relations: Female Intimacy in the Age of Enlightenment* (Stanford, 1999), 212-5, 317-8.

3. For a discussion of this antilesbian rhetorical tradition, see David Michael Robinson, "To Boldly Go Where No Man Has Gone Before: The Representation of Lesbianism in Mid-Seventeenth- to Early Eighteenth-Century British and French Literature," PhD dissertation, University of California-Berkeley, 1998), chapter 1.

4. Claude Courouve, *Vocabulaire de l'homosexualité masculine* (Paris, 1985), 35. I find it significant that d'Argenson applies to Murat and Nantiat an epithet, "abominable," frequently used to characterize *male* sodomites and their sexual activities in the seventeenth and eighteenth centuries, even by d'Argenson himself. For examples in

which this word is used to characterize male sodomites and male-male sodomy, see Courouve, 35-8. Small as it is, this detail suggests that a bi-gendered category encompassing both tribadism and sodomy may have been conceivable long before the mid-nineteenth-century "invention" of the term "homosexuality."

5. Robinson, "'For How Can They Be Guilty?': Lesbian and Bisexual Women in Manley's *New Atalantis,*" *Nineteenth-Century Contexts* (special issue on women's friendships and lesbian sexuality, forthcoming 2001).

6. Eve Kosofsky Sedgwick, "Privilege of Unknowing: Diderot's *The Nun,*" in *Tendencies* (Durham, 1993), 23-51.

7. Mary Delariviere Manley, *The New Atalantis*, ed. Rosalind Ballaster (New York, 1992), 154.

8. Madame de Villedieu (Marie-Catherine Desjardins), *Mémoires de la vie de Henriette-Sylvie de Molière* (1671-4), in *Oeuvres* (1702; reprint, ed. Michel Cuénin, Tours, 1977), 147-8.

9. On the subject of lesbianism and *les précieuses*, see Wahl, chapter 6.

10. For a particularly nuanced version of such a claim (distinguishing "femme-femme" love from the figure of the tribade), see Valerie Traub, "The (In)Significance of 'Lesbian' Desire in Early Modern England," in *Queering the Renaissance*, ed. Jonathan Goldberg (Durham, 1994), 62-83.

11. From Behn, *Lycidus* (1688), in *Chloe Plus Olivia: An Anthology of Lesbian Literature from the Seventeenth Century to the Present*, ed. Lillian Faderman (New York, 1994), 27.

12. For example, Faderman, 24-5, remarks briefly that "'To the Fair Clarinda' provides a provocative hint that 'romantic friends' may have sometimes laughed at the shield that convention allowed them in relationships that we would describe as 'lesbian.'" See also Arlene Stiebel, "Not Since Sappho: The Erotic in Poems of Katherine Philips and Aphra Behn," in *Homosexuality in Renaissance and Enlightenment England: Literary Representations in Historical Context*, ed. Claude Summers (New York, 1992), 161-2; and especially Wahl, *Invisible Relations*, 55-60. Wahl's analysis of the poem is particularly illuminating, although she reads it as less clearly radical than I do.

13. Rosalind Ballaster overlooks this important point in her discussion of the poem in *Seductive Forms: Women's Amatory Fiction, 1684-1740* (Oxford, 1992), 75-6. She acknowledges the possibility of a prolesbian reading but instead chooses to emphasize that "Another possible reading . . . is that the lover is a cross-dressing or transvestite man." Her reason for suggesting this interpretation is to show that "Behn allows us no easy solution to this riddle [the sex or identity of "Clarinda"], but rather encourages her reader to enjoy the play across both sexes and the subversive power of the image of the hermaphrodite." In addition, Ballaster introduces the poem as an example in which Behn's "narcissistic challenge to masculine exclusions reaches its height." According to Ballaster, then, Behn's poem is best understood not as lesbian, but as transgender and feminist. I find this reading interesting but unconvincing, mostly because the title of the poem signals that Clarinda is indeed a woman, and that the complex gender-shifting and gender-blending games in which the speaker engages are flights of imagination, of fantasy (Wahl's interpretation also occasionally loses sight of this point). But I am also suspicious of Ballaster's blithe willingness to delesbianize the poem without any acknowledgment either of Englit's tenacious resistance to admitting lesbian readings of any canonical author's work or the larger society's eagerness to erase every possible instance of lesbianism whether in literature or reality. I take the term "Englit" from Alan Sinfield's *Cultural Politics-Queer Reading* (Philadelphia,

1994), chapter 4. My point here is not that lesbian interpretations never can nor should be contested, but that such contestations must be undertaken with great care, lest they replicate or reinforce our culture's longstanding and widespread attempt to make lesbianism disappear by refusing to see any expression or representation of love between women (except, perhaps, male-authored pornographic representations) as lesbian.

14. This interpretation of "To The Fair Clarinda" is strengthened by Catherine Gallagher's reading of Behn's plays in *Nobody's Story: The Vanishing Acts of Women Writers in the Marketplace 1670-1820* (Berkeley, 1994), chapter 1. Gallagher argues that, contrary to what feminist critics often maintain, Behn does not directly contest dominant late seventeenth-century definitions of and strictures upon women, but instead accepts them in order to exploit their contradictions.

15. Joan DeJean, *Tender Geographies: Women and the Origins of the Novel in France* (New York, 1991), 258, n. 26. Note 28 on the same page alerted me to the representation of antilesbian accusation in Murat's novel. Wahl, *Invisible Relations*, 317, n. 17, notes this moment in passing, remarking that "Murat wrote a fictionalized defense of her behavior in her *Mémoires de Madame la comtesse de M**** that contains a coded reference to the accusation of a lesbian liaison but casts it as an attempt to slander her reputation."

16. *Les Memoires de Madame la Comtesse de M*** avant sa retraite, ou La Defence des Dames, dans lesquels on verra que tres-souvent il y a beaucoup plus de malheur que de déreglement dans la conduite des Femmes*, 2 vols. (Lyon, 1697), 2: 88-94. The phrase "Mademoiselle Laval's husband" is strange; it ought to be "Madame Laval's husband." It is as if the narrator or the text resists treating her as a married woman. I would not want to place too much emphasis on this particular inconsistency, however. Despite the husbands' return, the promised rendering of justice never takes place. Instead, the accusations of lesbianism are simply forgotten by both narrator and text.

17. Christopher Rivers, "Safe Sex: The Prophylactic Walls of the Cloister in the French Libertine Convent Novel of the Eighteenth Century," *Journal of the History of Sexuality* 5 (1995): 387.

18. Ibid., 388.

19. D'Argenson, *Rapports*, 94.

20. Sedgwick, "Paranoid Reading and Reparative Reading: or, You're So Paranoid, You Probably Think This Introduction Is about You," in *Novel Gazing: Queer Readings in Fiction*, ed. Sedgwick (Durham, 1997), 12-4. Strong theories strive for universal validity, weak theories for local validity. As Silvan Tompkins (quoted by Sedgwick, 13) puts it,

> Any theory of wide generality is capable of accounting for a wide spectrum of phenomena which appear to be very remote, one from the other, and from a common source. This is a commonly accepted criterion by which the explanatory power of any scientific theory can be evaluated. To the extent to which the theory can account only for "near" phenomena, it is a weak theory, little better than a description of the phenomena which it purports to explain. As it orders more and more remote phenomena to a single formulation, its power grows.

21. For an excellent example of these competing approaches to the question of exceptions, see the exchange between David M. Halperin and Ann Pellegrini on the one hand, and Bernadette Brooten on the other, on the question of whether apparently feminine/nonmasculine women who had sex with apparently masculine women would

have been perceived as tribades in the ancient world, in "Lesbian Historiography Before the Name?" *GLQ* 4 (1998): 557-630.

My thanks to Maxine Wolfe for originally pointing out to me the importance of exceptions in writing lesbian and gay history. Wolfe credits this insight into the importance of exceptions to geneticist Barbara McClintock, whose attention to them led to some of her greatest scientific discoveries. In McClintock's words, "If the material tells you, 'It may be this,' allow that. Don't turn it aside and call it an exception, an aberration, a contaminant. . . . That's what's happened all the way along the line with so many good clues"; "The important thing is to develop the capacity to see one [detail] that is different, and make that understandable. . . . If [something] doesn't fit, there's a reason, and you find out what it is." Quoted in Evelyn Fox Keller, *Reflections on Gender and Science* (New Haven, 1985), 162, 163.

22. James Creech, *Closet Writing/Gay Reading: The Case of Melville's Pierre* (Chicago, 1993).

23. Ibid., 50-1. See also Sedgwick's passage on camp vs. kitsch reading–particularly her appreciation of camp's understanding "that it is dealing in reader relations and in projective fantasy (projective though not infrequently true) about the spaces and practices of cultural production"–in *Epistemology of the Closet* (Berkeley, 1990), 156.

24. See, for example, Sinfield's brilliant (and wonderfully concise) *Cultural Politics*.

25. Sedgwick memorably lays out the variety of such rejoinders in *Epistemology of the Closet*, 52-3.

26. Creech, *Closet Writing*, 69.

27. Sedgwick, "Paranoid Reading," 23.

The "Italian Taste" in the Time of Louis XVI, 1774-92

Olivier Blanc

Editors' note: This is a translation of the original text.[1]

Amorous relations outside marriage have been tolerated to a greater or lesser extent in different times and places. They have accordingly been more or less acknowledged by participants and more or less visible to contemporaries. During the years preceding the French Revolution, people talked about the "audacity" with which women "flaunted their amours" and, depending on their point of view, about the "disorders" or the "sweetness of life" at court (Versailles) and in town (Paris).[2] It is surely not by chance that the modern meaning of the word "libertinism" evolved at this time, a period which was tolerant about sexuality and during which readers devoured Laclos's *Dangerous Liaisons*.

Inspired by nineteenth-century prudishness, many authors of memoirs skipped quickly over their own youths and avoided the subject of libertinism.[3] We must, therefore, go back to contemporary texts: correspondence (most commonly of foreigners living in France, such as Grimm, Kageneck, Meister, Métra, or Rivière) or works not published because of censorship, such as the celebrated *nouvelles à la main* (collections of news and gossip) that were later printed. The "free" press of the early 1790s provides additional details about the private live of Louis XVI's contemporaries, but these more or less defamatory texts, intended to ridicule and prejudice, must be used with caution. To these sources may be added notarial acts drawn up between lovers, often lifetime annuities. These documents, which have been little used until now, made amorous liaisons outside marriage, whether heterosexual or homosexual in nature, official in some sense.[4]

[Haworth co-indexing entry note]: "The 'Italian Taste' in the Time of Louis XVI, 1774-92." Blanc, Olivier. Co-published simultaneously in *Journal of Homosexuality* (Harrington Park Press, an imprint of The Haworth Press, Inc.) Vol. 41, No. 3/4, 2001, pp. 69-84; and: *Homosexuality in French History and Culture* (ed: Jeffrey Merrick, and Michael Sibalis) Harrington Park Press, an imprint of The Haworth Press, Inc., 2001, pp. 69-84. Single or multiple copies of this article are available for a fee from The Haworth Document Delivery Service [1-800-342-9678, 9:00 a.m. - 5:00 p.m. (EST). E-mail address: getinfo@haworthpressinc.com].

AN EXAMPLE FROM ABOVE

By 1780 libertinism in the sense of amorous relations outside marriage seems to have become common in Paris and, more generally, in urban environments, which were less subject than rural areas to the influence of the Church. The visibility of libertinism, previously restricted to private spaces, had expanded during the reign of Louis XV, who did not shrink from imposing upon the court first a married woman from the bourgeoisie (Madame de Pompadour, née Poisson), then a genuine commoner, an unmarried girl (the beautiful Jeanne Bécu). In doing so, he broke with the tradition of his ancestors, who had recruited their male and female favorites from the aristocracy. By the time of Louis XVI, all the great nobles, including members of the royal family, openly flaunted their mistresses. Not to be left behind, great ladies like the duchess de Mazarin publicly paraded lovers whose fortunes they sometimes promoted or debts they sometimes paid. The court and the city followed these examples, and, as the writer Chamfort observed, marriage among the aristocracy and the wealthy bourgeoisie in this period came down to economic and dynastic considerations.[5]

If the wealthy and the privileged flaunted themselves with impunity, ordinary people tended, on the contrary, to conceal adultery and liaisons outside marriage, which were looked down on by their peers, who were much influenced by the teachings of the Church and by generations of prohibitions and condemnations of a political and religious nature. Such liaisons were strictly repressed if they took a scandalous turn, and women were judged more severely than men. It was the same for relations between persons of the same sex, which were accepted in aristocratic and urban settings but not tolerated, in fact vigorously condemned, among the lesser bourgeoisie and the peasantry. The popular words for persons involved in such relations generally expressed scorn for them: "buggers," "bardashes," "anti-physicals," "tribades," and so forth.[6] A single phrase commonly used in the most advanced circles at the time, the "Italian taste," was straightforwardly positive.[7] The Italian peninsula, after all, was regarded by educated people as a cradle of civilization, as evidenced by the recently excavated remains of buried cities like Pompeii and Herculaneum and the newly fashionable tradition of lyric poetry.

A contemporary author, Coste d'Arnobat, commented that the authorities themselves made a clear distinction between what was tolerable in some (in this case Hérault de Séchelles, a young and rich prosecutor in the parlement of Paris), and illicit in others.

> At the time of this magistrate's first anti-physical passions, there was talk about expelling him from the parliament, but one of its members re-

> marked that the last execution, of a poor wheelbarrowman burned in the place de Grève for the crime of sodomy, had provoked the most violent grumbling; that several notable or very well known individuals, such as Elbeuf, Bauffremont, Villars, Bouillon, Chambonas, Thibouville, and Villette made a public profession of sodomy with impunity without being confined in the Incurables [one of several Parisian hospitals that also functioned as a prison], which had led to criticism of our lords of the parlement for dealing severely only with the rabble; and, besides, that Hérault was a magistrate. They contented themselves with a reprimand behind closed doors, which he paid no attention to, and returned to the day's agenda.[8]

Coste d'Arnobat remembered on this occasion that prince Charles-Roger de Bauffremont, a confirmed bachelor, had "tried rather publicly to violate a handsome Swiss Guard" not long before he was supposed to be decorated with the Cordon bleu. "This prank blocked his nomination." One wit said that Bauffremont had been only the thickness (of body or mind) of a Swiss away from the Cordon bleu.[9] Infatuated with a schemer named Rousseau who had tried to steal his fortune, Bauffremont drafted a will in his favor that was nullified by judgment of the Tribunal of Paris on 15 May 1797.[10] In addition to this great lord who made no secret of his tastes, Coste d'Arnobat mentioned the last duc d'Elbeuf, Emmanuel-Maurice de Lorraine, who could not, according to Casanova, spend a single night without one or the other of his minions.[11]

Much more well known was the duke de Villars. Along with Henri Lambert d'Herbigny, marquis de Thibouville, and the marquis Charles de Villette, he belonged to Voltaire's inner circle. No matter what has been said about the matter, Voltaire enjoyed the company of both men and women interested in their own sex. He had special affection for the writer Jean-Pierre de Claris de Florian, a regular visitor at Ferney. The baronne d'Oberkirch noted, not without irony, that he was "pleasant and attentive like a woman" and that he took the greatest pains to conceal his genuine tastes. "Monsieur d'Oberkirch gave an explanation of all this that the men accepted as undeniable and which I did not understand in the least and which I therefore prefer not to repeat."[12] Like many others inclined to homosexual amours, Florian cultivated what were then called "liaisons for show" and platonic passions. In the same vein, Voltaire advised his dear Villette, who was seen everywhere for a while with the singer Sophie Arnould, "to avoid envy and malice" and urged him to marry properly in order to stifle slander.[13] Villette married Voltaire's protégée Reine Philiberte Rouph de Varicour, which might have but did not put a stop to the persistent rumors about him spread by the *nouvelles à la main*. According to those sources Voltaire himself had been a "pederast" (in the sense of homosexual) or bisexual: "He also liked to tribadize women. His first passion was inherited by the marquis de Villette and the second by Baculard d'Arnaud, who tongued obliging prostitutes."[14]

Other celebrities to whom Coste d'Arnobat attributed "the Italian taste" included Scipion Charles Victor Auguste de La Garde, marquis de Chambonas, and Jacques-Léopold-Charles Godefroy de La Tour d'Auvergne, duke and then prince de Bouillon, who were apparently lovers at court and in town, providing the scandal sheets with plenty of material. Son of a couple known for their libertinism, Bouillon lived apart from his wife, in Paris or at the château de Navarre in Evreux, where he had a sort of "love circle" (from the medieval vocabulary of courtly love) and staged sumptuous entertainments for the celebrated, if not notorious, actress Mademoiselle Laguerre and others. Referring to the duke's efforts to conceal his sexual taste by taking mistresses just for show, one *nouvelliste* remarked that "a clever man wants to dispel even the appearance of suspicion about his conduct."[15] The marriage and separation case of his associate the marquis de Chambonas and his wife, the illegitimate daughter of the duke de La Vrillière and an actress married to the count de Langeac, delighted the *nouvellistes* and intrigued the police.[16] Chambonas had "many debts, little fortune, and a very questionable reputation," but he became mayor of Sens, then minister of Foreign Affairs during the Revolution.[17] Madame d'Oberkirch reported that he lived with his ex-lover Bouillon and that they both behaved foolishly. They had regular mistresses and occasional lovers, among them Mademoiselle Laguerre, the actor Colson-Bellecour, and the theatrical Dugazons, husband and wife.

To the incomplete list provided by Coste d'Arnobat one could add the names of many great nobles, such as marshal de Mouchy, who was known "to have the same tastes as Alexander, Caesar, and other great men."[18] Commandant of Versailles after having been involved in all of Louis XV's military campaigns, he could not do without the company of soldiers. His reputation for having "the taste for which Alexander and other great men were blamed" was known in Bordeaux when it was time, in 1780, to select a candidate for the position of city councilman. Marshal de Richelieu, commandant of the city, explained his choice between one Lamothe and one Lanus (literally "the anus") in this way. "For all sorts of reasons and in keeping with my inclination for the natural religion, I could have chosen Lamothe, but considerations related to my deference to marshal de Mouchy led me to prefer Lanus this time, without attaching any significance to it."[19] One could also mention the marquis de Polignac, the count de Besenval, and another one of Marie-Antoinette's friends, count Jean-Balthazar d'Adhémar de Montfalcon, French ambassador to England, who, it was whispered, "has the inclinations of Socrates: he needs Alcibiadeses."[20]

One might also review the names cited in a pamphlet published in 1790 under the title *The Children of Sodom to the National Assembly, or Deputation of the Order of the Cuff to the Representatives of All the Orders*. The list includes nobles with positions in the households of members of the royal family, several of them in charge of pages. It also includes Nicolas-Augustin de Montjoie de Briges, first equerry of the king's stable, and Marie-Octave, baron de Milleville, in the count d'Artois's guard. The most representative of them, because he was never afraid to flaunt his bent, was the marquis de Villette. He was all the more mocked and vilified by the versifiers of the time because, as a noble and an educated man, he seemed immune to slander and jeering. His promising political career in the *Chronicle of Paris* and then in the Convention was interrupted by premature death in July 1793. He was a man of spirit, the leading architect of the cult of Voltaire, and also a man of courage, the only elected representative who spoke out publicly against the September Massacres in 1792.

LOUIS XVI'S EXASPERATION

On 4 December 1784 a collection of news and gossip recorded the exasperation expressed by the prudish Louis XVI, who showed that he was hardly disposed to tolerate an activity that the Church and its devout supporters condemned in no uncertain terms.

> Pederasty, the stylish vice in fashion today, like tribadism among women, has been recently carried to such a such a scandalous extreme at court that His Majesty wanted to have several great nobles caught in flagrante delicto severely dealt with. There was talk about a sort of seraglio that they had established at Versailles, where bardashes intended for their use congregated. It was pointed out to the king that the scandal of a judicial punishment would be very dangerous, moreover would dishonor many great families, and finally would doubtless provoke even more taste for and curiosity about this sin. As a consequence of these objections, the king contented himself with exiling some of them. People mentioned the marquis de Crénolles, master of Madame [countess de Provence]'s household, in particular. He was accused of having debauched a heyduck [liveried attendant] of the queen. Since he had been away in his estates in Flanders for two months, this rumor gained so much currency that his friend Monsieur d'Angivilliers wrote him that it would be good to demolish the distressing rumors that were spreading about him by showing his face.[21]

In his memoirs Lioult de Chênedollé alluded to the exile of the marquis Germain-Hyacinthe de Romance de Mesmont, an officer in the regiment of the French Guards whom he described as a "gentleman whom an unfortunate adventure had obliged to withdraw from society."[22] The adventure in question was amply explicated in another collection of gossip, which provides an adulterated version of the incident: advances on the part of the marquis, on the terrace of the palace of Versailles, to a nineteen-year-old guard in the service of the count d'Artois.[23] In his correspondence Kageneck gives two versions, of which the young man's is the more plausible:

> I was strolling alone on the terrace. I encountered a man in a frock coat there. He accosted me, offered me money and gifts, and stuck his hands in my pants. I grabbed him by the collar while telling him whom he was dealing with. He stated his name and rank. We left the terrace, we fought, and I gave my bugger two big swordstrokes.

The marquis, who had eighteen years of service behind him and had been decorated, was required to resign his commission and ordered not to reappear at Versailles.[24] In the wake of this costly scandal, he married for form's sake and left the country.

LIBERTINE SALONS

In spite of such incidents, the Italian taste became more visible in the 1780s, just like heterosexual libertinism. The Paris of Louis XVI included a number of noteworthy salons where libertines of both sexes were welcome.

Theatrical and operatic folks were honored at the residence of the dancer and courtesan Marie-Madeleine Guimard, who had accumulated a fortune thanks to her lovers. One of her friends was her rival in dance, Victoire Dervieux, who was inseparable from her architect and lover Bélanger. She also welcomed famous dancers who, although some of them were duly married, had a reputation for cultivating the Italian taste, such as Maximilien Léopold Philippe Gardel, who had obtained a lifetime annuity from Villette and whose recognized lover was the handsome Richer de Sérizy, nicknamed the "royalist doll" during the Revolution. The latter subsequently married Gardel's widow for her fortune. Another regular, Jean-Etienne Despréaux, was not interested in women but entered into a marriage of convenience with Guimard in 1789.

The lawyer Grimod de La Reynière, meanwhile, threw dinners for men like the meals hosted by the actor Lekain. Lekain assembled guests who appreciated the company of other men in the presence of a token woman, in this case the obliging and retiring woman he finally married on Voltaire's advice.[25] Author of *Philosophical Reflections on Pleasure* (1782), which provoked much talk, Grimod vindicated celibacy and libertinism enthusiastically. In this essay he envisaged pleasure in all its forms, including the Italian taste (in the section "Sensual Love and Friendship") without stressing it. He also defended gastronomic pleasure, which he shared one night with seventeen unmarried men in the course of a memorable dinner intended to vindicate the "system of the anti-marriers."[26] On this occasion, the token woman, Madame de Nozoyl, was asked to disguise herself as a man. When he published his *Almanac of Gourmands*, Grimod dedicated it to a very dear friend who shared his tastes, Charles Jean Louis de Toussaint, marquis d'Aigrefeuille. Former royal prosecutor in the Cour des Aides of Montpellier, "he had wit, the ways of the world, exquisite manners, apt rejoinders, and learning."[27] Aigrefeuille was later close to the future chancellor Jean Jacques Régis de Cambacérès, whom he introduced to Freemasonry along with their mutual ex-lover, the witty Philippe Charles François de Pavée, marquis de Villevieille, capitain of the count d'Artois's Swiss guards. Former regimental comrade and perhaps lover of the moralist Vauvenargues, Villevieille was also a good friend of Voltaire. As for Vauvenargues, he was one of the first to expound the principles of sexual freedom: "What does not offend society does not fall within the jurisdiction of the courts."[28] He likewise rejected the concept of "against nature" that Montaigne had already criticized.

The men invited to Grimod's dinners also included Collin d'Harleville and his handsome lover Andrieux (whose features are known to us through the magnificent portrait by Delafontaine exhibited in 1798), Guillaume Imbert de Boudeaux, Villette, the painter Vigée-Lebrun's handsome brother, and the chevalier de Champcenetz. Champcenetz was a playful and caustic character who, according to Madame de Staël, always had a grudge against "the sex that wants nothing to do with him."[29] He harbored resentments stubbornly, and he settled many personal accounts in the *Journal of the Court*, the *Acts of the Apostles*, and especially the 1791 version of the *Scandalous Chronicle*. His relations with the marquis de Louvois, a notorious libertine who died prematurely in 1785, and his unfailing friendship for the writer Rivarol provoked gossip.[30] Rivarol was known to live apart from his English wife and was thought, rightly or wrongly, to look for men in the evening in the Palais-Royal.[31] Champcenetz was also thought to have the Italian taste. His name is listed in *The Children of Sodom*, but with the titles of his older half-brother, the marquis de Champcenetz.

The duchess de Villeroy, born Marguerite-Henriette d'Aumont, was known for organizing dinners for women. She publicly revealed her lesbian tastes by taking the side of Mademoiselle Clairon, whom she "loved tenderly," against her theatrical rival Mademoiselle Dumesnil, who was supported by Madame Du Barry.[32] She received many great ladies, including the elderly Madame Du Deffand, marquise de Luchet (the well-known writer's wife), présidente de Sauvigny (the intendant of Paris's wife), princess Galitzin (the Russian ambassador's wife and Clairon's former mistress), dowager countess de La Ferté, marquise de Sénecterre (née Crussol d'Uzès), and Madame Joly de Fleury (née Dubois de Courval). The husbands of almost all of these women were libertines, beginning with the duke de Villeroy himself. In 1782 a club of heterosexual libertines appeared that undermined the salon of "a certain duchess who abjured love fifteen years ago in order to surrender herself to strange whims that exclude all male creatures."[33] Many contemporaries mentioned the strong-willed duchess, who once had a girl whom she desired kidnapped.[34]

Keeper of the Royal Treasury like his father, Paul Savalette de Lange was a free-thinker and libertine, one of the most visible backers of Parisian Freemasonry, "a model of good manners, elegant civility, respect for established customs," a witty and worldly man whom Frénilly called the "old fox."[35] He married Geneviève Hatry and acknowledged paternity of four of her children, one of whom turned out to be a famous transvestite under the Empire and Restoration. Savalette de Lange had a passion for music and founded a Masonic lodge devoted to the promotion of music. He gathered around him music lovers, singers, composers, and patrons. His relative Florian was one of his regulars, and so was the marquis de Chambonas, his intimate friend and Masonic brother. Another frequent guest was the chevalier de Saint-Georges, a mulatto talented with a sword and the violin. Everywhere he went, he brought along the handsome Lamothe, who was regarded as his lover. Their friend Louise Fusil described them as Orestes and Pylades. "One never saw one without the other," usually surrounded by admiring young men.[36] Another couple met for the first time at Savalette's: the chevalier d'Allayrac, a member of the count d'Artois's guard and a composer as well, and Langlé, professor of composition and singing.

> Langlé greeted the young officer amiably, and d'Alleyrac used every method of seduction to ingratiate himself with him, whose favor he aspired to. He succeeded admirably. Langlé was witty and liked good company. He was charmed by the young guard's friendly and relaxed manners and especially by his enthusiasm for music. A sort of intimacy was already established between them.[37]

The elder Garat, Marie-Antoinette's singing teacher, also frequented Savalette's salon. Detractors of abbé Maury, an outspoken conservative in the National Assembly, often identified him as Garat's lover.[38]

Jean-André Vassal, seigneur de la Fossette, another wealthy financier, entertained libertine friends interested in their own and the opposite sex. Those with the Italian taste included his sons-in-law Joseph de Montglas and the baron de Carion-Nisas, both mentioned in *The Children of Sodom*, both friends of Cambacérès. When Cambacérès, whose sexual interests were well known, arrived in Paris, he frequented the Vassal salon, where he rubbed shoulders with Masons like his friends d'Aigrefeuille and Villevieille, who introduced him into their lodge in 1779. Many years later Cambacérès, then Napoleon's chancellor, founded a small lodge in the faubourg Saint-Germain, in modest quarters rented under an assumed name. Most of the members of this lodge shared the Italian taste: Jean-Olivier Lavollée (his faithful secretary and lover), Carion-Nisas, d'Aigrefeuille, Villevieille, Monvel (the adopted son of the actor), the viscount de Ségur, the magistrate Fesquet. It is clear that the chancellor's political career owed much to his Masonic friends and also to the fabric of friendships woven by men sexually interested in other men. Few historians have properly understood the importance of the "brotherly" friendship uniting Cambacérès and Barras, the only original member of the Directory still in office at the time of Napoleon's coup. Viscount Paul de Barras married in 1791, but he was seen in the gambling dens of the Palais-Royal looking for Italian amours. In 1793, during one of his stays in Draguignan, he noticed a young barber's assistant, named Victor Grand, "with a rather nice figure whom he took into his service and never abandoned."[39] Barras's Italian taste antedated the Revolution, and he probably frequented the Vassal salon, Mademoiselle Maningan's house in the rue Chantereine, and other libertine gatherings.

The Villette salon, last but not least, welcomed libertines of both sexes including Florian, d'Aigrefeuille, Villevielle, Thibouville, and Joseph Louis de Ponte, count d'Albaret, who imitated Voltaire's tics to perfection. During the Revolution it was frequented by the editors of the *Journal of Paris*, most notably Louis-Sébastien Mercier, the marquis de Condorcet, and baron Clootz du Val de Grâce, who made no secret of his interest in boys. "Anacharsis" Clootz wrote something about the subject in his paper, *The Orator of the Human Race*.[40] When he referred to the philosophic abbé Raynal as a *giton* (a male who took the passive sexual role with other males), the *Journal of the Court* retorted that he should know what he was talking about on that score. "If you want information [about him], you can apply to lady Sainville in the rue des Bons-Enfants, Madame Camille Desmoulins, Delaunay, Laperrière, and especially the little hermaphroditic marquis Villette, Gorsas, Gouttes, etc.," all of whom were suspected of having "equivocal" morals.[41] The entire homosexual society of the time knew about Villette, who attracted homophobic attacks from contemporaries of all political persuasions, but especially from the aristocratic party, who could not forgive him for betraying his class. Tolerance and openmindedness about morals and private life were much more widespread among the Girondins, who, during the Legislative Assembly, prepared and passed the law legalizing divorce.

LIBERTINISM FLAUNTED IN PUBLIC

Libertinism moved from the private space of the salons into the public space of clubs, gambling establishments, cafés, hotels, bath-houses, gardens, bookshops, and theaters. These sites of conviviality fostered a homosociability that evolved not in the margins of but in parallel with heterosexual society, whose norms changed little by little, taking into account the new model of "liberated" women embodied by the marquise de Merteuil in *Dangerous Liaisons*.

In dissident Masonic societies including both sexes and intended for amorous entertainment, libertines celebrated love with classical references, initiatory rituals, and mysterious ceremonies. Pidansat de Mairobert described the Sapphic initiation of a girl under the auspices of "Madame de Furiel," that is to say Madame Joly de Fleury, who was separated from her husband, advocate general in the Parliament.[42] Homosexual libertinism became more visible during these years, when women like Madame Joly de Fleury and Mademoiselle Raucourt did not shrink from dressing in men's clothes and going out with their mistresses at their sides.[43] At the famous Longchamp promenade in 1788, a rich man appeared before Parisians with his *giton* at his side, like any other illegitimate couple. Open public space became more and more an extension of closed private space, the traditional domain of aristocratic and bourgeois libertinism. Illegitimate couples joined and split in new public or at least semi-public spaces provided by clubs, which promoted the mixing of classes and sexes. Concerned about social and political disorder, the king ordered the closing of clubs and salons.[44] When the duke d'Orléans, who protected the clubs in and around the Palais-Royal, protested, the king backed down.[45]

Sometimes located inside clubs, gambling establishments constituted a convivial space valued by libertines. Gambling was a pretext for many who came to meet women or men for sexual encounters. Some gambling houses were much frequented by men of the Italian taste who made up most of the clientele. On the mezzanine at number 33 in the Palais-Royal there was a gambling den visited by "little bardashes, unemployed servants, and bad types." The second floor was "the rendezvous for all the buggers of the Palais-Royal," who congregated there around 10 and gambled all night.[46]

Cafés, much in vogue since the Regency, were open to everyone. Paris contained hundreds of these establishments by the time of Louis XVI, and many men interested in men found work in them. Some cafés seemed to have a clientele composed largely of men with the Italian taste, for example, the café Yon on the boulevard du Temple, between the café Goddet and the Associated Theater. Nicolas Yon, originally from Normandy, probably shared this taste. He was married, like most men, but he and his wife were separated in 1786. He came up with the idea of dressing up his rooms with a little musical show. Other cafés of the same type, with the same clientele, were located on the quai de la Mégisserie, for example, the café Maunoury and the café Devertu.

There were even hotels where men could have a good time together, but they were expensive. Men "in the opposition" reportedly paid twice as much as men involved in trysts with women for furnished rooms in the Palais-Royal.[47] Brothels like that of Madame Gourdan almost always had several male prostitutes. Right up until the Empire, there was a concentration of male prostitutes in the vicinity of the well-known establishment of Madame Hecquet, who outfitted men like women.

The numerous public baths in the capital combined opportunities for hygiene, conviviality, and pleasure as well. Men of the Italian taste liked to frequent the Poitevin baths near the Palais-Bourbon, not far from the former Deligny pool, which was one of the centers of Parisian homosexuality until recently.

On the other side of the Seine, the Tuileries gardens have always been a strolling and meeting place for male homosexuals. In these gardens the great actor Boutet de Monvel was questioned four times and threatened with imprisonment if he continued to indulge in "indecent acts." He prudently went into exile for several years at the court of Gustave III of Sweden, where no one thought of blaming him for his way of loving.[48] The passing repressive wave in 1780-5, of which Monvel was the most celebrated victim, did not have much effect on the regulars in the Tuileries, who crowded the terrace of the Orangerie again in the following years. The baron de Breteuil wrote about this situation to the official responsible for the management of the Tuileries:

> I have received, Sir, complaints about the large numbers of libertines who gather every evening in the Tuileries gardens, and it is to be feared that this disorder will get even worse as a result of the measures taken to expel from the Palais-Royal the rogues who also meet there. I therefore ask you to exercise the strictest surveillance in this regard, by having the Swiss and the veterans guards patrol all parts of the garden every day. At the same time, I charge the officer responsible for the policing of this royal residence to make diligent efforts to recognize the individuals who are accustomed to coming there to indulge in their infamous excesses.[49]

These instructions had little effect, judging from Kageneck's observations in August 1785 about "licentious nocturnal gatherings" in the Palais-Royal, where men sought other men in the d'Argenson walk on the side of the Valois wing.[50] "Arrests of pederasts were very common" under Lenoir, lieutenant general of police from 1776 to 1785, "and provided much work for and profit to those who were responsible for the business. There were many mistakes and abuses." Surveillance slackened after Lenoir, "and these gentlemen surrender themselves freely to their tastes."[51] Repression resumed in 1792, largely because of the zeal of commissioner Soltho-Douglas. In March of that year young Alexandre Coindet was arrested and imprisoned for several days but nothing more.[52] During the Terror round-ups in public places, especially the Palais-Royal, multiplied, and several men were subjected to legal prosecution.[53]

Men with the Italian taste also met in bookshops where they could find and read erotic or pornographic literature, for example, the shops of Letellier, Denis Volant, and Pierre Honoré Pain in the Palais-Royal or Claude-François Maradan, nicknamed "the doll of the quai des Augustins."[54] These booksellers supposedly shared their taste and, during the Revolution, sold pamphlets with titles like *The Children of Sodom to the National Assembly*, *Clandestine Loves*, *Secret Diversions*, *Sodom and Cythera*, and *Private Lives* of Mirabeau, Villette, Maury, and others.

The world of the theater and opera, finally, has always attracted devotees of good-looking boys. If Monvel, Fleury, and Lekain himself were known at the French Theater for their marked taste for men, the corridors of the Italian Theater and the Opera were full of attractive males. The actor Michu of the Italian Theater had such a "pretty face" that Grimod de La Reynière went on and on about him.

> You know that when he was almost fifty years old he still played the roles of Colin with all the charm, levity, and graciousness imaginable and that the youngest actors, those who had been most favored by nature, were outshined by his physical attractions. Yes, by his physical attractions. You must pardon me for using this word. Michu's face did not seem to be altogether that of a man, and anyone who saw him dressed like a shepherdess would have been completely fooled by his disguise.[55]

The Jewish banker Peixotto, who reportedly had the Italian taste and some unusual fantasies, did not mistake Michu for a girl when he gave him the generous sum of a thousand louis "to spend the night with him."[56] Other actors were also subjects of conversation, like Michu's colleagues Raymond, Granger, Dorsonville, and Solié, who, in order not to disappoint their female admirers, flaunted liaisons with pretty actresses.[57] Raymond went all the way and married an actress, Molé's adopted daughter, whom Tilly called "the Merteuil of the backstage."[58] She collected lovers and made a marriage of convenience, just like the pretty Carline (Gabrielle Malacrida) of the Italian Theater. This notorious lesbian, an intimate friend of Saint-Aubin and Madame Joly de Fleury, married the handsome dancer Nivelon. The Italian taste was very well represented in theatrical circles, which traditionally functioned as a breeding ground from which wealthy aristocrats like d'Aigrefeuille and the Venetian ambassador Zeno supplied themselves.

Mademoiselle Raucourt, who was probably one of the greatest tragic actresses of her time, embodied all by herself the world of Lesbos. If some dared to criticize her for it, others, like Marie-Antoinette and then Napoleon, praised and protected her. Like Villette, Raucourt preached by example and contributed to normalizing her sexual preferences by projecting the image of a woman fulfilled in her personal as well as professional life. Despite the case of Raucourt and also that of Cambacérès, both well received as they were in the new society, it seems that amorous activities outside marriage and their visibility were considered undesirable under the Empire. Talleyrand, Bignon, Berthier were urged to marry their mistresses (Mesdames Grant, Chevalier, and Visconti) or abandon them. The new social elites, enriched by the purchase of confiscated ecclesiastical or aristocratic property and by political circumstances, were marked by their rural or bourgeois origins and by the prohibitions of the Church that the former nobility had violated. As a result of the return to traditional domestic values, women were relegated to the private sphere and same-sex relations became much less tolerated than they had been at the end of Louis XVI's reign, in spite of the fact that there was no longer any law to criminalize them.

NOTES

1. Translated by Jeffrey Merrick.
2. Henriette Lucie Dillon, marquise de La Tour du Pin Gouvernet, *Mémoires* (Paris, 1913), 136; Alexandre, comte de Tilly, *Mémoires*, ed. Christian Melchior-Bonnet (Paris, 1986), 249; Charles Maurice de Talleyrand-Périgord, quoted in François Guizot, *Mémoires pour servir à l'histoire de notre temps*, 8 vols. (Paris, 1858), 1: 5-6.
3. The memoirs of Lauzun and Tilly are exceptions to the rule, but the authors died before their publication. The first was guillotined, and the second, who had accumulated gambling debts, committed suicide.
4. In the papers of Parisian notaries in the Minutier Central, there are many disguised gifts between lovers. To mention just a few, the deeds drawn up between the banker Laborde and the dancer Mademoiselle Allard, Olympe de Gouges and Jacques Biétrix, Madame Joly de Fleury and her mistresses, or the marquis de Villette and his lovers.

5. Olivier Blanc, *Les Libertines: Plaisir et liberté au temps des lumières* (Paris, 1987).

6. Other terms include *arracheurs de palissades* (from an incident in the gardens at Versailles in 1722), Ebugors (anagram of "buggers," coined in 1733), and Guèbres (from the title of a play by Voltaire).

7. Charles Théveneau de Morande, *Correspondance de Madame Gourdan* [1775], quoted in Pol André [pseudonym], *Le XVIIIe siècle galant et libertin* (Paris, n.d.), 140, 152; and Jean Hervez, *Les Sociétés d'amour au XVIIIe siècle* (Paris, 1906), 269, 274.

8. Charles Pierre Coste d'Arnobat, *Anecdotes curieuses et peu connues sur différentes personnes qui ont joué un rôle dans la Révolution* (Geneva, 1793), 6, 27.

9. Ibid, 27. See also Matthieu-François Pidansat de Mairobert, *L'Espion anglais ou Correspondance entre Milord All'Eye et Milord All'Ear*, 10 vols. (Paris, 1779-84), 10: 197, 228.

10. Aristide Douarche, *Les Tribunaux civils de Paris pendant la Révolution, 1791-1800*, 2 vols. in 3 (Paris, 1905-7), 2: 393. For the will see AN, Minutier Central, Etude Thion de la Chaume, 20 May 1791.

11. Giacomo Casanova, *Mémoires*, 8 vols. (Paris, 1879), 4: 146.

12. Henriette-Louise de Waldner de Freundstein, baronne d'Oberkirch, *Mémoires sur la cour de Louis XVI et la société française avant 1789*, ed. Suzanne Burkard (Paris, 1970), 353.

13. François-Marie Arouet de Voltaire to Charles-Michel de Villette, 20 September 1767, in *Correspondance*, ed. Theodore Bestermann, 107 vols. (Geneva, 1953-65), 67: 36.

14. "Recueil de lettres secrètes: Année 1783," BHVP, Ms 718, 237.

15. Théveneau de Morande, *Mélanges confus sur des matières fort claires* [1777], in *Le Gazetier cuirassé, ou Anecdotes scandaleuses de la cour de France*, ed. Jean Hervez (Paris, 1912), 315.

16. *Journal des inspecteurs de M. de Sartines*, ed. Camille Piton (Brussels, 1863), 171. On Chambonas and his career, see Frédéric Masson, *Le Département des Affaires étrangères pendant la Révolution (1787-1804)* (Paris, 1877), 181-3, 198, 206. On the separation case, see *Mémoires secrets pour servir à l'histoire de la république des lettres en France depuis 1762*, 36 vols. (London, 1780-89), 8: 147, 170-1; 29: 335-6; 30: 220; 31: 346.

17. Théveneau de Morande, *Mélanges confus*, 315.

18. Jacques Bruno de Kageneck, *Lettres au baron Alströmer sur la période du règne de Louis XVI de 1779 à 1784*, ed. L. Léouzon Le Duc (Paris, 1804), 192.

19. Ibid, 192; and *Correspondance secrète inédite sur Louis XVI, Marie-Antoinette, la cour et la ville de 1777 à 1792*, ed. Mathurin François Adolphe Lescure, 2 vols. (Paris, 1866), 1: 316-7.

20. "Recueil," 15, 104.

21. *Mémoires secrets*, 27: 57-8.

22. Charles-Julien Lioult de Chênedollé, quoted in Lescure, *Rivarol et l'émigration* (Paris, 1887), 445.

23. *Correspondance secrète inédite*, 1: 311-2.

24. Kageneck, *Lettres*, 181.

25. There is a disturbing portrait of Lekain dressed like a woman in the Carnavalet museum in Paris. On this actor, see Abraham-Joseph Bénard, known as Fleury, *Mémoires*, 2 vols. (Paris, 1844), 1: 279. Fleury, a successful actor himself, reportedly liked men. The malicious Marie-Antoinette wanted to have him marry Mademoiselle Raucourt.

26. "Recueil," 4.

27. Jean-Pierre Fabre de l'Aude, *Mémoires et souvenirs d'un pair de France*, 4 vols. (Paris, 1829-30), 3: 161-3.

28. Luc de Clapiers, marquis de Vauvenargues, *Maximes* (Paris, 1767), 164.

29. Anne-Louise-Germaine Necker, Madame de Staël, "Lettres aux rédacteurs . . . signée Un Androgyne," *Journal de Paris*, 18 October 1788; and *Mémoires secrets*, 36: 226.

30. "Where the vermin live, Rivarol does the cooking, and Champcenetz does the cleaning." Attributed to Beaumarchais in *Correspondance littéraire et critique par Grimm, Diderot, Raynal, Meister, etc.*, ed. Maurice Tourneux, 15 vols. (Paris, 1877-82), 15: 99.

31. "Recueil," 32.

32. Fleury, *Mémoires*, 81.

33. *Correspondance secrète, politique, et littéraire*, 18 vols. (London, 1787-90), 12: 191.

34. Kageneck, *Lettres*, 379.

35. Jacques Marquet, baron de Norvins, *Souvenirs d'un historien de Napoléon*, ed. L. De Lanzac de Laborie, 3 vols. (Paris, 1896-7), 1: 132; Auguste-François, baron de Frénilly, *Souvenirs*, ed. Arthur Chuquet (Paris, 1909), 196.

36. Years later, when she assumed they were dead, Fusil ran into them, still together, in the Tuileries. Louise Fusil, *Mémoires* (Paris, 1861), 129.

37. Adolphe Adam, *Souvenirs d'un musicien* (Paris, 1857), 245.

38. For example, *Courrier des 83 départements*, 17 May 1791.

39. Empress Josephine, *Correspondance*, ed. Christophe Pincemaille (Paris, 1996), 45. On the sexual taste of Barras, see Michel Missoffe, *Le Coeur secret de Talleyrand* (Paris, 1956), 96-8.

40. Number 179, 57-61.

41. 11 June 1791.

42. *Espion anglais*, 10: 230-47.

43. Blanc, *Libertines*, 163-80, 51-72.

44. Louis-Auguste Le Tonnelier, baron de Breteuil, minister of the royal household, to Louis Thiroux de Crosne, lieutenant general of police of Paris, 19 August 1787, in *Chronique scandaleuse, ou Mémoires pour servir à l'histoire de la génération présente* (Paris, 1785-91), 5: 177-8.

45. *Mémoire présenté au roi par Son Altesse Sérinissime le duc d'Orléans, le 20 août 1787, suivi de Lettre de Monsieur de Crosne au Club du Palais-Royal* (Liège, 1787).

46. Procès-verbal de descente dans une maison de jeu du Palais-Royal, 30 August 1791, APP, Sections de Paris, Section du Palais-Royal, procès-verbal des commissaires de police (Butte-des-Moulins).

47. *Chronique scandaleuse*, an IX (1801), 79. The period 1780-5 was marked by the brutal Pascal affair, which was emblematic of the history of the persecution of male homosexuality in France. After 1785, the repression of loitering for sexual purposes in the Palais-Royal as well as in the Tuileries gardens decreased.

48. *Mémoires secrets*, 17: 268-9, 274.

49. AN, M667, 17 November 1784.

50. Kageneck, *Lettres*, 165.

51. Jacques Peuchet, *Mémoires tirés des archives de police de Paris*, quoted in Claude Courouve, *Les Assemblées de la manchette* (Paris, 1996), 2.

52. AN, W251, dossier Soltho-Douglas, 26 March 1792.

53. For example, Philippe-Jacques Friez and Jean-Louis Lenoir, AN, F^{7}4713, II, 16 nivôse an II; Jean Mallerange and Robert Rémy, AN, F^{7}6776, 89.

54. *Les Enfants de Sodome à l'Assemblée Nationale, ou Députation de l'Ordre de la Manchette aux représentants de tous les ordres* (Paris, 1790), reprinted in *Cahiers Gai-Kitch-Camp* 1 (1989), 5.

55. *Revue des Comédiens*, 1808, 179.

56. Théveneau de Morande, *Correspondance*, 152.

57. Emile Baux, *Notes et documents inédits sur l'Opéra Comique* (Paris, 1909), 5-6, 35-42.

58. Tilly, *Mémoires*, 446. Raymond was sexually harassed by the actor Desessarts. Imbert de Boudeaux, "Recueil," 264.

"Brutal Passion" and "Depraved Taste": The Case of Jacques-François Pascal

Jeffrey Merrick

When the Austrian empress Maria Theresa asked the French king Louis XV for information about the preservation of order and repression of disorder in Paris, the task of explaining the work of the police fell to Jean-Baptiste-Charles Lemaire, one of the forty-eight district commissioners of the capital. In the section of his report devoted to morals, Lemaire noted that the police did their best to control luxury, drunkenness, misconduct in taverns, baths, and theaters, gambling, prostitution, curses and blasphemy, fortune telling, sorcery, and other forms of charlatanry, vagabondage, and everything that "might offend decency" or "tends to the corruption of public and private morals."[1] He did not include sodomy in this catalogue of transgressions, perhaps because he did not think it would be appropriate to mention the sin or crime "against nature" in a document addressed to such an exalted personage, but he undoubtedly intended it, as well as other kinds of sexual deviance, to be covered by the vague language at the end of the list. We do not know how many men the police arrested for sodomy in 1770, the year Lemaire composed his report, because of a sizeable gap between two surviving series of archival records. We do know, however, that they arrested hundreds of men between 1715 and 1750 and hundreds more in the 1780s.[2] Jean Charles Pierre Lenoir, the lieutenant general of police for the first half of that decade, characterized "pederasty" as an aristocratic vice, but he must have known that most of the "pederasts" ap-

[Haworth co-indexing entry note]: "'Brutal Passion' and 'Depraved Taste': The Case of Jacques- François Pascal." Merrick, Jeffrey. Co-published simultaneously in *Journal of Homosexuality* (Harrington Park Press, an imprint of The Haworth Press, Inc.) Vol. 41, No. 3/4, 2001, pp. 85-103; and: *Homosexuality in French History and Culture* (ed: Jeffrey Merrick, and Michael Sibalis) Harrington Park Press, an imprint of The Haworth Press, Inc., 2001, pp. 85-103. Single or multiple copies of this article are available for a fee from The Haworth Document Delivery Service [1-800-342-9678, 9:00 a.m. - 5:00 p.m. (EST). E-mail address: getinfo@haworthpressinc.com].

prehended by his subordinates were ordinary workingmen and that most of them spent no more than a few weeks in prison.[3]

The police of Paris arrested many men for solicitation in the parks and streets in the course of the eighteenth century, but the parlement of Paris sentenced only a few men to be executed for sodomy in the place de Grève, including Benjamin Deschauffours (1726), Jean Diot and Bruno Lenoir (1750), and Jacques-François Pascal, who assaulted an errand boy on 3 October 1783. Until now, the only sources of information about the case of Pascal have been the manuscript journal of the printer and bookseller Siméon-Prosper Hardy and several published collections of news and gossip about the court and capital in the last decades of the Ancien Regime, none of which even named the boy.[4] To the best of my knowledge, no one before me has located any of the criminal or judicial records other than the sentence. Previously unknown documents, most notably the transcript of the investigation conducted by commissioner Benjamin Bourderelle, shed new light on this case.[5] They do not tell us everything we might like to know, but they do allow us to correct the mistakes and reassess the comments in the contemporary accounts.

Having taken Pascal into custody, Bourderelle recorded testimony from ten witnesses at the scene of the crime in the rue Michel-le-Comte. Pascal, 42 years old, identified himself as a priest and Capuchin who had not worn his habit for a year and currently worked for a wine merchant under the name Chabanne. Pascal's victim identified himself as Jacques Gressier, 14, a native of the town of Saint-Flour in the Auvergne and resident of the rue Zacharie (today Xavier-Privas) on the other side of the Seine. He testified that the monk had accosted him nearby and given him a letter and a package to deliver to the porter of the house in which he now lay wounded. Weakened by loss of blood and perhaps consciousness as well, he related his story in a condensed and confused manner. He charged first that Pascal had taken 38 sous from his pocket, as if to suggest that he was more concerned about the theft than anything else. He then added that the monk had thrown him on a bed, unbuttoned his pants, and "put his penis into his ass."[6] Gressier resisted, so Pascal stabbed him many times with a knife and threatened to kill him "if he did not let him put his penis into his ass." The boy was obviously stabbed, but was he actually violated? He naturally felt "very sick," but because of the wounds on his head and in his back or because of the pain in his rectum or both?

The porter, Marie-Elisabeth Guarabi (widow Michaux), 46, provided a more detailed narrative. She had known Pascal all his life but lost track of him for a long time until the last two weeks. She was evidently not surprised when he showed up just after Gressier delivered the letter and the package, which the monk could undoubtedly have carried himself. She was evidently not concerned when he asked for a room so he could write a letter and for change so he could pay the boy. Having failed to get change nearby, Guarabi came back to the room on the third floor and found the door locked. When she knocked, Pascal opened it and asked her to bring him a bottle of beer. When she returned with the beer and the change, she had to knock more than once before he opened the door. She asked where the boy was, and he replied, "in the next room." When she went to pay Gressier, Pascal headed for the stairs. The porter retraced her steps, found the boy covered with blood, ran after the monk and cried out for help, caught up with him in the rue Transnonain (today Beaubourg), and, with the assistance of others, dragged him back to the house. Having examined the boy more closely, she noticed that his pants were undone and pulled down. She overheard commissioner Bourderelle send for a priest and a doctor, and she overheard Gressier telling Bourderelle that Pascal "wanted to put his penis into his rear" (more polite than the word "ass" used by the boy himself). All of the other witnesses, who lived in the neighborhood or worked for the police, used exactly the same words, either because they overheard and imitated each other or because the clerk standardized their language.

Bourderelle sent Gressier to the Hôtel-Dieu to be healed and Pascal to the Grand Châtelet to be tried. Five days later the Châtelet convicted the monk of having "surrendered himself to the excesses of the most criminal debauchery" and stabbed the boy, whose life was still in danger, many times. Pascal appealed the death sentence, but the parlement confirmed it, without identifying him in the written text as a member of the clergy. During the final interrogation on the tenth, he denied the charges against him one more time.[7] When he performed the *amende honorable* that afternoon, he finally acknowledged his crime in the words used in the sentence. Bareheaded and barefooted, with a rope around his neck, wearing a sign in front and back that stigmatized him as an "unnatural profligate and murderer," he knelt before the central doors of Notre-Dame and asked God, king, and justice to forgive him. He reportedly looked contrite and shed tears during this judicial ritual. He did not cringe or shriek in the place de Grève when the executioner broke his limbs and back on the wheel, and he was still alive when he was tied to the stake. After his body was consumed by the flames, his ashes were thrown to the wind.

Parisians talked about the case before and after the public spectacle of retribution. Hardy, who rented his quarters from one of the district police commissioners, recorded the most detailed account of the crime and the punishment, on the dates when they took place.[8] He collected information from his landlord, neighbors, friends, colleagues, or customers, and he also read the sentence promulgated and published by the parlement. According to Hardy's sources, Pascal was the son of a quarryman from the faubourg Saint-Jacques. After he was expelled from the Capuchins in the same quarter or the one in the Marais for unspecified "misconduct" and relegated to a provincial monastery, he left the order and the country. When he returned to Paris, he lived in a respectable house in the rue Michel-le-Comte where the owners "allowed him to occupy a room" under unspecified conditions. On 3 October, between 4 and 5 in the afternoon, Pascal came back from the rue de la Harpe, on the other side of the Seine, with an errand boy whose uncle worked as a dishwasher at the Sorbonne. He sent the porter to get him a bottle of beer "in order to get rid of her" and then assaulted the boy "in order to satisfy a brutal passion and gratify his depraved taste." The boy resisted, and Pascal stabbed him so forcefully that the blade broke in his body. When the porter encountered the monk in the courtyard, with wild eyes and bloody hands, she asked what had become of the boy. Pascal answered that he had left, but she suspected otherwise, so she went upstairs to check. When she collared the culprit in the street, she told people that he had just committed a murder. He protested that she was out of her mind, but they helped her drag him back to the scene of the crime.

Under questioning Pascal pretended to be insane himself, and people feared that the authorities might declare that he was, in order not to embarrass the clergy. Parisians, after all, were used to seeing "the most abominable crimes" go unpunished because of the rank or wealth of the individuals who had committed them. Hardy characterized the torture as "cruel" and the execution as "frightful," but he did not forget the victim of Pascal's "inconceivable brutality." People regarded the boy, who looked attractive and respectable, as a "martyr to innocence and virtue." The king promised to take him under his protection and grant him a pension if he recovered from his forty wounds. The archbishop of Paris promised him another pension to console him for "the frightful misfortune he had just experienced."

Hardy combined facts and fictions communicated by word of mouth. He was right about many of the particulars, but he was also wrong about others, for example, the dramatic confrontation in the courtyard. He provided additional details not included in Bourderelle's report, but he also left many questions unanswered. Did the boy live or die? Did the monk have a history of sexual relations with males inside or outside the monastery? Why did he leave the order and the country? What did he do during his travels in Italy (conventionally associated with sodomy) and elsewhere? What did the police ask him, and what did he say in his own defense? The other sources, unfortunately, do not provide any answers to these questions. The collections of news and gossip reported most sexual escapades with amusement, but they recounted this sexual tragedy with indignation. Since information about such cases was transmitted orally, and undoubtedly altered in the process, it is not surprising that they recorded somewhat different versions of this incident. Since they summarized the events after the fact, it is also not surprising that they omitted more details and added more comments than Hardy did.

The *Correspondance secrète* and the *Correspondance littéraire* did not agree about the particulars of Pascal's career in the clergy or the nature of his relationship with the porter.[9] Was he a defrocked monk or a suspended priest? Was she just an acquaintance or someone who had known him all his life? Neither implied that she was responsible in any way for what happened after she gave him a key and left him alone with the boy. Both reported that Pascal displayed rage and fury during the assault, to suggest not that he was temporarily insane but that he was naturally violent. Unlike Hardy, the editors of these sources charged that the monk had consummated the sexual crime. According to one, he had not only "the infamous plan" of "satisfying his brutality upon this young man" but also "the revolting atrocity to prostitute himself on this bloody victim." According to the other, who claimed melodramatically that the following clause made the pen drop from his hand, "this monster satisfied his brutality upon this child swimming in his blood." Without saying so in so many words, they meant that Pascal first subdued and then raped the boy. Neither one of these sources identified Gressier by name, but both of them added that the monk stole 38 sous from his victim.

The *Correspondance secrète* and the *Correspondance littéraire* used much the same scenario in telling the story, but they packaged it in different ways. In order to seize the attention of its readers, the *Correspondance secrète* began with a declamatory sentence announcing that a "frightful drama" had taken place in the rue Michel-le-Comte. It ended with a rhetorical sentence asking what tortures could "satisfy public scorn" in this case and deter "such monsters" in the future, as if to suggest that Parisians thought that Pascal had not suffered enough in the place de Grève and that others like him might repeat his crime at any time. The *Correspondance littéraire* began more sensationalistically and ended more philosophically. It declared that the "vice that offends nature and love by thwarting their wish," presumably for the reproduction of the species, was responsible for this crime of unexampled atrocity and fury. It concluded by invoking nature to denounce not only sodomy but also celibacy, which contradicted "the most sweet, necessary, and admirable wish of nature." Unnatural abstinence caused the "transport of desire" that exploded, in this instance, in the most "barbarous" way. This source, produced by advocates of Enlightenment, did not explain why only some priests and monks were interested in their own rather than the opposite sex, and it made no apologies for sodomites who were not members of the First Estate. It exploited resentment against the clergy, who did not produce children or pay taxes, in order to score polemical points. Reminding readers that the philosophes knew what was best for "the public welfare," the *Correspondance littéraire* read this case in the political and cultural context of decades of debate about issues involving church and state.

The *Mémoires secrets* combined the most extensive discussion of the social context with the most condensed account of the "horrible drama."[10] It exaggerated in asserting that the "villain" had committed the crime "almost in view of the whole neighborhood" and, perhaps, in observing that more people had witnessed his punishment than any other since that of the regicidal lackey who stabbed Louis XV in 1757. This source introduced the news about Pascal with remarks about the sodomitical subculture that did not really illuminate the case. It claimed that the vice in question, which used to be confined to aristocrats, wits, and Adonises, had become so fashionable that it now infected all ranks, "from dukes down to lackeys." It reported that there were almost as many "pederasts" as prostitutes in Paris and that there were places where they sold their services in public. In one section of the Tuileries garden, *gitons* (young males willing to play the passive role in sexual relations with other males) offered themselves to clients with money to spend. As in the cases of "the prince de Bauf******, the actor Monvel, and the notary Margantin," men arrested in flagrante delicto were "only" exiled, imprisoned, or reprimanded, depending on identity and circumstances. Charles-Roger de Bauffremont was undoubtedly subjected to nothing more than a reprimand. Jacques-Marie Boutet de Monvel of the Comédie-Française left the country in 1781 after he was arrested in the Tuileries, allegedly for the fifth time.[11] Perhaps Margantin was the unidentified notary apprehended in the same year by the guards who patrolled the Champs-Elysées and the "antiphysical notary" mentioned two years later in the apochryphal correspondence of Madame Gourdan, the most notorious procuress in Paris. And perhaps he, by process of elimination, ended up in prison for a while.[12]

In any case, the *Mémoires secrets* rightly observed that the authorities did not want to make "the sin against nature more common by making it more known" through exemplary public punishment but wrongly reported they had not executed anyone for this offense since 1726. It overlooked Diot and Lenoir, two consenting adults arrested in flagrante delicto, but remembered the notorious Deschauffours because he, like Pascal, molested boys and used violence, although he, unlike Pascal, also kidnapped and sold youngsters. The reference to Deschauffours, in the first sentence of the first paragraph, makes more sense than the transition from the remarks about the subculture to the news about the monk, in the first sentence of the third paragraph: "Justice thought it should finally wake up about a crime too widespread to have to worry about revealing it and not to demand a striking example." The preceding paragraph suggests that the widespread crime in question was seeking, selling, or having sex in public places, and yet Pascal was not arrested for that reason, and he did what he did behind closed doors. He did not assault the boy "in view of the whole neighborhood," a deceptive phrase apparently intended to bridge the gap between the remarks and the news. The following paragraph reduces the sexual element in this episode to the monk's unnamed "desires," without alleging that he consummated those desires. Given that silence, it implies that the real crime was the stabbing, and yet such violence was hardly common in same-sex encounters. Why would the execution of Pascal intimidate sodomites in the parks and streets who were not guilty of the offenses that had led him to the stake? The "striking example" sounds no more effective, in the last analysis, than the awkward effort to connect the incident with the subculture.

Whatever its shortcomings in logic, this source provided more information about the subculture than the others. Hardy alone mentioned Pascal's "taste," which suggested that the monk might have been different from most other men not only because of what he did but also because of who he was. The *Mémoires secrets* employed more explicit and specific language. It did not bother to define *giton*, derived from the name of a character in the *Satiricon* of Petronius, and evidently assumed that readers would understand its meaning in this context.[13] It also used two more common terms to label men who committed "the sin against nature": the more traditional and pejorative "sodomist" (usually "sodomite"), derived from the name of the city destroyed, according to the book of Genesis, because of the sins of its inhabitants, a word used in theology, law, and medicine since the Middle Ages, and the more modern and neutral "pederast," derived from the Greek noun for institutionalized educational and erotic relations between adult and adolescent males in ancient city-states, the word used by the police in the last decades of the eighteenth century without regard to age.

The *Correspondance secrète* and the *Correspondance littéraire* did not label the villain in this way and did not seem to know what to call his victim: "young savoyard" (literally, person from Savoy but loosely, errand boy) or "young man." Either they were not sure how old he was, or, more likely, they were not sure how to describe this particular adolescent, who was no longer a child but not yet an adult. Less concerned about sexual sins than urban disorder by this time, the police were quite concerned about age differences in the sodomitical subculture. Judging from the papers of commissioner Foucault, who was responsible for the surveillance of "pederasty" in Paris between 1780 and 1783, they routinely assumed that sodomites were interested in locating and involved in corrupting young males, who therefore needed to be rescued from or at least protected against predatory adults. It is abundantly clear from their own reports that some teenagers propositioned or allowed themselves to be propositioned by older males, not infrequently in order to make money, but this evidence did not make the police rethink the victimization model.

Most of the cases documented in Foucault's papers do not fit that model, but some do. The police, for example, recorded depositions from five witnesses against a thirty-nine-year-old cook named Percheron. The three adults, all of whom described him as a dangerous character, testified that he had bragged about keeping a "young man," attempted to seduce a servant with gifts and drink, and lured a boy into his house. A fifteen-year-old reported that Percheron had made him "various propositions," caressed him, and unbuttoned his pants in front of him. A sixteen-year-old reported that the cook had thrown him onto a bed, undone his pants, fondled him, and encouraged him to do likewise. Both adolescents testified that they had not only resisted his advances but also struggled with him.[14] An apprentice cook named Jean-Marie Paris, also fifteen or sixteen years old, was not able to defend himself against the unknown individual who raped him. When he returned to an address where he had made a delivery, in order to retrieve the dishes, this man caressed him "a lot" and suggested that they "have a good time together." When he refused, the man locked the door and knocked him down, then picked him up, threw him onto a bed, undid his pants, and had his way with him. Having satisfied his "passion," he gave Paris some money and sent him away. According to his brother, who made the deposition against the assailant, the victim told his confessor about "the crime he had committed in spite of himself" and used the money to have several masses said.[15] The police interrogated Percheron about the charges against him and a disreputable character named Valoux about the rape of the apprentice. It is not clear from Foucault's papers if these individuals were convicted and punished in some way, but they were certainly not executed.

The execution of Pascal was no more typical of French jurisprudence in the second half of the eighteenth century than the executions of the Protestant Calas and the blasphemous La Barre in the 1760s or the last punishments of suicides in the 1770s. Long before 1783, the police and the magistrates had abandoned any efforts to eradicate sodomy and confined themselves to controlling sodomitical activity in public places without publicizing the cases or the crime. They routinely dealt with "pederasts" in the late eighteenth century in much the same way that they would in the early nineteenth century, by arresting individuals who violated the standards of decency or corrupted the morals of minors. Why did they execute Pascal? Because he was *not* typical of the majority of "pederasts," who involved themselves in consensual (including venal) relations, because he acted out the victimization model that embodied collective anxieties, because he did so in a way that made him guilty not only of (attempted or completed) sodomy and rape but also of (attempted or completed) murder, and because he was apprehended in a very public way.

The author of the articles on sodomy in the standard encyclopedias of jurisprudence published during the 1780s ratified the verdict of the judges and the public by adding Pascal's name to the list of men executed for that offense against nature and society.[16] At the beginning of the Revolution, which decriminalized sodomy in principle but did not revolutionize the way it was handled in practice, an unknown pamphleteer incorporated the monk into a different history. In the satirical address of "the children of Sodom" to the National Assembly, published in 1790, he identified Pascal as a martyr of the Order of the Cuff (a collective nickname for sodomites) who was executed "for having attempted, by consent or through force, to make away with the virginity of a bootblack." In doing so he had allegedly followed the example of Jesus, "dead like our brother Pascal in the service of the faith." The author reported that Jesus had welcomed Saint John into his arms with the words "Come, my son, come my beloved, rest on my breast," and then asked, "Can anyone doubt the true meaning of these phrases?"[17] With tongue in cheek, he used Scripture not to vilify but to vindicate the monk. Without knowing anything more about Pascal's sense of himself than we do, he located Pascal in a collective history that would not be claimed for many years to come. Two centuries after the fact, in 1981, a member of the French National Assembly mentioned the execution of a monk who had committed a "homosexual act" with a boy without mentioning the violence involved in the incident.[18] Like the Revolutionary pamphleteer, she miscast Pascal in the role of a martyr and made him sound more modern, as well as less guilty, than he really was.

DOCUMENTS

Investigation

AN, Y11800, 3 October 1783

Official investigation conducted by us, Benjamin Bourderelle, counsellor of the king, commissioner, investigator, and examiner of the Châtelet of Paris, at the request of Monsieur the royal prosecutor in said Châtelet, in the matter of the murder committed upon the person of Jacques Gressier, errand boy in Paris, of which is accused Jacques Chabanne, a wine merchant's assistant, dressed in a gray coat and vest, with a rounded haircut, blue trousers, and an oilskin hat, who apparently calls himself Pascal.

In which investigation we heard the witnesses produced to us and drafted their depositions one after another in private as follows.

On Friday, 3 October 1783, at 7 p.m.

1. Jacques Gressier, 14 years old, native of Saint-Flour in Auvergne, errand boy living in Paris on the rue Zacharie, at the residence of Madame Jacques, innkeeper, who, after taking the oath to tell the truth, told us he

is not a relative, in-law, servant, or domestic of the parties, after his statement was read to him.

Testifies that this afternoon, near the rue Michel-le-Comte, an individual gave him a letter and a package in order, said individual told him, to have them delivered to the porter of the house we are in, that said individual took 38 sous from the pocket in his pants in the room where we are, that he threw him on the bed where he is now, unbuttoned his pants, then put his penis into his ass, that because of the deponent's resistance the individual took out his pocket knife and struck him several times with it on the head and in the back, that the individual told him that if he did not let him put his penis into his ass, he would kill him, that he, the errand boy, felt very sick. The deponent adds that if he saw said individual, he would recognize him, that said individual has a gray coat, that he has an oilskin hat, a rounded haircut, trousers, and that he is of medium build, which is all he said he knows. His deposition having been read to him, said it contains the truth, reaffirmed it, did not claim a fee, and, asked by us to do so in keeping with the ordinance, stated that he could not write or sign, given the weakness of his hand caused by his state of weakness, and we, the commissioner, signed the present deposition.

2. Remy Miguet, 43, first clerk of Sieur Santerre, police inspector
3. Louis Ravet, 24, apprentice jeweler
4. Guillaume Grisse, 25, apprentice jeweler
5. Jean-Baptiste Fauconnet, 51, sergeant of the city guard
6. Germain Lefranc, 35, under-brigadier of the city guard
7. François Maneglier, 30, employee of the city guard
8. Marie-Elisabeth Guarabi, 40, widow of Monsieur Colas Michaux, master carpenter, porter of the house we are in and where she lives, who, after taking the oath to tell the truth, told us she is not a relative, in-law, servant, or domestic of the parties, after said minutes were read to her, with the exception of the interrogation contained in them.

Testifies that she has known the arrested individual since his birth, that she lost track of him for a long time, that she saw him, however, several times, that in the last two weeks he came to see her at various times and that she had no familiarity with him, that it was known to the deponent that said arrested individual had taken monastic vows in a Capuchin monastery in the faubourg Saint-Jacques, that he was arrested in Dijon and imprisoned because he was not supplied with a passport, that at this same time he wrote to the witness to get her to find someone with influence to get him released from prison, that he came back after this time to see said deponent, whom he told he was soliciting a priory, that on this day, at 4 p.m., said individual, whom the deponent told us calls himself François Pascal, sent the murdered errand boy to her with a letter and a package, which said errand boy delivered to the deponent in asking her if it was not she who was Madame Michaux, that as soon as the deponent asked said errand boy where the person was who had given him the letter and package, said errand boy responded to her, the deponent, that this person was in the street, and at once said individual appeared and asked the deponent to lend him the key to the room we are in because, he told the deponent, he had an important letter to write, that said deponent did not think she should refuse him the key to this room, that after said deponent handed said key to said Pascal, the latter took an écu worth three livres from the pocket of his pants and handed it to the deponent to go get change in order to pay said errand boy here present, that said Pascal went upstairs to said room where we are with said commissioner, and the deponent went to get change for him, that not having found any, she came back and went to the door of the room where we are, in which door the deponent did not find a key, which made it necessary for her to knock on said door, which was opened for her at once by said Pascal, whom she told that she could not find change, that said Pascal immediately told the deponent that since she could not find change, she had only to go get a bottle of beer, which the deponent did, that having returned to said house and to the door of said room where we are, she again did not see a key in said door, such that she knocked, that since it was not opened for her at once, she knocked again more vigorously, that said door was finally opened for her by said Pascal, whom the witness asked where said errand boy was in order to pay him, that said Pascal told her immediately that he was in the room next to the one we are in, that she, the witness, having gone into the next room, did not see said errand boy, heard said Pascal leave the room we are in, that said deponent came back right away to the room where we are, where she saw said errand boy on the edge of said bed in said room where we are, that the deponent ran after said Pascal right away, calling for help, that she caught up with said Pascal in the rue Transnonain, stopped him and had him arrested and brought back to the house where we are, that the guard having arrived, several persons helped said deponent hand said Pascal over to said guard, which led him to the door of our residence, that we went with said guard, which led said Pascal, along with said deponent, to said house in which said Pascal had just committed said murder and that having all gone upstairs to said room where we are, she noticed that said errand boy was covered with blood, that there was also lots of blood on the front of the mattress on the bed in said room where we are, also on a piece of needlework tapestry that was on said bed, that having examined said errand boy closely, the witness noticed that he had received various stabs on the head and one in the back, that the vest, waistcoat, and shirt in which said errand boy was dressed were pierced at the spot of the wound he received in the back and that said errand boy's clothes were covered with blood, just like his head, that said errand boy was dressed in a blue vest, gray waistcoat, and had his pants undone and pulled down, that our first concern was to send for the holy oils and two surgeons, who, having arrived, administered to said errand boy the care appropriate to his condition, that said deponent then saw that we had said Pascal's pockets searched and that she saw taken out of the right pocket of said Pascal's vest a large knife with a black handle, the blade of which was covered with blood and broken at the end, that she noticed that said Pascal was dressed in a gray coat and vest on which there was a little blood, that he had trousers made of white linen and an oilskin hat, that it is known to the deponent that said Pascal has a rounded haircut, that she noticed that he had blood on his shirt, on the front and the back, and that he had a lot of it on the sleeves and cuffs of his shirt. The deponent adds that she heard said errand boy say that the individual who had stabbed him was dressed in a gray coat, trousers, and had an oilskin hat, that the same individual had thrown him on the bed in the room where we are, had undone his pants, stolen 38 sous from him, and then wanted to put his penis into his rear, that after the resistance that said errand boy offered to said individual, the latter stabbed him, that after our procedure was completed, we instructed the guard to have said errand boy taken to the Hôtel-Dieu, which is all that the deponent said she knows. Her deposition having been read to her, said it contains the truth, reaffirms it, claim a fee fixed for her at 6 livres, and signed the present deposition with us, the commissioner.

9. Claude-Pierre Poulleau, 37, employed by Sieur Santerre, police inspector
10. François Boncourtois, 47, employed by Sieur Santerre, police inspecteur

Interrogation

AN, X^2A 1147, 10 October 1783

If he had not given a package and letter to an individual to carry this package and letter to the widow Michaux. No.

If he had not asked the widow Michaux for the key to a room to write an important letter? No.

If he had not tried to commit horrors against the individual and stabbed him a number of times? No.

If his shirt was not covered with blood and the knife found on him? Yes, but does not know how that happened.

If the shirt was not stained and bloody in front and in back? That might be.

If he did not wash his hands in a basin? No.

Why he did not sign the proceedings and interrogations? Because he is innocent and did not want to sign what was false.

Siméon-Prosper Hardy

"Mes Loisirs, ou Journal des événements tels qu'ils parviennent à ma connaissance"
BN, Ms, Fonds Français 6684

3 October 1783

[359] Between 4 and 5 o'clock in the evening, a priest who was not yet known by name and title, a so-called secularized Capuchin, living in a respectable house in the [360] rue Michel-le-Comte kept by a single porter and where the owners, who were in the country, had allowed him to occupy a room, having engaged in the rue de la Harpe, near the rue de la Parcheminerie, a young errand boy who was said to be the nephew of a dishwasher at the Sorbonne, on the pretext of having him carry a small package, having led him to said house, started, upon his arrival, by sending said porter to get a bottle of beer in order to get rid of her, attempted to violate said young errand boy to satisfy a brutal passion and gratify his depraved taste, but encountering the most spirited resistance on his part, made the cruel decision to murder him with several strokes of a knife whose blade broke in the unfortunate lad's body, left him on the floor, and went down to the courtyard, where the porter, on her way back, found him with a bewildered look, washing his bloody hands in a washbin, asked him what had become of the errand boy, and after his reply that he had gone away, having decided that she should go up to the room and having found him still alive but soaked with his own blood, went back down, ran after the ecclesiastic, who had already reached the rue Transnonain, grabbed him by the collar and brought him back to the house, assisted by several passers-by whom she engaged to help her by telling them that this wretch just committed a murder, while he did not stop shouting that she had lost her mind. This incident caused a great deal of commotion in the neighborhood. Monsieur the lieutenant crimi-

nal informed, went to the scene at once to begin the procedure by subjecting to interrogation the guilty man, who began by trying to take the easy way by pretending to be insane. People really feared that if it happened that he did not play his part in such a way as to be able to convince others that he was actually insane, that they would pass him off as such in order not to compromise the clergy, so accustomed were people to seeing the most abominable crimes go unpunished on account of the rank or wealth of the accused. All the judicial formalities necessary in such circumstances having been completed, the ecclesiastic was taken to the prison of the Grand Châtelet and the young errand boy was transferred to the Hôtel-Dieu, in the ward of the wounded, with a strong injunction that he receive there all the care that his condition required.

10 October 1783

[363] On this day, about 4 o'clock in the afternoon, by virtue of the sentence handed down the same morning by the criminal chamber of the parliament, verified by Gollien and signed by Lacousturier, confirming the verdict handed down two days before by the lieutenant criminal of the Châtelet, a man named Jacques-François Pascal, who was said to be about fifty years old, a priest and former Capuchin from the monastery of Saint-Jacques, which he had left several years before, and son of a master quarryman from said faubourg, who had taken the name Jacques Chabanne, and whose sentence did not mention the titles out of respect for the ministers of the faith, was taken in a tumbril, accompanied in the usual way by a doctor of the Sorbonne, first in front of the main door of the cathedral of Paris to perform the *amende honorable* there, having signs in front and back with these words on them, unnatural profligate and murderer, then to the place de Grève to be broken on the wheel and then thrown into a burning woodpile to be reduced to ashes and have his ashes scattered to the wind, for having been duly charged with and convicted of "having surrendered himself to the excesses of the most criminal debauchery toward an errand boy fourteen years old whom he had lured, on the third of this month, into a room and, provoked by his resistance, of having murdered him by stabbing him many times, both on the head and in the back, which stabs had put and still put the young errand boy's life in danger."

Having reached the place de Grève, said Jacques-François Pascal, a sturdy, large, stout man, with short graying hair, wearing a gray vest and blue and white cotton and silk pants, who had been seen to shed many tears in front of Notre-Dame and who seemed contrite and repentant, although he still had a pretty steady gait, asked to go into the city hall, from which he emerged after half an hour, after having finally confessed his crime, which he had tried up until that moment to deny in an audacious manner, having even attempted at the time of his imprisonment to inculpate the porter of the house in which he committed it. People were surprised by the extraordinary steadiness with which he undressed himself and stretched out on the wheel and that, receiving the blows slowly and at intervals, no sort of exclamation escaped from him. He was carried immediately after this cruel torture to the woodpile still alive, and the tranquil spectators of such a frightful drama [364] even noticed that in spite of the precaution taken of attaching an iron ring around his neck to hasten the end, he knocked down, by the agitation and violence of his movements, the first logs thrown onto his body.

It was said that this unfortunate ecclesiastic had returned not long ago from a trip he had taken to Italy and various other foreign countries, after having been caretaker of the Capuchins in the Marais, from which his misconduct had forced the superiors to relegate him to a provincial monastery that he had left in voluntarily renouncing his frock and choosing to live as an adventurer. Also that the young errand boy, the victim of his inconceivable brutality, as attractive for the features of his face as for a certain air of breeding, and who was treated with the greatest care in the ward of the wounded in the Hôtel-Dieu, had on his body forty wounds that did not look as good as they did the first few days, suppuration seeming to want to take place in them. People affirmed that if this martyr to innocence and virtue escaped from the danger of death with which he was threatened, the king, who had declared that he took him under his protection, would grant him a pension drawn on the royal domain, independently of another pension that Monsieur the archbishop of Paris, deeply touched by the fate of this child, also proposed, they said, to offer him to console him, as much as it was within his power, for the frightful misfortune that he had just experienced.

Correspondance secrète, politique, et littéraire
18 vols. (London, 1787-90), vol. 15, 15 October 1783

[166] A frightful drama has just taken place in the rue Michel-le-Comte. A sort of defrocked monk presented himself to a porter of his acquaintance, accompanied by a young savoyard who carried a little package for him. He asked permission to write a letter in any room in the house. He was given a key, he went upstairs, and his errand boy followed [167] him. Having entered the room, his first care was to close its door, in order to accomplish the infamous plan he had conceived of satisfying his brutality upon this young man. Encountering resistance, his passion turned to rage, frenzy, fury. He stabbed this unfortunate several times, both on the head and in the back, and all the same he had the revolting atrocity to prostitute himself on this bloody victim. He did more, and here is what goes beyond all measure and which you will undoubtedly find hard to believe. He took wickedness so far as to rob this unfortunate

of 38 sous that he found in his pocket. But so many crimes are beyond human strength. His mind got confused. He went down to the porter's to wash his hands stained with blood. His bewildered look alarmed and frightened. He tried to flee, but he was stopped. Proof of guilt for his crimes was obvious, so his execution followed quickly. But great God, for such monsters, what tortures would satisfy public scorn and inflict enough terror on their kind?

***Correspondance littéraire, philosophique, et critique* ed. Maurice Tourneux, 16 vols. (Paris, 1877), vol. 13, October 1783**

[388] This vice that offends nature and love by thwarting their wish has just caused to be committed a crime of a character of atrocity and fury that perhaps no man has yet given an example of.

A man named Jacques-François Pascal, a former Capuchin, then unbeneficed priest at the church of Saint-Nicolas-des-Champs, finally barred from performing ecclesiastical functions a year ago, a few days ago led a young savoyard to a house whose porter had witnessed his birth, on the pretext of having him carry a package. He asked this woman for the key to a room in order to write, he said, an urgent letter, got rid of her by sending her to buy beer and cakes, and tried to seize the occasion of her absence to violate this young man. The cries and resistance that this unfortunate opposed to the efforts of this villain, instead of frightening him, filled him with rage and fury. He grabbed him by the hair, threw him on a bed, and, having stabbed him seventeen times without taking his life, this monster. . . . Fear and modesty make the pen drop from my hands. . . . This monster satisfied his brutality upon this child swimming in his blood and left him only after having stolen 38 sous from him. In going downstairs he met the porter, whom he told that he was going to return, stopped in the courtyard to wash his bloody hands in a bucket of water, and did not run off until he heard this woman, who had found the unfortunate child drowned in his blood and hardly breathing, come down shouting "murderer!" Sixty-six years old, she followed him and was the first to stop him in the street.

[389] This wretch was sentenced to be broken on the wheel and thrown alive on a pyre. Conflict over ecclesiastical jurisdiction was avoided by trying him under the assumed name he had taken in the first interrogations, and the sentence, in restoring his true name, did not, contrary to custom, mention his status as a priest. In this way they avoided part of the scandal of a crime that it would have been as desirable to conceal as to punish.

What is more, philosophy, which seeks to console itself for and perhaps to put a stop to such horrors by going back to their cause, sees nothing in this double crime but the inevitable result of the law of celibacy imposed on Catholic priests, an almost forced taste, since the law thwarts in them the most sweet, most necessary, and most admirable wish of nature, finally a fury, a transport of desire that must have been increased by the resistance that blood could not calm and that such a barbarous pleasure alone could satisfy.

How many secret crimes could be prevented, what blessing to the human race could be given by the ruler who commanded so many men to take advantage both for themselves and for their country of a right that nature and the public welfare do not cease to demand in their favor!

Mémoires secrets pour servir à l'histoire de la république des lettres en France depuis 1762 jusqu'à nos jours 36 vols. (London, 1777-89), vol. 23, 13 October 1783

[241] Since the execution of Deschauffours, no sodomist had been executed. The government had been afraid of making the sin against nature more common by making it more known. It is thus that the prince de Bauf******, the actor Monvel, the notary Margatin, and so many others caught in flagrante delicto were punished only with exile, prison, Bicêtre, or a simple reprimand from the police, depending on their identities and the circumstances.

This vice, which used to be called the fine vice because it was affected only by great aristocrats, wits, or Adonises, has become so fashionable that today there is no rank in society, from dukes down to lackeys and the populace that is not infected with it. Commissioner Foucault, recently deceased, was responsible for this area and used to show his friends a thick book in which were written [242] all the names of pederasts known to the police. He claimed that there were almost as many of them as prostitutes in Paris, that is to say about forty thousand. There are also public places of prostitution of this kind, and in the Tuileries gardens there is a known section assigned solely to gitons who come there looking for good luck.

Justice thought it should finally wake up about a crime too widespread to have to worry about revealing it and not to demand a striking example. The day before yesterday it had burned a pederast named Pascal, who had taken the surname Chabanne. It seems sure that he had been a Capuchin and that he was a priest. He was not given any title in the sentence in order to spare the clergy and, moreover, not provoke its objections.

This villain was first broken on the wheel because, having encountered resistance on the part of a young savoyard who did not want to give in to his desires, he stabbed him seventeen times and put him in danger of death. It was on the first of October that this horrible drama took place, in full daylight and almost in view of the whole neighborhood.

Since Damiens a more well attended execution had not been seen. There were people up to the rooftops.

NOTES

1. "La Police de Paris en 1770: Mémoire inédit composé par ordre de Gabriel de Sartine sur la demande de Marie-Thérèse," ed. Augustin Louis Gazier, *Mémoires de la Société de l'histoire de Paris et de l'Isle-de-France* 5 (1878): 14. The author wishes to thank Bryant Ragan and Michael Sibalis for comments on this article.

2. See Michel Rey, "Les Sodomites parisiens au XVIIIe siècle," Mémoire de maîtrise, Université de Paris III, 1980; idem, "Parisian Homosexuals Create a Lifestyle, 1700-1750: The Police Archives," in *'Tis Nature's Fault: Unauthorized Sexual Behavior during the Enlightenment*, ed. Robert Maccubbin (New York, 1987), 179-91; idem, "Police and Sodomy in Eighteenth-Century Paris: From Sin to Disorder," in *The Pursuit of Sodomy: Male Homosexuality in Renaissance and Enlightenment Europe*, ed. Kent Gerard and Gert Hekma (New York, 1989), 129-46; Maurice Lever, *Les Bûchers de Sodome: Histoire des "infâmes"* (Paris, 1985); Jeffrey Merrick, "Commissioner Foucault, Inspector Noël, and the 'Pederasts' of Paris, 1780-3," *Journal of Social History* 30 (1998): 287-307. For sample documents from both series, see *Homosexuality in Early Modern France: A Documentary Collection*, ed. Jeffrey Merrick and Bryant T. Ragan, Jr. (New York, 2001).

3. Quoted in Jacques Peuchet, *Mémoires tirées des archives de police de Paris*, 6 vols. (Paris, 1838), 3: 39.

4. In *Bûchers de Sodome*, 384-7, Lever combined information from several sources into a straightforward narrative without acknowledging the differences in the accounts or analyzing the commentaries on the case. The case is not mentioned, unfortunately, in the *Correspondance secrète inédite sur Louis XVI, Marie-Antoinette, la cour et la ville de 1777 à 1792*, ed. Mathurin François Adolphe de Lescure, 2 vols. (Paris, 1866), or the *Recueil de lettres secrètes: Année 1783*, ed. Paule Adamy (Geneva, 1997).

5. AN, Y11800, 3 October 1783.

6. If the boy used slang, then the clerk must have substituted the more proper word [*verge*] for the male organ.

7. AN, X^{2}A 1147, 10 October 1783.

8. "Mes Loisirs, ou Journal d'événements tels qu'ils parviennent à ma connaissance," BN, Ms, Fonds Français 6684, 359-60, 363-4.

9. *Correspondance secrète, politique, et littéraire*, 18 vols. (London, 1787-90), 15: 166-7; *Correspondance littéraire, philosophique, et critique*, ed. Maurice Tourneux, 16 vols. (Paris, 1877), 13: 388-9.

10. *Mémoires secrets pour servir à l'histoire de la république des lettres en France depuis 1762 jusqu'à nos jours*, 36 vols. (London, 1777-89), 23: 241-2.

11. See *Correspondance secrète*, 11: 328, and *Mémoires secrets*, 17: 274, as well as François Marie Mayeur de Saint-Paul, *Le Désoeuvré, ou L'Espion du boulevard du Temple* (London, 1782), 66; and Roselyne Laplace, *Monvel: Un Aventurier au siècle des Lumières* (Paris, 1998), 137-8.

12. AN, O^{1}1589, 2-9 July 1781. The guard released the notary, on this occasion, out of deference to his status and out of consideration for his wife. Letter dated 2 January 1783, in Charles Théveneau de Morande, *Correspondance de Madame Gourdan*, ed. Octave Uzanne (Brussels, 1883), unpaginated. Margantin is included not only in the list of notaries to the Châtelet in the *Almanach royal* but also in the list of sodomites in *Les Enfants de Sodome à l'Assemblée Nationale, ou Députation de l'Ordre de la Manchette aux représentants de tous les ordres pris dans les soixante districts de Paris et de Versailles y réunis* [1790], reprinted as *Cahiers Gai Kitsch Camp* 1 (1989): 5.

13. For more on *giton* and other terms, see Claude Courouve, *Vocabulaire de l'homosexualité masculine* (Paris, 1985).

14. AN, Y13410, 29 March 1783.

15. AN, Y13408, 25 January 1781.

16. André Jean Baptiste Boucher d'Argis, "Sodomie," in *Repertoire universel et raisonné de jurisprudence civile, criminelle, canonique, et bénéficiale*, ed. Pierre Jean Jacques Guillaume Guyot, 17 vols. (Paris, 1784-5), 16: 337; idem, "Sodomie," in *Enyclopédie méthodique: Jurisprudence*, 10 vols. (Paris, 1782-91), 7: 615.

17. *Enfants de Sodome*, notes 4 and 5. John 13:25 indicates that John, who repeatedly described himself as the disciple whom Jesus loved, leaned against his chest but mentions no explicit invitation to do so.

18. Janine Mossuz-Lavau, *Les Lois de l'amour: Les Politiques de la sexualité en France de 1950 à nos jours* (Paris, 1991), 361.

"*Au sein de vos pareilles*": Sapphic Separatism in Late Eighteenth-Century France

Susan Lanser

Echappée dès votre tendre jeunesse aux séductions des hommes, goûtez le bonheur de vous trouver réunie au sein de vos pareilles.[1]

Donna con donna, femme à femme: so Pierre Brantôme designates the "art" of "lesbian ladies" at the close of the sixteenth century. "Woman with woman" certainly seems to suggest the desire of like for like, but Brantôme places man as the shadowy similitude beneath this same-sex coupling: Tribades "give themselves to other women in the very way that men do."[2] What Marie-Jo Bonnet identifies as the first entry for "tribade" in a French dictionary echoes Brantôme's suggestion that "woman with woman" is somehow also "woman with man." In Richelet's dictionary of 1680, the tribade is one "who mates with another person of her sex and imitates a man."[3]

This understanding of the tribade as man-like carries us into, but does not carry us out of, the eighteenth century. In the larger project of which this essay forms a part, I argue that during the "Age of Enlightenment" new concerns that women might align themselves with other women become crucial in creating the ideology not simply of sexual but of heterosexual difference on which modern patriarchy grounds itself. Representations of female homoeroticism, which intensify dramatically during the late seventeenth and eighteenth centuries, perform complicated cultural work of both incitement and containment as European societies struggle with new challenges to male dominance. In ways

[Haworth co-indexing entry note]: " '*Au sein de vos pareilles*': Sapphic Separatism in Late Eighteenth-Century France." Lanser, Susan. Co-published simultaneously in *Journal of Homosexuality* (Harrington Park Press, an imprint of The Haworth Press, Inc.) Vol. 41, No. 3/4, 2001, pp. 105-116; and: *Homosexuality in French History and Culture* (ed: Jeffrey Merrick, and Michael Sibalis) Harrington Park Press, an imprint of The Haworth Press, Inc., 2001, pp. 105-116. Single or multiple copies of this article are available for a fee from The Haworth Document Delivery Service [1-800-342-9678, 9:00 a.m. - 5:00 p.m. (EST). E-mail address: getinfo@haworthpressinc.com].

largely overlooked in such brilliant scholarship on sexual difference as Thomas Laqueur's *Making Sex* and Geneviève Fraisse's *Reason's Muse*, sapphism (the term through which I am designating the new conception of *donna con donna*) serves at once as stimulus and sign of the reconfigured gender identities that Enlightenment generates.[4] In late eighteenth-century France, one important effect of this reconfiguration is a changed sense both of the tribade's "likeness" and of the "bosom" in which she rests.

The movement that I am tracing operates alongside and sometimes inside "libertine" fictions that both legitimate and circumscribe women's erotic relationships.[5] From the *Académie des dames* (1680) and *Venus dans le cloître* (1683), through d'Argens's *Thérèse philosophe* and Diderot's *Bijoux indiscrets* (both 1748) and reaching forward to the writings of Sade, the prolific and primarily French tradition of what Robert Darnton has called "philosophical pornography" commonly incorporates sexual acts between women.[6] Even as these narratives validate female pleasure, they nearly always give tribadism a dependent status as either substitute or supplement: Sex between women usually occurs in a cloister or from the chance sharing of a bed, prepares a woman for a man, or involves a man as voyeur or participant. If libertine discourse seems to contain tribadism through integration, however, it also suggests that any woman can enjoy another woman when circumstances conspire.

This implicit pan-homoeroticism may explain why, although libertine fiction seems rather comfortable with the female intimacies that it both recognizes and regulates, dictionary definitions of the *tribade* begin by the mid-eighteenth century to reveal a certain distress.[7] In a significant departure from definitions like Brantôme's and Richelet's, the 1755 *Manuel lexique ou dictionnaire portatif des mots françois* designates *tribade* as the "name given to lascivious women who try to obtain among themselves pleasures they can receive only from the other sex."[8] Here the tribade is defined by a pleasure rendered both obscene and unattainable precisely because the tribade is not a man. The 1762 *Dictionnaire de l'Académie française* erases even that pleasure by making the tribade a "woman who violates another woman," so that female homoeroticism becomes predatory rather than consensual.[9] And notwithstanding Diderot's radical suggestion that sexual pleasure can be valid with any "like being male or female," the *Encyclopédie* defines the tribade as "a woman with a passion for another woman; a type of peculiar perversion as inexplicable as that which inflames a man for another man."[10] The range of concerns embedded in these definitions indicate that *donna con donna* has by mid-century become a more troubled site. And as sex between women becomes unsuccessful and incomprehensible, man no longer hovers as the tribade's *pareille*.

I want to suggest that these vexed definitions herald a shift whereby the tribade will be envisioned less as desiring women in manlike ways than as rejecting men and creating spaces that exclude them. Elizabeth Wahl and Domna Stanton have shown that same-sex desire was sometimes inferred from the "masculine" ambitions and feminist leanings of the seventeenth-century *précieuses*. But the texts of the later eighteenth century go beyond implying that feminism is potentially sapphic to suggest that sapphism is essentially feminist.[11] The new configuration is especially visible in a group of writings of the late 1770s and 1780s that depict tribades not simply as predatory individuals or amorous couples but as members of voluntary communities and secret societies.

The best known and most influential of these texts is the "Confessions d'une jeune fille" [Confessions of a Young Girl] (1778), which first appeared as four episodes in the *Espion anglais*, a collection of scandalous tales probably created by the journalist and royal censor Mathieu-François Pidansat de Mairobert. The "Confessions" purports to expose an all-female community featuring such actual Parisians as Mademoiselle Raucourt, renowned actress of the Comédie française, and Madame Joly de Fleury, whose husband and father were members of the parlement of Paris. Its narrator is the precocious young provincial "Mademoiselle Sapho," plucked from a brothel to be the mistress of Madame de Furiel (Fleury) and eventually evicted when she becomes pregnant by a young man who has entered the community in female disguise. While the text certainly contains prurient moments, what most interests me here are its description of an elaborate secret ritual that initiates Sapho into the lesbian community and its extensive "Apologie de la secte anandrine" [Apologia for the Anandrine Sect] putatively delivered by Raucourt "on 28 March 1778." As the "Apologie" makes especially vivid, the tribade constructed by the "Confessions" is motivated not simply by sexual passion but by intellectual and spiritual commitment to women and by distrust of men. A tribade, Sapho is instructed,

> is a young virgin who, having had no commerce with men, and convinced of the excellences of her own sex, finds in women the true and pure pleasures of the flesh, devotes herself entirely to them, and renounces that other sex who is as treacherous as it is seductive. Or she is a woman of any age who, having fulfilled the wish of nature and the nation that she propagate the human race, recovers from her error, abhors and abjures crude pleasures, and dedicates herself to forming pupils for the goddess.[12]

From this position comes a new definition and rationale for same-sex affinities. The "Apologie" designates the group's official name as "the *Anandrine* sect, or tribades as they are commonly called," and a footnote, taking liberties with etymology, claims that "this word, which I believe comes from the Greek, means in French *anti-male*."[13] A lover of women is now a hater of men, devoted not only to her own erotic pleasure but to preserving other women from male perfidy. Sapphism has become feminist separatism, as it were.

But the "Apologie" goes beyond simply depicting tribades as women in revolt against men. Enacting secret rituals that it dates to the vestal virgins but which it claims have continued throughout history and around the world, the community also presents itself as a social utopia. "Peace, harmony, serenity, and unity" are its "basic foundation." It is structured as a large family of "sisters," with young adherents treated maternally by their elders and "with no hierarchy but that established by nature itself for its preservation, and necessary for its governance." Benevolence toward the unfortunate is a distinctive trait; all goods are held in common, differences between rich and poor disappear, and the temporary distinction of "mother" and "pupil" replaces patriarchy's fixed system of male supremacy. Relationships between women are deeply erotic but also tenderly mutual. A "true" tribade will want every member of her sex to share her happiness, all the more as tribadism here is declared the purest and most natural of choices, the "safeguard of the virtue of girls and widows," and the consolation of old age. And it is through the happiness and beauty of the "pupils" that the group propagates itself, for as the women appear in public, displaying genteel manners and regal dress regardless of their birth, they "will attract others to the sect; you will plant in the hearts of those who are like you and will admire you, the desire to imitate you by sharing your fate."[14]

Clearly this representation goes far beyond a notion of *donna con donna* as sexual coupling, though sexual coupling is certainly a significant feature of the community and an explicit constitutent of the "Confessions" that frames the "Apologie." The society's manifesto reads rather like a feminist-separatist *Social Contract*, with its own brand of maternity and its pastoral space, and it seems no accident that some of the Anandrine members are described explicitly as "philosophes." If for Brantôme tribadism concerns what one does (one's "art"), and if for the *Encyclopédie* the term designates whom one (inexplicably) desires, here tribadism is an entire social program involving what one believes, how one presents oneself, and where one dwells. The "Apologie" thus interpolates women into a collective sapphic subjectivity in ways that challenge both the historical presumptions and the conceptual distinctions between "acts" and "identities" that have tended until very recently to guide the history of sexuality.

Although the "Confessions d'une jeune fille" is almost certainly fictitious and probably meant to be mocking, and although "Mademoiselle Sapho" herself ends up outside the sapphic community (back in the brothel, pregnant, and not necessarily better off), the complex representation of the Anandrines exceeds satire. It is not surprising that belief in its veracity, encouraged by the text's use of realist devices and characters *à clefs*, seems to have been fairly widespread in its own time and has not disappeared in ours. Extensively circulated in and beyond France, the "Confessions" was frequently reprinted, excerpted, parodied, imitated, and evoked. Mirabeau's *Erotika Biblion* (1783) describes the vestal virgins as "the most famous seraglio of tribades that ever existed," no "vulgar establishment" but an "august society with high-ranking priestesses, high privilege, and limitless power."[15] Jouy's libertine *Galerie des femmes* (1799) frames its one sapphic portrait, "Sappho, or the Lesbians," around the scene of three women enacting ritual "mysteries" in secret space.[16] Such renditions suggest that sapphic separatism was a site of curiosity, if not of concern, in the late eighteenth century. Moreover, the term "anandrine" rather quickly caught on as a synonym for "tribade." In the 1789 novel *La Curieuse impertinente*, for example, "Anandrine sect" designates the convent, where female community is not simply circumstantial but serendipitous. Its cloistered women have a "natural" passion for one another, and their understanding of women's needs makes them superior lovers rather than men's pale likenesses. The nuns are "the happiest of all creatures, and also the most considerate," for "men don't know how to love; always occupied by business, irrelevant matters, and pointless speculations, they are incapable of those attentions that the heart requires and that women alone are fit to possess." The speaker of these words goes on to say that her own convent experiences provided:

> more tenderness, more ecstasy, more pleasure, than I have ever experienced in the arms of a man. With what attentiveness and tenderness did my little friend take care of me! with what concern every morning for the state of my health! what pleasure in teaching me everything she knew!

Having learned from each other "the most hidden mysteries of nature and love," these young women have no reason, she says, to long for men.[17] Marie-Jo Bonnet describes what seems to be a similar dynamic in Restif de la Bretonne's 1780 *La Duchesse ou la femme Sylfide*, whose eponymous protagonist takes young "nymphs" into a convent for their own protection: "Their feelings were based on a real or feigned contempt for men in general. The duchess especially took this so far that she was persuaded men were by nature women's inferiors."[18]

A sustained effort to defuse this kind of philosophical separatism motivates another novel of the period, *Les Chevalières errantes, ou les deux sosies femelles* [The Female Knights-Errant or the Two Twin Girls] (1789). Like the *Curieuse impertinente* a purported translation of an English work, this text is typically English in being sapphic only by innuendo. Yet it incorporates the

Anandrine ritual with a similarity of detail that could hardly be coincidence. Its "Raucourt" is Miss Eleanora Finch, a single, mannish "Amazon" who hunts and shoots and in other ways fails to "adhere to the ways of her own sex," and these "bizarreries" are attributed directly to Miss Finch's perceived antipathy for men. As one male character puts it, such amazons are not exactly "enemies of the human race, but they are very openly enemies of the more wretched [i.e., male] half of humankind," and he accuses Miss Finch not only of influencing her niece Clara and Clara's friend Bella against marrying but of "initiat[ing]" them "into the mysteries."[19] Miss Finch herself tells Bella that men are "the natural enemies of women, whom they view as born to satisfy either their lust or their greed, and sometimes both."[20]

Ultimately, however, the *Chevalières errantes* rejects any possibility of sapphic society. Midway through the novel, Miss Finch does induct Bella and Clara into a "sect" dedicated like the Anandrines to Vesta, with Miss Finch's servant Polly presiding as its egalitarian "sovereign." Although the sect is named the Order of Chastity, sexuality is never explicitly ruled out, for this chastity is explicitly designated as a matter of the *heart* rather than "chastity as vulgarly understood." This sect, however, is merely a tiny remnant rather than the widespread secret society claimed by Raucourt. Miss Finch explains that there are only thirteen members world-wide, and, as if revising the agenda of the Anandrines, she stresses that the group does not "chase after proselytes" and refuses women who are likely to become mothers (yet Clara and Bella are admitted despite their obvious marriageability).[21]

Ultimately, however, the *Chevalières errantes* does away with separatism entirely. Although Clara and Bella have joined this society of what Bella's nurse calls "crazy virgins," and although they even run off to France on horseback to escape the men who are in love with them, the young women end up renouncing their "vows" and marrying their suitors after Miss Finch reveals that the sect into which she initiated them does not even exist. It was merely a device she invented to humor the young women lest they run off to a Catholic convent.[22] Indeed, the novel explicitly dissolves the all-female society, creating in its place a heterosocial Order of Chastity in which the prospective male-female couples swear to be faithful, loyal, and benevolent, thereby reinscribing qualities associated with the Anandrine community into private domestic partnerships.

Although the "Confessions d'une jeune fille" pretends to describe an actual sect and the *Chevalières errantes* insists that no such sect exists, the dialogic implication of these texts is that some separatist threat looms in the cultural imagination of late eighteenth-century France. As I earlier suggested, this is, of course, not the first time sapphism has been connected to female resistance or female power. But I see in these late eighteenth-century French texts a new dynamic, one that makes sapphism a foundation for, and not simply a consequence or danger of, female utopia. Although the narrating Sapho of the "Confessions" is herself evicted from the Anandrines, there is no sense of a failure of the community itself; if the story suggests a "natural" heterosexuality on Sapho's part, it upholds an equally "natural" homosexuality in the women who remain. And at the end of the *Chevalières errantes*, Miss Finch remains a resistant if lone amazon.

It makes sense that female separatism and female community might be appealing and threatening in a climate of ideological and material challenges to traditional conceptions of woman's nature and woman's place. I am only now beginning to explore the more specific cultural meanings that might lie beneath the coding of sapphism as both social and separatist. I do not yet know, for example, how these sapphic texts might have influenced, or been influenced by, the pamphlets that, as other scholars have noted, began around the same moment to attack Marie-Antoinette and the women around her and to connect their political manipulations with alleged sapphic tastes.[23] In one pamphlet, for example, the queen's intimate friend the duchess de Polignac is represented as being ready to wipe out millions of French citizens in exchange for power; the two women "rest from our fatigues of lovemaking" only by "working with ardor to destroy a people who have the insolent pride to despise us. . . . And who cares, indeed, if thousands of men are destroyed? Paris is overflowing with inhabitants; let's purge them from the kingdom and ensure our bliss."[24] In another text, Polignac blames herself for having "poisoned" Marie-Antoinette "through my perverted advice": "It is I and my kind who have collaborated in swelling the national debt; it is our doing that the State has for so long now been turned upside down."[25] And in another, the princess de Lamballe, whose presumed intimacies with the queen proved fatal, is said to give advice "dictated by a truly diabolical politics."[26] A later and longer book, the *Cadran des plaisirs de la cour*, depicts Marie-Antoinette and Polignac as "treat[ing] men like oranges; when [they] have sucked the juice, [they] toss the peel far away."[27]

Given these connections between sapphism and politics, the "Anandrine" texts may have been linked to the court in the popular imagination. Documented connections between the queen and known sapphists such as Raucourt, which also turn up in some of the pamphet literature especially during the Revolution, suggest as much; and the "Confessions d'une jeune fille" is, suggestively, appended to at least one edition of the *Cadran des plaisirs de la cour*. I want to propose, however, that the pre-Revolutionary texts may not only reveal and foster a general anxiety about women's power and a particular anxiety about the Queen, but also a concern about another phenomenon: the place of women in Freemasonry. Janet Burke and Margaret Jacob have argued (individually and together) that although eighteenth-century Freemasonry usually "effectively excluded" women, France was exceptional in authorizing female Masonic groups.[28] Although women's lodges were never wholly independent but were "adopted" by male clubs, and although, as Dena Goodman argues, their actual power may have been very limited, these groups resembled the men's lodges in their ethos of friendship and exclusivity and in their "enlightened" philosophy. What Burke and Jacob describe as a "woman-centered celebration" seems to have characterized some of the initiation ceremonies, and at least one lodge featured a utopian oration in its initiation rite. The highest Masonic degree for women, they report, was called the *Amazonnerie anglaise* and its leader "the Queen of the Amazons." This platform of the *Amazonnerie* called for the equal distribution of wealth between the sexes and urged women "to throw off the yoke of the men and regard as tyrants those who refused to submit to the female order," deploying language evoking both the *Chevalières errantes* and the Anandrine "Apologie."[29]

French Freemasonry officially admitted women (over some protest, apparently) in 1774, and most of the "lodges of adoption" were founded in the mid-1770s and 1780s, when most of the texts I have been citing also appear. Several scholars have noted that the Anandrine rites, with their emphasis on secrecy, mystery, and initiation ceremonies that test the applicant's virtue, vividly evoke the rites of Freemasonry, which also shares the utopian discourse of equality, humanity, and friendship around which the fictional Raucourt centers her "Apologie." Jean Reuilly in 1909, and Marie-Jo Bonnet and Joan DeJean in the 1990s, have recalled the entry in the 1775 *Correspondance littéraire* that supports this link between masonic and anandrine societies: "They say there exists a society known as the *Lodge of Lesbos*, but whose meetings are even more mysterious than those of the Freemasons have ever been, with initiations into all the secrets that Juvenal described so frankly and openly."[30]

I want to press this connection further than scholarship has currently taken it by proposing that use of Masonic tropes to represent sapphic community reflects anxiety not only about sapphism but Freemasonry as well. The threat of a "Lodge of Lesbos" signifies the potential initiated by the masonic movement for women to convene apart from men as self-authorizing communities. The "lodges of adoption" actually instituted by French Freemasonry may not have given women this kind of effective power: Where Burke and Jacob see female agency, Goodman sees a mechanism for "includ[ing] women while maintaining moral and political authority over them."[31] Goodman may be right to argue that the lodges of adoption were not egalitarian projects, since, as Burke and Jacob also acknowledge, the Masonic lodges were in fact "mixed rather than wholly female"; women were never truly alone in their lodges, and, indeed, "there were no totally female formal organizations in eighteenth-century

France."[32] Burke and Jacob attribute this absence to the eighteenth-century conception that men had a "duty to protect women in public situations. To leave women alone in their lodges, however private they may seem to us, would have been considered desertion; probably the women themselves would have felt abandoned."[33] Goodman sees Freemasonry as perpetuating a discourse of "gallantry, seduction, and sex" that leads directly to the Republican ethos of wifely submission and domestic harmony.[34] Both arguments, however, suggest a culture in which a "Lodge of Lesbos" that entirely excludes men could loom as a threatening next step in women's efforts for equality. The fact that male Freemasons were sometimes charged with sodomy, and sometimes felt the need to repudiate in their ceremonies "the mysteries and 'indecencies' associated with Saturn, Bacchus, and Priapus," already connects Freemasonry with anxieties about single-sex gatherings.[35] I am suggesting, in short, that the sapphic texts I have been discussing represent the threat of a genuine female autonomy not yet necessarily offered by Freemasonry but made imaginable by the possibilities that the "lodges of adoption" opened, in their ritual and discourse if not in fact. It is worth recalling that, as Burke has shown, Marie-Antoinette's intimate and putatively sapphic friend, the princess de Lamballe, was deeply dedicated to the principles of Freemasonry.[36] And it may not be inconsequential that when the Revolutionary Republican Women's Clubs were shut down in 1793, its members were charged (among other appellations) with being *chevalières errantes*.[37]

A culturally specific anxiety about women's separation from men helps to explain why representations of sapphic enclaves seem at this particular historical moment to be particular to France.[38] Goodman and Burke/Jacob seem to agree that the "single-sex sociability" of Freemasonry disrupted the heterosocial culture of the salons. It seems to me that the social separation of women from men is much less conventional in France than, say, in England; as a shorthand, one might compare the French salon with the English coffeehouse. While representations of sapphism in England proliferate throughout the eighteenth century, I have not found evidence that they take during the 1770s and 1780s a specifically separatist form. The notion of the tribade as separatist may suggest that in France, women's social withdrawal from men may have seemed more dangerous than merely sexual, even homosexual, philandering. Indeed, this national difference might also help to explain the fact that several of these sapphic separatist texts evoke England or the English, just as the more sexualized sapphic texts of England often evoke things French.

In the end, sapphic separatism may have been the unintended consequence of an even larger social change. The ideology of sexual difference that gained prominence in the eighteenth century attempted to reconstruct patriarchy on the ground that men and women were dramatically different, both physically and mentally, and thus to proclaim that each sex merited its own "sphere." Sapphic writings that present men as women's enemies or at least as their opposites, insisting that women are "naturally" better attuned to other women than men can be, legitimate *donna con donna* precisely on the ground of sexual difference. The sapphic separatism I am describing here is thus inseparable from, and arguably created by, the very constructions of femininity on which modern patriarchy comes to rely. In this context, the call of the Anandrines becomes an ironic warning: if women are going to be segregated "like to like," they may end up preferring the happiness of union in the "bosom" of their *pareilles*.

NOTES

1. "APOLOGIE de la secte anandrine, ou Exhortation à une jeune tribade, par Mlle de Raucourt, prononcée le 28 mars 1778," in *L'Espion anglais, ou Correspondance secrète entre Milord All'Eye et Milord All'Ear*, 10 vols. (London, 1786), 10: 284. Excerpts from the "Confessions" appear in *Homosexuality in Early Modern France: A Documentary Collection*, ed. Jeffrey Merrick and Bryant T. Ragan, Jr. (New York, 2001), 137-51. Merrick and Ragan translate my epigraph as follows: "Having escaped the seductions of men since your tender youth, enjoy the happiness of finding yourself joined to the bosom of those like you" (144).

2. Pierre Brantôme, *Recueil des Dames*, ed. Etienne Vaucheret (Paris, 1991), i, 361, 363.

3. Quoted in Marie-Jo Bonnet, *Les Relations amoureuses entre les femmes du XVIe au XXe siècle* (Paris, 1995), 89. A first version of Bonnet's pioneering study was published in 1981 under the title *Un choix sans équivoque*. Bonnet's work broke new ground in documenting and analyzing representations of female homoeroticism from early to late modernity. It remains the most comprehensive French-language source on eighteenth-century sapphism and one of few scholarly books to focus on French representations of female homoeroticism across several centuries.

4. Thomas Laqueur, *Making Sex: Body and Gender from the Greeks to Freud* (Cambridge, MA, 1990); and Geneviève Fraisse, *Reason's Muse: Sexual Difference and the Birth of Democracy*, trans. Jane Marie Todd (Chicago, 1994). While working from different paradigms, both scholars (and numerous others writing either independently or in their wake) locate in the eighteenth century a change in gender relations that instantiates a discourse of difference as the primary mechanism for articulating male-female identities and relationships, both personal and political.

I use the term "sapphism" to denote a shift that eighteenth-century terminology does not readily capture. The term "tribade" continues to dominate French writings into the nineteenth century. In the eighteenth century, however, earlier and more frequently in England than in France, both the figure of Sappho and the terms "sapphist" and "sapphic" begin to gain currency as sexual signifiers. My choice of term underscores my contention that in the course of the eighteenth century, female homoeroticism was already beginning to take on the characteristics usually associated with "sapphism" but dated only to the nineteenth century.

5. Libertine fiction is not the dominant medium for representing sapphism in England or, to my knowledge, elsewhere. For discussions of other forms of representation,

see my "Sapphic Picaresque and Sexual Difference," forthcoming in *Textual Practice* (November 2001); and " 'Queer to Queer': The Sapphic Body as Transgressive Text," forthcoming in *Lewd and Notorious: Female Transgression in the Eighteenth Century*, ed. Katharine Kittredge (Ann Arbor: University of Michigan Press, 2001).

6. Robert Darnton, *The Forbidden Best-Sellers of Pre-Revolutionary France* (New York, 1996), chapter 3 and *passim*.

7. In ways that I do not have space to pursue here, this anxiety is also evident in such "realist" novels as Diderot's *La Religieuse* (1760) and Rousseau's *Julie, ou La Nouvelle Héloïse* (1762).

8. *Manuel lexique ou dictionnaire portatif des mots françois dont la signification n'est pas familière à tout le monde*, ed. abbé Prévost, 2 vols. (Paris, 1755), 2: 502.

9. Also in *Dictionnaire royale français-anglais et anglais-français*, ed. A. Boyer, 2 vols. (Lyon, 1780), 1: 610. Interestingly, a 1796 *Dictionnaire Royal, Français-Anglais, et Anglais-Français tiré des meilleurs auteurs qui ont écrit dans ces deux langues*, ed. P. M. Fierville, repeats the 1762 definition but gives a quite different English version that removes the sense of violation and even the certainty of sexuality: "Tribade (*femme qui abuse d'une autre femme*): a woman who loves her own sex, a woman-lover."

10. Denis Diderot, *Le Rêve de d'Alembert*, in *Oeuvres philosophiques*, ed. Paul Vernière (Paris, 1964), 379; and "Tribade," in *Encyclopédie, ou Dictionnaire raisonné des sciences, des arts et des métiers*, 28 vols. (Paris, 1751-65), 16: 617. Although it is "depravation" that I am stressing here, Bonnet, 112, is certainly right to underscore the fact that the *Encyclopédie* pioneers in crediting the tribade with "passion" in its positive, Enlightenment sense.

11. For a very rich exploration of French (and English) representations of female homoeroticism in the seventeenth and eighteenth centuries, see Elizabeth Wahl, *Invisible Relations: Representations of Female Intimacy in the Age of Enlightenment* (Stanford, 1999). On sapphism and the *précieuses*, see Wahl, chapter 5; and Domna Stanton, "The Fiction of *Préciosité* and the Fear of Women," *Yale French Studies* 62 (1981): 107-34.

12. *Espion anglais*, 10: 113.

13. Ibid., 238. As Bonnet, 159, points out, *anandrine* might more properly denote the absence of a husband than hostility to men.

14. *Espion anglais*, 265-6.

15. Honoré-Gabriel Riquetti, comte de Mirabeau, *Errotika Biblion* [sic] (Rome, 1783), 92-3.

16. Etienne de Jouy, *Galerie des femmes: Collection incomplète de huit tableaux recueillis par un amateur* (Paris, 1799).

17. *La Curieuse impertinente, traduite de l'anglais* (n.p., 1789), 101.

18. Restif de la Bretonne, *Les Femmes titrées*, cited in Bonnet, *Relations amoureuses*, 181.

19. *Les Chevalières errantes, ou Les Deux sosies femelles*, 3 vols. (Paris, 1789), 2: 6-7.

20. Ibid., 2: 16-7, 29-30.

21. Ibid., 2: 47-51.

22. Ibid., 2: 102, 105.

23. Several scholars have explored representations of Marie-Antoinette as sapphist. For a superb discussion particularly relevant to my arguments, see Elizabeth Colwill, "Pass as a Woman, Act Like a Man: Marie-Antoinette as Tribade in the Pornography of

the French Revolution," in *Homosexuality in Modern France*, ed. Jeffrey Merrick and Bryant T. Ragan, Jr. (New York, 1996), 54-79.

24. *Les Imitateurs de Charles IX*, initially entitled *La Destruction de l'aristocratisme, drame en cinq actes en prose, destiné à être représenté sur le théâtre de la Liberté* (Chantilly, 1789), 110. "Men" here, of course, could mean people in general or males in particular, though in context the former is more plausible.

25. *Confession et repentir de Mme de P***, ou La Nouvelle Madeleine convertie* (1789), reprinted in Hector Fleischmann, *Madame de Polignac et la cour galante de Marie-Antoinette* (Paris, 1910), 130.

26. *Mémoires secrets*, 21 February 1776, quoted in Fleischmann, *Les Maîtresses de Marie-Antoinette* (Paris, n.d.), 26.

27. *Le Cadran des plaisirs de la cour, ou Les Aventures du petit page Chérubin, pour servir de suite à la Vie de Marie-Antoinette, ci-devant Reine de Franc, suivi de la Confession de Mademoiselle Sapho* (Paris, n.d.), 81-2. The British Library dates this text to 1795, but the text's reference to Marie-Antoinette as the "ci-devant Reine de France" would suggest a date before her execution in October 1793.

28. Among their relevant publications, see Janet M. Burke, "Freemasonry, Friendship and Noblewomen: The Role of the Secret Society in Bringing Enlightenment Thought to Pre-Revolutionary Women Elites," *History of European Ideas* 10 (1989): 283-93; and Burke and Margaret C. Jacob, "French Freemasonry, Women, and Feminist Scholarship," *Journal of Modern History* 68 (1996): 513-49.

29. Burke, "Freemasonry."

30. *Correspondance littéraire et critique par Grimm, Diderot, Raynal, Meister, etc.*, ed. Maurice Tourneux, 15 vols. (Paris, 1877-82), 11: 159. See Jean Reuilly, *La Raucourt et ses Amies: Etude historique des moeurs saphiques au xvIIIe siècle* (Paris: H. Daragon, 1909), 13; Bonnet, *Relations amoureuses*, 158; and Joan DeJean, *Fictions of Sappho 1546-1937* (Chicago, 1989), 119.

31. Dena Goodman, *The Republic of Letters: A Cultural History of the French Enlightenment* (Ithaca, 1994), 258.

32. Burke and Jacob, "French Freemasonry," 545-56.

33. Ibid., 546.

34. Goodman, *Republic of Letters*, 258.

35. Burke and Jacob, "French Freemasonry," 527.

36. See Burke, "Freemasonry," the latter part of which is devoted specifically to Lamballe and her loyalty to the queen which, Burke argues, stems from her Masonic ideals.

37. The charge of "knight-errantry" is cited in Lynn Hunt, *The Family Romance of the French Revolution* (Berkeley, 1992), 119.

38. My larger project will attend to the ways in which English discourse often associates sapphism with France; conversely, some French figurations of sapphism, especially in this period, carry English references.

The Palais-Royal and the Homosexual Subculture of Nineteenth-Century Paris

Michael Sibalis

It is more or less a truism among historians that "[t]he first queer spaces of the modern era were the dark alleys, unlit corners, and hidden rooms that queers found in the city itself."[1] Any history of gay or queer space in eighteenth- and nineteenth-century Paris is likely to stress the concealed sites of the (male) homosexual subculture, most of which came to life only after dark: the city's parks and gardens, the quays and banks of the Seine, and the public urinals along the boulevards.[2] And yet perhaps the most startling feature of Paris's homosexual subculture in this earlier period is not how invisible it was, but, on the contrary, how conspicuous it could be, at least at certain times and in certain places. Indeed, it is precisely the conspicuousness of "Paris-Sodom," a visibility that many people found profoundly disturbing, that explains the increasing attention that police, judicial, and medical experts paid to the phenomenon over the course of the nineteenth century. By the 1880s, and 1890s, their concerns were widely echoed by social commentators and by journalists working for the new mass-circulation press.[3]

One of the key sites of homosexual visibility for almost a century, between approximately 1780 and 1870, was the Palais-Royal, a complex in central Paris comprising a palace, its gardens, and adjacent shops. Far from being one of Paris's "unlit corners," the Palais-Royal was for a time the very heart of the city. Built for himself (beginning in 1627) by Cardinal Richelieu, who left it to Louis XIII on his death in 1642, the Palais-Royal passed to Louis XIV's

---

[Haworth co-indexing entry note]: "The Palais-Royal and the Homosexual Subculture of Nineteenth-Century Paris." Sibalis, Michael. Co-published simultaneously in *Journal of Homosexuality* (Harrington Park Press, an imprint of The Haworth Press, Inc.) Vol. 41, No. 3/4, 2001, pp. 117-129; and: *Homosexuality in French History and Culture* (ed: Jeffrey Merrick, and Michael Sibalis) Harrington Park Press, an imprint of The Haworth Press, Inc., 2001, pp. 117-129. Single or multiple copies of this article are available for a fee from The Haworth Document Delivery Service [1-800-342-9678, 9:00 a.m. - 5:00 p.m. (EST). E-mail address: getinfo@haworthpressinc.com].

brother, Philippe, duke d'Orléans, in 1692 and remained the property of the duke's descendants until the Revolution of 1848. In the 1780s, the family transformed the palace gardens, which had always been open to the public for leisurely strolling, into a lively center of leisure and commerce. They built a covered promenade on three sides of the garden, along which they rented out shops, restaurants, cafés, and gambling dens. Idlers, gamblers, prostitutes, pickpockets, and casual strollers of every sort and all classes were soon flocking there. Mercier described the Palais-Royal in the 1780s as "the capital of Paris" and "the temple of sensual pleasure." Historians agree. The Palais-Royal became a focus of Parisian cultural and political life in the late eighteenth and early nineteenth centuries. Robert Isherwood has written that, on the eve of the French Revolution, the Palais-Royal was "the logical playground of the highborn" and "equally seductive to the lowborn," a place where popular culture and elite culture converged. For James Billington, it was "the center in Paris not just of high politics and high ideals, but also of low pleasure," in whose cafés "distinctions of rank were obliterated and men were free to exercise sexual as well as political freedom." Indeed, the garden and its cafés developed so rapidly into places for political debate and popular mobilization in the late 1780s that Joseph Cerutti, a deputy to the National Constituent Assembly of 1789-1791, could quite reasonably assert that "the [French] revolution was born in the Palais-Royal."[4]

The crowd that thronged the Palais-Royal in the 1780s was doubly transgressive–in both the private and the public sphere–by combining sexual licence with political radicalism. It was this that made the Palais-Royal so disturbing a symbol to so many people in its heyday and gave it an enduringly bad reputation thereafter. For instance, when the Englishman Henry Redhead Yorke visited the Palais-Royal in 1802, he described it as "that hotbed of revolution and crime, that nursery of every loathsome vice, that abomination of all virtue and profanation of all religion." It had been only recently (during the Revolution), he said, "the rendezvous of the desperate, the ambitious and the cut-throat," and "the arsenal wherein were forged the instruments of anarchy and murder." But what most drew his ire now, in Napoleon's day, were the thieves, prostitutes, and gamblers who continued to frequent this "infected lazar house . . . which has reduced the whole of [Parisian] society to degradation and corruption." He added that after visiting "every part of this Temple of Sin," he and a friend had concluded "that as long as it existed it will be vain to look in Paris for any sincere demonstration of either moral probity, decency in private or honesty in public life."[5]

Neither Yorke, nor, for that matter, any subsequent visitor to the Palais-Royal, whether French or foreign, ever alluded directly (at least not in print) to the presence of either homosexually inclined men or teenaged hustlers among the palace's many debauchees. Such men were certainly present, however, conspicuous enough and in sufficient number for a newspaper in far-away New York City to remark on the fact in 1842. Denouncing the sodomites who frequented one of New York's parks, the newspaper declared "their [sic] is no difference between the doings of these fiendish agents of the Palais Royale [sic] and the sodomites of New York."[6]

Certainly, sodomites were gathering in the Palais-Royal gardens well before the nineteenth century. In 1724, a man named Gromat, interrogated by the police about other sodomites of his acquaintance, "declare[d] that he knows a large number of them; that he has seen . . . a large number of them at the Palais-Royal; that he has seen several in action along the walls and in the corners of the stairwells."[7] Sixty years later a police report mentioned the Palais-Royal among the "suspicious places" where pederasts habitually went in the evenings.[8] Twenty-year-old Louis Le Beaux, for example, visited the Palais-Royal every day in the spring of 1787 "to solicit men in order to engage in pederasty and to earn money from it" (he apparently also had an accomplice with whom he robbed and blackmailed the men whom he picked up there).[9] Nonetheless, the palace and its gardens do not usually show up in eighteenth-century police reports as places regularly "cruised" by sodomites, perhaps simply because, as the private property of the Orléans family, they were off limits to police patrols. But there can be little doubt that hustlers and their customers were already there before 1789, and the celebrated polemical pamphlet *The Children of Sodom to the National Assembly* (1790) referred to "the young bardashes of the Palais-Royal" as if their existence were common knowledge.[10]

The French Revolution, which (temporarily) changed the name of the palace (it became the Palais-Egalité), could not dissipate the sexual licence prevalent there, and indeed may even have increased it. In the late 1790s the police repeatedly expressed alarm that the Revolution had brought in its wake rampant sexual immorality, including an unprecedented incidence of pederasty and both male and female prostitution: "Sodomite love and Sapphic love are as impudent as prostitution and are making deplorable progress."[11] They expressed particular concern about juvenile prostitutes who worked the Palais-Égalité, which was flourishing as a centre for gambling, prostitution, and night-life much as it had before 1789: "One still sees in the Palais-Égalité a considerable number of young people of both sexes, aged from about twelve to fourteen, who engage publicly in the excesses of debauchery and libertinage."[12] Thirty years later, a study of French morals had this to say about Paris during the Revolution and under Napoleon: "Another kind of debauchery, which we shall not name, was exercised under the wooden galleries of the Palais-Royal, and in several remote spots in the capital. Thus not a night went by that National Guard patrols did not surprise in flagrante delicto, several men guilty of this vile pleasure."[13]

Mehmed Sa'îd Hâlet Efendi, Constantinople's ambassador to Paris from 1803 to 1806, has left a description of prostitution in the Palais-Royal during Napoleon's reign:

> By dint of hearing all the Greeks and Armenians in the world say "the Muslims are pederasts, such a shameful thing cannot exist in the country of the Franks . . ." we have come to believe it. But [the French] do nothing else! There is a place in Paris like a bazaar called Palais-Royal, a very large place with shops along the four sides where one finds all sorts of things. Above [the shops] there are rooms and in these rooms there are one thousand five hundred girls and one thousand five hundred boys who earn their daily bread by debauchery. . . . As soon as one enters [the palace], women and men on all sides distribute specially printed sheets on which it is written: "I have so many girls, my room is at such a place, it costs so much," or "I have so many boys, of such and such an age, at such and such a price." . . . These girls and these boys besiege every person from all four sides, asking which among them he prefers. . . . Thanks be to God, there are not so many boys and so many pederasts in all the Muslim countries put together.[14]

Although Hâlet Efendi, who belonged to a political faction in Turkey extremely hostile to the Occident, undoubtedly exaggerated the scenes that he witnessed, male prostitutes certainly did work the Palais-Royal in the Napoleonic period. On 2 November 1811, the police interrogated one of them, an eighteen-year-old unemployed hairdresser named Magloire Garet. Garet came to the police station late one evening to report that a man whom he did not know had just collapsed and died in the youth's fourth-floor room on the rue Saint-Honoré. The dead man's children eventually identified him as sixty-seven-year-old Jean François Bernot de Congy, a property owner and widower. Garet at first claimed that Bernot had come up to his room only "to talk with me" after the two had met in the Palais-Royal and Bernot obligingly offered to help him find a job. The police did not believe his story, and Garet quickly cracked under their questioning:

> Question: It seems very peculiar to us that you took home in this way a man who was unknown to you; did you not accost him in order to engage in acts of pederasty?
>
> Answer: That is true, Monsieur, I had accosted him and had taken him home for that purpose.

Q: So you carry on this trade?

A: Yes, Monsieur, I am obliged to do it ever since I found myself without work. . . . We were fooling around, this individual and I, on the bed: he was groping me and trying to get close to me; he ejaculated, and it was at that moment that he cried out: *Oh My God, I feel sick*; he no longer showed any signs of consciousness.

Q: Did this individual pay you for accommodating him?

A: No, Monsieur.

Q: But you are undoubtedly in the habit of getting paid by the men whom you take home, because you say that you carry on this trade for lack of work?

A: I do not ask them for anything; I expect everything from their generosity.

Although Garet had violated no existing law, the prefect of police decided on his own considerable authority to incarcerate him in Bicêtre prison until the spring and then to send him back to Normandy, to his native village of Arc (department of the Seine-Inférieure).[15]

The importance of the Palais-Royal to Parisian leisure activities increased in the following decades, especially after the construction of the Galerie d'Orléans in 1828-1830. This was one of the many covered commercial passages or arcades that developers built in the city in the first part of the nineteenth century.[16] The English tourist, Frances Trollope, who visited "the superb Galerie d'Orléans" in 1835, described it as "a gay and animated scene at any time of day. . . . Paris itself seems typified by the aspect of the lively, laughing, idle throng assembled there."[17] But she did not mention (and may not even have noticed, although this seems somewhat unlikely) one particular element among that "idle throng": the hustlers who do turn up regularly in the police reports from these years. Other observers did notice them, however. For example, in July 1830, one irritated Parisian praised the prefect of police for ridding the streets of female prostitutes, but also drew the prefect's attention to "another kind of debauchery even more disgusting and which exists in total freedom, this is pederasty." According to his letter, "Every evening, in the Palais-Royal, in the new Grand Galerie [d'Orléans] and around it, young boys, in jacket and morning coat, individually accost men."[18] In 1839, another Parisian sent the prefect an anonymous letter on the same subject:

> How can it be that . . . in a city like Paris every evening among the strollers in the Galerie d'Orléans [at the] Palais-Royal, you let a troop, that is the word, of young boys from eighteen to twenty, all in cap and smock . . . carry on a trade . . . that rejects all morals? These are *male whores* who sell themselves to the inhabitants of Sodom and do so publicly. How can you let this disgusting traffic go on every evening?[19]

The police were hardly unaware of the problem. In October 1837, for example, the police commissioner for the quarter, in a report about the thieves, pickpockets, and pederasts who congregated at the Palais-Royal, noted that "the number of these young people has been increasing, and . . . those known as pederasts have had the effrontery to fondle and caress each other in the presence of the public, [who are] scandalized by their conduct."[20]

It is precisely the attention that the city's police began paying to the public flaunting of homosexuality at the Palais-Royal that makes the phenomenon so interesting to the historian. "Pederasty patrols" to repress homosexual cruising were nothing new (they had begun in the eighteenth century), but the reports and interrogations generated by this activity had been filed away and left to gather dust in the archives.[21] In the mid-nineteenth century, however, police officials and forensic scientists began to write about what they observed, and in books usually intended for the general public. Of course, they did not base their conclusions entirely and solely on what they witnessed at the Palais-Royal, but there can be no doubt that their experiences with this one particular place did contribute to molding their views and thus ultimately the public perception of homosexual behavior.

Eugène-François Vidocq (1775-1857), head of the Security Brigade at the Paris Prefecture of Police (1811-1827, and again in 1832) was one of the very first to give widespread publicity to the homosexual subculture of Paris. He knew it well enough from his early days in prison (he had been a criminal before the police recruited him), but also from his work policing the Palais-Royal. Vidocq may have been the first police official to issue explicit instructions for the repression of homosexual activity at the Palais-Royal. As he reported to the prefect of police:

> On the 7th [of September 1832], I gave the order to several agents to establish a surveillance around the Palais-Royal and in the neighborhood, in order to arrest all the individuals without papers and known to engage in the disgusting taste for pederasty, which they have made their sole means of existence.[22]

The police arrested eighteen men, presumably male prostitutes, as an immediate consequence of Vidocq's order, and police surveillance remained in place for at least another fifty years.

And yet this surveillance apparently had minimal effect. In 1843, the Palais-Royal shopkeepers, especially those in the Galerie d'Orléans, were complaining "loudly" (as one policeman noted) "about the pederasts who abound there, and who by their behavior and their appearance drive away the respectable people who come to stroll there."[23] A year later, "licensed [shopkeepers], domiciled in the Galerie d'Orléans, Palais-Royal," petitioned the prefect of police that:

> they have the honor of informing you that for a long time the Galerie d'Orléans has been infested by a crowd of good-for-nothings who have chosen it for carrying on their hideous business, which one is ashamed to name. Every day they come to flaunt there a shamelessness that revolts everyone, even the least fastidious; thus the petitioners have acquired the certitude that many people, and even foreigners, fearing to rub elbows with this horde of vagabonds, carefully avoid crossing this gallery, which causes a great prejudice to the undersigned.
>
> The Palais-Royal has been purged of the female prostitutes that dishonored it, but today these vile beings whom we denounce to you are worse: they accost men![24]

Once they had made contact with clients, hustlers could take them to any one of a number of disreputable taverns or rooming houses that served as *maisons de passe* (hotels commonly used for prostitution). The most conveniently located in the 1840s were two cabarets very near the Palais-Royal, one on the rue Montpansier, the other on the rue des Bons-Enfants: "they find [here] small private rooms, [while] the owners profit from selling bad wine at a very high price."[25]

The newspapers soon picked up on the problem and gave it even wider publicity. The *Gazette des Tribunaux* carried several reports in 1846 and 1847.[26] It denounced "these vile and suspicious prowlers with which the busiest galleries and passages swarm" (5 June 1847) and portrayed "these miserable young people" as potential criminals of the type who had blackmailed and murdered the Englishman Ward in 1845 or who belonged to the gang of blackmailers subsequently prosecuted in the affair of the rue du Rempart (30 October 1846). The newspaper even suggested (5 March 1847) that it was time for the government "to introduce a reform to the law as it exists, and to decree a stiffer penalty than that which [currently] applies to public offenses against morals."

Paul-Louis-Adolphe Canler (1797-1865) became a policeman in 1820 and eventually succeeded Vidocq as head of the Security Brigade (appointed in 1849, he served for most of the 1850s). His memoirs (first published in 1862) offer a vivid picture of the young men who hung around the Galerie d'Orléans and some of the city's other arcades. He labeled them *persilleuses* (a slang term ordinarily, as its feminine gender suggests, applied to female streetwalkers) and made them the first of his four subcategories of "antiphysicals" or "aunties," i.e., homosexuals in general. "In the evening," he wrote, "they habitually frequent the passage des Panoramas and passage de l'Opéra, and the Galerie d'Orléans at the Palais-Royal, where they stroll about in pairs." They were "young people belonging mostly to the working class, and who have been brought to the lowest degree of abjection by their desire for luxury and for pleasure, by gluttony or by laziness." In other words, unwilling to live honestly and decently, they sought to earn their income or perhaps merely extra pocket money by selling their bodies; moreover, whereas Canler specified that men in his other three categories engaged in homosexual activity "by taste," he made no such observation as far as the *persilleuses* were concerned, which suggested that at least some of them might have done so purely for economic advantage. Canler provided a physical as well as a moral portrait of the *persilleuses*:

> These young people differ entirely from other men by appearance, language, dress, behavior, and bearing. They can be easily recognized from the following model: the beard is close-shaved, the hair is worn long, almost always rolled from the bottom; the gaze is soft, languorous; the drawling, weak, and feminine voice add to the illusion.

As for clothing, they usually wore a peaked cap, necktie, short frock coat or jacket to emphasize their (often corseted) waist, and tight-fitting trousers.[27]

These young men and their clients made an appearance in another contemporary book, a study of indecent assault published in 1857 by Ambroise Tardieu (1818-1879), a specialist in forensic medicine. Tardieu's study conflated homosexuality and prostitution: "the most common and also the most dangerous conditions in which pederasty is practiced take the form of a veritable prostitution." Although he declined to say precisely where this prostitution occurred, he explained that "it is not relegated to the shadows of remote and deserted places," but rather took place at "certain places on the public streets." Given the historical context, it is more than likely that the Palais-Royal was at least one of these places. Tardieu also physically examined 212 arrested homosexuals, of whom a good number must have been prostitutes. He calculated that half of them were under twenty-five. Some 22 percent were domestic servants, 14 percent clerks, 5.7 percent tailors, and 5.7 percent soldiers, while the remainder worked in sixty different occupations.[28]

Surviving documentary evidence cannot confirm Canler's physical description of the *persilleuses*, which may have been biased but which certainly derived from his personal experiences policing them. However, the records can flesh out what Canler had to say and also partially validate Tardieu's statistics with additional information about their ages and social class. The men who prostituted themselves in the Galerie d'Orléans were apparently young (the vast majority had not yet reached their mid-twenties) and otherwise employed (or perhaps unemployed: the sources do not mention this) in a wide variety of trades. These conclusions come from an analysis of arrest records and newspaper reports, which give the names and occupations of some seventy-seven men (and the ages of all but one of them) arrested, generally for "offending morals" or "provocation to pederasty," in the Galerie d'Orléans from the late 1830s to the early 1850s: eight on 1 December 1839, nine on 15 October 1844, seven on 26 September 1844, eighteen in October 1846 (no precise date was reported), three on 13 October 1851, and thirty-two on 20 and 21 February 1852.[29] These men (and adolescents) ranged in age from fifteen to fifty-five (the older ones were presumably either pimps or customers). Their median age was only twenty, however, and seventy-five percent of them were less than twenty-five years old. Three teenagers said that they had no occupation. The others reported working in thirty-six different occupations in the unskilled, semi-skilled, and skilled trades. They included nine waiters, six street peddlers, five printers, five tailors, four jewelers, four clerks, three butchers, three book-binders, two shoemakers, and two domestic servants. The only pattern here is the total absence of factory workers (still relatively rare in Paris of the time) and of artisans doing heavy physical labor, such as those in the building trades.

Unfortunately, by their very nature, arrest records cannot answer the really important and interesting questions. Were these young men sexually attracted to other males or did they engage in sexual relations only for the money? Was prostitution a way for them to make a living (perhaps in a period of unemployment) or did they sell their bodies just to pick up extra cash and perhaps even for the pleasure it brought them? Did they also engage in criminal activity, like many of the young men in the 1870s studied by William Peniston?[30] Certainly, the authorities worried, and for good reason, that they were all potential blackmailers. In the mid-1830s, for instance, the police reported on a gang of men who lived from "the kind of industry that is called in slang 'make the fag sing.' "[31] The gang members hung about the Galerie d'Orléans every day until midnight but could usually be found in the gardens themselves between 6:00 and 9:00 p.m. Ten or twelve youngsters, aged ten to sixteen, accosted potential clients, "as impudently in the day as at night," while another ten or twelve older men, aged twenty-five to forty, then stepped in to blackmail anyone imprudent enough to succumb to temptation and pick up a youngster.[32] Gangs like this one were still operating at the Palais-Royal in the 1850s, as one of the Czar's advisers discovered to his dismay in 1852 when a group that he met there tried to extort money from him.[33]

By then, however, the Palais-Royal was entering into decline as Parisians increasingly searched for pleasure in other quarters of the city, like the boulevards and the Champs-Élysées, thoroughly modernized by Baron Haussmann's urban renewal under Napoleon III in the 1850s and 1860s. As Johannes Willms has written (but, ignoring the significance of the Galerie d'Orléans, he dates the decline to the 1820s, too early by a generation): "The motley crowd for which the Palais-Royal had become too small . . . flooded the arcades, cafés, restaurants, public reading rooms, theaters, balls, gardens, and boulevards."[34] One city guidebook included the following sad, even nostalgic, comment on the Palais-Royal:

> This abandoned palace, these galleries frequented by indifferent passers-by, this garden . . . were, for a century, the scene of the sumptuous festivities, the passions, the love affairs, and the vices of a civilization [that was] refined to the point of depravity. One could write on the frontispiece of this palace: "Here once was Paris!"–Today it is no more than a province.[35]

Significantly, Félix Carlier's study of "anti-physical prostitution," published in 1887 but for the most part written just after his retirement as head of the Paris vice squad from 1860 to 1870, does not even mention the Palais-Royal. The *persilleuses*, he told his readers, liked to practice their trade in "well lit and busy places, like the Bois de Boulogne in the day, the passages and *grands boulevards* in the evening."[36] Even so, Parisian homosexuals had not entirely abandoned the place. Thus, according to one police report from 1874, "Men of this sort still meet in the same areas, that is to say in the Champs-Élysées, under the bridges and at the Palais-Royal."[37] Or, to take another example, a moralistic study of Parisian "vice" published in 1888 noted that "the [homosexual] soliciting occurs more or less generally in the same way, whether it takes place around the passages, near the Grand-Hôtel, under the arcades of the rue de Rivoli, at the Palais-Royal, in the Tuileries [gardens], on the boulevards or at the Luxembourg [Palace]."[38] Other reports, however, suggest that cruising in the Palais-Royal was now a function of the weather. The arcades and the gallery provided shelter in Paris's cold, wet winters, but once the spring came in 1874, "the Galerie d'Orléans has been deserted in the evening; one sees a few strollers, but the pederasts have abandoned it to meet near the cafés-concerts on the Champs-Élysées where arrests are carried out every evening."[39] Clearly, by the 1870s, the Palais-Royal was, at best, no more than one (and by no means the major) among many different sites for homosexual cruising and prostitution. Not surprisingly, then, only two percent of the approximately nine hundred men whom the police charged or considered charging with a public offense against decency between March 1873 and March 1879 had been arrested in the Palais-Royal.[40]

But the Palais-Royal did leave a lasting trace in the public image of the Parisian homosexual. Tens of thousands of Parisians must have observed for themselves at least some of the conspicuously public homosexual activity that took place there, but of course not only there, in the late eighteenth and early nineteenth centuries, and thousands more would have read about it in books and newspapers in the mid-nineteenth century. What the experts wrote about and what the public witnessed were effeminate and flamboyant young men (often hustlers) and older, usually monied gentlemen who sought their favors. These two groups became the stereotypical homosexuals–one group shamelessly brazen, the other timidly secretive–and they gave shape to the notion that homosexuality was most often venal and usually involved the corruption of idle youths by cynical older men (who were usually bourgeois or aristocratic). The fact that this type of homosexuality eventually spread out from the Palais-Royal to other quarters of Paris only reinforced such misconceptions.

NOTES

1. Aaron Betsky, *Queer Space: Architecture and Same-Sex Desire* (New York, 1997), 141.
2. Michael Sibalis, "Paris," in *Queer Sites: Gay Urban Histories since 1600*, ed. David Higgs (London, 1999), 10-37.
3. Sibalis, "Paris-Babylone/Paris-Sodome: Images of Homosexuality in the Nineteenth-Century City," in *Images of the City in Nineteenth-Century France*, ed. John West-Sooby (Mooroka, Queensland, Australia, 1999), 13-22.
4. Musée Carnavalet, *Le Palais-Royal* (Paris, 1988) [catalogue of an exhibition, 9 May-4 Sept. 1988]; Maurice Garçon, "Les Métamorphoses du Palais-Royal," *Miroire de l'histoire* 126 (1960): 712-8; Louis Sébastien Mercier, *Tableau de Paris*, 12 vols. (Amsterdam, 1782-88), 10: 220; Robert Isherwood, *Farce and Fantasy: Popular Entertainment in Eighteenth-Century Paris* (New York, 1986), 214-49 (quotation, 248); James H. Billington, *Fire in the Minds of Men* (New York, 1980), 25-33; Darrin M. McMahon, "The Birthplace of the Revolution: Public Space and Political Community in the Palais-Royal of Louis-Philippe-Joseph d'Orléans, 1781-1789," *French History* 10 (1996): 1-29 (Cerutti quotation, 2); Johannes Willms, *Paris: Capital of Europe. From the Revolution to the Belle Époque* (New York, 1997), 5-10.
5. Henry Redhead Yorke, *France in Eighteen Hundred and Two*, ed. J.A.C. Sykes (London, 1906), 69-70, 64-75.
6. "The Sodomites," *The Whip and Satirist of New-York and Brooklyn*, 29 January 1842, 2. I am grateful to Jonathan Ned Katz for this reference.
7. Quoted in Michel Rey, "L'Art de 'raccrocher' au XVIIIe siècle," *Masques* 24 (1984/85): 93.
8. AN, Y 11723, 25 April 1784; and Y 11724, 17 July 1784, translated in *Homosexuality in Early Modern France: A Documentary Collection*, ed. Jeffrey Merrick and Bryant T. Ragan, Jr. (New York, 2001), 81-4.
9. AN, Y 11729, 2, 3 April 1787.

10. Translated in Merrick and Ragan, *Homosexuality*, 183.

11. AN, F^7 7409, dossier 4577, and F^1c III Seine 20, "Tableau analytique de la situation du département de la Seine pendant le mois de prairial an VII" (May/June 1799).

12. AN, F^7 7579A, dossier 25, Floréal Year VII (April/May 1799).

13. Antoine Callot, *Mémoires pour servir à l'histoire des moeurs et usages des français*, 2 vols. (Paris, 1827), 1: 52.

14. Enver Ziya Karal, *Halet Efendi'nin Paris büyük elçiligi 1802-1806* (Istanbul, 1940), 32-4, quoted in Morali Seyyid Alî Efendi and Seyyid Abdürrahim Muhibb Efendi, *Deux Ottomans à Paris sous le Directoire et l'Empire: Relations d'ambassade*, ed. Stéphane Yerasimos (Paris, 1997), 37-8.

15. APP, Aa 125, pièces 34-36, 2 November 1811; AN, F^7 3137, 7 November 1811.

16. Bertrand Lemoine, *Les Passages couverts en France* (Paris, 1990); and Patrice de Moncan and Christian Mahout, *Les Passages de Paris* (Paris, 1991).

17. Frances Milton Trollope, *Paris and the Parisians in 1835*, 2 vols. (London, 1836), 2: 52, 59.

18. APP, dossier 25,396-MR [in an unclassified series], Bonnetat to prefect, 15 July 1830.

19. APP, dossier 25,396-MR, letter to prefect, 25 November1839.

20. APP, dossier 25,396-MR, Police commissioner for Palais-Royal quarter to prefect, 9 October 1837.

21. Jeffrey Merrick, "Commissioner Foucault, Inspector Noël, and the 'Pederasts' of Paris, 1780-83," *Journal of Social History* 32 (1998): 287-307.

22. APP, Da 230, 9 September 1832. For Vidocq's discussion of pederasty, see E. F. Vidocq, *Les Voleurs: Physiologie de leurs moeurs et de leur langage*, 2nd ed., 2 vols. (Paris, 1837), especially 1: 53-5, 60-4; 2: 160-5, 241-2. For his life and career, see Paul Metzner, "Vidocq, Detective," in *Crescendo of the Virtuoso: Spectacle, Skill, and Self-Promotion in Paris During the Age of Revolution* (Berkeley, CA, 1998), 84-112.

23. APP, dossier 25,396-MR, 8 September 1843.

24. APP, dossier 25,396-MR, undated petition [c. Oct. 1844] and police report, 19 October 1844.

25. APP, dossier 25,396-MR, 28 January 1844.

26. *Gazette des Tribunaux* 5812 (21 February 1846): 397; 6038 (12 November 1846): 39; 6136 (5 March 1847): 461; 6203 (22 May 1847): 735; 6215 (5 June 1847): 783; 6390 (26 December 1847): 199.

27. Paul-Louis-Adolphe Canler, *Mémoires de Canler, Ancien chef de service de sûreté*, ed. Jacques Brenner (Paris, 1986), 318-9.

28. Ambroise Tardieu, *Étude médico-légale sur les attentats aux moeurs* (Paris, 1857). Other editions, with additional material, appeared in the following years.

29. *Gazette des Tribunaux* 5812 (21 February 1846): 397; APP, BB/5, ledger entitled "Pédés No. 2," 106-7, 253-73; dossier 25,396-MR, 1 December 1839, 15 October 1844, 26 November 1844. I have not included thirteen men (of similar ages and occupations) arrested as "thieves and pederasts" (19 December 1838).

30. See his essay in this volume; also "Love and Death in Gay Paris: Homosexuality and Criminality in the 1870s," in *Homosexuality in Modern France*, ed. Merrick and Ragan (New York, 1996), 128-45.

31. The expressions *faire chanter* ["to make sing"] for "to blackmail" and *maître chanteur* or *chanteur* ["master singer" or "singer"] for "blackmailer" originated in the nineteenth-century homosexual subculture of Paris and rapidly became standard French.

32. APP, Da 230, pièce 25, "Note transmise à M. le chef de la 1ère division," 28 June [ca 1835]. The first printed use of the word *chanteur* in this sense is apparently Vidocq, *Voleurs*, 1:60-4.

33. APP, BB5, Register entitled "Pédés No. 2," 300-1.

34. Willms, *Paris*, 183.

35. Auguste Villemot, "Le Jardin et les galeries du Palais-Royal," in *Paris Guide par les principaux écrivains et artistes de la France, Deuxième partie: La Vie*, new ed., 2 vols. (Paris, 1868), 2: 1304.

36. Félix Carlier, *Etudes de pathologie sociale: Les Deux prostitutions* (Paris, 1887), 355.

37. APP, Da 230, pièce 372, 4 August 1874.

38. Pierre Delcourt, *Le Vice à Paris*, 2nd ed. (Paris, 1888), 289.

39. APP, dossier 25,396-MR, May 1874. Similar observations in report dated 10 August 1875.

40. Sibalis, "Paris," 21.

Les Chevaliers de la guirlande: Cellmates in Restoration France

Nicholas Dobelbower

On the cold winter morning of 9 January 1836, throngs of onlookers gathered at the place Saint-Jacques to witness the double execution of Pierre François Lacenaire and his accomplice Pierre Victor Avril.[1] The crowd was composed of people from all classes and walks of life. They came humbly, as if to church, to witness the solemn ceremony that would publicly unite in death two men who had sought in life to hide from society the nature and goals of their complicity. Lacenaire and Avril were brought together by the prison system, and their relationship was indelibly colored by that fateful encounter. Their joint execution spectacularly confirmed popular beliefs about the intimacy and loyalty of the criminal class, whose members were "thick as thieves." In fact, the doomed couple uncannily resembled the chainmates who had become major attractions in vaudeville and boulevard comedies, inseparable to the very end. The celebrity of prison couples like Lacenaire and Avril, as well as their literary counterparts, draws attention to the numerous discourses that collectively articulated a fatal connection between crime, the prison, and visible forms of male homosexuality in early nineteenth-century France.

Homosexuality lay at the heart of the double murder of the passage du Cheval-Rouge for which Lacenaire and Avril were executed. One of the victims was identified in the press as Tante (Auntie) Chardon because he was known to be a homosexual. The investigation of his death "naturally" focused on "these sordid men," according to chief of police Louis Canler. It was, in fact, the inspector's discovery that Lacenaire shared his bed with another man that proved to be the first piece of evidence incriminating him: "I learned that the two individuals in question had occupied but a single bed, and soon I gained

[Haworth co-indexing entry note]: "*Les Chevaliers de la guirlande*: Cellmates in Restoration France." Dobelbower, Nicholas. Co-published simultaneously in *Journal of Homosexuality* (Harrington Park Press, an imprint of The Haworth Press, Inc.) Vol. 41, No. 3/4, 2001, pp. 131-147; and: *Homosexuality in French History and Culture* (ed: Jeffrey Merrick, and Michael Sibalis) Harrington Park Press, an imprint of The Haworth Press, Inc., 2001, pp. 131-147. Single or multiple copies of this article are available for a fee from The Haworth Document Delivery Service [1-800-342-9678, 9:00 a.m. - 5:00 p.m. (EST). E-mail address: getinfo@haworthpressinc.com].

the certainty that it was indeed them that I had the mission to arrest."[2] Additional information about Lacenaire's "intimate" connections with other criminals, including his relationship with Avril, would later be provided by an inmate named Leblond in the La Force prison. He too was known as a *tante*, Tante Rasoir. Finally, Lacenaire's full confession was motivated by his desire to strike back at Avril for betraying him. The execution could thus be read as a crime of passion, or at least a murder-suicide.

Lacenaire had used his trial as a forum to stage a virulent attack on the hypocrisy of Restoration society, thereby effectively elevating his already sensational stature from that of the "dandy of crime" to a revolutionary hero of the people. In an effort to preserve his legacy as a defiant figure of anticonformism, he dedicated his last days to orchestrating the posthumous publication of his memoirs. Whether the political objectives he offered in justification of his crimes were accurate or merely an attempt to make a name for himself, even an infamous one, is less significant than the general terms in which he characterized his particular form of social resistance. For Lacenaire, the rejection of society required not only an attack upon its laws through crime, but also the abandonment of traditional family ties as engendered by heterosexuality. To embrace crime was to espouse an alternate form of solidarity organized around same-sex companionship. Lacenaire wrote from his prison cell that he had vowed at a young age to become the "scourge of society," but that in order to do so he recognized the dual needs for knowledge and a helpmate. His immediate instinct was to seek them both in prison: "I had made an idea for myself of what this class in continual hostility against society was like. There, I said to myself, there is where I must go to find an arm to back me up; only there will I find him."[3] Lacenaire staged a crime in order to get himself imprisoned for theft. It was in the La Force prison that he met Avril and was initiated into the mysteries of the criminal subculture, including its peculiar language and mores. Lacenaire's desire to wage a moral war by joining the ranks of the criminal class raises several questions: What notions circulated in the public sphere regarding men who had done time in prison? What role did homosexuality play in the infamous solidarity known to exist among former cellmates? Was their reputation for homosexual activity a possible incentive for men like Lacenaire to seek imprisonment, whether actively or unconsciously?

THE CONVICT'S BODY

At a time when the problems of criminality and penology were being aggressively debated by learned societies, prison administrators, reformers, and philanthropists, the convict was a subject of sustained interest. He represented a new and exotic cultural identity, one that was shaped by incarceration and whose most salient feature was an exclusive reliance upon other men for social support and intimacy. In fact, it may be as a direct result of the explicit debate surrounding the undesirable effects of the prison system that a non-aristocratic form of homosexuality came to the public's attention. Despite the universal condemnation of the vices inculcated in prison, the public obsession with prison mores suggests that convicts were objects of curiosity and even of erotic interest for certain segments of the reading public.

The convict sentenced to hard labor was first and foremost a guilty body. He was exhibited as such, marked by the brand with the letters T. F. (*travaux forcés*, forced labor), and ceremoniously paraded across the countryside as he was led off to the *bagne*, the forced labor prison. This publicity was intended to be a source of shame and to serve as an example to others. The accounts of these events that blackened the pages of the press indicate instead that these disciplinary rituals had a carnivalesque atmosphere.

Exhibition and branding drew large crowds, and onlookers were eager to see the bare-chested convict receive his mark and to learn the nature of his crime. The abbé Molitor, convicted of theft, forgery, and aggravated sexual assault, "was exhibited to the public and received the mark at Versailles. It was a market day. The crowds of spectators were immense and pressed all about the scaffold with avid curiosity. Everyone was trying to read the sign placed above the convict's head. . . ."[4] The brand that convicts carried with them the rest of their lives was an inscription of the shame experienced during the exhibition and a public sign of their infamy.

The long journey from Bicêtre to the penal colony that followed was also an occasion for spectators to ogle their half-naked bodies and even engage them in confrontational jeering and gesticulating. The single-file line of prisoners on foot or in carts was known as the chain. "They are treated like ferocious beasts; the carts on which they are transported are like circus wagons designed to satisfy the curiosity of the towns through which they pass."[5] The chain was intended as a further source of humiliation, but the convicts turned it instead into a theatrical affirmation of their vice.

> The final stage of the journey . . . was a spectacle whose horror cannot be expressed in human words. Imagine, one hundred and fifty or two hundred miserable souls . . . half clothed or covered in fetid rags . . . impure minstrels, standing upright in their carts, rattling their chains like trophies, and crying out to the public, laughing, and making obscene gestures toward the populace that had rushed there from the town and countryside to serve as a retinue to their arrival.

The crowd goaded them on, cheering the most lascivious among them and "extravagantly catcalling those who didn't have the courage in their shame that they had shown in their crime." The scene was described as an "orgy of the most unbridled and base, the most disgusting and foul passions."[6] Descriptions of the chain invariably insist on the licentiousness of both convicts and spectators but remain vague concerning the content of the exchanges and the nature of the gesticulations. It is clear, however, that both were decidedly sexual.

Benjamin Appert, secretary of the philanthropic Society for Christian Morality and a member of the Royal Society on Prisons, explained that every facet of the convict's life during the three-week journey was lived before the eyes of the public. Routine personal hygiene and daily inspections of each convict's body were performed in the open: "Even in the harshest of climates, they have to undress outside in the open fields, in front of avid spectators, where they are subjected to the most indecent exam, requiring the most degrading movements; and all that with sang-froid."[7] The daily medical exam apparently included inspection of the prisoner's genitals and anus.[8]

Convicts showed no evidence of shame: the humiliation of public exhibition had ironically stripped them of the very bourgeois values it sought to inculcate. For Appert, however, the most disturbing aspect of the chain was the absolute effacement of all the tokens of social propriety and class distinction. They "accept the comrade whom the chain imposes upon them with a stupid smile of satisfaction, striking up conversation, which necessarily requires that their minds descend to a common level." Appert's disgust for mixing individuals from different classes or chaining hardened criminals to first-time offenders masks an implicit paranoia concerning homosexuality as a form of filiation. The chain symbolized a new type of community: "all become equally ignominious . . . the chain of one man is also the chain of the other; in short, a perfect equality assimilates all the convicts."[9] This absence of distinction, which sounds distinctly like a form of Jacobinism, also raises the specter of a single-sex or homosexual nation. Freed from the regulating pressures exerted by conventional social identities, figuratively and literally stripped, chainmates symbolized the prospect of unregulated intercourse between men.

Once behind the prison walls, the convict's body was not necessarily hidden from the public eye. He continued to be made accessible through accounts of prison visits made by novelists, artists, and reformers. It was not uncommon for public figures to obtain permission to visit the prisons and penal colonies in order to conduct interviews with inmates or to sketch or paint them. These visits were subsequently published in journals or monographs. Sketches found their way into illustrated editions. Just as the criminal's physical body provided the public with a visual spectacle of flesh through the ceremonies of exposition, branding, and the chain, his virtual body was also a source of titillation. The description of prison conditions allowed writers to discuss nudity and sexuality more directly than was permitted in novels. Although the explicit description of sex acts was still the sole purview of medical literature, the paraliterature that flourished around the prison made its own case for the need to address the "realities" of carceral life.

The journalist and author Joseph Méry and the artist Henri Monnier made just such a visit to a penal colony, and Méry published a step-by-step account of their descent into a subterranean dungeon cell. Far from a mere exposition of the lamentable conditions in which prisoners lived, the text is a careful narrative intended to give the reader the sensation of taking a journey to a mysterious world peopled with fantastic creatures who live according to an exotic moral system: "We showed our tickets to the usher, and we were permitted to enter. We were equipped with torches like those used in the catacombs; it took time for the light to illuminate these dense black shadows. . . ." Once in the depths of the pit, the two artists distinguished seven forms in the darkness. Monnier's sketch of the scene, which was reproduced with the article, shows the prisoners huddled closely together, one bare-chested and another reclining languidly in front of the others. The figures loom eerily out of the darkness thanks to Monnier's use of chiaroscuro. The scene may well have been posed, but the accompanying text makes the physical proximity of the convicts even more striking. It explains that one of the men, "young, lively, and cheerful," was "completely nude, save for his chains." Méry compares his quick movements to those of a "wild animal" and specifically to the fierce and beautiful mandrill. Monnier "was forced to sketch him in mid-air" as he leapt up and down. We learn that the naked young man was "the hero of the prison" and that "his comrades gave him a certain deference."[10] Méry and Monnier bartered with the naked youth, who placed the tobacco he received in exchange for conversation in the middle of the group. Each convict took a modest share for himself, careful not cheat his cellmates.

The author and artist found these men beast-like but also tender and caring. From an outsider's perspective, the scene is striking: established members of Parisian society converse through the prison bars with half-clothed men who are presented as their primitive or atavistic alter egos. In a society struggling to find new stability through discourses advocating moral purity and familialism, criminal bodies were paradoxically constituted as legitimate objects of prurient interest and public voyeurism. The moralizing intentions that were advanced to justify the spectacular representation of convict bodies were as much a pretense as the disclaimers offered in the prefaces to erotic novels of the eighteenth century.

THE MORES OF THE BAGNE

Convicts doing time in prison were chained together in pairs. In the argot of the prison, they were known as *chevaliers de la guirlande*, knights of the garland, a colorful expression conjuring romantic images.[11] Applied as it was to prisoners, it produces a strange set of discordant images: infusing an all-male social space, presumably populated by the most despicable members of society, with overtones of nobility, courtly love, and even femininity. For whom, one wonders, might these knights have performed feats of gallantry, and what was their code of conduct? It also echoes the other chivalric designation applied to homosexuals during the Ancien Régime: knights of the cuff. The term "garland" actually refers to the chain worn by convicts, which reached from one convict's foot to his belt, then extended about one meter to his partner's belt and foot. The length of chain between the two individuals hung in a semi-circle. Repeated allusions to the "shameful relations" encouraged by this form of pairing were intended to convince the public of the need for prison reform. At the same time, the style of description, whether in juridico-administrative or purely fictional texts, tended compulsively towards the romantic register.

Maurice Alhoy's *Les Bagnes* is typical of the mixed discourse articulated around the prison: its style is literary and sensational, though it purports to be documentary. The administration at Rochefort referred to the convicts as couples, Alhoy explained, because the act of chaining them together was called coupling. The connotations evoked by the term were not lost on Alhoy. The chain, he explained, served as a "sort of exhortation to the most shameful excesses in this forced union. . . ."[12] The French word for "coupling" means linking, but it also refers to mating in reference to animals. Alhoy's text returns repeatedly to the topos of animality, referring to the prison cell as a lair and to the convict himself as a savage beast.[13] His description of a prison couple fighting for dominance sounds remarkably like two animals caged together for the express purpose of being mated.

> This fraternity of chains possesses something repugnant. It is painful to think of the influence that a stronger, crueler, more perverse mate's treatment can have upon a weaker comrade. So many times have I been witness to these acts of despotism on one side and to base submission on the other! So many chained struggles have I seen where the will of one led the other towards a goal to which his own desire did not direct him. So many torments, so many humiliations, so many clashes, so many annoyances committed that the eye of the guard was unable to catch! Exasperation is born of these conflicts; their blood is always agitated and so close to fermenting! The only moral lessons to be derived from the system of coupling are the instigation to crime and the invitation to the most shameful passions. . . .[14]

Echoing the political rhetoric employed by Appert, Alhoy assimilated a debased form of "fraternity" to homosexuality, thus stigmatizing the bonds that united the People during the popular uprisings of the Revolution and calling into question the founding principles of the Republic. Although Alhoy never explicitly mentioned sex in this passage, the reference is made clear by his use of polysemous words and metaphors: mate, agitated blood that ferments, shameful passions, etc. The bombastic style, heavy with exclamation points and anaphora, seems to involve an attempt to bring the reader to a similar state of agitation. Alhoy proceeded to condemn the prison administration for not letting convicts receive conjugal visits: "If this man, sentenced to the *bagne*, becomes guilty of the most shameful vices, should the guilt be his alone?"[15] Though his language was often periphrastic, there can be little doubt about which vices he was referring to.

Alhoy's later edition of *Les Bagnes* is significantly less explicit in discussing prison sexuality because the new richly illustrated Harvard edition was clearly destined to a public beyond that of prison administration. Unlike the first edition, it could not claim to be scientific. Its language had to be more veiled and circuitous. The expunged references to sexuality, nonetheless, reemerge visually in the lascivious attitudes of prison couples captured by its illustrators, Jules Noële and Horace Vernet. Alhoy's language also became more sensational and commercial since the edition was sold in installments by subscription. The author, it was claimed, "has not overlooked anything . . . and if the mysteries of the *bagne* are hidden behind a veil of bronze, it has not remained impenetrable to the eye of the writer."[16] This language shows the negative gestures of a rhetorical style that must be highly implicit, the ellipsis replacing what could previously be stated explicitly.

Texts published for the express purpose of ameliorating the prison system allowed readers to pass through the prison walls as well as the barriers of censorship. Those whose interest had been piqued by stories in the press could find more detailed and usually more racy accounts of prison sex in philanthropic and professional publications. This was true of publications on both ends of the political spectrum. Benjamin Appert focused on the prevalence of same-sex intimacy in almost every issue of his *Journal of Prisons* (1825-33). Boldly naming the evil was part of his strategy to win support for prison reform.

> Pederasty is frequent among these men, deprived of the greatest comforts one can experience. That explains the arguments, I would even say extravagant battles, that they engage in sometimes when there is a question of whom a Ganymede . . . might prefer. This crime is severely punished, but the dreadful results it produces are worse (I am referring to the disorder created in the hall when several of the individuals fight).[17]

At the same time, Appert clearly took pleasure in stylizing numerous descriptions of sexual promiscuity. As in the passage cited above, Appert often described sex in prison as involving a titanic battle in which man was pitted against man for dominance or in order to win the prized Ganymede. This fanciful language lends an air of timelessness and magnitude to these epic struggles that can be construed either as mocking the importance that they assume in the prison community or as reflecting the writer's ability to be seduced by them.

Dr. Hubert Lauvergne did not fail to observe the frequency of sexual intimacy in his well-known study of convicts serving in the *bagne* of Toulon. He labeled these relations as prostitution despite the absence of monetary remuneration.

> These men in the *bagne* organize prostitution among themselves, making converts and even enthusiasts. No one knows what their depraved passions are capable of. It seems that nature, a weak mother and an accomplice of her children who have been robbed of liberty, has inspired a peculiar morality in them, with its own vices, furors, disappointments, and nights of tears and struggles. It is deplorable but true.[18]

At the same time that he spoke of prostitution, he ascribed to prison relationships all the passionate excess found in Petrarchan sonnets. Lauvergne refused to describe them as marriages; in a discussion of the problems plaguing conventional heterosexual marriage, he referred only obliquely to same-sex relationships at the Toulon *bagne*.

Félix Carlier, head of the vice squad during the Second Empire, likewise referred to all sexual relations between men as a form of prostitution in order to evacuate rhetorically the possibility that they might be construed as loving relationships. He broadly defined the individuals targeted in his book on "antiphysical" prostitution as those men who, "having the ability to satisfy their desires naturally, nevertheless seek out other men," rather than those interested in paying or being paid for sex. This reflected a conscious effort to distance same-sex relationships from heterosexual ones, which alone were presented as loving. According to Carlier, "if reproduction is impossible because the two lovers are of the same sex, then it is no longer love, rather it is its negation." He reiterated this distinction throughout the treatise: "Unnatural relations do not derive from affection nor from true love."[19] It seemed only logical to him, since he considered homosexuality as purely carnal, that it should be treated as a form of prostitution. This novel nomenclature had the additional benefit of bringing under police jurisdiction activities that the laws did not expressly prohibit.

Other observers, however, marveled at the devotion seen in some convict couples. Their commitment rivaled that of any heterosexual couple. Adolphe Dauvin declared in a tone of astonishment, "Love reigns there in all its furor, and there's only one sex!" Some convicts, he explained, could not tolerate being separated from their mates. "Convicts separated from their love by freedom or the scaffold have been known to wither from despair and from languor when faced with their powerlessness to be reunited with him if he was freed, or to perish by the executioner if he had perished by the executioner."[20] The tropes of Romanticism that prevailed in the early nineteenth century caused the description of prison friendship to be invariably tinged with a pathos that was indistinguishable from passionate love. If sex was the only thing missing from romantic friendship, one could suspect that in the case of cellmates their friendship was in fact "consummated."

Doctor Villermé was one of the first public officials to use the word "marriage" to describe the relationships between prisoners.

> Everything would lead you to believe that one of the first effects of these circumstances in which prisoners find themselves is the extinction of the desires of love. This is in fact what happens at first among the very small number of those whose moral character has not yet been degraded by the irons; but it is far from being so among those depraved and brutish beings who are together! Shall I paint a picture of the morals that result? In what terms can I explain that in the absence of an individual of another sex, the prisoner "marries" (that is the accepted word in prisons) another prisoner? It is hard to believe the degree to which pederasty and masturbation are common in prisons. Young and old, they give into it with such zeal. . . .[21]

Marriage was in fact the metaphor used by both inmates and prison officials to refer to the shackling together of two prisoners, but it did not specifically denote their emotional or sexual intimacy. Of course, the term was always subject to double entendre, but it was Villermé who first suggested that the "marriage" of prisoners was a surrogate for heterosexual marriage and referred expressly to their sexual union. His description of prison mores also illustrates the predominance of a heterosexual conception of sex. Once woman was absent, the various means by which desire could be satisfied became indistinguishable: homosexuality and masturbation were equivalent. Whenever a male seed was spilled rather than used for insemination, it constituted an onanistic or masturbatory act. Oral sex, for example, was commonly referred to as "buccal onanism." Throughout the century, doctors continued to regard homosexual acts as equivalent to other practices that similarly "deceived" the reproductive instinct.

Vidocq included in his slang dictionary a reference to "marriages" that were actually celebrated in prison. He explained with some astonishment that prison officials tolerated these marriages, implying that they believed that bonds created within the prison community reduced the number of escape attempts. "In the *bagnes* and prisons, you often see audacious thieves attached to young pederasts because then they no longer seek to escape; the prison wardens and staff even permitted marriages to be celebrated with a certain pomp."[22] Others feared that this type of social organization would be perpetuated beyond the confines of the prison as convicts were released back into society. It was along these lines that Appert solicited the confession of a young convict who declared that he, like everyone else, had sexual relations with his fellow inmates: "If a saint were here, he'd be forced to do like the others, and what is even more unfortunate is that one gets so accustomed to that vice that the majority of men who are released retain it and propagate it in society."[23]

THE FAMILY OF CRIME

The convict was more than a social type; he was described as a member of an independent class or subculture. Louis Mathurin Moreau-Christophe, inspector general of prisons in 1837, called the public's attention to the existence of a "criminal class" invisibly woven into the fabric of mainstream society. Moreau-Christophe characterized this class as the inverted or negative image of mainstream society. Every moral value in the one had its counterpart in the other. In this scheme of antipodes, vagrancy replaced the home, while "a community of prostitution" replaced marriage. The particular form of prostitution to which he alluded did not, of course, involve women. It had instead "an unheard of character."[24] A class is defined by more than distinctive traits; it displays sociality, solidarity, and, most importantly, the reproduction of its values. Making use of an epidemiological metaphor, official discourse described the cultural reproduction found in prisons as a form of moral contagion. "Contact with great criminals is contagious for those who are predisposed to their mental aberration."[25] In like manner, sexual intimacy was referred to as vice or perversion, both of which suggest etymologically a turning away from conventional practices. "Men, it is said, leave the *bagne* essentially perverted."[26]

The prison cell, like the chain that led convicts to the penal colonies, was most vehemently criticized by public officials and reformers for lumping together individuals of all natures and social positions. Appert declared categorically that "the dangerous contagion of vice" always resulted from "the mixing of all the convicts, and especially of old and young ones."[27] Moreau-Christophe invited his readers to imagine what it must be like to spend day and night in a cell packed with the "human flesh collected in all the gutters, in all the hovels of Paris": "One shudders to think that there is not a father implicated in an unfortunate affair, not a student leaving a ball or a café, not an honest citizen caught in the street during a fight or a riot, who does not risk being thrown into this vile place and given to the beasts." The prison cell, as a closed space where inmates ate, slept, and satisfied "all their natural needs," was ripe to "engender physical corruption and moral contagion."[28]

This perverse education posed a danger not only to prisoners but also to the society into which they would be returned at the end of their sentences. Their release was equated with an invasion of vice. One judge lamented the problem of recidivism, asking, "Will our *bagnes* always be a school of perversity, where the voice of regret is always muffled by the audacious excitement of crime, and where moral standards will always wander away discouraged?"[29] Conceived originally to rehabilitate criminals, incarceration had ironically facilitated the emergence of this new community, substantiating its unique culture and facilitating its transmission. After spending years in an environment where the "most urgent needs of nature are repressed," and in which inmates were forced to "offend the laws of nature and society," how could they be expected to respect them once their chains were removed?[30]

To return to the questions raised at the beginning of the article, it appears that Lacenaire was attracted to the inhabitants of the prison as a direct result of the knowledge that circulated about them in public discourse. Among the works that influenced him most, he cited the memoirs of Vidocq, the convict turned informant who created the security police during the reign of Napoleon and who inspired Hugo's Jean Valjean and Balzac's Vautrin.[31] Vidocq returned the gesture by mentioning Lacenaire and Avril in his slang dictionary. The reference occurs significantly in the article *Tante*. A *tante*, Vidocq explained to the reader, "is the woman of male prisons." The pair of convicts had been found guilty of killing Tante Chardon, but by evoking the crime in his article, Vidocq was doing more than clarifying an unusual term. The gesture pointed metonymically to the presumed homosexuality of the murders.

Although Lacenaire did not admit in his own memoirs to intimate relationships with other men, part of what drew him to the prison was the alternative it offered to conventional social relations. It was there that he learned a new language and a new culture and also where he met the type of man with whom he desired to wage his war against Restoration society. Once a part of the community of convicts, he felt so at home that it seemed to him as though he had been born among them. He described himself significantly as a "new Alcibiades," a comparison that was not without certain connotations.[32] It is fair to say that if Lacenaire had not been attracted by the prison's reputation for sexual immorality, he had certainly not been repelled by it. He had welcomed the guillotine as a means punishing Avril for his betrayal, but in the end he did not hold a grudge against his companion in crime. The two ultimately reconciled their differences and were even allowed to celebrate their reunion by sharing a dinner together in prison. Before they approached the guillotine, they embraced warmly and each cried out for the other to take courage. The intimate relationship they shared and their joint execution struck a chord with the public; it reflected popular images of other devoted convict couples they had seen on the stages of the boulevard theaters.

One journalist complained, in fact, that during Lacenaire's trial, it was impossible to speak of anything else in the Parisian salons. "Lacenaire! this hero straight out of a novel and a melodrama. . . ."[33] Lacenaire seemed to be proof that life imitated art and that consumer culture could render the simulacrum more vital than the real. "The Lacenaires and others like him," argued Lauvergne, "are but the offshoots of a more noble race whose role they learned to play through written tradition and which they in turn perfected."[34] Jules Janin claimed that

> today, by dint of melodramas, the terrible prestige of the guillotine has been stripped away; today criminals in the place de Grève offer their heads smugly and with lugubrious folly, following the example of the criminals of the boulevards; today, Robert Macaire and Bertrand are becoming tragic realities in their elegance and in their crimes, in their cynicism and in their social graces; in short, by dint of making us touch the executioner with our hands, we have turned this red-cloaked man, whose name alone made a man's hair stand on end a hundred years ago, into an actor like any other.[35]

The most famous fictional convict in the nineteenth century was certainly Robert Macaire, mentioned by Janin. Unlike the lone rebels later made famous by Hugo and Balzac, Macaire had a constant companion named Bertrand, his former chainmate. The couple made its début in a play entitled *The Inn of the Adrets*, first performed at the Théâtre de l'Ambigu-Comique on 6 December 1823. Macaire subsequently inspired the eponymous play *Robert Macaire*, which was made famous by the dramatic talent of Frederick Lemaître, who played the title role at the Théâtre des Folies-Dramatiques. The fantastical play *A Riot in Paradise* also featured Macaire and Bertrand, who mug Saint Peter and con their way into heaven. In a series of sketches entitled "The Hundred Robert Macaires" and published in *The Charivari*, Daumier pointed out the hypocrisy of French society by showing Macaire disguised as a member of each of the most important professions of the time. Even at the end of the nineteenth century, Macaire was still a very well known figure.[36] Productions, adaptations, and references to the convict "multiplied in a remarkable way," proving that "at certain moments a trivial character can express latent ideas and serve as a mechanism to express hidden feelings."[37]

Between the performance of *The Inn of the Adrets* and *Robert Macaire*, Vidocq had published his memoirs. He cast himself in terms that made him appear very much like the dramatic character, which may in fact have been inspired by Vidocq himself. There was certainly some degree of mutual influence between Vidocq's life, his memoirs, and the boulevard plays being produced during the 1820s and 1830s. What is particularly remarkable is the way that Bertrand was pushed farther out of the spotlight with each subsequent work, as if the figure of Vidocq influenced the relative importance of the two stage criminals. Still, convicts always appeared on stage in couples. In each of the plays, Macaire and Bertrand insinuate themselves into the lives of a self-important bourgeois family. Macaire, we learn, had sold out his wife and daughter, leaving them to take the rap for his crimes. By the end of these plays, the family they had planned to swindle turns out to be Macaire's own. He once again abandons his family, choosing to remain with Bertrand instead, and the two set out for the open road. On the one hand, the plays present their fraternal devotion as a danger to the family structure so dear to conservative and counterrevolutionary political factions. On the other hand, the bourgeois family is presented as a sham itself, since it turns out to be Macaire's own illegitimate family.

The most interesting play of the genre is *The Two Convicts*. Like *The Inn*, the story involves two convicts who were chainmates. The main character, François, arrives as a stranger in a small town in Auvergne. He has escaped from a chain of convicts and refuses to talk about his past, but the villagers assume he is just a military deserter. On the day of his wedding to a young widow, Thérèse, his former chainmate shows up in their barn. He recognizes François and plans to blackmail him. François wants to help his former mate but fears that revelations about his past will destroy all his dreams of a normal life. Meanwhile, the villagers and little Louis, a son whom Thérèse is raising on her own, are decorating the house for the marriage celebration. They adorn the rooms with garlands and try to place them around the groom's neck, which provokes a reaction of horror in the former convict. Since the play's dialogue does not explain this violent reaction, it must be assumed that spectators in the 1820s recognized the wedding garland as a metaphor for the convict's chain. Further strengthening the symbolic connection between conventional and prison marriage, the stage directions explain that "Garlands of flowers are placed all around the room, two medallions depicting the initials T. F. decorate the back of the theater."[38] Louis explains to François that he even drew the letters T. F., surrounded by a garland of flowers on all the walls of the house. The initials T. and F. stand for Thérèse and François: "these names that love has joined will always remain united." François is, of course, traumatized by what he interprets instead as the "horrible sign of opprobrium and dishonor."[39]

The chainmate suddenly shoots François in anger, and when the wedding guests strip off his shirt, the crowd (and the audience) sees the mark T. F. on his shoulder. As some of the villagers recall that François had always avoided swimming with them in the river, his valet exclaims that he must quickly leave the ex-con's service because of the adage, "Like master, like servant." He continues, "What! Stay in a house like this? . . . a house so badly mixed! . . . It's pretty mixed-up."[40] Might this be another reference to the presumed homosexuality of convicts? Once again, crime and homosexuality become indistinguishable as sources of shame. In literary discourse, sexuality had to be suggested implicitly, communicated to the reader through a highly coded, but nonetheless recognizable, web of tropes and images. The garlands of the wedding celebration parallel the symbolic chains that still bind François to his former chainmate. The valet fears people will gossip about his relationship with his employer. At the same time that literature must be allusive, plays about criminality had more license than those about other forms of social impropriety. A discernible homosexual theme would probably not have been tolerable in a play treating something other than crime. In fact, many of the gestures and words that particularly shocked and titillated the audience were not included in their printed versions.[41] Appert noted that these plays were

> far from giving moral instruction to the majority of spectators who were attracted by the disgusting jokes of these famous thieves: while the authorities allowed the presentation of these regrettable plays, they showed ridiculous severity towards authors who skillfully depicted the mores of courtesans and social climbers.[42]

These plays systematically place the prison couple in direct conflict with the traditional family, creating a symbolic tension that is only subtly perceptible in the rhetoric of more scientific texts. Thus, a homosexually troped form of fraternal solidarity, which can be read as implicitly Jacobin, appears at odds with a counterrevolutionary conception of the family as the true foundation of social unity. While the protagonist invariably chooses to honor his commitment to his chainmate rather than to his wife and children, the subtext cannot be read as univocally affirming revolutionary ideals of popular sovereignty. The convict, after all, remains a self-interested criminal, and his homosocial affinity for his chainmate is devalued as much as the insubstantial basis of his heterosexual marriage. It is nonetheless significant that the convict as social rebel is aligned on the side of liberalism and republicanism while the nuclear family is positioned on the side of traditionalism and legitimism. Homosexuality and heterosexuality are mapped accordingly and as a consequence have a politically charged signifying potential.

Literature may be less explicit than juridico-administrative or medical texts in the depiction of the convict's sexuality (neither Robert and Bertrand nor François and his chainmate have a clearly sexual relationship), but it more accurately reveals the social signification of the convict's identity in Restoration society. The criminal's secret identity and his talent for disguise suggest the latent potential for social unrest that may be hidden beneath the calm surface of conventional society. Homosexuality is likewise a figure for invisible threats to the family and thus to the social order. It reveals itself to be the primitive affective bond that unites the people as a mass rather than as a codified and regulated society.

The *chevaliers de la guirlande* stand out among the faces of crime because they convey strong notions of commitment and solidarity.[43] They were always presented in pairs, unlike Mandrin, Cartouche, and other great bandits of the previous century who were lone figures in life and on the stage. The convict created by the new prison system underwent a paradoxical "familialization," as did many other identities in the social discourse of Restoration France. He too existed as a partner in a devoted and usually monogamous couple, but one whose particular form of solidarity threatened the general social order. Convicts were represented through a sexually charged semiotic system that deployed specifically homosexual signs and tokens. The flowers of the convict's garland may be at the origin of the pansy tattoos used by homosexual men as a symbol of commitment in the latter half of the nineteenth century. Some had themselves tattooed simply with the words "*bagne* flower."[44] One wonders if they influenced the symbolic system of a writer like Jean Genet in whose work flowers become a leitmotif.[45]

The penal system, through its prisons and *bagnes*, created a new type of (anti)social body. It also created a subculture, or at least radically reified what was formerly only a loose fraternity of bandits and robbers. In discursive depictions, the social solidarity of convicts was often tinged with eroticism, when not overtly described as sexual. The analogy drawn between prison couples and marriage harbored a twofold significance. Prison "marriages" were seen as a novel form of social reliance, but this bond was perceived as a direct challenge to the monogamous heterosexual couple that legitimist ideologues were raising up as the bulwark of a divinely ordained society. The vices believed to lead men to imprisonment and to make them susceptible to the sexual depravity that flourished there were ironically attributable to the failings of heterosexuality. Lauvergne argued that a lack of religious sensibility produced defective marriages that in turn produced defective offspring who filled prisons: "People no longer marry like our fathers did. The oddly matched unions are too often strange grafts that produce fruit that is mongrel, abortive, thin, and degenerate."[46] Amid the tumult of post-Revolutionary society and the resulting fragmentation of formerly fixed class structures, a great deal of anxiety surrounded the viability of the family as the new foundation of social solidarity.[47] The loyalty of prison couples was sometimes admired as a fraternal ideal, but the reality of men sharing their lives together was also taken as an affront to the institutions they seemed to flout.

NOTES

1. The scene is described in the *Gazette des Tribunaux*, 10 January 1836; and in Eugène François Vidocq, *Voleurs, physiologie de leurs moeurs et de leur langage* (Paris, 1837), 160.
2. Louis Canler, *Mémoires*, 3rd ed. (Paris, 1862), 95-7.
3. Pierre François Lacenaire, *Mémoires et autres écrits* (Paris, 1991), 104, 109.
4. *Gazette des tribunaux*, 7 November 1827.
5. Benjamin Appert, *Bagnes, prisons et criminels* (Paris, 1836), 119.
6. Adolphe Jules Dauvin, "Les Forçats," in *Les Francais peints par eux-mêmes: Encyclopédie morale du dix-neuvième siècle*, 8 vols. (Paris, 1842), 6: 69.
7. Appert, *Bagnes*, 119-20.
8. Eugène François Vidocq, *Mémoires*, ed. Jean Burnat (Paris, n.d.), 150.
9. Appert, *Bagnes*, 112, 114.
10. Joseph Méry, "Les Forçats: Le Cachot," *Revue de Paris* 16 (1835): 276-84.
11. Maurice Alhoy, *Les Bagnes: Rochefort* (Paris, 1830), 8, n. 25.
12. Ibid., 138.
13. Ibid., 103.
14. Ibid., 138-9.
15. Ibid., 44.
16. Alhoy, *Les Bagnes: Histoire, types, moeurs, mystères* (Paris, 1845), 2-3.
17. Appert, *Journal des prisons, hospices, écoles primaires et établissements de bienfaisance* 1 (1825): 224.
18. Hubert Lauvergne, *Les Forçats considérés sous le rapport physiologique, moral et intellectuel, observés au bagne de Toulon* (Paris, 1841), 287.
19. Félix Carlier, *Etudes de pathologie sociale: Les Deux prostitutions* (Paris, 1887), 280, 286-287, 301.
20. Dauvin, "Forçats," 93.
21. Louis-René Villermé, *Des prisons telles qu'elles sont, et telles qu'elles devraient être* (Paris, 1820), 95-6.
22. Vidocq, *Dictionnaire argotique* (Paris, 1837), 163-4.
23. Appert, *Journal* 4 (1828), 85-6.
24. Louis Mathurin Moreau-Christophe, "Les Détenus," in *Français peints par eux-mêmes*, 4: 1-3.
25. Lauvergne, *Forçats*, 198-9.
26. Alhoy, *Rochefort*, 2-3.
27. Appert, *Journal* 4 (1828): 42.
28. Moreau-Christophe, "Détenus," 12-3.

29. *Gazette des Tribunaux*, 2 October 1829.
30. Alhoy, *Rochefort*, 8.
31. Jean Savant, "Portrait de Vidocq," in Vidocq, *Mémoires*, 14-44.
32. Lacenaire, *Mémoires*, 109.
33. *Mercure de France* 11 (1835): 169.
34. Lauvergne, *Forçats*, 198.
35. Quoted by Moreau-Christophe, "Détenus," 37-8.
36. Ludovic Celler, *Les Types populaire au théâtre* (Paris, 1870), 181.
37. The Goncourt brothers cite Robert Macaire as one of the most important "types" of the century, comparable even to Goethe's Werther. Edmond and Jules Goncourt, *Charles Demailly* (Paris, 1876), 262.
38. Eugène Cantiran de Boirie and Pierre-Frédéric-Adolphe Carmouche, *Les Deux Forçats, ou la Meunière du Puy-de-Dôme* (Paris, 1823), 24.
39. Ibid., 29, 25.
40. Ibid., 32.
41. Léon Gozlan, "Robert Macaire," *Revue de Paris* 19 (1835): 118-29.
42. Appert, *Journal* 5 (1829): 417.
43. Victoria Thompson has noted this special bond between inmates in "Creating Boundaries: Homosexuality and the Changing Social Order in France, 1830-1870," in *Homosexuality in Modern France*, ed. Jeffrey Merrick and Bryant T. Ragan, Jr. (New York, 1996), 109-13.
44. Several criminologists note the discovery on the bodies of known homosexuals tattoos representing two pairs of hands holding a pansy with two sets of initials. Alexandre Lacassagne, *Les Tatouages: Etude anthropologique et médico-légale* (Paris, 1881), 61, fig. 36; Charles Perrier, *Du Tatouage chez les criminels* (Lyon, 1897), 30-3; and Emile Laurent, *Les Habitués des prisons de Paris* (Lyon, 1890), 514-17.
45. The opening shot of Genet's silent film *Un Chant d'amour* shows the exterior of a prison wall. One prisoner reaches through his cell window and swings a garland of flowers in an attempt to pass it to the prisoner in the neighboring cell. One of Genet's novels is entitled *Notre-Dame-des-Fleurs* and another *Miracle de la rose*.
46. Lauvergne, *Forçats*, 237.
47. Roddey Reid, *Families in Jeopardy: Regulating the Social Body in France, 1750-1910* (Stanford, 1993), chapter 1.

Homosexuals in the City: Representations of Lesbian and Gay Space in Nineteenth-Century Paris

Leslie Choquette

The Victorian Age, as Michel Foucault demonstrated in his *History of Sexuality*, was not simply a period of sexual repression, but rather a time in which discourses about sexuality multiplied at a dizzying rate.[1] Homosexual behavior, for example, received increasing attention from sources as diverse as experts in medicine and law enforcement, newspaper reporters, writers of fiction and poetry, visual artists, and even lesbians and gays themselves. This essay will examine the multiple printed and iconographic representations of Parisian homosexuality from the 1830s to the end of the century, in keeping with Foucault's admonition to try to determine what can and cannot be spoken, who can and cannot speak. What emerges first from the cacophony of voices is a sense of the obsessions, anxieties, and taboos of the age regarding public homosexual behaviors. For instance, gay spaces, which concerned experts at least as much as lesbian venues, were less visible than the latter in literature and almost, if not entirely, absent from the visual arts. Portrayals of lesbians clearly had a voyeuristic appeal to straight men, while those of gay men produced discomfort. At the same time, the cross-class nature of lesbian space took longer to acknowledge than that of gay space, owing to a focus on prostitution. Upper-class lesbians became visible only in the 1880s, after the fall of the Empire had stripped the veneer of virtue from women of the imperial elite.

Secondly, the sources, despite their limitations, present a composite picture of the vibrant urban subcultures of lesbians and gays in nineteenth-century

[Haworth co-indexing entry note]: "Homosexuals in the City: Representations of Lesbian and Gay Space in Nineteenth-Century Paris." Choquette, Leslie. Co-published simultaneously in *Journal of Homosexuality* (Harrington Park Press, an imprint of The Haworth Press, Inc.) Vol. 41, No. 3/4, 2001, pp. 149-167; and: *Homosexuality in French History and Culture* (ed: Jeffrey Merrick, and Michael Sibalis) Harrington Park Press, an imprint of The Haworth Press, Inc., 2001, pp. 149-167. Single or multiple copies of this article are available for a fee from The Haworth Document Delivery Service [1-800-342-9678, 9:00 a.m. - 5:00 p.m. (EST). E-mail address: getinfo@haworthpressinc.com].

Paris. Unlike police reports and judicial records, which detail the surveillance and prosecution of either gay men or female prostitutes (whose lesbian behavior was sometimes noted), they reveal these homosexual subcultures to have been both distinct and overlapping. The intersection, as opposed to the uniqueness, of lesbian and gay space has been too often overlooked by scholars interested primarily in either lesbian or gay history.

In the 1830s and 1840s, lesbianism moved beyond the fantastic realms of pornography and romantic fiction into that of urban sociology, as men of science increasingly turned their attention to social problems. The inventor of the new discourse, Alexandre Parent-Duchâtelet, viewed Parisian lesbianism as a nefarious by-product of prostitution, which herded debased women into the promiscuity of prisons and brothels. Although he raised the subject "only with an extreme reserve," he provided a vivid and influential portrait of lesbian mores, including the frightening image of older lesbians initiating young acolytes.[2] His description apparently inspired a new police ruling against apartment sharing by streetwalkers in 1843.[3]

The 1850s witnessed the emergence of another new discourse about lesbian Parisians. In this age of romantic individualism, the first quasi-autobiographical voice made itself heard in the memoirs of Céleste Mogador, a prostitute and actress turned writer.[4] While Céleste was obviously attracted to men (she eventually married her true love, count Lionel de Chabrillan), she also portrayed a world in which abused prostitutes turned to each other for emotional and sexual solace. Her firsthand experience of prison and brothel confirmed that lesbian liaisons were common there, some of them between young girls and middle-aged women.[5] More importantly, she made clear that such relationships were not confined to institutions, but spilled out onto the city streets. Independent streetwalkers and courtesans, who multiplied as the century progressed, brought same-sex intimacy to their residential neighborhood, the Bréda quarter. Here they shared apartments, regardless of the police ruling, and even patronized their own restaurants, the prostitutes' *tables d'hôte*.[6] These *tables d'hôte*, which were run by older procuresses, sometimes catered to women who announced their sexual preference through cropped curly hair and a boyish appearance.[7] Beyond the Bréda quarter, lesbianism was also visible among the women of the theater world, the singers, dancers, and actresses who were often indistinguishable from courtesans.[8]

Three years after the publication of Mogador's memoirs, gay men became objects of the medical gaze for the first time. Ambroise Tardieu, presenting himself as a reluctant successor to Parent-Duchâtelet, authored a landmark study of Paris's gay subculture, focusing on its purported links to crime.[9] As the reference to Parent-Duchâtelet would indicate, Tardieu was chiefly concerned with male prostitution, although, unlike his predecessor, he was unable to ignore the clientele. He pointedly refused to identify the places associated with gay solicitation, noting only that it occurred in certain "well-known" locations "on the public way" and in brothels. At least some of the latter were female brothels that provided male prostitutes alongside the ordinary merchandise.[10] Ironically, then, the brothel, that heterosexual institution par excellence, was an important locus of both the lesbian and gay subcultures.

Tardieu was more specific in describing the physical appearance of male prostitutes, since he was training forensic specialists to recognize them. Some of them worked in drag, but the standard uniform was curly hair, make-up, open collar, tight clothes, lots of jewelry (rings, earrings, necklaces), strong perfume, and something in hand, whether handkerchief, flowers, or needlework. Their customers were a diverse lot, gay men being found in every class of society.[11]

Just as Parent-Duchâtelet's concern with criminality was echoed by Tardieu, so Mogador's autobiographical voice was mirrored in the memoirs of Arthur Belorget, a male prostitute. They were written in the 1860s, although not published until 1896.[12] Belorget, whose mother was a dressmaker and perfume seller in the Bréda quarter, emulated her clients and became the courtesan Pauline de Floranges at age sixteen. He was mentored in his new role by Paula, a lesbian courtesan and dancer not unlike Mogador. As "mistress" to a marquis, Belorget continued to live in the notorious neighborhood. When the marquis tired of him, he followed Paula onto the stage, becoming the Countess in a music hall on the Champs-Élysées. He supplemented his income by turning tricks in his costume after the concerts.

Among the most enthusiastic members of his audience, "every night, in the front rows," "were the principal tribades of Paris." Next to them, and equally avid in their appreciation, were "the most elegant of the *complaisants* [Belorget's word for gay courtesans] of the boulevard and grand quarters." Belorget stressed the affinity between the two groups, both of which enjoyed drag shows and dressing in drag. His "baptism" as the Countess, which celebrated his move to the chic new neighborhood around place Saint-Augustin, was attended by both lesbians and gays.[13] Belorget was a talented artist, and he made numerous drawings to accompany his memoirs. His lesbians, who wear men's clothes and haircuts for fun, also don the working costume of luxurious courtesans. He and his fellow "minions" do not correspond exactly to Tardieu's description. Part-time drag queens do wear their hair long and curly when dressed as males, but they also have ties and loose, dress-like coats. Some of their friends, the "boys," are in ordinary working-class garb. Perhaps Tardieu's insistence on tight, distinctive clothing to accentuate large buttocks and wasp waists had less to do with reality than with an emerging model of homosexuality as inversion.[14]

Although Belorget's manuscript languished unread for many years, the 1860s did see the publication of another detailed description of the gay subculture, this one by a former police chief. Canler, who wrote his memoirs to capitalize on the public taste for crime stories, had none of Tardieu's reticence. He drew for the first time a detailed map of gay prostitution, which included the Champs-Élysées and contiguous areas (place de la Concorde, faubourg Saint-Honoré, and quai des Tuileries), the boulevards (passage des Panoramas and passage de l'Opéra), and also the Palais-Royal. In addition, a lower class of hustlers worked on quai des Invalides and quai de Billy. According to Canler, the male prostitute's costume included a tie and visored cap, both of which were indeed depicted by Belorget. Like Tardieu, however, he maintained that the coat was cinched tightly at the waist. As for the hustler's clientele, Canler concurred with Tardieu in emphasizing social diversity. What made the gay subculture so dangerous, even apart from its connection to crime, was this promiscuous blurring of class lines.[15]

In the aftermath of the Commune, the spotlight returned to lesbians, as anxiety about female prostitutes peaked in a discourse making these viraginous "arsonists" responsible for the carnage.[16] With the concurrent rise of naturalist literature, lesbian prostitutes were portrayed as invaders of another type of public space, the café. In "The End of Lucie Pellegrin," a short story written in 1875 by Paul Alexis, the dying courtesan of the title spends twenty francs a day to keep Chochotte, a leather-jacketed lesbian hoodlum.[17] The loathsome Chochotte maintains headquarters at a café, the Rat-Mort, where, like a pimp, she endlessly plays cards and smokes cigars. Alexis, a young disciple of Zola, claimed to have based the story on an actual conversation between four prostitutes, overheard in an inferior restaurant in Montmartre. In any case, the Rat-Mort was a real café, located at 7 place Pigalle and 16 rue Frochot, on the outskirts of the Bréda quarter. Dating from the Second Empire, it served a mixed clientele of well-heeled businessmen, political radicals, avant-garde artists, cutting-edge writers, prostitutes from the neighborhood, and lesbians.

"The End of Lucie Pellegrin" was an enormous critical success, as a result of which the Rat-Mort's lesbians gained notoriety. A few years later, when artist Félicien Rops decided to make a print of a lesbian in drag, he entitled his preliminary drawing "Rat-mort, 1879, Sister of the Pale Hoodlum." The image resembles those of Arthur Belorget, with the difference that Rops's lesbian, like a man or a prostitute, is smoking.[18]

In the 1880s and 1890s, as gender anxiety reigned and naturalism gained force in art and literature, the trickle of discourses on Parisian homosexuals turned to a flood, particularly where lesbians were concerned. Émile Zola's *Nana*, which became a *succès de scandale* in 1880, launched the upsurge by confirming lesbians as legitimate, if distasteful, subjects of the literary gaze. A central scene in the novel unfolds at a lesbian *table d'hôte* on rue des Martyrs, the main commercial artery of the Bréda quarter. In *Nana*, visual detail replaces the earlier innuendo of Mogador.[19]

Zola's notebooks reveal that he based his description on an actual visit to Louise Taillandier's *table d'hôte* at 17 rue des Martyrs. His laconic scribbles, which he simply expanded for the novel, provide a vivid picture:

> 3 dining rooms, Friday busy day, sometimes 150 women and 10 men. In couples the women. All of them kiss Louise on the mouth. Mistresses of grave bourgeois who come to have fun. The girl dressed as a man. 3 francs for the dinner, lots of dishes, chicken with rice that they stuff themselves with, leg of lamb with beans, old-fashioned chic: vol au vent. Not great. Wine undrinkable. Maternity of the Taillandier, of this fat monster. The maid skinny, infirm dyke. Ham actresses. Fortunes earned dyking it up in town. An old slut, as soon as she finds a pretty novice, brings her there, and all the fat women woo her. Horrible fat women.[20]

The notebooks also contain the observation that Louise moved her restaurant during the summer to her "large and beautiful property" just outside the city in Asnières, where she kept house with seven or eight other women. The public presence of these lesbians at nearby bathing stations inspired Zola to visit one of the most popular, the Grenouillère, in preparation for a scene of *Nana* that he eventually cut.[21]

Nonetheless, fans of naturalist fiction did not have long to wait to learn where Parisian lesbians went on holiday, for Guy de Maupassant published his short story "La Femme de Paul" in 1881. Like Zola, Maupassant had done some firsthand research, in his case through a liaison with the bisexual bohemian Gisèle d'Estoc.[22] In "La Femme de Paul," the Grenouillère is the summer home of four notorious lesbians, two of whom dress as women and two as men. Their many female visitors include famous actresses, not to mention the mistress of the aggrieved Paul.[23]

Shortly after the release of Maupassant's story, two satirical drawings appeared in the *Little Journal for Laughs*. Both, by an artist named Lafosse, were entitled "Along the Banks" and featured summering lesbians. In the first, an elegant woman asks her cross-dressed, cigarette-smoking companion whether her new boat club is taking shape, to which her friend replies, "You bet it has shape, real shape! It has 200 members." The second shows a clueless young man accosting two garishly dressed, hatless women walking brazenly arm in arm, only to be told, "I'm telling you, sir, we can't accept anything, we've just finished eating. . . ."[24]

Further revelations about homosexual space appeared the same year in the memoirs of Claude, another ex-police chief. In keeping with the fashion of the day, Claude, unlike Canler, included lesbians as well as gays in his rogues' gallery. From him, readers learned what Zola had discovered but declined to reveal in *Nana,* that women as well as men patronized brothels.[25] Claude's discussion of gay prostitutes both expanded and updated the map provided by Canler. The once-popular Palais-Royal had given way to the Hôtel Drouot, boulevard, and theater lines by day, the perennial Champs-Élysées by night. The favor of the latter was enhanced by the proximity of two male brothels, located on allée des Veuves (now avenue Montaigne) and rue Marbeuf. Tales of two gay murders, both associated with the barren northern outskirts of the city, reinforced the association of homosexuality with crime.[26]

Claude's recollections of the theater world, whose surveillance he had overseen before becoming police chief, clearly reveal the interconnectedness of the lesbian and gay subcultures. One of his nemeses as theater inspector was Tante Malaga (*tante* or "auntie" was ordinarily a derogatory term for a gay man), a cross-dressing lesbian ticket seller, claque leader, and loan shark with whom "the old generation of authors was also well acquainted." Malaga adored actresses, attended premiers with young cross-dressing women, and lived with one (going so far as to murder her, with a male lover, when she found them together at her summer place in Asnières). Along with her other activities, she worked as a procuress for gay men, providing customers to the male prostitutes of the Palais-Royal and keeping an old vaudeville writer supplied with young actors.[27]

A less criminal form of lesbian and gay interaction, the Mardi Gras ball, was also portrayed for the first time in 1881, in a minor naturalist novel by writer Edouard Rod. The ball, held at Bullier in the Latin Quarter, counted among its attendees an Italian model who is "well known at the Rat-Mort," two girls in drag who dance the mazurka together in a close and loving embrace, and "some young men dressed as pages" who walk "with languorous poses." By the last quarter of the nineteenth century, the traditional Mardi Gras masked ball had been appropriated by the lesbian and gay subcultures and turned into a public community celebration for both groups.[28]

The 1880s witnessed qualitative as well as quantitative changes in the depiction of lesbian Paris. Only then did writers acknowledge the cross-class nature of the urban subculture, after portraying it as involving only prostitutes and actresses. Although earlier authors, from Balzac to Adophe Belot, had written fiction about wealthy, upper-class lesbians, they had imagined the activities of these women entirely within the private sphere.[29] Not so Marguerite Bellanger, the boyish former mistress of Napoleon III, who published her memoirs in 1882. Bellanger, a prostitute of peasant origins, did not come out herself; she scarcely needed to, given her predilection for male attire. Instead, she was at pains to prove that courtesans of her ilk were no worse than society ladies, hence her tales of lesbian women-about-town who visited brothels.[30] Already, in Zola's version of the corrupt Empire, countess Sabine had been a mirror image of Nana, but in Bellanger's version, the corruption of the elite woman became explicitly (homo)sexual.

Readers of Bellanger's memoirs probably had higher expectations of entertainment than veracity, but they may have been more impressed with the report of prostitution expert Louis Fiaux to the Paris Municipal Council the following year. It contained a deposition from Dr. Paul Dubois to the effect that the Chabanais, the city's premier deluxe brothel, admitted not only *demi-mondaines* but authentic *femmes du monde*, who "came with the unique aim of satisfying abnormal tastes with the feminine personnel of the establishment."[31] Meanwhile, journalist Catulle Mendès revealed in his *chroniques* (hybrids of fiction and reportage) that aristocratic ladies also picked up prostitutes in the Bréda quarter's millinery shops.[32]

In 1885, the new society lesbian entered the popular novel, cruising in public places and crashing the gates of the lesbian *demi-monde. Parisian Women: Two Friends* by René Maizeroy featured voracious ladies in wool jackets, starched collars, and straight, tweed skirts, who pick up women in the theater, the Rat-Mort, arcade boutiques, the flower market, even the church of the Madeleine. Their assignations are as likely to take place in the private rooms of expensive restaurants as in the brothels and *tables d'hôte* of the Bréda Quarter.[33] Maizeroy was the pseudonym of baron René Toussaint, a prominent journalist, man-about-town, and frequent escort of the popular actress Elzéar, mistress of Mathilde de Morny, marquise de Belbeuf.[34] His novel, a best seller, earned him a one-thousand-franc fine for obscenity.[35] The frightening convergence of high and low, long a cliché in representing gays, had nonetheless become a staple of discourses on lesbians.[36]

Between 1885 and 1890, writers elaborated on their portrayal of classless lesbian space, while also describing gay space in more detail. Significantly, the first naturalist novel to focus on the gay subculture was published in 1888, and it in turn inspired a rare visual representation.

Lesbians received their due from Jean Lorrain, an up-and-coming journalist who picked up where Mendès and Maizeroy had left off. In a hypocritical column of 1887, Lorrain, who was flamboyantly gay himself, further traced the boundaries of lesbian Paris under the guise of lambasting his two colleagues for pandering to lesbians.[37] For Lorrain, the subculture still centered on the Bréda quarter (now rebaptized Montmartre) and its suburban extension Asnières, but along with prostitutes and entertainers, it now attracted authentic ladies from the fashionable quarters, and even stolid bourgeoises from the city center. Regardless of class, the prescribed costume consisted of short, curly hair worn with a stiff collar, man's jacket, wool frock coat, and dress of "androgyne" cut. Besides the *tables d'hôte*, popular venues for cruising included the Rochechouart pool, which held a ladies' day every Friday. Contact was made by a slow, fixed, mutual stare or eloquent finger squeeze.[38] There seemed little to add, although Ali Coffignon managed to offer up a few more journalistic tidbits in time for the World's Fair two years later. Lesbian pedophiles, he claimed, could hire child prostitutes, the little flower girls who made the rounds of boulevard cafés. Those seeking adult company could explore the Bois de Boulogne by morning or wait to try their luck later at the city's races, art exhibits, or dance halls.[39]

Jean Lorrain was less forthcoming about the gay subculture, despite his personal commitment to it. He did, however, portray it in several poems from his collection *Modernities*, published in 1885. His snapshots of nocturnal cruising, whether on the ritzy Champs-Élysées or the sinister outer boulevards, emphasize once again the transgression of class boundaries; they celebrate the furtive couplings of top-hatted gentlemen with stable boys, workers, street urchins, and soldiers.[40]

Lorrain's designation of the outlying quarters as theaters of cruising was new, nor was it echoed two years later in the reminiscences of former vice squad chief Félix Carlier. Carlier, however, added two more sites to the map of familiar hot spots in central Paris: public toilets and public baths. Notorious toilets included those around the Halles, while a particularly suspect bathing establishment flourished in the Countess's old neighborhood of Saint-Augustin, on chic rue de Penthièvre.[41]

Lorrain's poems and Carlier's book may have inspired the young Henri d'Argis, who in any case decided to make a name for himself by writing the first realist novel devoted to "Sodom." He was not the first novelist to try to capitalize on the scandalous topic; Joseph Méry's bestseller, *Monsieur Auguste*, had followed upon the heels of Tardieu in 1859. Méry's book, however, was a light, boulevard-style comedy, utterly devoid of scabrous detail.[42] D'Argis's *Sodom* would instead be a naturalist compendium of information on the Parisian subculture, harnessed to a preposterous and moralistic tragic plot.

The novel opens, portentously, in a recently founded establishment of Turkish baths near the Opera, where the depressed protagonist ponders his unhappy past. His homosexuality, the combined result of heredity and environment, has become full blown only recently, owing to a chance encounter with a hustler on the Champs-Élysées. The young man, who corresponds neatly to Tardieu's description, invites him to have sex on a park bench behind the music hall, the Ambassadeurs. Without waiting for a response, he explains that he also hustles around the Grand-Hôtel, the Palais-Royal, and the Tuileries, then proceeds to escort his client to a male brothel "not far from rue La Boétie." The brothel, the first such to be described, features heavy red velvet curtains, divans with cushions, a table littered with nun costumes, corsets, women's trousers, peacock feathers, and dildos, a mannequin in a corner, and a Great Dane on a chaise-lounge. Only the engravings on the walls, with their pornographic images of men, would appear to distinguish it from an ordinary brothel. Although Jacques flees in horror, he encounters "a beautiful adolescent" at the baths, and their relationship completes his decline into murder and madness.[43]

D'Argis's sensational novel was popular, going through no fewer than six editions within the year. It also gave rise to one of the rare visual images of contemporary gay space, Jean-Louis Forain's drawing "The Third Sex."[44] Forain no doubt chose his Balzacian title as a guarantee of legitimacy, but he also added the inscription, "To the author of *Sodom*."[45] The drawing, which took up a full page of *The French Courrier* in October 1888, unmistakably depicts a gay hustler on the Champs-Élysées by night (he walks in the middle of the roadway, with the equestrian statue marking the entrance from place de la Concorde on his right). The gas lamps are lit, casting a garish glow on his costume and visage. Though he wears an ordinary frock coat, he has drawn his coattails forward to reveal a pair of very tight pants. The viewer's eye is pulled first to his buttocks, then his face, both portrayed as round and feminine. A soft hat and pointy shoes contribute to the effeminate effect.[46]

Forain never returned to the subject of hustlers after his salute to d'Argis, although he portrayed countless female prostitutes and went on to make several satirical drawings of lesbians. The only other artist to allude to the subject in the 1880s was Adolphe Willette, and he did so more ambiguously. Willette, the illustrator of *Paris Nights* (essentially a naughty guidebook for visitors to the World's Fair), chose to depict the obliging doorman of a boulevard restaurant, described in the text as ready "for all sorts of errands, pretty and well-groomed, as pleasing to men as to women." In the image, a clean-shaven young man in uniform simply passes an envelope to an elegant lady; however, his tight pants reveal an ample rump, which he further accentuates by leaning forward with his hand squarely on it. Yet Willette, who had no qualms about sketching the lesbians of the Rat-Mort in the same work (they were alluring after all), refrained from illustrating the more pointed passage devoted to the disturbing hustlers of the Folies-Bergère: "dubious young men, curly-haired, perfumed, dressed in the latest fashion, with fine shoes, monocle in eye or hand, walk[ing] in an equivocal manner, smiles on their lips and in their eyes."[47]

As the previous quotes suggest, authors divulged a few more haunts of gay prostitutes in time for the World's Fair. Others who added to the familiar list included ex-police chief Macé, for nighttime cruising spots (Bois de

Boulogne, Bois de Vincennes, and boulevard Bourdon), and scandal-monger Coffignon, for daytime ones (Bourse, military concerts, and Palais de Justice). Coffignon was also the first to call attention to the regular social venues of gay Parisians, citing the wine shops and cheap restaurants of the Halles together with a French fry joint at the bottom of rue Monge.[48] Policemen, of course, had long kept an eye on suspect establishments in certain neighborhoods, and yet the gay hangout had never before captured the public imagination, unlike its lesbian counterpart.[49] Only at the time of the World's Fair, with its upsurge in voyeuristic tourism, did gay men, like lesbians, become part of the urban spectacle as they were going about their ordinary business.

The 1890s, for both lesbians and gays, were characterized by ever greater visibility in the city. In 1890, reporter Jules Davray broke new ground by describing the successor to the prostitute's *table d'hôte*, the lesbian *brasserie. Brasseries*, cheap restaurants offering alcoholic beverages (especially but not exclusively beer) and limited meals, sprouted up all over Paris at the end of the century. While some of them were actually brothels for a male clientele, in which the waitresses did double duty, others took the opposite tack.[50] Davray introduced his readers to the *brasserie* of Mother G., a latter-day Louise Taillandier, near place d'Anvers in Montmartre. He wrote, "The proprietor is the ideal type of the lesbian aged in the saddle; massive, tall, masculine features, short hair, cigarette dangling from her lip, she comes and goes in her *brasserie*, amiable to male and female alike, encouraging about the start of a new girl." The many patrons of the establishment exchange kisses on the mouth, grope one another without modesty, and fail to modulate their voices; to this voyeur they are "the poet's dream." Davray was almost certainly describing a *brasserie* called the Souris, at 29 rue Henri-Monnier (formerly rue Bréda), owned by the indomitable Palmyre. Out of discretion, he simply shifted the address from the environs of place Pigalle to those of place d'Anvers, and he changed Palmyre's initial to G., conveniently suggestive of *gousse, gougnotte*, and *gouine* (terms equivalent to dyke). He was even more discreet, however, when broaching the subject of gay male *brasseries*. While admitting that they existed, particularly in the same neighborhood, he noted only that "the shameful looks of these individuals turn the stomach, and we wouldn't know how to enter into more ample details with regard to the houses that exploit this specialty."[51]

Press reports were not always so coy. The same year, for instance, newspapers apprised their inquiring readers of a raid on a gay tavern at 9 rue Roy near place Saint-Augustin.[52] This address, in the neighborhood where the Countess resided in his prime (and where Marcel Proust would arrive in 1906), is around the corner from the brothel described by d'Argis and a block away from the baths on rue de Penthièvre. The baths themselves were in the news in 1891, following a bust involving eighteen men who represented, according to the newspaper reports, "an amazing confusion of races and social classes."[53]

The affair of the baths, which received widespread publicity from the arrests of April 8 to the convictions on 2 May, is also notable for inspiring another rare visual image, satirist Louis Legrand's "That's your uncle . . . but he's an auntie!"[54] Published in *The French Courrier* on 31 May, the drawing makes no reference to the baths, depicting as it does another public venue, the café. Yet its timing must have been more than coincidental, and likewise Legrand's choice of subject, not a gay prostitute as in Forain's study, but a client reminiscent of the affluent patrons of the bathhouse. In Legrand's ordinary café scene, only the caption unequivocally distinguishes the elegant gentleman from his straight counterparts. As Canler first admitted, such homosexuals "dress like everyone else," so that "the observer, to see through them, requires the greatest attention joined to the greatest experience."[55] This uncle is certainly a dandy. Seated before his coffee cup in top hat and frock coat, umbrella and shiny shoes, he appears more dapper than his female companion, never mind the balding man reading a newspaper at the next table. Except for the slender waxed mustache, his complexion resembles a woman's, with perhaps even a hint of eyebrow pencil or eyeliner.

Legrand's drawing, like Forain's, was singular in his oeuvre, which included legions of drawings of lesbians. Several of his lesbian images from the 1890s also feature cafés, notably the etchings "Parisian Profiles" and "At the Café." The first shows a tough butch in cycling costume topped by the extravagantly plumed headgear of a boulevard whore, smoking at a table, her radiant lady friend beside her. In "At the Café," the two girlfriends, both in the unmistakably gaudy attire of prostitutes, sit together as one prepares to inject herself with a hypodermic needle.[56] In stark contrast to Forain's lonely hustler or Legrand's aloof "auntie," both couples exude an air of defiant intimacy. George Bottini's woodcut "At the Café" (1897), in which two lesbians eye each other amorously across a table, similarly transforms the viewer into a voyeur.[57]

Viewing and voyeurism are also conflated in the lesbian brothel scenes that multiplied during the decade.[58] Louis Legrand contributed his share, as did Félicien Rops, but the master of the genre was incontestably Henri de Toulouse-Lautrec, who spent the better part of two years (1893-1894) actually living in brothels.[59] Based on his experiences in the tony establishments of rue d'Amboise and rue des Moulins, Lautrec produced a series of images in the mid-1890s with titles such as "The Two Girlfriends," "Abandon or the Two Girlfriends," and "Debauchery." Several of these scenes of prostitutes in the throes of passion feature Gabrielle, a well-known denizen of rue des Moulins, who moonlighted as a dancer at the Moulin-Rouge. As early as 1891, Lautrec had painted a portrait of Gabrielle in the strict black jacket and white shirt of the lesbian.[60]

Many verbal and visual images of lesbians from the 1890s focus on major entertainment spots, big music and dance halls like the Folies-Bergère, Moulin de la Galette, and Moulin-Rouge. In Albert Cim's novel *Blue Stockings*, lesbians (who ominously include a new breed of newspaper woman alongside the familiar *mondaine* and *demi-mondaine*) parade brazenly through the galleries of these meat markets, but it is in Toulouse-Lautrec's lithographs and paintings that they truly come alive.[61] His pictures of Moulin-Rouge dancers La Goulue and La Môme-Fromage (1891-1892) require insider knowledge to be read as lesbian images (albeit knowledge that any self-respecting observer of the Montmartre scene would have). But no one could mistake his portrayals of Mademoiselle Cha-U-Kao in lesbian costume at the Moulin de la Galette, waltzing in the arms of a girlfriend on the dance floor of the Moulin-Rouge or boldly escorting Gabrielle down the Moulin-Rouge gallery.[62]

Gay men were also a part of this mix, as connoisseurs of Paris nightlife testified. For example, reporter Charles Virmaître wrote of the Moulin-Rouge in 1897, "There is something for everyone in this place: women for women, men for women and women for men: rent boys, queers, fags, fairies, and homos. The choice for the taker is as marvellous as it is abundant."[63] Gay prostitutes, like ordinary ones, clearly worked these indoor venues; however, no novelist's or artist's pen recorded their presence.[64]

A disproportionate amount of attention was likewise paid to lesbian as opposed to gay *brasseries*. Charles Virmaître, in 1894, became the first person to identify two of them by name, noting that the Souris and the Hanneton, like the Rat-Mort, were hangouts for "women who love each other with an ardent passion and in consequence detest men."[65] That same year Toulouse-Lautrec chose the *brasserie* over the café to illustrate the "sapphic loves" of Maurice Donnay's poem, *Exhausted Eros*.[66] His drawing portrays two lesbians seated at the counter, one in regulation tailored jacket, the other, drink in hand, clearly recognizable as Moulin-Rouge performer and militant sapphist May Milton.[67]

In 1897, Lautrec, too, gave the *brasserie* a name, doing numerous on-site sketches in preparation for his lithograph, "The Souris, at Palmyre's Place." The following year he did the same thing for Palmyre's main competitor, Armande Brazier of the Hanneton, at 75 rue Pigalle. In "The Souris," the gruff proprietress shares center stage with a middle-aged fem, who smokes and drinks at her side, her rotund assistant, Monsieur Brunswick, and the backside of her beloved bulldog Bouboule. If the stuccoed walls are suggestive of fin-de-siècle luxury, the impression is tempered by the massive, rough-plank table at which (or in Bouboule's case, on which) they sit. "The Hanneton, at the *Brasserie*," in contrast, doubles as a portrait of Madame Brazier, shown seated on a banquette at her counter, having a cigarette and a beer (she too has a little dog). Her blowzy squint, extravagant hat, and abundant ruffles mark her as an over-the-hill courtesan, an image in sharp contrast to the persona she adopted outside her restaurant. In "La Grande Loge," a Lautrec painting and lithograph of 1897, she shares a theater box with lesbian courtesan Émilienne d'Alençon, but here she wears the white shirt, bow tie, and severe jacket associated with the lesbian, not the professional costume of gallantry.[68]

By the end of the century, the Souris and the Hanneton were included in the so-called "Grand Dukes' Tour" (a tour of Parisian nightspots for affluent slummers) as legendary gathering places for lesbians. Beautiful people went up to Montmartre with the idea, as Jean Lorrain put it, "We must dine in Lesbos to see."[69] This emphasis on voyeurism may explain why so little attention was paid to the gay men who also frequented the Souris, if not the Hanneton. Lautrec did portray Palmyre's right-hand man, Monsieur Brunswick, in his lithograph, but his rough sketches of her gay clients, young men with long curly hair and delicate features, languished forgotten in his notebooks.[70]

Nevertheless, verbal details about gay establishments continued to accumulate. In 1894, the indefatigable Virmaître revealed that a "*brasserie* for aunties" existed on a street adjoining rue Fontaine, and, in 1896, naturalist novelist Huysmans informed sex researcher Raffalovich about similar establishments on rue Vauvilliers and rue des Vertus.[71] According to Huysmans, the taverns near the Halles differed from those of Montmartre in catering to a macho crowd of "market porters, butchers' apprentices, slaughterhouse workers, and heavy-weight wrestlers." This urban scene, though acknowledged by the Countess and adored by Jean Lorrain, had scarcely registered among straight writers and artists preoccupied with sexual inversion.[72]

The Halles were identified as gay, if not macho, space in two interminable but sociologically interesting serial novels of the fin-de-siècle: Aristide Bruant's *Lower Depths of Paris* (1897) and Jean-Louis Dubut de la Forest's *Latest Scandals of Paris: Hitherto Unpublished Great Dramatic Novel* (1898-1900).[73] Bruant had built his career as a songwriter on conjuring those lower depths, and he deployed the same investigative zeal to compile a dictionary of popular slang and churn out his atrocious melodrama. Likewise Dubut de la Forest, a police official turned successful hack, assured his readers that for twenty years, "we have spared neither sleepless nights, nor documentary research, on the spot, and in the midst of nature."[74] For both Bruant and Dubut, gay men were an unsavory but ubiquitous component of the urban wilderness.

Bruant described two gay brothels in the vicinity of the Halles, the first in the form of a *brasserie*. My Aunt's Place, as he nicknamed it, was run by a thin young man with a monocle, who called himself the *patronne*. His three or four male employees, a mix of old and young, made themselves available for tricks just like the waitresses of ordinary *brasserie*-brothels. The second establishment, on rue d'Aboukir, belonged to a former hustler known as la belle Arsène. "Infinitely more discreet" than My Aunt's Place, it was open only to gay men, a few "intrepid" men of letters, and female prostitutes. Arsène furnished the inevitable "young men in curly hair and make-up," but his best customers, ironically, were the women: "for the sentimental thing, it's the little woman with whom you're *doubled up* in the joint. Days when there was enough dough unknown to the pimps, the little couple went to live it up at la belle Arsène's. . . . They bought champagne. It was their turn to be johns."[75]

Dubut de la Forest also described the gay brothel on rue d'Aboukir, which he called the Fairies' Dance Hall. Like Bruant, he agreed that it welcomed "gracious lesbians," just as Palmyre was happy to serve gay men. Certain businesses, while geared primarily toward either gays or lesbians, clearly belonged to the city's wider homosexual community. The Fairies' Dance Hall, a long, dimly lit room with bar, tables, and dance floor, is managed by a fat old queen assisted by a thin ephebe. The gay clientele, a mix of gentlemen, esthetes, hustlers, bicycle messengers, servants, doormen, and apprentice printers, sip mixed drinks at their tables, waltz amorously to a three-piece orchestra, and visit the rooms upstairs.[76] Although unsympathetic, this depiction dovetails with one produced ten years later by gay writer Lucien Daudet, except for a pianist in the place of the orchestra.[77] With Daudet, however, the representation of gay space crosses the threshold into the twentieth century.

In conclusion, the lesbian and gay spaces of nineteenth-century Paris gave rise to multiple discourses, a din of voices that also concealed multiple silences. As medical-legal experts, reporters, writers, artists, and lesbians and gays themselves portrayed urban homosexual subcultures, certain subjects remained relatively taboo. Among experts, the focus on prostitution meant that upper-class lesbians would be largely overlooked until the 1880s. Among writers and artists, a penchant for voyeurism made gay men a less compelling subject than lesbians throughout the century. Certainly the words and images examined here reflect widespread and growing anxieties about the nature of same-sex sexuality in the modern city.

At the same time, happily for the social historian, they provide a precious window, however clouded, onto the vibrant and interrelated urban worlds of lesbians and gays. While it may be more accurate to map gay, and perhaps even lesbian, space based on the archival record, the printed sources have the advantage of revealing more clearly the interpenetration of the two communities. Certainly some places were distinct: Gay men congregated around Saint-Augustin, lesbians in Asnières, for example. Yet they also shared many neighborhoods and institutions, from Montmartre and the boulevard to the brothel (gay or otherwise), the theater, the masked ball, the *brasserie*, and the dance hall.

NOTES

1. Michel Foucault, *Histoire de la sexualité: La Volonté de savoir* (Paris, 1976).
2. Alexandre Parent-Duchâtelet, *La Prostitution à Paris au XIXe siècle*, ed. Alain Corbin (1836; Paris, 1981), 113-9. Fantastical treatments of lesbianism included Balzac's *La Fille aux yeux d'or* (1834-5) and Gauthier's *Mademoiselle de Maupin* (1835-6). A popular pornographic work was Musset's *Gamiani* (1833).
3. Victoria Thompson, "Creating Boundaries: Homosexuality and the Changing Social Order in France, 1830-1870," in *Homosexuality in Modern France*, ed. Jeffrey Merrick and Bryant T. Ragan, Jr. (New York and Oxford, 1996), 113.
4. Céleste Mogador, *Adieux au monde: Mémoires*, 5 vols. (Paris, 1854); *Mémoires de Céleste Mogador*, 3 vols. (Paris, 1858); *Mémoires de Céleste Mogador*, 2 vols. (Paris, 1876); and Countess Lionel de Chabrillan, *Un Deuil au bout du monde: Suite des mémoires de Céleste Mogador* (Paris, 1877). The first edition ends in midstream, interrupted by Mogador's marriage. The second and third editions provide new details about her life just prior to her marriage, while the sequel deals with her years as wife and widow.
5. Mogador, *Adieux*, 1: 42. Céleste, however, was seduced by a girl her own age, whom she met in prison as a fifteen-year-old runaway. This Denise, "a real boy" with short hair and a side part, convinced her that they should enter a brothel together.
6. For example, after leaving the brothel, Céleste moved in with one of Denise's girlfriends, who had an apartment on rue de Provence. A *table d'hôte* provided simple fare at modest prices to clients who might or might not be lodged by the hostess. See Mogador, *Adieux*, 4: 59.
7. *Mémoires de Céleste Mogador*, 1: 235. Later in the century, the Bréda quarter and its landmark churches were virtual shorthand for lesbian prostitution, as was *the table d'hôte*. Émile Goudeau, "Sapho-Lorette à Lesbie-Trinité," *Le Chat Noir*, 22 December 1883, 197-8; and Jean Lorrain, *Une Femme par jour* (Paris, 1896), 201.
8. For example, Mogador hinted about the lesbian proclivities of La Reine Pomaré and Rose Pompon, two well-known dancers, and of actress Alice Ozy.
9. Ambroise Tardieu, *Étude médico-légale sur les attentats aux moeurs*, 7th ed. (Paris, 1878), 194-276. This edition features new statistics based on a larger number of case studies, but the analysis remains that of 1857.
10. Ibid., 198, 200, 204, 207 (cited).
11. Ibid., 205, 208, 216, 218.
12. H. Legludic, *Notes et observations de médecine légale: Attentats aux moeurs* (Paris, 1896). Legludic reproduced Belorget's memoirs, drafted in prison in the 1860s and entrusted to the doctor in 1874, under the title "Confidences et aveux d'un Parisien." Belorget, to whom Legludic referred as Arthur W., was identified in Philippe Lejeune, "Autobiographie et homosexualité en France au XIXe siècle," *Romantisme* 56 (1987): 79-100.
13. Legludic, *Notes*, 302, 305. This neighborhood would soon be known for its abundance of gay institutions, from bars to baths to brothels.
14. In this regard, it should be noted that Belorget's lesbians have amply endowed female bodies, regardless of their attire. For Belorget's illustrations, see Legludic, *Notes*, passim.
15. *Mémoires de Canler, ancien chef du service de sûreté* (1862; Paris, 1968), 317-8, 322, 331.

16. Leslie Choquette, "Degenerate or Degendered? Images of Prostitution and Homosexuality in the French Third Republic," *Historical Reflections/Réflexions historiques*, 23 (1997): 205-28.

17. Paul Alexis, *La Fin de Lucie Pellegrin* (1875; Geneva, 1979).

18. *Félicien Rops* (Brussels, 1998), 188. The lesbians of the Rat-Mort continued to fascinate artists and writers in the 1880s and 1890s. See, for example, Émile Goudeau, "Le Rat-Mort," *Le Courrier français*, 24 October 1886, 3; A. Lagarde, "Cafés artistiques de Paris," *Le Courrier français*, 14 July 1889, 3-4; Rodolphe Darzens, *Nuits à Paris* (Paris, 1889), 91-3; Jean-Louis Forain, "Au Rat," *Le Courrier français*, 14 December 1890, 3; and Phillip Dennis Cate and Patricia Eckert Boyer, *The Circle of Toulouse-Lautrec: An Exhibition of the Work of the Artist and of His Close Associates* (New Brunswick, 1985), color illustration 19.

19. Émile Zola, *Nana*, in *Les Rougon-Macquart*, 5 vols. (Paris, 1960-), 2: 1300-3.

20. BN, Ms, Nouvelles Aquisitions Françaises 10.313, folios 76-7, Émile Zola, *Nana*, Dossiers préparatoires, 1878.

21. Ibid., folios 76-7, 253-4, 333-6.

22. See letters to Gisèle d'Estoc in Guy de Maupassant, *Correspondance*, ed. Jacques Suffel, vols. 1-2 (Geneva, 1973).

23. Guy de Maupassant, "La Femme de Paul," in *La Maison Tellier* (1881; Paris, 1991), 61-82.

24. G. Lafosse, "Le Long des berges," *Petit journal pour rire (Troisième série)*, 300 (1881): 5, and 301 (1881): 4. Also Ferdinand Lunel, "A la Grenouillère," *Le Courrier français*, 31 July 1887, 11; and Catulle Mendès, *Lesbia* (Paris, 1887).

25. *Mémoires de Monsieur Claude, chef de la police de sûreté sous le Second Empire*, 10 vols. (Paris, 1881-83), 7: 203-7. Zola had written of brothels in his notebooks, "People go there to dyke it up with the whores." *Nana*, Dossiers préparatoires, folio 260.

26. Ibid., 1: 52-3; 3:101; 5:17; 9:74-5, 115.

27. Ibid., 3: 85-97. If only a fraction of Malaga's story is true, the silence of those authors who knew her is to be regretted.

28. Édouard Rod, *Palmyre Veulard* (Paris, 1881), 277-8. On Mardi Gras balls, see also Ali Coffignon, *Paris vivant: La Corruption à Paris* (Paris, [1889]), 337; Marie-François Goron, *L'Amour à Paris: Nouveaux mémoires: Les Parias de l'amour* (Paris, [1899]), 133; and Jean Lorrain, *La Ville empoisonnée: Pall-Mall Paris* (Paris, 1936), 11.

29. For example, in Balzac's *La Fille aux yeux d'or* and Adolphe Belot's *Mademoiselle Giraud ma femme* (Paris, 1870), the lesbians make love only in their private apartments, while maintaining a public façade of respectability.

30. *Confessions de Marguerite Bellanger: Mémoires anecdotiques* (Paris, [1882]), 141.

31. Cited in Léo Taxil, *La Prostitution contemporaine* (Paris, 1884), 374.

32. Catulle Mendès, *Monstres parisiens* (1882; Paris, 1902), 210-3.

33. René Maizeroy, *Les Parisiennes: Deux amies* (Paris, 1885).

34. Claude Francis and Fernande Gontier, *Mathilde de Morny, 1862-1944: La Scandaleuse marquise* (Paris, 2000), 149-50.

35. Nicole Albert, "Books on Trial: Prosecutions for Representing Sapphism in *fin-de-siècle* France," in *Disorder in the Court: Trials and Sexual Conflict at the Turn of the Century*, ed. George Robb and Nancy Erber (New York, 1999), 128-9.

36. Nonetheless, the only man of science to consider lesbians in these years continued to focus exclusively on prostitutes. He particularly deplored their latest fad of dressing as "little sisters," in twin dresses and accessories, thereby advertising their public presence in *brasseries*, dance halls, public gardens, and on the boulevards. Louis Martineau, *La Prostitution clandestine* (Paris, 1885), 94.

37. Lorrain's hypocrisy is compounded by the fact that he had himself portrayed lesbian Paris in his poems "Coquines," "Little Boy," and "Adultère" in *Modernités* (Paris, 1885).

38. Jean Lorrain, *Dans l'oratoire* (Paris, 1888), 47-55. The article first appeared in *L'Événement* on 14 April 1887.

39. Coffignon, *Paris vivant*, 309-12.

40. See the poems "Modernités," "Copailles," and "Prince héritier."

41. Quoted in Pierre Hahn, *Nos Ancêtres les pervers: La Vie des homosexuels sous le Second Empire* (Paris, 1979), 145, 150. The police were much less visible in outlying neighborhoods, which probably explains Carlier's failure to discuss them.

42. Joseph Méry, *Monsieur Auguste* (Paris, 1859). The plot revolves around the farcical attempts of a bourgeois pater familias to marry off his daughter to the homosexual Auguste.

43. Henri d'Argis, *Sodome* (Paris, 1888), 11, 199-201, 213. Rue La Boétie is one block north of rue de Penthièvre. One wonders, from this description, whether d'Argis simply transposed a visit to a heterosexual brothel.

44. I know of only one earlier image, an anonymous illustration entitled "The Pederasts" that appeared in Taxil, *Prostitution*, facing page 310. Its five men, however, are shown in a boudoir, a private rather than a public space.

45. In *Splendeurs et misères des courtisanes*, Balzac had employed the term "the third sex" to designate homosexuals in the prison system.

46. Jean-Louis Forain, "Le Troisième Sexe," *Le Courrier français*, 14 October 1888, 9.

47. Darzens, *Nuits à Paris*, 149, 192. Willette's illustration appears on 193.

48. Gustave Macé, *La Police parisienne: Gibier de Saint-Lazare* (Paris, 1888), 18; idem, *La Police parisienne: Mes lundis en prison* (Paris, 1889), 160-1; and Coffignon, *Paris vivant*, 333, 346-7.

49. On police surveillance, see William Peniston, "Love and Death in Gay Paris: Homosexuality and Criminality in the 1870s," in *Homosexuality in Modern France*, 128-45.

50. Turn-of-the-century establishments falling into this category included, among many others: Brasserie du Caprice, 131 rue Saint-Denis; Grande Brasserie de l'Ile d'Amour, 13 rue Grange-Batelière; and the Sacré-Coeur, 59 rue Rochechouart. *Guide secret de l'étranger célibataire à Paris* (Paris, [1889]); and *Guide complet des plaisirs mondains et des plaisirs secrets à Paris* (Paris, n.d.).

51. Jules Davray, *L'Amour à Paris* (Paris, 1890), 109-11.

52. Émile Chautard, *La Vie étrange de l'argot* (Paris, 1931), 558.

53. Michael Sibalis, "Defining Masculinity in Fin-de-Siècle France: Sexual Anxiety and the Emergence of the Homosexual," *Proceedings of the Western Society for French History: Selected Papers of the Annual Meeting*, 25 (1998): 251.

54. Louis Legrand, "Ça ton oncle . . . mais c'est une tante!" *Le Courrier français*, 31 May 1891, 11. The drawing covers three-quarters of the page, with the remainder devoted to advertisements for venereal disease remedies.

55. *Mémoires de Canler*, 319.

56. Camille Mauclair, *Louis Legrand: Peintre et graveur* (Paris, 1910), 155, 159, 248 (facing page). Former police chief Goron also called attention to morphine addiction among lesbian prostitutes, in *Amour*, 130-1.

57. Edna Carter Southard, *George Bottini: Painter of Montmartre* (Oxford, OH, 1984), 52-3. Ironically, this last image was acquired by lesbian poet H.D.

58. Although Degas included lesbian images among his brothel monotypes (c. 1879), he kept them completely private. In 1884, an anonymous picture of a cat fight among cathouse lesbians appeared in Taxil, *Prostitution*, but that work was withdrawn from circulation in the wake of obscenity proceedings. Only in the 1890s did it become common to portray the brothel lesbian visually with impunity. Euguenia Parry Janis, *Degas Monotypes: Essay, Catalogue and Checklist* (Cambridge, MA, 1968), 30; and Taxil, *Prostitution*, 174 (facing page). On the obscenity proceedings, see Annie Stora-Lamarre, *L'Enfer de la IIIe République: Censeurs et pornographes (1881-1914)* (Paris, 1990), 197-8.

59. "En Visite" of Félicien Rops depicts a half-dressed prostitute pleasuring her mostly naked friend on a chair. Louis Legrand's abundant images are mostly untitled. *Audacious Eroticism: The Unconventional Art of Félicien Rops (1833-1898)* (New York, 1983), catalogue number 124; and BN, Cabinet des Estampes, Oeuvre de Louis Legrand, vols. 17-8.

60. M. G. Dortu, *Toulouse-Lautrec et son oeuvre* (New York, 1971), paintings 549, 550, 598, 601, and 602. For "La Débauche," see Jean Adhémar, *Toulouse-Lautrec: His Complete Lithographs and Drypoints* (New York, 1965), 213.

61. Albert Cim, *Bas bleus* (Paris, 1891), 313.

62. Dortu, *Toulouse-Lautrec*, paintings 428, 429, and 583. Cha-U-Kao (an orientalized version of *chahut-chaos*, a version of the can-can) was an acrobat, dancer, and later clown at the Moulin-Rouge. She also starred in Toulouse-Lautrec's earliest lesbian sex scenes of 1892. Ibid., paintings 436, 437, 438, and 439.

63. Charles Virmaître, *Trottoirs et lupanars* (Paris, 1897), 146.

64. Lautrec did, however, portray Oscar Wilde at the Moulin-Rouge, in his décor for La Goulue's stall in 1895. Dortu, *Toulouse-Lautrec*, painting 591.

65. Charles Virmaître, *Dictionnaire d'argot fin-de-siècle* (Paris, 1894), 4.

66. Maurice Donnay, *Eros vanné* (Paris, 1894). The poem was made famous in dramatic reading by Yvette Guibert.

67. Reinhold Heller, *Toulouse-Lautrec: The Soul of Montmartre* (Munich and New York, 1997), 83, 89.

68. Adhémar, *Toulouse-Lautrec*, 229, 252, 290. See also Dortu, *Toulouse-Lautrec*, painting 651.

69. Jean Lorrain, *Madame Baringhel* (Paris, 1899), 269.

70. Dortu, *Toulouse-Lautrec*, drawings 4.193 and 4.322, for example.

71. Charles Virmaître, *Paris-impur* (Paris, 1894), 193.

72. Louis Allen, "Letters of Huysmans and Zola to Raffalovich," *Forum for Modern Language Studies*, 2 (1966): 215. Marc-André Raffalovich published Huysmans's material in "Les Groupes d'uranistes à Paris et à Berlin," *Archives d'anthropologie criminelle* 19 (1904): 926-36. Huysmans was particularly dismissive of Zola, whom he accused of failing to notice that "the Halles are the real den of deviant loves." "From this point of view," he wrote, "*Le Ventre de Paris* of Zola, who only saw comestibles for sale there, is really worthless and devoid of all serious study."

73. Aristide Bruant, *Les Bas-fonds de Paris* (1897; Paris, 1902); and Jean-Louis Dubut de la Forest, *Les Derniers scandales de Paris: Grand roman dramatique inédit,* 37 vols. (Paris, [1898-1900]).

74. Dubut de la Forest, *Derniers scandales*, 15: 4.

75. Bruant, *Bas-fonds*, 736-41.

76. Dubut de la Forest, *Derniers scandales*, 1: 20, 13: 4-8.

77. Lucien Alphonse-Daudet, *Le Chemin mort* (Paris, [1908]), 72-3. Daudet called the place the Rat-Musqué, perhaps in deference to the Rat-Mort.

Pederasts, Prostitutes, and Pickpockets in Paris of the 1870s

William A. Peniston

Under the presidency of marshal Patrice de MacMahon, from 1873 to 1879, the French government sought to impose a "Moral Order" on the country. During these years, the Prefecture of Police in Paris kept a ledger of arrests for public offenses against decency and other minor crimes. Entitled "Pederasts and Others," this ledger listed male prostitutes, thieves, and vagrants, as well as men who sought the company and sexual favors of other men. The police believed that these men represented a threat to society. Although same-sex sexual activity was not illegal in France in the nineteenth century, the police assumed that it led to crimes against both property, such as theft, blackmail, and extortion, and persons, such as assault and murder. The police, therefore, patrolled certain areas of the city that they considered dangerous, looking for any kind of unusual activity, which they often found, whether that activity was truly dangerous or not. They arrested men about whom they had received information, whom they had followed, and whom they had caught performing various sexual acts. Some of these men they arrested two or three times over the years and occasionally released after questioning them. From these interrogations, the police gathered a great deal of information about the male homosexual subculture of Paris in the 1870s.[1]

Even though the ledger reflects the concerns of the police more than it does the experiences of the men arrested, it remains a valuable source of information about their vital statistics, relationships, and way of life. It gives their names, addresses, occupations, ages, and other personal details. It records the dates, times, and places of their arrests, as well as the activities in which they

[Haworth co-indexing entry note]: "Pederasts, Prostitutes, and Pickpockets in Paris of the 1870s." Peniston, William A. Co-published simultaneously in *Journal of Homosexuality* (Harrington Park Press, an imprint of The Haworth Press, Inc.) Vol. 41, No. 3/4, 2001, pp. 169-187; and: *Homosexuality in French History and Culture* (ed: Jeffrey Merrick, and Michael Sibalis) Harrington Park Press, an imprint of The Haworth Press, Inc., 2001, pp. 169-187. Single or multiple copies of this article are available for a fee from The Haworth Document Delivery Service [1-800-342-9678, 9:00 a.m. - 5:00 p.m. (EST). E-mail address: getinfo@haworthpressinc.com].

were engaged. Finally, it lists any penalties imposed on them by the law courts. It reveals that most of the men were in their teens, twenties, or thirties, working in unskilled, skilled, clerical, or service positions. Most of them were from the provinces, struggling to make a living and to form friendships and relationships in a difficult urban environment. Sometimes they resorted to prostitution and theft in order to support themselves, but mostly they were just pursuing their own sexual interests.[2]

This article focuses on the extensive network of relationships that revolved around a man by the name of Arthur Dechatillon. His friends and lovers and their associates were involved in several same-sex sexual scandals that were investigated by the police. Their friendships with one another and their sexual relationships with older, wealthier men reveal a variety of experiences. Their contacts with the police demonstrate that these men lived in a dangerous world, subject to interference by the authorities, as well as betrayal, whether intentional or not, by their associates. Despite these hazards, they managed to find one another, to form lasting relationships, and to build a community of support.

Known as La Mogador, the name of a famous nineteenth-century actress, Dechatillon was a 24-year-old waiter from the department of the Aisne in northern France.[3] He first came into contact with the police in May 1875, when he was brought in for questioning about a theft. The police also took into custody 20-year-old Sénateur-Arsène Lebaillif, who lived with Dechatillon, and one of their friends, 19-year-old Théophile-Louis Rousseau. The police found the three of them sleeping together in Dechatillon's apartment. They did not charge them with a crime, however, because they could not characterize the trio's activities as a public offense against decency. Besides, they were more interested in questioning them about their friend, Henri Boquet, a 23-year-old commercial clerk, who, according to the police, had robbed a priest named Delaisne. After the interrogation, the police set Dechatillon, Lebaillif, and Rousseau free but placed them all under surveillance. Boquet, the subject of the original police investigation, was not charged with a crime, most likely because the police were unable to find him.[4]

Several months later, in October 1875, the police arrested Lebaillif for solicitation in the passage Jouffroy and the passage Verdeau in the Ninth Arrondissement, two notorious meeting places for sexual encounters.[5] This time the police charged him with a public offense against decency, and the court sentenced him to six months in prison.[6] A month later the police arrested Rousseau on the boulevard des Italiens with Louis-Adrien Petit, a 19-year-old commercial clerk. According to the police, these two young men were trying to attract the attention of pedestrians "by means of obscenities." They were promptly charged with a public offense against decency and sentenced to four and thirteen months in prison, respectively.[7] The police clearly kept a close watch on these men, especially after they had recorded their names in the ledger.

Boquet's name appeared in the ledger again in March 1878, almost three years later. In this case, he was himself the victim of a theft while staying at the Hôtel de la Côte-d'Or. According to the police, he had picked up a man who threatened him and stole his gold watch.[8] From the point of view of the police, Boquet's sexual behavior led him to steal at the age of twenty-three, when he was probably a male prostitute, but it also exposed him to the same danger, when, as a client, he himself was robbed three years later. The change in role from perpetrator to victim merely confirmed the police's conclusion that "pederasts" were threats to each other and to society.

The ledger does not make it clear whether these cases involved male prostitution or not, but it does imply it. Male prostitution is a difficult subject to study, especially in the nineteenth century, because, unlike female prostitution, it was not regulated by police officers and medical examiners. Consequently, the sources are very vague. In many respects, the authorities did not even acknowledge its existence. They considered female prostitution, on the other hand, a necessary evil, an evil because of its association with the criminal underworld, but a necessary one because of its socially useful function in providing an outlet for men's sexual urges. In order to protect clients from theft, violence, and venereal disease, the police established an entire regulatory system that involved registration of prostitutes, periodic examinations, medical treatments, strict administrative rules, and punishment if those rules were violated. In many respects, the regulatory system was not completely legal, as several critics then and scholars since have pointed out. "In the nineteenth century," Jill Harsin has written, "the control of prostitution became a matter of deliberate decisions to violate systematically the rights of prostitutes as well as women who were merely suspected of prostitution."[9]

Harsin and others have shown that the regulatory system created a new professional category, that of the "public girl" who got caught up in the cycle of police surveillance and harassment, from which she was frequently unable to escape. Not all female prostitutes, however, were registered with the police. Most of them, in fact, were poor working-class women, down on their luck, who resorted to prostitution only temporarily. They moved in and out of the world of prostitution casually, rarely coming to the attention of the police. The police feared these unregistered prostitutes more than the registered ones because they were outside their control. They were always on the alert for suspected prostitutes, and, in their haste to find them, they frequently violated the rights of working-class women found in public. They escaped criticism for their actions because the individuals they arrested were "members of the working class, made vulnerable by their economic powerlessness," and "women ... [whose] legal invisibility cut so deeply" in the society of nineteenth-century France.[10]

Although the authorities suspected certain men of being involved in prostitution, their attitude toward and treatment of those individuals were very different from their surveillance and harrassment of women suspected of prostitution. In the first place, most of the men suspected of prostitution told the police that they were employed as clerks, servants, artisans, or laborers in a variety of ordinary occupations. The police evidently believed them, since they recorded these occupations in their reports. They listed nobody as a "male prostitute," whereas they frequently used the term "public girl" for a working-class woman suspected of female prostitution.[11] In the second place, the police made a sharp distinction between female prostitutes and their clients, but not between male prostitutes and theirs. They referred to both male prostitutes and their clients as "pederasts," suggesting that they were very different kinds of men from those who visited female prostitutes.[12] No doubt many of these men supplemented their meager earnings with money from venal sexual encounters, but others probably indulged their own sexual interests. In any case, it is difficult to tell whether arrests for public offenses against decency involved a male prostitute and his client or merely two men looking for a sexual adventure. In either case, both men were generally treated in the same manner.[13] In the third place, whereas the police routinely violated the civil rights of working-class women suspected of female prostitution, they were much more careful to respect the rights of working-class men. For the most part, they charged working-class men with a misdemeanor and turned them over to the courts. Still, they often felt that the maintenance of public order required the invasion of the private lives of certain individuals, especially if those individuals were engaged in socially unacceptable, albeit not illegal, activities.

In an article on male prostitution in England, Jeffrey Weeks has argued that the social and legal restrictions on same-sex sexual behavior created an environment in which a male homosexual subculture developed. In this subculture, male prostitution played a significant but subordinate role. "The 'deviance' of prostitution," he wrote, "was supplementary to the 'deviance' of homosexuality." Thus, "for the young man who prostituted himself, the choices were effectively between retaining a conventional self-concept . . . or accepting a homosexual identity. . . ." Weeks reasoned that "the more casual the prostitution, the less likely was the individual to identify himself as homosexual or as a prostitute. . . . Conversely, the longer the person stayed in the homosexual subculture, the more likely he was to accept its values and to identify himself as primarily homosexual."[14] In all likelihood, Dechatillon and his friends were so deeply involved in a series of interconnected relationships that they identified not only with one another, but also with a wider community, and this identification was not so much as prostitutes but as pederasts.

Even if some of these men were prostitutes, many of them also maintained ongoing relationships with other men that were clearly not based on monetary gain. Others may have been willing to accept gifts as part of the "dating" ritual without considering themselves prostitutes or their partners clients. Kathy Peiss has described the working-class women in New York City who adopted such an attitude as "charity girls." These "respectable" young women engaged in a variety of sexual activities ranging from flirtation to intercourse in exchange for gifts, treats, or simply a night on the town. The level of sexual intimacy usually, but not always, depended upon the length of time that the women knew the men.[15] Perhaps their male counterparts in Paris and elsewhere should be considered "charity boys": young working-class men who accepted meals, drinks, or an evening's entertainment from interested sexual partners. In most cases, the pursuit of sexual pleasure seemed to be their overriding concern.

Dechatillon's involvement in the world of male prostitution becomes clearer from subsequent entries in the ledger. In October 1876, according to the police, he was the "lover" of François-Joseph Coco, a 17-year-old waiter with whom he probably worked. Known as The Russian Kid, even though he had been born in the department of the Nièvre in Burgundy, Coco was caught performing oral sex on Hippolyte-Michel Lemoine, a 56-year-old hatter, on the quai de la Tournelle. A third person, whose identity remained unknown to the police, managed to elude them.[16] Coco's encounter with Lemoine was probably just a one-time-only meeting involving the exchange of money for sexual favor, although the police were silent on this point. His relationship with Dechatillon, although certainly emotional and sexual, according to the police, was probably economic as well. Perhaps Dechatillon was fixing him up with potential clients and sharing the profits.

Several months later, in early 1877, the police came to an attic apartment in the Eleventh Arrondissement in order to interrogate Dechatillon about his involvement in a case known as the Voyer affair.[17] There they found him sleeping with Coco, whom they also interviewed. Once again, Dechatillon found his privacy violated by the police because they were interested in obtaining information from him.

During his interrogation, Dechatillon told the police that Louis-Marcel Voyer, a 33-year-old former artillery captain known for his Catholic charity work, his musical abilities, and his interest in young men, had had a sexual relationship for over two years with Albert Exmelin, a 20-year-old valet.[18] Exmelin had introduced Voyer to Lebaillif, the former lover of Dechatillon, who had been involved in the Delaisne affair. According to Dechatillon,

Lebaillif had been sexually involved with Voyer during a five-month period in 1875 and 1876. Dechatillon also told the police that Hippolyte-Marie-René David, a 17-year-old engraver, had received fifteen francs from Voyer on three different occasions. Known as The Little White Girl, David would later be listed as the lover of Dechatillon in another entry in the police ledger.[19] Yet another friend, 18-year-old Louis Pelletier, had also been paid by Voyer for sexual favors. He was living with 20-year-old Edouard Gallienne at 28 rue de la Parcheminerie, in a building where several men whose names appeared in the ledger lived.[20] Gallienne had a prior conviction for masturbating Henri Lecomte, 52, a man of independent means, in May 1876 outside the Café des Ambassadeurs on the Champs-Elysées.[21] Finally, according to Dechatillon, Rudolphe-Frédéric Langer, a 23-year-old bellhop, the last man involved in this affair, had been sodomized by Voyer on four different occasions and, as a result, had contracted a venereal disease.

This case obviously involved male prostitution. Voyer, the older man from the upper class, was clearly paying these five working-class men for sex. The age and class differences between them reenforced the social and economic inequalities that made male prostitution an option for them. The five young men obviously knew one another and had other mutual friends. They were probably little more than friends, although both Lebaillif and David had a close personal relationship with Dechatillon, who was also intimate with Coco. Nevertheless, these relationships did not preclude other associations with older, wealthier men, like Voyer, Lemoine, and Lecomte, who sought casual encounters on the city streets or arranged temporary affairs in their private homes. In the Voyer affair, none of the young men was charged with a crime because their activities took place in private at Voyer's residence on the rue de Beaune in the Seventh Arrondissement. Nevertheless, the police placed all of them under surveillance, including Voyer, and they subsequently arrested several of them for public offenses against decency. Because of Voyer's social prominence (he was a good friend of Madame MacMahon), his arrest for a public offense against decency in 1880 would cause a public scandal covered in all of the Parisian newspapers.[22]

Dechatillon's relationship with the police was quite complicated. He was frequently questioned and, in order to avoid a prison term, was willing to give them information that he thought might be of interest to them. In addition to identifying the young men involved in the Voyer affair, on 4 March 1877 he also identified the sculptor Gesler, the actor Léopold, and the clerk Vigneau as "pederasts," implying that they were clients of adolescent prostitutes. Since clients, as well as prostitutes, were of interest to the police, the names of these three men were duly recorded in the ledger, but, in this case, the police were unable to obtain any further information about them.[23] As an informer, Dechatillon's statements were not always very helpful. The police, on the one hand, believed that they could coerce the information out of Dechatillon and others through intimidation or promises of better treatment. Dechatillon, on the other hand, believed that he could manipulate the police by giving them just enough information to satisfy their curiosity, but not enough to get his friends in serious trouble. This combination of coercion and manipulation did not always work to the advantage of either the police or the men arrested.[24]

The next entry for Dechatillon is dated three weeks later, on 26 March 1877. On that date, the police arrested his lover, François Coco, and a 17-year-old groom named Alfred Reeves in the passage des Panoramas, another site of many arrests for public offenses against decency.[25] A third person, identified as Ernest Duquesne, a 16-year-old driver, escaped the police but was subsequently arrested on 20 April. Along with Duquesne, the police also questioned four other young men, whom they eventually released, after listing them as "pederasts."[26] The three main characters in this case, Coco, Reeves, and Duquesne, were accused of accosting men in the commercial arcade. In addition to this public offense against decency, Coco was suspected of stealing a pipe from Monsieur Bornet de Coton and a gold watch from Mademoiselle Durville. The pipe was found in the possession of Ernest Giblin, whom the police arrested on 27 March but later released due to lack of evidence. The watch had been pawned for twenty francs by Dechatillon. The police first questioned Dechatillon on 27 March and then arrested him on 7 May.[27]

From the point of view of the police, Coco was guilty not only of prostituting himself by soliciting on the street, but also of stealing small items from his clients and other citizens. If he could not earn enough money from prostitution, they assumed, he would resort to theft. Dechatillon, his friend and lover, not only profited from Coco's business transactions but also helped him find clients and dispose of stolen merchandise. Nor did these two men act alone. They both knew others engaged in similar criminal activities. Together they formed a community that the police felt obliged to watch closely.

The court sentenced Coco and Duquesne to eight months in prison, the former for theft and a public offense against decency and the latter for two public offenses against decency and for resisting arrest. It sentenced Dechatillon to four months in prison for complicity in the theft and Reeves to four months in prison for a public offense against decency.[28] This sentence was not, however, the end of Dechatillon's troubles with the police.

After his prison term, Dechatillon returned to Paris and took up residence with René David, who had already been implicated in the Voyer affair. On 10 November 1877 David and two 16-year-old tailors, Georges-Louis Gallet and Léon-Frédéric Rousselle, confessed in an interview with the police to having had sex with Félix Brochad. A 20-year-old grocery clerk, Georges-Louis

Mullot, served as the informer. The police issued a warrant for the arrest of Brochad for incitement of youths to debauchery, although these young men were hardly novices. In any event, the police did not follow up on this case, perhaps because they were unable to find Brochad. Instead, they released the four young men without charging them with a crime because the acts they had committed had not taken place in public.[29]

Three of these young men, however, soon came into contact with the police again, all for public offenses against decency. On 15 December 1877 the police arrested David, Dechatillon's lover, along with a neighbor, 21-year-old Alfred-Joseph-Emile Beauvisage, whose nickname was The Terror. The arresting officer said that he had seen these two individuals, along with several others, on the boulevard Montmartre near the passage Jouffroy, where they were provoking passers-by with "obscene gestures" and "effeminate allures." From the passage Jouffroy, they proceeded to the Café des Ambassadeurs near the Champs Elysées, and there they entered one of the nearby urinals. Inside the urinal, David displayed his buttocks, while Beauvisage kept watch. Beauvisage, however, was apparently not a good watchdog, for it was in this state of disarray that the arresting officer finally caught the two young troublemakers. The court sentenced them to a year in prison and a fine of sixteen francs.[30]

The arresting officer's allusion to David's and Beauvisage's "effeminate allures" indicates that, in the opinion of police, male prostitution and male same-sex sexuality were inseparable from effeminacy in men, which they associated with physical, intellectual, and moral weaknesses. It was, from their perspective, partly responsible for the military defeat of France by Prussia in 1870-71. One police officer, referring to male prostitutes and their clients during the Second Empire, wrote that they "all have, as a distinctive sign, a feminine appearance, enticing ways, and mincing manners that they exaggerate to a ridiculous degree."[31] As evidence, he cited their many feminized nicknames, a practice that continued in the Third Republic. For example, David himself, as already noted, was known as The Little White Girl. Two of his friends in the Voyer affair were called The Girl from Nice and The Girl with Flaxen Hair, while his acquaintances in the Brochad affair were known as The Charmer, Georgette, and The Negress.[32]

The members of the male homosexual subculture used these nicknames and adopted effeminate mannerisms for a variety of reasons. Some of them no doubt linked their sexual behavior to an effeminate personality, which they considered a fundamental identity. Others probably used effeminacy as a way of signalling their sexual availability to potential partners. Male prostitutes may have appropriated these nicknames and mannerisms because they thought that their clients expected them to be effeminate. However, many clients expected them to act as men in order to contrast with their own effeminacy, because they wanted to reproduce in their own relationships the sharp distinction between masculine and feminine behavior that was part of the separate sphere ideology of the nineteenth century. Others probably used the nicknames and the mannerisms in a humorous way to make fun of the dominant cultural representations of masculine and feminine behavior.[33]

According to Randolph Trumbach and Theo van der Meer, such effeminacy indicates the development of a new concept of same-sex sexuality as a third gender that began to appear within the male homosexual subcultures of the eighteenth century.[34] Other historians disagree, claiming that effeminacy was mostly linked to the aristocracy in the eighteenth century and that it became associated with same-sex sexuality only in the nineteenth century.[35] Gert Hekma suggests that the model of the "queen" was only one of many different kinds of same-sex sexual behavior that existed throughout the eighteenth, nineteenth, and twentieth centuries.[36] Whether these young men adopted effeminacy as a serious identification or as a cultural signifier or as a mocking representation bordering on "camp," they, nevertheless, clearly associated it with same-sex sexuality in a much more positive way than the police and the public did.

The two tailors in the Brochad affair, Gallet and Rousselle, were arrested on 29 January 1878, just two months after their initial encounter with the police. They were accused of accosting men in the passage Jouffroy and the passage des Panoramas. The police had undoubtedly kept an eye out for them for quite some time, waiting for the right moment to arrest them and charge them with a crime. The court sentenced them to prison terms of six months and fines of sixteen francs.[37]

The "innocent" witness in the Brochad affair, Mullot, was actually not all that innocent. He had already been convicted in 1876 for his involvement in the affair of the Bains du Gymnase, a bathhouse on the rue du Faubourg Poissonnière, the street separating the Ninth from the Tenth Arrondissement.[38] That affair began on 14 April with the arrest of seven individuals in the Galerie d'Orléans in the Palais-Royal. Antoine Lampre, a 22-year-old day laborer, was the oldest, and Eugène-Ferdinand Malherbe, a 14-year-old waiter who lived with Lampre, was the youngest. The others were George-Alphonse Maillot, Jules-Emile-François Noget, Marie-Aimé-Georges Sarciron, Pierre Serré, and, of course, Georges-Louis Mullot. The police charged all of them, except for Noget, with public offenses against decency for solicitation, and the court convicted and sentenced them to one to six months in prison.

Noget had escaped the criminal justice system by telling the police that these individuals, whom he identified as male prostitutes, frequently took their clients to the Bains du Gymnase. He also identified five individuals named Lasenne, Lutheroth, Marlet, Rouffle, and Rousselot as clients of the bathhouse and hosts of private receptions for "pederasts." With this information, the police raided the bathhouse the very next day and arrested its owner, Manuel-Prosper Brunel, his wife, and stepdaughter; his assistant, Ferdinand Bureau, and his wife, Léontine; and Adolphe Adam, another attendant in the bathhouse. The prosecutor dropped the charges against the women, but he indicted the men for incitement of youths to debauchery. The court dutifully convicted them. Bureau and Adam, the employees, spent six months in prison and paid a 50-franc fine, while the owner, Brunel, spent two years in prison and paid a 200-franc fine. With reference to this case, the press declared, "Decidedly these are times of scandalous affairs!"[39]

Another commentator on this case was Georges Herelle, the future translator of Gabriel d'Annunzio. He included the Bains du Gymnase in his list of special places for same-sex sexual encounters. "I have visited this bathhouse several times," he wrote.

> I have heard it said that tricksters often arranged rendezvous there, that patrons knew them well, that boys were there, etc. Actually I have seen several times young boys waiting there for someone in the corridor . . . [and] I have heard suspicious sounds. One day a boy asked me if I needed someone to hand me my dressing gown, and as he handed it to me, he touched me in a significant manner. Finally, on another day, someone made some propositions to me by opening the door that connected the adjacent cabins.[40]

The bathhouses of Paris were well-known meeting places for men interested in same-sex sexual activities. Originally established for purposes of personal hygiene, they served an essential need, especially for members of the working classes, who often had no place else to go to wash themselves. The bourgeoisie and the aristocracy also frequented them, although not so much for hygienic reasons as for social purposes. Whether public or private, catering to the upper or lower classes, bathhouses often offered services other than washing or provided places for activities other than cleaning. For their patrons, bathhouses offered some degree of privacy for a variety of sexual activities that were more difficult to pursue on the street. Sometimes the sexual encounters in bathhouses involved prostitutes and clients or two men out for a sexual adventure. Sometimes these encounters were brief and anonymous, and at other times they developed into lasting friendships or intimate relationships. Occasionally they involved good friends or lovers who had no place else to go.[41] In this particular case, according to the police, the patrons of the Bains du Gymnase were male prostitutes and their clients, and the owner and his workers were deliberately catering to these kinds of customers.

Rousselot, one of the patrons, whose nickname was Rousselotte, the feminized form of his last name, was already well known to the police because of his involvement in the affair of the Republican Guards in February 1875. At the center of this investigation were two soldiers named Villaron and Velfringe stationed at the Caserne Tournon, a military barracks on the outskirts of Paris. They had reportedly had sexual relations with the following individuals: Edouard de Boisseuil, baron de la Roche, an archivist; 28-year-old Frédéric Boullié, whose profession was not listed; and Louis Haumond, a 33-year-old day laborer. Villaron had also been sexually involved with Claude-Marie Desmures, a 38-year-old hairdresser, and Jules-Charles-Maximillien Ménétier, a 28-year-old glove salesman. According to the police, Desmures and Ménétier had apparently argued over Villaron. All of them were frequent visitors to Rousselot's boarding house on the rue Greneta in the Second Arrondissement, where Rousselot not only hosted several parties for them, but also rented them rooms for short periods of time. He later sold this building to Lasenne, another patron of the Bains du Gymnase.[42]

Although the police did not say so in so many words, they apparently thought that Rousselot was running a male brothel of sorts. They believed that he was allowing his friends, some of them quite wealthy and others relatively poor, to use his boarding house as a meeting place. There they could privately encounter other men, especially soldiers, about whom a popular fantasy had already developed. According to the head of the vice squad during the Second Empire, houses of prostitution specializing in virgins, workers, or soldiers sprang up all over Paris, because "pederasts," as they grew older, developed obsessive tastes for particular kinds of men. "When the rich *amateur* has reached a certain age," he wrote, "his tastes become difficult to satisfy, [and] his sick brain forms an ideal without which there is no longer any possible pleasure."[43] This particular officer would have recognized Rousselot and his friends as "the rich *amateurs*," and Villaron and Velfringe, the soldiers, as their ideal type of man.

Also implicated in this scandal were Eugène Dumont, 21, known as The Brunette Girl, and Louis Nesme, a valet. Dumont was a street hawker who obtained military medals from Villaron and Velfringe and then peddled them on the city streets. Most likely, then, Villaron and Velfringe were trying to supplement their military wages by selling medals to Dumont and sexual favors to the other men involved in this case. However, they may have simply found a small group of friends with whom to pass the time while on leave from the garrison.[44]

The subject of same-sex sexual behavior in the French army has not been studied, even though it was considered one of the "privileged sites of pederasty."[45] Other historians have studied the phenomenon in other countries and at other times.[46] Gert Hekma, for example, has found that same-sex sexual behavior was the most common sexual crime prosecuted by the military authorities in the Dutch army in the nineteenth century. He explained this behavior by postulating that soldiers, being at their sexual prime and living in an all-male environment, had few sexual outlets other than contract with one another. He also believed that this kind of behavior had little or no impact upon the sexual identity of the soldiers.[47] In another study, Jeffrey Weeks pointed out that the all-male society of the English Brigade of Guards was often an entry point into the world of male prostitution. In his analysis, the Guardsmen found it easy to make a few extra pounds through prostitution because upper-class clients found the Guardsmen attractive since they associated their duties with masculine behavior. In other words, the clients were looking for what they considered "masculine" men, and the soldiers fit the bill.[48]

This analysis tends to confirm the opinion of the head of the Parisian vice squad during the Second Empire. He believed that "with military men, the antiphysical tastes are no more common than with any other class in society," but that "a soldier, whose moral sense is faulty, rarely lets an occasion escape that presents itself to him of procuring a little money." Military men were frequently involved in male prostitution, not so much out of personal preference but simply out of greed.[49] In the affair of the Republican Guards of 1875, the soldiers, Villaron and Velfringe, seemed to have been interested in making a few extra francs, but the clients, Rousselot and his friends, seemed to have been interested in forming a social circle that could meet in their own apartments as well as the bathhouses of Paris.

Another scandal involving same-sex sexual activity in the army centered on Voyer, the ex-captain of the artillery who was associated with Dechatillon's friends in 1877. This second scandal made it into the press and an annual series on celebrated court cases.[50] It began on 18 June 1880 when the police arrested Voyer and a soldier named Louis-Nicolas Megnin on the avenue du Polygone near the Fort de Vincennes. The police officers declared that they had seen Voyer "brushing against Megnin's pants in an indecent manner." They also told the court that they had received several complaints against him for his "bad habits" and that they had, consequently, placed him under surveillance.[51]

Voyer claimed that the police had completely misinterpreted his actions. He told the court that he had met Megnin, whom he already knew as a cadet in the artillery school, after dinner at a restaurant in Vincennes. Realizing that he was being followed and fearing that he was in danger, he thought that he would be safer in the company of the young soldier. When it began to rain, they stopped under a tree, and he took the artillery man's hand because Megnin was afraid.

Upon hearing this explanation, Megnin immediately adopted it and recanted his original confession to the police, in which he said that Voyer had indeed made an indecent proposal to him. He claimed that this original confession had been given under threats, an excuse frequently heard in court. Given the police's reputation for coercive methods, this excuse should not be dismissed lightly, although the presiding judge did not want to hear it.[52]

The judge also did not like Voyer's explanation because it sounded unpatriotic. "What you say there," he chided Voyer, "does not flatter the French army. Afraid! A soldier? And of whom?" Following the defeat of the Franco-Prussian War, this judge was not going to allow some "pervert" to defame brave French soldiers. Besides, even if Megnin had been afraid, Voyer's behavior was inappropriate and unmanly. "Between men," the judge continued, "one does not take another's hand in order to reassure him."[53]

Other witnesses gave good reports of Voyer's character. One friend, an ex-soldier from Voyer's former regiment and a police officer, said, "Never have I seen men coming to [Voyer's] house, but I have seen women."[54] In his opinion, Voyer's relationships with women must have been sexual and, therefore, acceptable, even though they would have been illicit, since Voyer was not married. Such heterosexual behavior would have been typical for, even expected of, an officer. Finally, Georges Bergeron, a medical expert for the police department, testified that Voyer had absolutely no physical traces of any "shameful habits," such as an elongated penis or an infundibuliform anus.[55]

Doctors like Bergeron had been using medical reports to establish themselves as experts on a variety of subjects, such as mental health, penal reform, and criminal and sexual behavior. During the middle years of the nineteenth century, Ambroise Tardieu was the leading French medical expert on "pederasty." In his *Medical-Legal Study of Offenses against Morals*, first published in 1857, he devoted considerable attention to the physical signs of sodomy and pederasty, but he also claimed to be able to deduce from these physical signs the mental and moral characteristics of the sodomite or pederast. Until the 1880s, Tardieu and his disciples dominated the medical discourse on pederasty in France, and they also exerted their influence on the criminal justice system by instigating medical examinations of many of the suspects arrested by the police and tried by the courts. Usually the medical reports supported the prosecution's arguments, but in Voyer's case, the defense used it in its own presentation.[56]

After hearing all of these witnesses, the Court of Criminal Corrections acquitted the two defendants. The Court of Appeals, however, overturned the decision. It felt that the testimony of the arresting officers and the initial testimony of Megnin far outweighed Voyer's defense, Megnin's retraction, the character witnesses, and the medical report. It consequently sentenced Voyer to a prison term of six months and a fine of 200 francs. Megnin received a prison term of three months and a fine of sixteen francs.[57]

Voyer had clearly been the subject of a police investigation for a number of years. The police pursued him on and off until they were able to catch him in a compromising situation. At first they simply gathered information from the young men with whom he was associated. Several of these young men they arrested at later dates, but in 1877 the police did not have enough evidence to charge Voyer with any kind of crime. In 1878, just a year later, they placed him under surveillance again, this time for his part in a duel involving his brother and Paul Bloch.[58] This case apparently had nothing to do with "pederasty," but into the ledger the names of these three men went. From the point of view of the police, the duel was just another sign of Voyer's illicit activities. Only in 1880 were the police able to charge him with a public offense against decency. Unfortunately for them, the lower court acquitted him, but the police, along with the prosecution, were unwilling to settle for this verdict. They appealed to the upper court and managed to convince it of Voyer's guilt. In this way, after all their work, they made sure that he was convicted.

The cases discussed above demonstrate that Dechatillon was at the center of a group of men, many of whom were prostitutes and thieves. All of them, whether prostitutes, clients, or sexual adventurers, came into contact, either directly or indirectly, with the police at one point or another. Many of them were arrested two or three times, sometimes only to be released after questioning, and other times to be tried and sentenced by the courts. Most of them were willing to give the police, or were pressured into revealing, information about other men, usually their friends, associates, or clients. They did so when they believed that their cooperation with the police would get them out of their own predicaments. In some cases, it helped them avoid a prison term, but in most cases, it did not.

The police diligently recorded all of the information gathered from these men. Sometimes they pursued the information vigorously, as in the affair of the Bains du Gymnase. Sometimes they merely noted names and addresses, hoping to catch the men in a compromising situation at a later date, as they did in the case of Voyer. All in all the police kept a close watch on the activities of "pederasts," especially when those activities took place in public areas like the *grands boulevards* and the commercial arcades. The research, surveillance, and harassment of "pederasts" were part of the police's attempt to maintain social and political order, as well as sexual and gender order, which seemed so precarious in the early years of the Third Republic.

Many historians and commentators have assumed that the 1791 repeal of the ancient law against sodomy ushered in an era of toleration. Theoretically, before the Revolution, the law of Valentinian II, Theodosius, and Arcadius from 390 was still on the books in the southern provinces, whereas the *Institutes of Saint Louis* from 1272-73 expressed the legal customs of the provinces in the north.[59] In actuality, in the eighteenth century, the police rarely enforced these laws, which called for the death penalty for sodomites. Instead, they developed a policy of surveillance and harassment which treated same-sex sexual behavior as a misdemeanor.[60] In the nineteenth century, they continued to keep under surveillance and to harass men who engaged in such behavior by interpreting broadly the new laws against public offenses against decency, incitement of youth to debauchery, and sexual assaults, and applying these laws loosely.[61]

The young working-class men who created the male homosexual subculture of Paris in the 1870s, especially the friends and associates of Dechatillon, lived, worked, and socialized together. Dechatillon himself, over a two and a half year period, lived with Lebaillif, Coco, and David. As waiters, he and Coco probably worked together. His friends and neighbors included Boquet, Rousseau, and Beauvisage. His lovers' acquaintances included the young men in the Delaisne, the Voyer, and the Brochad affairs. These men, in turn, had relationships with one another, involving them in a number of other cases, such as the affairs of the Bains du Gymnase and the Republican Guards. Their relationships were complex, involving money, desire, love, and friendship, and forming a series of interconnected social circles upon which they could rely for emotional and financial support.

Historians like Colin Simpson, Lewis Chester, David Leitch, and Montgomery Hyde have dismissed such young working-class men in other countries as mere prostitutes who engaged in same-sex sexual activities only for monetary gain. They have assumed that their association with each other was only temporary, involving no permanent identity.[62] This study of working-class youths in Paris in the 1870s has shown that the networks of relationships developed by these men fulfilled several important functions. As friends, lovers, and acquaintances, they chose to associate with one another for emotional support, entertainment, and other reasons. As co-workers and neighbors, they either recognized one another as kindred spirits or helped one another find jobs and housing. They formed a community based on emotional ties, financial support, common experiences, and shared identities. In many respects, these men were the ones who created and sustained the male homosexual subculture of Paris throughout the nineteenth century.

In addition to their relationships with one another, many of these young men also confessed to having had relations with other men, usually older and wealthier than themselves, who gave them gifts or money in exchange for sexual favors. These older men, usually in their thirties, forties, or fifties, included a priest, a hatter, a man of independent means, an ex-captain in the artillery, a sculptor, and an actor, as well as a clerk, a hairdresser, and a salesman. Some of these older men were from the upper classes, but others had quite modest occupations. Like Lemoine's encounter with Coco, the liaisons of these men with these youths were usually brief, casual, one-time adventures, but Voyer's relationships with his young men all extended over a period of several months or even years. Whereas a few of these older, wealthier men were arrested and convicted of a crime, most of them were merely investigated by the police. The police were clearly suspicious of the suspected clients of male prostitutes, as much as the prostitutes themselves, both of whom they considered "pederasts," but the position of the clients in society allowed them a little more protection.

The elites have been the focus of much of the research on same-sex sexual behavior in the past. They were the ones, after all, who articulated new sexual identities at the end of the nineteenth century. They based these identities upon the philosophies of ancient Greece, the humanistic traditions of the Renaissance, and the scientific theories of the modern world. Since they were frequently on the periphery of the networks of relationships that constituted the male homosexual subcultures of Paris and other cities, they did not always share the same attitudes toward their behavior as the members of the subcultures. Hence, an analysis of their attitudes is only part of the story. The other part, which has not received as much attention as it should, is the construction of communities by young working-class men like Dechatillon and his friends.

NOTES

1. APP, BB6, Pédérastes et divers. On the police, see Louis Canler, *Mémoires de Canler, ancien chef du service de sûreté* (Paris, 1968), 264-95; Felix Carlier, *La Prostitution antiphysique*, ed. Dominique Fernandez (Paris, 1981); and William A. Peniston, "'Pederasts and Others': A Social History of Male Homosexuals in the Early Years of the French Third Republic," PhD dissertation, University of Rochester, 1997, 40-85.
2. Peniston, "Pederasts and Others," 86-205.
3. The actress was Céleste de Chabrillan (1824-1909), who took the name Mogador from a city in Algeria.
4. APP, BB6, #594-6 and #839-40. In these entries, the name appears as Buquet or Buguet.
5. Peniston, "Pederasts and Others," 206-41.
6. APP, BB6, #679.
7. Ibid., #728-9.
8. Ibid., #1477. In this entry, the name is Henri Boquet.
9. Jill Harsin, *Policing Prostitution in Nineteenth-Century Paris* (Princeton, 1985), 57.
10. Ibid., xviii.
11. Peniston, "Pederasts and Others," 86-144.
12. On the meaning of the word "pederast," see Claude Courouve, *Vocabulaire de l'homosexualité masculine* (Paris, 1985), 169-78.
13. On male prostitution, see H. Montgomery Hyde, *The Cleveland Street Scandal* (New York, 1976); Colin Simpson, Lewis Chester, and David Leitch, *The Cleveland*

Street Affair (Boston, 1976); and Jeffrey Weeks, "Inverts, Perverts, and Mary-Annes: Male Prostitution and the Regulation of Homosexuality in England in the Nineteenth and Early Twentieth Centuries," in *Hidden from History: Reclaiming the Gay and Lesbian Past*, ed. Martin Bauml Duberman et al. (New York, 1989), 195-211.

14. Weeks, "Inverts," 210-1.

15. Kathy Peiss, " 'Charity Girls' and City Pleasures: Historical Notes on Working-Class Sexuality, 1880-1920," in *Passion and Power: Sexuality in History*, ed. Kathy Peiss and Christina Simmons (Philadelphia, 1989), 57-69. See also Peiss, *Cheap Amusement: Working Women and Leisure in Turn-of-the-Century New York* (Philadelphia, 1986).

16. APP, BB6, #995-6.

17. Ibid., #1058-67.

18. Christian Gury, *L'Honneur musical d'un capitaine homosexuel en 1880: De Courteline à Proust* (Paris, 1999).

19. APP, BB6, #1376-80 and #1384-5.

20. Peniston, "Pederasts and Others," 162-3.

21. APP, BB6, #854-5.

22. Gury, *Honneur musical.*

23. APP, BB6, #1111-3.

24. Benjamin F. Martin, *Crime and Criminal Justice Under the Third Republic: The Shame of Marianne* (Baton Rouge, 1990), 39-124.

25. Peniston, "Pederasts and Others," 206-41.

26. APP, BB6, #1126-9, 1159-61, 1177. The four young men were named Besserat, Dunessey, Renault, and Stodel.

27. Ibid.

28. Ibid.

29. Ibid., #1376-80.

30. Ibid., #1384-5. See also *Gazette des Tribunaux*, 17 January 1878.

31. Carlier, *Prostitution antiphysique*, 120.

32. The Girl from Nice was Langer; The Girl with Flaxen Hair was Pelletier. APP, BB6, #1058-67. The Charmer was Gallet, Georgette was Mullot, and The Negress was Rousselle. Ibid., #1376-80.

33. Weeks, "Inverts," 205-6.

34. See Randolph Trumbach, "The Birth of the Queen: Sodomy and the Emergence of Gender Equality in Modern Culture, 1660-1750," in *Hidden from History*, 129-40; and Theo van der Meer, "Sodomy and the Pursuit of a Third Sex in the Early Modern Period," in *Third Sex, Third Gender: Beyond Sexual Dimorphism in Culture and History*, ed. Gilbert Herdt (New York, 1994), 137-212.

35. Alan Sinfield, *The Wilde Century: Effeminacy, Oscar Wilde and the Queer Moment* (New York, 1994).

36. Gert Hekma, "Sodomites, Platonic Lovers, Contrary Lovers: The Backgrounds of the Modern Homosexual," in *The Pursuit of Sodomy: Male Homosexuality in Renaissance and Enlightenment Europe*, ed. Kent Gerard and Gert Hekma (New York, 1989), 433-55; and idem., "Wrong Lovers in the Nineteenth-Century Netherlands," *Journal of Homosexuality* 13 (1986-87): 43-56.

37. APP, BB6, #1411-2.

38. Ibid., #807-19.

39. *Gazette des Tribunaux*, 18 June 1876.

40. Georges Herelle, *Anecdotes contemporaines. Ex diariis, 1858-1889*, Bibliothèque Municipale de Troyes, Ms 3395-6.

41. Michael D. Sibalis, "Defining Masculinity in Fin-de-Siècle France: Sexual Anxiety and the Emergence of the Homosexual," *Proceedings of the Annual Meeting of the Western Society for French History* 25 (1998): 247-256; and George Chauncey, *Gay New York: Gender, Urban Culture, and the Making of the Gay Male World, 1890-1940* (New York, 1994), 207-25. See also Julia Csergo, *Liberté, égalité, propreté: La Morale de l'hygiène au XIXe siècle* (Paris, 1988).

42. APP, BB6, #551-60.

43. Carlier, *Prostitution antiphysique*, 182.

44. APP, BB6, #551-60.

45. The phrase is from Christian Bonellos thesis, but he applied it to the asylums and the prisons of France. See Bonello, "Discours médical sur l'homosexualité en France au XIXe siècle," Thèse de doctorat de 3ème cycle, Université de Paris VII, 1984, 186-217.

46. Arthur N. Gilbert, "Buggery and the British Navy, 1700-1861," *Journal of Social History* 10 (1976-77): 72-98; George Chauncey, Jr., "Christian Brotherhood or Sexual Perversion? Homosexual Identities and the Construction of Sexual Boundaries in the World War I Era," in *Hidden from History*, 294-317; and Allan Bérubé, "Marching to a Different Drummer: Lesbian and Gay GIs in World War II," in *Hidden from History*, 383-94.

47. Gert Hekma, "Homosexual Behavior in the Nineteenth-Century Dutch Army," *Journal of the History of Sexuality* 2 (1991): 266-88.

48. Weeks, "Inverts," 203.

49. Carlier, *Prostitution antiphysique*, 182.

50. *Gazette des Tribunaux*, 31 July, 23 September, and 20 November 1880; and Albert Bataille, *Causes criminelles et mondaines* (Paris, 1881), 150-61. See also Gury, *Honneur musical.*

51. Bataille, *Causes criminelles*, 151-3.

52. Martin, *Crime and Criminal Justice*, 39-124.

53. Bataille, *Causes criminelles*, 155-7.

54. Ibid., 154-5.

55. Ibid., 158.

56. Ambroise Tardieu, *Etude médico-légale sur les attentats aux moeurs* (Paris, 1857, 1858, 1859, 1862, 1867, 1873, 1878). On Tardieu and his critics, see Bonello, "Discours médical," 77-118; Robert A. Nye, "Sex Difference and Male Homosexuality in French Medical Discourse, 1830-1930," *Bulletin of the History of Medicine* 63 (1989): 32-51; and Vernon A. Rosario II, "Pointy Penises, Fashion Crimes, and Hysterical Mollies: The Pederasts' Inversions," in *Homosexuality in Modern France*, ed. Jeffrey Merrick and Bryant T. Ragan, Jr. (New York, 1996), 146-76.

57. Bataille, *Causes criminelles*, 159-61.

58. APP, BB6, #1448-9.

59. Marc Daniel, "Histoire de la législation concernant l'homosexualité," *Arcadie* 8 (1961): 618-27, 9 (1962): 10-29.

60. Michel Rey, "Les Sodomites Parisiens au XVIIIe siècle," Maîtrise d'histoire, Université de Paris VIII-Vincennes, 1979-80; idem., "Police and Sodomy in Eighteenth-Century Paris: From Sin to Disorder," in *Pursuit of Sodomy*, 129-46; idem., "Parisian Homosexuals Create a Lifestyle, 1700-1750: The Police Archives," *Eighteenth-Century Life* 9 (1985): 179-91.

61. Michael Sibalis, "The Regulation of Male Homosexuality in Revolutionary and Napoleonic France, 1789-1815," in *Homosexuality in Modern France*, 80-101; and Peniston, "Pederasts and Others," 40-85.

62. Simpson et al., *Cleveland Street Affair*; Hyde, *Cleveland Street Scandal*; and Hekma, "Wrong Lovers." Weeks and Chauncey give more nuanced interpretations of working-class same-sex sexual behavior in "Inverts" and "Christian Brotherhood."

Drames d'amour des pédérastes: Male Same-Sex Sexuality in Belle Epoque Print Culture

Michael L. Wilson

In his sweeping 1889 survey of "vice" in Paris, the social observer and hack writer Ali Coffignon devoted several chapters to an attempt to explain why, "in the past twenty years, pederasty has gained so much ground in Europe." To confirm the menace of this growing phenomenon and to guarantee his broader conclusions, Coffignon offered a personal anecdote. One of his "intimate friends" was co-owner of a building in the rue Monge to which he paid only fitful attention until he heard that one tenant, a vendor of fried potatoes, had installed a piano and acquired an all-male clientele that he allowed to dance until two in the morning. It was "impossible to know" what occurred inside the establishment, since "each evening, the shutters were closed, the windows blocked, and the door covered by curtains." Shocked by this attempt to "revolutionize" not only his building but also the neighborhood, Coffignon's friend appealed to the authorities for help in removing the undesirable tenant but, as the police reminded him, "All that is not forbidden [by law] is permitted." Desperate but unwilling to resort to violence, the unhappy landlord was forced to pay his tenant a considerable sum to move elsewhere.[1]

While we may have reason to be skeptical of both the veracity and the moral of Coffignon's brief tale, his anecdote is emblematic of the difficulties of trying to reconstruct popular understandings of male same-sex sexuality in the late nineteenth and early twentieth centuries. An impressive body of scholarly literature has greatly enlarged and clarified our own understanding of male

[Haworth co-indexing entry note]: "*Drames d'amour des pédérastes*: Male Same-Sex Sexuality in Belle Epoque Print Culture." Wilson, Michael L. Co-published simultaneously in *Journal of Homosexuality* (Harrington Park Press, an imprint of The Haworth Press, Inc.) Vol. 41, No. 3/4, 2001, pp. 189-200; and: *Homosexuality in French History and Culture* (ed: Jeffrey Merrick, and Michael Sibalis) Harrington Park Press, an imprint of The Haworth Press, Inc., 2001, pp. 189-200. Single or multiple copies of this article are available for a fee from The Haworth Document Delivery Service [1-800-342-9678, 9:00 a.m. - 5:00 p.m. (EST). E-mail address: getinfo@haworthpressinc.com].

same-sex sexuality in this period by focusing on medical discourse, the legal-juridical system, and canonical French literature.[2] Outside of elite discourses, and despite impressive efforts by social historians, however, much about same-sex sexuality in this period remains "impossible to know," because it was barely discerned by contemporaries and its traces are fragmentary and scattered, often noted only by hostile and outraged opponents.[3] My aim in this essay is to suggest some directions for further research. More particularly, in examining a period that saw the triumph of the mass-circulation newspaper and a crisis of overproduction in book publishing, I advocate a focus on print culture as offering cultural historians our best chance of moving beyond official and elite sources to discover how "popular" understandings of same-sex sexuality were articulated, shaped, and circulated.[4]

As my use of Coffignon suggests, we might profitably begin our investigations with guidebooks to metropolitan life. The guides to touristic Paris are of little use for our purposes. Starting in the 1890s, they increasingly include mention of the institutions of the lesbian subculture, but even those volumes explicitly promising to reveal the hidden erotic delights of Paris-Babylon omit mention of male same-sex activities. Instead, we have to turn to what might be termed works of popular sociology focusing on the urban underworld, popular guides to the Parisian "lower depths." The three representative and well-known titles that I examine here are Coffignon's *Corruption in Paris* (1889) and Charles Virmaître's *Streets and Brothels* (1882) and *Impure Paris* (1900).[5] These three works have as their major focus the revelation to a supposedly ignorant audience of "the places of debauchery in the capital" and the burgeoning world of prostitution.[6] Prostitution was accorded great prominence in the imagination and social relations of nineteenth-century Paris and was the focus of a variety of official, medical, legal, and artistic discourses.[7] It is hardly surprising, then, that it is under the sign of prostitution–a potent symbol of the vagaries of sexuality, commerce, and modernity–that we find extensive investigation of another marginal but highly charged form of sexual commerce: "pederasty." The association of same-sex sexuality with crime or criminality is, of course, very ancient. The association with prostitution is seemingly more recent but by this point commonplace. The basic outlines of the identification between prostitution and pederasty were formally established in two memoirs written by former officials of the Paris police, Louis Canler and Félix Carlier.[8] In both memoirs pederasty was identified as a major social problem, and the two texts are marked by a consistent effort to explain the phenomenon of pederasty as the inverted double of prostitution.[9]

The influence of Canler and Carlier on the guides to the underworld was quite direct. Not only did the authors acknowledge their debt to the writings of the police officials, but they aspired to a similar level of expertise and "insider" knowledge. They listed the many terms used to designate pederasts in slang, they detailed the settings and professions in which pederasts were most commonly to be found, and they offered suggestions on how to spot a pederast. Both writers were adamant in their identification of pederasty as a source of intense social disruption that overturned the most fundamental social hierarchies:

> It is no exaggeration to say that pederasts of all nations form a sort of freemasonry.... The shared vice effaces all social differences. The master and the manservant are on the same footing; the millionaire and the beggar fraternize; the functionary and the repeat offender exchange their ignoble caresses.[10]

Coffignon went even further in his emulation of his predecessors by formulating a taxonomy of pederasts to replace those conceived by Canler and Carlier. Like theirs, Coffignon's taxonomy had as its first principle that pederasty must echo normative heterosexuality in being divided into two "sexes": Pederasts were either active or passive. Coffignon divided each of the two primary classes of pederasts into three subdivisions: active pederasts were either *amateurs*, older, more established men living a double life; *entreteneurs*, the "hardened" pederasts for whom the dangers of this life were part of its appeal; or *souteneurs*, habitual offenders who had acquired the taste for pederasty in prison. Passive pederasts were divided into the *petit-jésus*, adolescents or young men who have been introduced into prostitution; or the *jésus*, prostitutes or kept boys in their 20s. Finally, the *tante* was the pimp of a female prostitute whose business dealings brought him into contact with pederasts, with whom he had sex for money.[11]

What is most striking about Coffignon's delineation of sexual roles and identities is that they were not derived from ascribed gender, that is, activity or passivity, alone. Age, class, and financial need formed important vectors, as did innate orientation and acquired taste. The internal incoherence of this panorama of pederastic life derived not only from the competing claims of what Eve Sedgwick has called universalizing and minoritizing views of homosexuality, but from the uneasy mapping of male same-sex behavior onto the presumed roles of prostitute, pimp, and customer.[12] In assigning sexual roles putatively analogous to the positions taken in a commercial transaction, Coffignon dislodged the basic gender binarism that was supposed to undergird the taxonomy. In trying to account for what united the spectrum of pederasts, he abandoned his previous classificatory criteria and had recourse to an affective state, "savageness," by which he seems to have meant an excess of emotion, irrationality in private relations, and a lack of personal control.[13]

This stress on savageness signaled something of the interest of these authors in the exemplary or symptomatic dimension of pederasty and its amenability to narrative inscription. Despite their sociological ambitions, these texts devoted surprisingly little space to the "factual" description of male same-sex activity. Instead, they told stories about it, inevitably cautionary tales centering on criminal activity. The most common form of criminality mentioned was blackmail; for these authors it is the most basic fact of a pederast's life, and "the anonymous letter [was] the grand weapon of combat."[14] Both authors suggested that the constant threat of blackmail also seemed to encourage more serious crimes because the victim was unlikely to report them; the savageness of pederasty combined with the constant exposure to criminality could even escalate to murder.

In order to make clear the "passion," "rage," and moral state of pederasts, Coffignon devoted an entire chapter to an exemplary "Love Drama of Pederasts."[15] The tale began with the robbery of a grocery store; the main suspects for which crime were the Simon brothers, who were not actually brothers but a male couple. In order to clear their names, the "husband" Simon led the police on a tour of cafés. At one café, a police officer observed a frightened young man, whom Simon unconvincingly denied knowing, throwing away a wad of paper. Retrieved, it was found to be a letter written by someone named Blum from Mazas prison. When summoned by the authorities, the prisoner Blum, who had just been sentenced to eight years of hard labor, refused to discuss either the robbery or what the police now believed to be a conspiracy of pederasts. By chance, as Blum was being interrogated, one of the officers noticed that the man who had thrown away Blum's letter had just arrived at the prison, arrested for swindling. Brought together in the same room, the two men "fell into one another's arms and embraced with effusion."[16] When the police separated them again, Blum continued to refuse to speak, but his partner, Thomas, confessed not only to the robbery of the grocery store, but to forty-seven additional robberies and to the murder ten years earlier of a furniture-store owner. Thomas confessed, it turned out, because he could not bear to be separated again from his "wife," Blum, and hoped that, if he implicated them both in this series of crimes, they would be sent together to the penal colony in New Caledonia. For Coffignon, the final irony was that, though the men were indeed spared the scaffold and sent to the South Pacific, they had by that point broken up.

This "love drama" recapitulated all the sociological themes raised by Coffignon in his explication of pederasty. These themes were realized, though, through a highly stylized narrative replete with all the thwarted investigations, false identities, secret alliances, and unexpected coincidences of a mid-century popular novel. But, similar as this and the other stories narrated by Virmaître and Coffignon are to the genre of the crime novel, they were tied formally much more closely to the *faits divers* (brief news items in the daily press).

We are only beginning to explore the importance of the *faits divers* as one of the crucial means deployed to shape and satisfy what Vanessa Schwartz has identified as "the public taste for reality" in late-nineteenth-century France.[17] The *faits divers* recounted incidents from modern urban life, from the banal to the titillating, in concise, dramatic form. The *faits divers* had paradoxical effects, offering readers a comfortable distance from the socially marginal yet creating a pervasive sense of impending social disruption. The *faits divers* thus merit, but have not yet received, systematic examination to establish how they represented male same-sex desire. We do have, though, a survey made of *The Journal* by a contemporary German writer who discovered 27 *faits divers* concerned with male same-sex behavior in this daily newspaper in the years between 1900 and 1913.[18] The majority of these items reported the arrest of men engaged in sexual conduct of some sort; most of those arrested were having sex with partners of significantly disparate age or social status. Most articles concern either soldiers or sailors or men of social standing, such as lawyers, judges, or teachers. Prostitution was mentioned explicitly only four times, and blackmail, robbery, suicide, and murder were each mentioned once.

Though these short articles did not attempt to reconstruct a larger social milieu in the manner of Virmaître and Coffignon, they reiterated the thematics of pederastic criminality. The journalists who wrote the *faits divers* thus seemed to reproduce even more directly the view of male same-sex desire formulated by the judicial system: pederasty drove men to the crime of public sexual expression, with that expression itself providing an opportunity for an escalation of criminal behavior, either as victim or perpetrator. That pederasty was a crime against the social order was further confirmed by the inappropriate and socially asymmetrical couplings uncovered by arrest. Such a confluence of attitudes between the police and journalists is hardly surprising, given that the former were a primary source of information for the latter. I think, though, that our reading of the larger social meanings of the *faits divers* will be found by placing these articles within the fragmented and discontinuous text of the newspaper itself. In their original setting, the *faits divers* were juxtaposed to, and may have become alarming instantiations of, contemporary social and political issues such as the depopulation crisis, fears of national degeneration, and tensions between France and Germany.

Indeed, the social and political anxieties implicit in the *faits divers* became much easier to identify in the more extended narratives occasioned by the outbreak of scandals involving same-sex sexuality. Take, for example, the Germiny affair, which in outline could pass for a *fait divers*. In December 1876, the Count de Germiny, a thirty-five-year-old lawyer from a distinguished family, was arrested for a public offence against decency, along with an eighteen-year-old jeweler, in a public urinal on the Champs-Elysées. As Christian Gury has shown, Germiny's trial (unusual in such cases and perhaps politically motivated) was covered in detail by the Parisian daily press.[19] The case occasioned an examination of the role and influence of traditional elites. The press stressed in its coverage the disparity in age and rank between Germiny and his co-defendant. The newspapers also noted the striking difference in the judicial system's treatment of the two men (although Germiny received a much more severe sentence, he was allowed to remain at liberty during the trial and could thus flee the country). The press regarded Germiny's sexual relations with a worker as an unnatural breaching of social hierarchy, and it treated this disruption as coterminous with the alleged dysfunctionalism of the French system of justice. One remarkable consequence of the trial was that "Germinism" became a popular euphemism for same-sex sexuality, reinforcing the long-standing association of "vice" and the aristocracy.

In newspaper accounts of foreign scandals, the treatment of same-sex sexuality as a symptom of cultural malaise was even more pronounced. As Nancy Erber has demonstrated, the initial response of the French press to the 1895 trials of Oscar Wilde was to cast this scandal in stridently nationalistic terms.[20] At first, French newspapers depicted the Wilde scandal as the embodiment of British puritanism and hypocrisy; later, some writers suggested that male same-sex sexuality was little-known in France while widespread in England. Similarly, Gury has documented the French response to the 1903 suicide in a Paris hotel room of Sir Hector Macdonald, one of the most visible figures of British imperial rule, after he had been accused of having sexual relations with young native men in Ceylon.[21] The French press saw the British army's treatment of Macdonald, which drove him to suicide, as representative of English mores in all their rigidity and hypocrisy and took the opportunity to examine anew the nature of military honor (itself a controversial topic in the wake of the Dreyfus affair). The Eulenburg affair of 1907-1909, a series of journalistic exposés and libel trials concerning the purported homosexuality of the German chancellor and members of the Kaiser's entourage, was also covered extensively by the French press.[22] Taking place during a period of heightened diplomatic tension between France and Germany, the Eulenberg Affair permitted the French press to mock the German military and to locate "the German vice" in the highest reaches of German society. Scandal, then, allowed for the representation of male same-sex sexuality as an unnatural transgression of the social order (undermining distinctions of class, age, and even culture) carried out by those Others for whom such transgression was characteristic, even natural.

The condemnatory conflation of male same-sex desire with criminality and social disorder can also be identified in the fiction of this period. From at least the 1830s, literature served as an arena in which "same-sex sexuality became an important metaphor for discussing the organization of society."[23] While the invocation of gender transgression and sexual ambiguity by Decadent writers such as Jean Lorrain and Rachilde has been much remarked upon, less attention has been paid to the role of male same-sex sexuality in naturalist fiction.[24] Generally, pederasty appears fleetingly in those naturalist works that examine and criticize homosocial environments. One telling example is Zola's 1903 novel, *Truth*, one of a series of books in which the author rebuked the Catholic Church. Here, in a crime clearly meant to be both literal and symbolic, a priest rapes and then strangles a choirboy.[25] A more detailed depiction of the sexual sins of the Church is found in Octave Mirbeau's *Sébastien Roch* (1890), the story of a doomed bourgeois youth from childhood through to his death in the Franco-Prussian War. Sébastien is sent by his indifferent parents to a boarding school where students whisper of the "filthy things" boys do together; but his spiritual life is destroyed by the sexual advances of his trusted confessor: "That hand ran over his body, at first gentle and timid, then impatient and bold. It groped, it clasped, it squeezed."[26] A more equivocal response to male-male sexuality can be found in Lucien Descaves's controversial novel, *Sous-Offs* (1889), an indictment of the corruption and debasement found within the French Army. Late in the narrative, the protagonist, Favières, realizes that one of the warrant officers, Laprévotte, is involved in furtive sexual relations with other soldiers. His response is ironic amusement: finally Laprévotte's "misogyny, his constant isolation" can be understood. Only at the disillusioned conclusion of his military service could Favières recognize such behavior as a minor instance of the Army's pervasive corruption.[27]

A very few novels went beyond such glancing treatments and took as their protagonist a "pederast" or "invert." The first of these was *Sodom* by Henri d'Argis, published in 1888 with a somewhat apologetic introduction by Paul Verlaine.[28] Drawing on both naturalist and Decadent conventions, this work is striking for its interest in the psychology of sexual dissidence. Like *Sébastien Roch*, d'Argis's novel traces the life of a bourgeois, Jacques Soran, from childhood to premature death. Soran in his youth develops a desire, encouraged by his confessor, to find romantic love with a woman and platonic union with a man who is his intellectual equal. After his mother's death, Soran retreats to a provincial mining town where he is surprised to meet and befriend a young woman who proves to be both his ideal of physical beauty and his mental and spiritual peer. The young woman insists that their relationships be chaste, but Soran, driven mad by physical and intellectual infatuation, forces himself on his beloved, only to "recoil, stunned" from the discovery that she has a penis.[29]

After this trauma, Soran flees to Paris, where his confessor arranges a marriage for him to a respectable young bourgeoisie. While initially content with his wife, Soran begins to wander Paris at night and one evening encounters Henri Laus, a seventeen-year-old orphan who strongly resembles the young woman whom he befriended in the provinces. Soran makes Laus his protégé, ignoring and finally abandoning his wife when he moves with Laus back to the mining town that was the scene of his greatest happiness. Soran struggles to insure that their companionship remains "chaste," and only when an unnamed disease causes Soran to disintegrate mentally and physically does Laus begin to intuit the nature of Soran's affection for him. Laus does not reject Soran, even after the elder man is confined to an institution and hallucinates about the hellfire that awaits him. *Sodom* treats its protagonist with almost clinical detachment: Soran is destroyed by his "aberration," though the text remains unclear about whether its origin lies in Soran's genetic inheritance, his loveless childhood, or the formative experience of loving a woman with a penis. The narrative endorses Soran's attempts at chastity and heterosexuality and presents him as justifiably repulsed by the criminal underworld in which other pederasts must travel. Though Soran is shown as incapable of developing relationships with either sex that conform to social norms, the character is himself troubled by this debility. D'Argis did not attempt to make Jacques Soran sympathetic to the reader, but merely to illuminate how the character must struggle with forces stronger than his will.

We might contrast this portrayal with a later work, Francis Carco's *Jésus-la-Caille* (1914). This novel established Carco's reputation as a chronicler of "the milieu," the underworld of petty criminals and social marginals inhabiting lower Montmartre.[30] At the beginning of the novel, Jésus's lover, Bambou, has just been arrested by the vice squad in a trap set by Dominique-le-Corse, a powerful pimp. As his nickname would suggest, Jésus is characterized as young, effeminate, and timid, with "the pretty face of a girl, hardly made up." He thinks of confronting le Corse about Bambou, but knows he would be "weak as a girl, cowardly and trembling like a girl before him."[31]

Jésus, though, develops an unexpected alliance with Fernande, le Corse's lover. Fernande is intrigued by Jésus, attracted by his effeminacy, drawn to "this delicious and tempting equivocator, this little kid, this spoiled and sentimental doll."[32] Though Fernande is unsure of what their relationship could be–"He was too much a woman for a woman"–she and Jésus become sexually involved. Unbeknown to both, le Corse is himself arrested as Fernande and Jésus spend their first night together. The relationship between the two is doomed to failure, not least because Jésus spends a good deal of his time when in Fernande's company daydreaming about his romance with Bambou. Moreover, their coupling begins to take on the character of all her previous liaisons: Fernande supports Jésus, though he grows less interested in her. Only the reappearance of Pépé-la-Vache, a rival thug who helped put le Corse in jail, enables Fernande to end the relationship with Jésus. She and la Vache begin a romance and Jésus, in turn, starts to live with the *petit-jésus* la Puce, who is the brother of his jailed lover, Bambou. The final third of the novel is concerned with describing these parallel romances, the more enduring of which, surprisingly, is that of Jésus and la Puce. Fernande leaves la Vache when she learns that he is not only a police informer but also the one who helped send le Corse to jail. In the novel's tragic ending, le Corse returns from prison only to kill la Vache, a crime for which Fernande, in a desperate act of loyalty, takes the blame.

Carco's uneasy melange of naturalism, torch songs (*chansons réalistes*) and journalistic accounts of street toughs (*apaches*) revised earlier popular texts identifying crime and pederasty in two significant ways. Though Jésus in most ways conforms to the stereotype of the youthful pederast, his affairs, first with Fernande and then with la Puce, break down the generalizations and typologies underlying most popular texts. His moving between same- and opposite-sex couplings and between passive and active roles does not admit of any conventional developmental narrative. The fluidity of Jésus's sexual behavior, moreover, is motivated by his shifting emotional needs, not economic necessity, advancing age, or debauched sensibilities. The book's narrative also describes at length the physical and affective dimensions of Jésus's same-sex relationships. These passages are remarkably frank in their recounting of sexual desire, particularly Jésus's attraction to Bambou, a former circus acrobat, but link sexuality with the habits of domesticity and emotional intimacy. The character of Jésus thus possesses an interiority, a represented subjectivity, explicitly positioned as equivalent to that of Fernande. The thematic doubling of Jésus and Fernande is itself an ambivalent move, stressing the emotional lability and social marginality of both characters and reiterating the trope of gender inversion; but, hemmed in by what Carco calls the "instinctual hatred" of "Bambou, la Caille and those of their species,"[33] the novel expresses considerably more identification with and sympathy for such men than the other popular sources can generate.

To conclude, I would like to hazard a few preliminary observations. Even in so limited a selection of popular printed texts, we can see the repetition of some familiar tropes in the representation of male same-sex sexuality: the description of same-sex relations as perversely imitative of normative heterosexuality; the strong association of pederasty with urban criminality, particularly prostitution; and the stress on the socially disruptive consequences of such sexual practices and identities. However, we might also note a few surprises. First, I would point out how consistently the popular discourses take up the construction of male same-sex sexuality promulgated by the police and the penal system and how many of these texts are untouched by, even resistant to the influence of, the emerging scientific or medical discourse. Few of these writers betray any interest in investigating the origins or etiology of pederasty. This points to a second observation: how incompletely and inconsistently these popular texts characterize male same-sex sexuality. The texts are marked by the very difficulty their authors faced in trying to make sense of their subjects. Indeed, the greatest anxiety in these texts frequently centers not on those men who are recognizably pederasts but on those who are not. The sometimes contradictory assumptions about pederasts that animate these texts–the shifting attention paid to the contingency of sexual acts, the persistence of affective orientations, the vagaries of gender emulation, and the imprecise social location of pederasty–suggest that there did not yet exist a coherent, popularly accepted model of sexual identity.

The absence of such clarity may also in part explain the regularity with which representations of same-sex sexuality took the form of narratives, particularly highly convention-laden genres of narrative, such as the *faits divers*, the crime story, the case history, the moral fable, and (however ironically) the love story. The narrative conventions may have worked to render male same-sex sexuality much more comprehensible to both their producers and consumers by depicting it in the terms of established social typologies and their attendant values. The ability of the arrests, and, at a higher social level, the scandal, to force male same-sex sexuality into an otherwise elusive visibility and, further, to cast that visibility in the moral terms of judgment and punishment may also account for the pervasiveness of legal-juridical discourses in popular texts. Finally, I would like to stress the degree to which in these texts pederasty is "discovered" as a phenomenon of urban modernity. Same-sex sexuality is located, described, and judged as yet another of the pleasures and dangers of the crowded metropolis, a symbol of social confusion, illicit sensation, and unimaginable possibilities. In particular, the Paris that emerges in these texts is an unpredictable social arena in which appearances are surprisingly, sometimes dangerously deceiving, and relationships are intense but ephemeral and untrustworthy. Thus, these representations are freighted not only with the moral disapprobation that has historically been visited on sexual dissidence, but also with the allure of forbidden knowledge and vicarious sensation, and the anxieties of people struggling with the forms and customs of modern civil society.

NOTES

1. Ali Coffignon, *Paris vivant: La Corruption à Paris* (Paris, 1889), 328, 348-51.
2. Robert A. Nye, *Masculinity and Male Codes of Honor in Modern France* (New York, 1993); idem, "Sex Difference and Male Homosexuality in French Medical Discourse, 1830-1930," *Bulletin of the History of Medicine* 63 (Spring 1989): 32-51; Vernon Rosario, *The Erotic Imagination: French Histories of Perversity* (New York, 1997); Pierre Hahn, *Nos ancêtres, les pervers* (Paris, 1979); Antony Copley, *Sexual*

Moralities in France, 1780-1980: New Ideas on the Family, Divorce and Homosexuality (New York, 1989); William Peniston, "'Pederasts and Others': A Social History of Male Homosexuals in the Early Years of the French Third Republic, PhD dissertation, University of Rochester, 1997; Paul Schmidt, "Visions of Violence: Rimbaud and Verlaine," *Homosexualities and French Literature: Cultural Contexts/Critical Texts*, ed. George Stambolian and Elaine Marks (Ithaca, 1979); Patrick Pollard, *André Gide, Homosexual Moralist* (New Haven, 1991); J. E. Rivers, *Proust and the Art of Love: The Aesthetics of Sexuality in the Life, Times, and Art of Marcel Proust* (New York, 1980); Eve Kosofsky Sedgwick, *Epistemology of the Closet* (Berkeley, 1990).

3. Michael Sibalis, "Paris," in *Queer Sites: Gay Urban Histories since 1600*, ed. David Higgs (New York, 1999) 10-37; Francesca Canadé Sautman, "Invisible Women: Lesbian Working-Class Culture in France, 1880-1930," in *Homosexuality in Modern France*, ed. Jeffrey Merrick and Bryant T. Ragan, Jr. (New York, 1996), 177-201.

4. Christophe Charle, *La Crise littéraire à l'époque du naturalisme* (Paris, 1979).

5. Coffignon, *La Corruption*; and Charles Virmaître, *Trottoirs et lupanars* (Paris, 1882) and *Paris impur* (Paris, 1900).

6. Coffignon, *Corruption*, 8.

7. Alain Corbin, "Commercial Sexuality in Nineteenth-Century France: A System of Images and Regulations," *Representations* 14 (1986): 209-19.

8. Louis Canler, *Mémoires de Canler, ancien chef du service de sûreté* (Brussels, 1862); Félix Carlier, *Études de pathologie sociale: Les Deux prostitutions, 1860-1870* (Paris, 1887).

9. Peniston, "'Pederasts and Others,'" 53-64.

10. Coffignon, *Corruption*, 328.

11. Ibid., 332-6.

12. Sedgwick, *Epistemology of the Closet*, 82-6.

13. Coffignon, *Corruption*, 336.

14. Ibid., 335.

15. Ibid., 355-66.

16. Ibid., 360.

17. Vanessa R. Schwartz, *Spectacular Realities: Early Mass Culture in Fin-de-Siècle France* (Berkeley, 1998), especially chapter 2.

18. Numa Praetorius, "Homosexuelle Ereignisse in Frankreich," in *Jahrbuch für sexuelle Zwischenstufen*, cited in Pollard, *André Gide*, 131-2.

19. Christian Gury, *L'Honneur perdu d'un politicien homosexuel en 1876: Des clés pour Flaubert, Maupassant, et Proust* (Paris, 1999). See also William Peniston, "A Public Offence Against Decency: The Trial of the Count de Germiny and the Moral Order of the Third Republic," in *Disorder in the Court: Trials and Sexual Conflict at the Turn of the Century*, ed. Nancy Erber and George Robb (New York, 1999), 12-32.

20. Nancy Erber, "The French Trials of Oscar Wilde," *Journal of the History of Sexuality* 6 (1996): 549-88.

21. Christian Gury, *L'Honneur suicidé d'un général homosexual en 1903* (Paris, 1999).

22. John Grand-Carteret, *Derrière "Lui": L'Homosexualité en Allemagne* [1908] (Lille, 1992).

23. Victoria Thompson, "Creating Boundaries: Homosexuality and the Changing Social Order in France, 1830-1870," in *Homosexuality in Modern France*, 104.

24. Jennifer Birkett, *Sins of the Fathers: Decadence in France, 1870-1914* (New York, 1986).

25. Emile Zola, *Verité* (Paris, 1903).
26. Octave Mirbeau, *Sébastien Roch* (Paris, 1890), 183.
27. Lucien Descaves, *Sous-Offs* (Paris, 1889), 417. The title means "non-commissioned officers."
28. Henri d'Argis, *Sodome* (Paris, 1888).
29. Ibid., 123.
30. Francis Carco, *Jésus-la-Caille* [1914] (Paris, 1953).
31. Ibid., 23-4.
32. Ibid., 42.
33. Ibid., 12-3.

Homosexuality in the French Colonies

Robert Aldrich

The links between sexuality and European overseas expansion have attracted increasing attention from historians and other scholars in recent years. They have explored the European encounter with diverse sexual practices in other parts of the world, the sexual opportunities presented by the colonies, the gendered nature of imperialism, the incidence of prostitution, the eroticized images of indigenous people in art and literature, interracial liaisons, and *métissage*.[1] Work has concentrated on heterosexuality in colonial contexts, but homosexuality is no less interesting. European explorers and adventurers came into contact with cultures in which sexual relations between men or between women (but this essay does not discuss lesbianism) were not subject to the same kind of legal, medical, and religious condemnation as in the West, or where formal disapproval had less effect on actual behavior. In some societies, those who contravened Western notions of sexual propriety (the *berdaches* of North America, the *maheus* of Polynesia, or those who participated in homosexual initiation rituals in Melanesia) enjoyed recognized and accepted status in their communities.[2]

The "new imperialism" (1880s to 1914) occurred at the same time as the emergence of new forms of same-sex identification: the invention of the word "homosexuality," the first movements of homosexual emancipation, and the establishment of modern patterns of homosexual sociability. Europeans overseas in this period sometimes engaged in "situational" homosexuality, particularly in all-male military battalions, in penal colonies, or on the frontier, which was often marked by a dramatic imbalance in the sex ratio between men and women. European homosexuals often met willing indigenous partners in societies with non-Western mores, while others found the male environments of

[Haworth co-indexing entry note]: "Homosexuality in the French Colonies." Aldrich, Robert. Co-published simultaneously in *Journal of Homosexuality* (Harrington Park Press, an imprint of The Haworth Press, Inc.) Vol. 41, No. 3/4, 2001, pp. 201-218; and: *Homosexuality in French History and Culture* (ed: Jeffrey Merrick, and Michael Sibalis) Harrington Park Press, an imprint of The Haworth Press, Inc., 2001, pp. 201-218. Single or multiple copies of this article are available for a fee from The Haworth Document Delivery Service [1-800-342-9678, 9:00 a.m. - 5:00 p.m. (EST). E-mail address: getinfo@haworthpressinc.com].

expeditions, cantonments, or colonial administrations congenial to intimate friendships with their compatriots. In the larger colonial cities, homosexual subcultures emerged with identifiable meeting-places and networks of contacts.

The relationship between the colonizer and colonized was seldom, if ever, an egalitarian one. Colonial domination clearly played a role in liaisons between Europeans and non-Europeans, homosexual as well as heterosexual, with Europeans exchanging power, privileges, status, and money for sexual favors. Some relationships differed little from prostitution or included coercion and violence, yet many indigenous men could derive material and emotional advantages in the form of income, social promotion, or closer association with the colonial ruling order from partnerships with Europeans. It would be illogical to suppose that none of the relationships involved affection, the pleasure of companionship, or love.

Relatively little scholarly work on homosexuality in the European colonial world has appeared, and almost none on the French overseas empire.[3] This silence mirrors the absence, until very recent years, of work on homosexuality in France itself. Overseas conquest, colonial rule, and decolonization have preoccupied colonial historians, and the history of sexuality has not yet attained the academic legitimacy and popularity in France that it enjoys in other countries. For historians of homosexuality, colonies do pose problems. Traditional writers often prove unwilling to admit that major figures were or might have been homosexual, regarding that orientation as a stigma on their subjects and, by extension, on colonialism (or anti-colonialism). Biographies, autobiographies, and memoirs show reticence in revealing homosexual experiences. Decriminalization of homosexuality in post-Revolutionary France and its colonies (though various statutes, such as those outlawing any "public offense against decency," made it possible to prosecute homosexuals) meant that the records of arrests and trials which have been so revealing elsewhere are less common in France and its domains. Yet there is no reason to suppose that homosexual activities were less common in the French colonies than in possessions of other powers or in France itself. Given the very license granted by colonialism to all sorts of dissident behavior, the opposite might well be true.

Writing about the history of homosexuality in the French colonies involves piecing together information, often about the colonial elite and, in particular, about writers who recorded their adventures in fictionalized accounts; it requires careful inferences from sometimes circumstantial evidence. The aim should not be to "out" famous figures of the colonial past or to argue that homosexuality forms a hidden linchpin of colonialism. Rather, this essay will suggest that the French discovered new sorts of sexual variance during their colonial expansion, that homosexuality was omnipresent in the colonial world (despite efforts by contemporaries and later commentators to avoid the issue), that concerns about homosexuality among "natives" or Frenchmen occasionally troubled observers and policy-makers, that homosexuality played a significant role in the lives and works of several colonialists and anti-colonialists, and, finally, that homosexuality formed a theme (albeit a minor one) in the imaginative literature of the colonial period.

L'ART D'AIMER AUX COLONIES

In 1893, Les Editions Georges-Anquetil, in a series on "the Art of Love," published *The Art of Love in the Colonies* by one "Dr. Jacobus X.," who identified himself as a medical doctor in the French Navy with twenty-five years of experience in the colonies. He declared that his volume was "not an obscene work but a psychological document on the general history of love in the human race," a claim somewhat belied by sixteen illustrations of naked "native" women. In almost four hundred pages, the author discussed sexual behavior in Indochina, the French West Indies, Africa, and Oceania, basing his statements on clinical observations made during his travels and on evidence supplied by colleagues (though the book contains no scholarly apparatus).[4]

The Art of Love in the Colonies provides an inventory of sex as practiced within indigenous societies and in liaisons between Europeans and colonized peoples. Jacobus X. described the genitals of women and men in voyeuristic detail and was especially assiduous in phalloplethysmography, measuring the size of penises and comparing dimensions across "races." He listed the various positions assumed in sexual intercourse, discussed brothels and other venues of sexual pleasure, and speculated as an amateur anthropologist on the causes of behaviors. He quoted from novels, such as those by Pierre Loti, to evoke the sexual temptations and opportunities of exotic lands.

Most of Jacobus X.'s study was devoted to heterosexuality, but rather more than might be expected focused on homosexuality, despite his affirmation that he found homosexual practices repulsive. He judged homosexuality most prevalent in Southeast Asia. In Cochinchina, where he served in the 1860s, homosexuality appeared endemic among Vietnamese and Chinese.

> The Annamite is a pederast because he is lascivious. Here is a sophisticated old race, which was already corrupted [before the arrival of Europeans]. [Pederasty] is an innate stigma, which the European discovered in full bloom and from which a few (a small number, let us hope) have profited.

The Frenchman in Indochina "could become a sodomite or a pederast because he found, without even having to search for them, women and children who presented him with the opportunity." Thus, the Indochinese had corrupted Europeans, especially in the early colonial period when there was a scarcity of European women.

> Formerly, the European pederast was far from a rarity and a goodly number of men, including some of the most respectable, still had this sad reputation. However, they were not despised, or even thought badly of, because of it. In the cafés when the most scandalous stories were told about them, everyone laughed.

A quarter of a century later, after another visit, Jacobus X. noted an improvement in morals, though he offered no explanation other than the increased presence of French women in the colony.

> European pederasts . . . hardly exist except as a memory. Those who have kept this reputation are old traders or bureaucrats. . . . They are regarded as a curiosity by new arrivals. It is possible that among this latter group, there are those who have a penchant for Greek love, since that exists in Europe, too.[5]

Jacobus X. went on to say that *boys* (youths employed as household servants) or *nays* (porters or errand-boys) were readily available for sexual activity. They offered fellatio and anal intercourse and proved versatile in providing services for a modest recompense.

> One must not think that the depraved Asiatic feels any repugnance whatsoever to engaging in this turpitude [fellatio]. He has even less than the *belle de jour* who performs the same operation. Whether the European reclines in a long planter's chair or lies on his bed, the *boy*, kneeling or squatting, *kisses and sucks his penis, and takes the emitted semen into his mouth, down to the last drop.*[6]

Jacobus X. claimed to have found physical "evidence" of homosexual practices in the mouths of youths distorted by frequent fellatio and the distended anuses of those who engaged in passive sodomy. He reported only two cases of passive sodomy among Europeans whom he cured of anal gonorrhea, one a seventeen-year-old. Although Jacobus X. was vague about the period to which he referred, he noted that *boys* were available in more or less open meeting-places, including male brothels *cum* opium dens in the suburbs of Saigon. He also cited the case of one of his old school friends, a Navy officer, who developed a "deplorable reputation because of his too little concealed taste for boys."[7]

Jacobus X. found morals similar elsewhere in Indochina: "The Tonkinese race . . . is basically lascivious, lubricious, pederastic and sodomitical." By contrast, he observed almost no sodomy among Africans and *métis* in French Guiana, though he treated a fifteen-year-old black boy who had "accepted the impure offers of an Arab" who had got him drunk and taken advantage of him, leaving the youth with an anal fissure (the boy's mother had first pretended that the adolescent had been stuck by the horn of a goat that had been chasing him). The reason for lack of sodomitical activity was "the ease of procuring women in this fine country."[8] The story was altogether different with the Indians brought to the Caribbean and French Guiana as indentured laborers and with European and North African prisoners transported to Devil's Island. Some homosexuality among prisoners was inevitable, because of scarcity of women, but for others it was, he said, "hereditary." Almost all of the Indian "coolies" between the ages of fifteen and twenty indulged in pederasty, often with European or Arab partners, in return for money. As for North Africans, "The Arab is an inveterate pederast, even in his own country, where women are not lacking.... All the travelers writing about morals in Arabia and Turkey have commented on this fact."[9]

In sub-Saharan Africa, Jacobus X. commented in detail on the large size of the men's penises, which he curiously attributed to circumcision. Homosexual activity among men was not frequent, except among slaves or *tirailleurs sénégalais* (French troops recruited throughout western Africa). He again attributed this homosexuality to absence of women partners, but he met two *tirailleurs*, "a true Negro Castor and Pollux," who had enjoyed an "unnatural" relationship until they found a woman, whose sexual favors they then shared.[10]

On his last stop, the South Pacific, Jacobus X. noted homosexual contact among Melanesians in New Caledonia, once again when women were unavailable, and recorded male homosexuality and lesbianism among transported prisoners. Indeed, he remarked on the "vices of Sodom and Gomorrah in full flower" there. Sometimes enduring partnerships formed among transportees and freed convicts, characterized by jealousy, violence, and revenge for infidelity. In Tahiti, homosexuality was rare, although the Tahitian in his twenties, he admits, was "a superb man and, in my opinion, one of the most perfect specimens of human beauty."[11]

The Art of Love in the Colonies was specious anthropology and sexology, punctuated with racist views and personal prejudices, voyeuristic soft-porn masquerading as science. It nonetheless remains a unique travel guide to sexual practices in the heyday of imperialism. It revealed European fantasies about foreign peoples, venturing no original interpretations but circulating commonly held views. It embodied typical late nineteenth-century attitudes, popularized by the author's acknowledged mentor, Ambroise Tardieu, about homosexuals and how to identify them, particularly by their enlarged anuses.[12] It repeated stereotypes about the small genitals, sexual licentiousness and sexual passivity of Asians, the oversized penises and lustiness of Africans, and the widespread penchant of Arabs for sodomy. It ascribed much homosexuality to the lack of women. Jacobus X. argued that "natives" could corrupt the French, but recognized that, among indigenous and migrant populations, various types of homosexuality flourished; he admitted that some men, including colonists, had a preference for homosexuality. The book showed awareness of homosexuality among indigenous peoples, indentured laborers and migrants, transported prisoners and free settlers, including men of high social standing, and even adolescents. Homosexual sex, he observed, was available both for money and without charge and could be obtained from youths encountered in the streets, domestic servants, fellow prisoners, or "sex workers" in brothels. The gamut of sexual pleasures was on offer. Though homosexual activities occasionally caused medical problems and Jacobus X. claimed to find them revolting, he mounted no campaign against immorality, whether homosexual or heterosexual.

IN THE ARMY

Jacobus X. was not the sole commentator to express distaste for homosexual practices in the colonial world, and although French officials had the reputation for being broad-minded about sexual peccadilloes, several wondered about the effects of colonial conditions on upright Frenchmen. In 1894, a criminologist observed a homosexual orgy among soldiers in Algeria and worried about the lasting effect of such excess.[13] Gérard Zwang argued that "a certain type of career officer was absolutely homosexual," a phenomenon seen among Roman centurions, Janissaries, and French marshals: "The choice of such a profession is made knowingly, and those who enlisted in the [French Foreign] Legion, the African rifles or the 'Colo' [colonial army], were not unaware of what they were getting into."[14] Colonel Weygand, a general's son and former Legionnaire, testified that commanders had to turn a blind eye to what went on between Legionnaires during rest-stops in desert oases.[15]

Georges Saint-Paul claimed that men who were not homosexual "become homosexuals there [in the colonies] and sometimes remain so," a situation he ascribed, predictably, to the shortage of women and corrupt native morals.[16] René Jude expressed concern about the frequency of homosexuality in the notorious *bataillons d'Afrique*, regiments of prisoners. He argued that troopers had adopted homosexual practices in civilian prisons and persisted in such behavior in the battalions. He hypothesized that two-thirds of those in the *bataillons* were homosexual and described the couples they formed. The "wife" shined the shoes, made the bed, and sewed on buttons, while the "husband" lounged about smoking but occasionally did the heavier chores; sometimes good friends shared the "woman." The "husband" usually remained very protective of his partner, however, and jealous of rivals.[17] Paul Rebierre concurred. Among the *Joyeux*, as soldiers of the *bataillons d'Afrique* were called, "We found almost all forms of sexual inversion." The reasons, he reiterated, were circumstantial. In the Islamic world, "homosexuality is certainly as common as heterosexuality. In Algeria and Tunisia . . . this 'pederastic atmosphere' [and] the real lack of women had an effect on our indigenous troops and our special action forces are made up of men who are inclined to let themselves be tempted." Other factors he enumerated were curiosity, fear of impotence or venereal disease (it was widely believed that men could catch venereal diseases only from women), and violence. Rebierre added that climate possibly had an influence, as "hot climates, by decreasing will-power, certainly play a preponderant role in sexual perversity."[18] In 1911, two writers (one an army doctor) reported:

> When we arrived in Algeria, under the influence of the climate and because of the total lack of women . . . [soldiers] could not resist imitating the ways of the locals, and soon their bad reputation for having 'African morals' had reached France. . . . Homosexuality in the [French] African army corresponded to a physical necessity, but not, in general, to a form of erotic folly.[19]

Such theories were hardly new; the notion of a connection between climate and homosexuality recalls the "Sotadic zone" described by Richard Burton. What seems noteworthy in these descriptions of colonial sexuality is the idea that homosexual relations took place by necessity in the absence of women (despite the presence of "native" female prostitutes near military camps) and the argument that the French learned homosexuality from "natives." But none of the writers ever really explained why a shortage of white women should compel Frenchmen to turn to native men rather than native women (except to imply fear of venereal disease). Of course, in some of the desert oases and military camps of North Africa, there probably were not many native women, because the Arabs would have tried to keep their women, at least respectable ones, away from the Frenchmen. A second point about the descriptions is the relative absence of hysterical indignation; writers did not demand disciplinary action or a morals campaign to end homosexual behavior. They assumed that such "vice" would not risk army morale but would disappear in due course.

Occasional problems did arise, however. For instance, in 1891, Lieutenant Boyer, a medical doctor in the first company of *spahis* in Algeria, denounced Captain Bouïs for having "brutalised his soldiers, stolen from them and for committing immoral acts on them." Authorities tried to hush up the affair, announcing that Bouïs would be removed and Boyer transferred. Bouïs then insulted Boyer, trying to provoke him into a duel. Boyer refused, "saying that he would not fight a thief and a pederast" but that he would fight against any other officer who cared to take Bouïs's place. No one offered to do so. A council of enquiry judged that Boyer had forfeited his honor by refusing to fight the duel and forced him out of the army.[20] Bouïs's violence seemed of more concern than his pederasty, and his accuser suffered the punishment: dishonorable conduct was more serious than immoral behavior.

Several French military officers of repute seem to have been homosexual, though absolute proof is lacking. General Lamoricière, one of the conquerors of Algeria, is quoted as having said, rather matter-of-factly, "There [in Africa] we were all [pederasts]," and adding that General Changarnier, unlike others, remained so once back in France. General Gallieni, who served in Indochina and Madagascar, was rumored to be homosexual. In the last years of the empire, General de Lattre de Tassigny was probably bisexual.[21] The most famous officer said to be homosexual was Marshal Hubert Lyautey, who was posted as a young officer to Algeria, then served with Gallieni in Indochina and Madagascar, became the first French Resident-General of Morocco, and was appointed commissioner of the Exposition Coloniale in 1931. With a patrician background, impressive bearing, keen intelligence, and wide-ranging interests, Lyautey was the most famous colonialist in France. Christian Gury has recently published a book arguing that Lyautey was homosexual and the model for Proust's Baron de Charlus in *Remembrance of Things Past*.[22] Gury's evidence is circumstantial but convincing. Lyautey married only late in life and fathered no children; he had no known affairs with women during his long life, something of an anomaly among Frenchmen of his background. Gury quotes the homoerotic descriptions Lyautey penned of Arabs, Greeks, Africans, and Ceylonese, as well as fellow officers, descriptions that went well beyond the usual admiration of "natives." Even given Lyautey's manifest interest in the world of Islam and other foreign cultures, these descriptions bespeak aesthetic and eroticised appreciation of the physical beauty of men. Moreover, Lyautey liked to surround himself with handsome young officers, with whom he formed close relationships, though whether professional, paternalistic, or something else can never be completely known. Gury refers to Lyautey's taste for accouterments and furnishings that later generations would consider "camp," proclivities not common among fellow soldiers; Lyautey was a dandy of a very *fin-de-siècle* sort.

Many of Lyautey's contemporaries, like André Maurois, Jean Cocteau, Julien Green, Abel Bonnard, and Daniel Guérin, remarked on Lyautey's preference for comely subalterns and hinted at (or mentioned outright) his homosexuality. Madame Lyautey has often been quoted for a remark to Lyautey's young officers after she had spent a night with the marshal: "Gentlemen, I have the pleasure of informing you that last night I cuckolded you all." Prime Minister Georges Clemenceau reputedly said of Lyautey, in a remark that defies full translation: "Voilà un homme admirable, courageux, qui a toujours eu des couilles au cul . . . même quand ce n'étaient pas les siennes" ("He is an admirable and courageous man who has always had balls between his legs, even when they weren't his own!").[23] Even if such quotations are apocryphal, they indicate the marshal's reputation among his peers.

Less significant than finding incontrovertible proof of Lyautey's homosexual leanings is suggesting that his sexual inclinations may have influenced his colonial vocation and policies. This does seem to be the case, as his attraction to the colonies, Morocco in particular, was bound up with a view of the regenerative nature of imperialism as led by courageous, hardy, and intelligent men such as himself, bound together by manly *esprit de corps* and dedication to their ideals. His attitude towards the North African population reflected a mystical appreciation of the desert, the sights of Morocco, and the attractiveness of its population. His writings cast his world-view in almost exclusively masculine (and masculinist) terms, suffused with homoerotic imagery.

LIVES AND LETTERS

A number of cultural figures associated with overseas activities dabbled in homosexuality. Gustave Flaubert, visiting Egypt, went to a hammam and implied in letters that he had tried sodomy but did not find it to his liking. Arthur Rimbaud, once he abandoned poetry to become a colonial trader on the horn of Africa, formed a very close friendship, which may well have been sexual, with an African named Djami Ouaddei, to whom he wished to bequeath his possessions. The ambisexual nature of Pierre Loti could hardly be bound by the confines of heterosexuality on his many travels. The composer Camille Saint-Saëns was said to have enjoyed North African youths while in Algeria. The Orientalist painter Etienne Dinet lived in an emotionally significant and intimate friendship with a Maghrebin man. Paul Gauguin, best known for his seduction of young Tahitian women, confessed in *Noa Noa* that he had almost given in to temptation with a comely Polynesian man.[24]

Homosexuality appears in several colonial novels. One example is a work by Claude Farrère, a novelist much honored during his lifetime but now little known. Gury asserts that he was homosexual. In 1905, Farrère published *The Civilized Ones*. Set in Indochina, it paints the portraits of two colonial groups: the "barbarians," those of impeccably good morals, and the "sophisticates," men and women who live in the world of opium, alcohol, and debauchery. One main character is Torral, a mathematician and engineer, who is homosexual. Whatever the author's own sexual inclinations, his portrayal of Torral's sexual activities rings true and confirms views expressed by Jacobus X. Torral's sexuality causes no concern among his friends, with whom he goes out, drinks, and carouses. Torral, thirty years old, retiring and intellectual, nevertheless detests other colonials, and chooses to live in the native quarter rather than in a European neighborhood. He straightforwardly affirms: "The woman question is not in my field of competence." "I've chosen for my lot," says Torral, "the splendor of perfect numbers and transcendent forms. And so I do mathematics, and my private *boy* takes care of settling my nerves when necessary–and I don't have to worry about that." Torral, who announces happily, "We're in Sodom here" in Saigon, "calculated his pleasures according to Epicurean arithmetic. . . . [E]ven in broad daylight he paraded his masculine liaisons, and walked about with his intimate boys Ba and Sao." His open homosexuality advertises his "condescending hatred of those whom he scandalized." Another character asks him: "Do you not wish for anything better? Is that enough–to sleep, eat, drink, smoke cigarettes and opium, make love to women–I mean, to boys?" Torral answers grandly, "Yes," and takes his leave. At the end of the novel, however, Torral is arrested and then flees, paying the price for a debauched life. For Farrère, the colonies offered a hospitable environment for excess, but such living does not come cheap.[25]

The most important and familiar example of homosexual colonial experiences is in the life and work of André Gide, the most openly homosexual literary figure in early twentieth-century France and the author of *Corydon*, an articulate defense of homosexuality.[26] It is well known that Gide was excited by youths from North Africa, where he experienced his own homosexual initiation, and that he transmuted his experiences into his writings. *The Immoralist*, published in 1902, tells the story of Michel, who journeys to North Africa for his honeymoon but is more attracted to village boys than to his wife. In 1926, a quarter century after *The Immoralist*, Gide published an autobiography, *If It Die . . .* , in which he spoke about his own journey to North Africa in 1893 and the loss of his virginity with a young Arab. Gide regularly returned to North Africa thereafter; on his second trip in 1895, he cruised boys with Oscar Wilde and Lord Alfred Douglas. The Maghreb remained for Gide, as for Lyautey, a place of desire and a veritable obsession.

Another homosexual writer (and artist) whose life and work touched on North Africa was François Augiéras.[27] In 1944, after a childhood spent in the United States and France, Augiéras did his military service in Algiers and after demobilisation spent the rest of the decade wandering around North Africa. A major stop was the small town of El Goléa and the house of his uncle, Marcel Augiéras, a former colonel and well-known explorer.[28] The nineteen-year-old François began a sadomasochistic affair with his uncle, then in his sixties; he willingly allowed himself to be beaten by his uncle, with whom he regularly had sex. He wrote about the relationship (making himself appear younger than he actually was) in *The Old Man and the Child*, a short book that he had privately printed under the *nom de plume* of Abdallah Chaamba. He boldly sent copies to a number of intellectuals, including Gide, who was impressed with the account. The book was commercially published in 1954.

The Voyage of the Dead, one of Augiéras's most accomplished books, records his life in North Africa in the 1950s. Full of lyrical descriptions of landscape and sexual encounters, it testifies to the transcendental nature of his experiences in the Atlas mountains, El Goléa, the oasis of Gardaia, the Moroccan port of Agadir, and a river voyage through Mali. He recounted easy sexual contacts with young Maghrebins, shepherds in the mountains, and city youths in Agadir. Some were "one-night stands," furtive pleasures taken in bushes or at the beach, often in a climate of extreme danger, which added an extra *frisson* to Augiéras's enjoyment, in the years leading up to Morocco's independence and in the midst of the Algerian war. Other relationships were longer-lived, and Augiéras told of falling in love with an Arab named Alec, whom he met outside a cinema and for whom he tried to find employment on the same ship where he was working. Among other partners were fellow Frenchmen, as well as the women whose services he procured in brothels.

North Africa and sex were almost synonymous for Augiéras, the pleasures of one reinforcing the other. "I dislike women, it is the young man who is beautiful, moving and truly sexual," he admitted. He celebrated the night sky and stars and the "caresses of young nomads," the virile young Arabs "whose clothes have the odor of the desert," who "smell of *chir* and thyme." Easy, unashamed sex–oral, anal, sadomasochistic, plus tender affection–was readily at hand with the Algerian or Moroccan youths whom other Frenchmen so despised. Augiéras found, briefly, in Alec, "the companion whom I had always hoped to find and keep for eternity." In North Africa, he located the "last laboratory for the Occident," the place where "it is possible that a new definition of man will more clearly appear."[29]

Augiéras claimed to despise France, the French, and French colonialism, preferring the vast expanses and uncomplicated sex of North Africa. He was another "barbarian" or "savage" (words he proudly applied to himself), disingenuously overlooking the benefits of travel, education, and opportunities that his status as a European provided, and finding more stimulation than danger in the "gay-bashing" that saw bands of local men attack Europeans as they cruised on the outskirts of cities. Homosexuality, for Augiéras, represented a vital component of his adventure-seeking, anti-modern persona; he argued that there are "two types of pederasty, one which issues from a surfeit of vitality, the other from decadence.... [T]he first type certainly appeared in the youths of Greece, healthy, robust, noble, useful to society, with unconstrained desires fed by an all-powerful flood of liberty." Only in a venue such as North Africa, a romanticised and mythologized North Africa, could a man find true happiness. What marks *The Voyage of the Dead*, in particular, is the transcendental feeling that Augiéras expresses about North Africa, the sense of being receptive to the beauties of the region, the joys of solitary contemplation, the excitement of market-places, cafés, and brothels, the pleasures of sex. All come together in physical and poetic enjoyment in a way reminiscent of the experiences of Lyautey and Gide in the "Oriental" desert.

A third example of homosexual fascination with North Africa and the Arab world, and the same coalescence of sexual and literary life as in Augiéras, is Jean Genet. Genet's links with Arabs spanned his life and appear in many of his writings. An introduction to the Islamic world came in 1930, when, as a young soldier, he was sent to Damascus, in the French protectorate of Syria. In the months he spent in the Middle East, Genet experienced the "exoticism, freedom, [and] army [life which] defined Damascus," and he fell in love with a sixteen-year-old hairdresser. The next year, Genet was sent to Morocco, where he fell for a Legionnaire, who let Genet have sex with him but would not or could not reciprocate his affections. By the early 1950s, Genet became involved in political affairs, taking part in protests against the Algerian war in 1955, a move which led to his being attacked in the press as a "professional pederast." The same year, he met Abdallah Bentaga, with whom he formed one of the most significant relationships in his life, and who, Edmund White has said, of all Genet's lovers, "would leave the deepest mark (one might say scar)" on him.

When they met, Genet was forty-five, and Bentaga eighteen. Bentaga was the son of an Algerian man and a German woman, and he followed his father into the circus to become a high-wire walker (his lessons paid for by Genet). By 1957, Genet dedicated to Bentaga *The Tightrope Walker*, a meditation on the danger and possible accidental death faced by a high-wire walker; Genet borrowed aspects of Bentaga's personality for a character in *The Folding Screens*, which he began at this time. Genet encouraged Bentaga to desert from the French army after he was called up to serve in Algeria; since Bentaga faced arrest for doing so, the two spent several years travelling around Europe. Genet pushed Bentaga to pursue his performing career, becoming, in White's phrase, the Pygmalion for the half-literate young acrobat, then coming to his aid when he fell and injured himself, but still hoping that he would return to the high-wire. By the early 1960s, Genet's affections turned towards another man. Bentaga became increasingly depressed because of both Genet's waning interests and his own physical inability, after injuries, to continue an acrobatic career. He committed suicide in 1964, leaving Genet distraught.

In 1970, Genet took his first trip to Palestinian camps in Jordan and made the acquaintance of a man called Hamza. Although Genet saw Hamza for only twenty-four hours, the young Palestinian haunted him afterwards. Genet made him a character in his book about the Palestinians, *A Captive in Love*, and later returned to the Middle East to search for Hamza after he was captured and tortured by Jordanian soldiers. The book was suffused with homoerotic descriptions of the virile young Palestinian warriors whose cause Genet espoused and who welcomed him into their camps. The Palestinian men and their campaign for a homeland in the 1970s, just like Bentaga and the way that he had symbolized the Algerian struggle for independence two decades before, became conjoined for Genet. Genet affirmed the connections between eroticism and revolution, between sex and anti-colonialism, his emotional and political seduction. Meanwhile, in 1974, in Tangier, Genet met Mohammed El Katrani, a Moroccan whose father had served in the French army; El Katrani became his final companion. They lived together in Tangier and Paris; Genet built houses for El Katrani and his wife and young son, of whom Genet became very fond, and for Genet himself, in Larache, Morocco. When Genet died in 1986, he was buried there.[30]

HOMOSEXUALITY AND ANTICOLONIALISM

Genet's life illustrates the fact that, in a way that is perhaps only initially paradoxical, many homosexuals with sexual interests overseas became firm critics of colonialism, even though colonies afforded them sexual opportunities and benefits. Gide's *Voyage to the Congo* and *Return from Chad* exposed and condemned exploitation of laborers in France's colonies in Black Africa. Genet's opposition to French rule in Algeria and his support for Palestinians (and American Black Panthers) created much controversy. Augiéras's disenchantment with Western mores hardly made him an apologist for imperialism. Other notable French anti-colonialists were also homosexual. Pierre Herbart, who journeyed with Gide to the Soviet Union in the 1930s, then visited Indochina before returning to criticize French rule in Vietnam, was sexually more attracted to Soviet workmen than to colonial "natives," but sexual dissidence, political rebellion and opposition to colonialism clearly combined in his life and work.[31]

An even more obvious case of the union of homosexuality and anti-colonialism is Daniel Guérin. Guérin rebelled against his privileged Parisian upbringing (his family were heirs to the Hachette publishing fortune), joined the socialist movement, and, throughout his long life, participated actively in libertarian, socialist, and anarchist politics. In the late 1920s, Guérin worked in Beirut, in the French protectorate of Lebanon, just after the Druze rebellion; soon afterwards, he visited Indochina and found himself in Vietnam during the Yen-Bay rebellion of 1930. Overseas experiences made him aware, he recalled, of the evils of colonial rule and imbued him with a deep-seated anti-colonialism. Guérin had several homosexual experiences overseas: a relatively long-lasting liaison with a French sailor in Beirut, a night with a Moroccan *spahi* stationed in the Levant, and a tryst with a servant in a Vietnamese hotel.[32] Although, like Herbart, he was sexually more attracted to proletarian Europeans than to Arabs or Asians, Guérin's sexual tastes, like his political sympathies for the victims of capitalism and colonialism, were broad.

In the early 1950s, Guérin established contacts with North African nationalists and wrote articles and books damning colonialism in Indochina, North Africa, and elsewhere. He took part in protests against French policy in North Africa in the 1950s, signed the "Appeal of the 121" against military conscription for the Algerian War in 1960 (for which he was arrested), attended meetings in post-independence Algeria, and investigated the death of Ahmed Ben Barka and others victims of the Boumediene coup d'état in 1965. In the last years of his life, Guérin espoused the nationalist cause of Kanaks in New Caledonia.

Guérin became involved in gay causes, writing about his sexual adventures in his autobiographies and living an openly homosexual life, although he had several heterosexual affairs and was briefly married. He was a longtime member of the French homophile emancipation organisation Arcadie, founded in 1954, but the more radical ideas of the sexual revolutionaries of 1968 and afterwards, including the Homosexual Front for Revolutionary Action, were congenial to him, and Guérin, then in his sixties, enthusiastically attended gay liberation meetings in Paris.

For Guérin, his personal life, including his homosexuality, and his political beliefs (socialism, anarchism, anti-racism, anti-colonialism) were inseparable. As he wrote in an epigraph to one volume of his autobiography, "I believe for my part, that a single and identical vital force . . . has propelled my existence, both political and carnal." His "revolutionary options" and his "amatory penchants" were two sides of the same coin, which, he affirmed, he had no ability or need to separate and which embodied "the two parts of the same vital flux:

one, the priority, was aimed towards a radical transformation of society; the other, in complementary fashion, but just as urgent, was directed at the love of men."[33]

A similar cohabitation of sexual, political, and literary life, with North Africa the arena, occurred with Jean Sénac. Born near Oran, Algeria, Sénac was a *pied-noir* (white settler) whose mother was of Spanish ancestry (he knew nothing of his father except that he was a hairdresser). After growing up in poverty, Sénac served in the French air force in the Second World War, then spent several years in a sanatorium, suffering from typhoid. By the early 1950s, he had moved to Algiers to make a name for himself as a poet. His first book appeared, thanks to the help of Albert Camus, in Paris in 1954, the year that marked the start of the Algerian war of independence. Sénac spent the war years in France, where he continued writing poetry and essays, including poignant open letters asking fellow *pieds-noirs* to support the National Liberation Front and independence for Algeria. This position caused Sénac, and those who shared his views, to be branded as traitors during a time of strife that almost reduced France itself to civil war. When Algeria gained independence in 1962, Sénac returned to Algiers, moving against the current which saw a million *pieds-noirs* flee Algeria. He worked as a radio presenter and compiled anthologies of French-language Algerian poetry, encouraging young poets in his entourage, and writing his own verses, but increasingly he was out of step with the authorities, especially after the 1965 coup. Sénac's dream of a multicultural, modern, and prosperous Algeria now seemed betrayed, and he became more and more marginalized. In 1973, he was murdered, though it remains uncertain whether by a former sexual partner or on the order of authorities who found it intolerable that the man acclaimed as Algeria's leading French-language poet was a political dissident of European and Christian background and an open homosexual.[34]

Sénac's prose and poetry celebrate the beauty of Algeria and its revolutionary fervor and the beauty of the adolescents whom he met on the beach or at the cinema and who became his sexual partners. Sex and revolution, for Sénac, as for Guérin, were inseparable. His most famous poem, "Citizens of Beauty," begins:

> And now we shall sing about love
> Because there is no Revolution without Love,
> There is no morning without a smile. . . .
> We must sing of Revolution,
> The eternally renewed body of the Woman,
> The hand of the Friend.

Sexual pleasure for Sénac formed an integral part of his commitment to Algeria, though sometimes he was disappointed by both. In words that were almost unheard of at the time–lines such as "Cum in my mouth" and poems with such titles as "Directory of the Anus"–Sénac recounted his sexual adventures. One poem, the elliptical but beautiful "The Race," echoes the disappearance of French Algeria and the burning of the Algiers library by the viciously anti-independence OAS in the closing phase of the war, but also evokes the seashore and describes oral sex with an Arab youth. Sénac's poetry is filled with the sun of the Mediterranean and the joys of sex, but his works enunciate a coherent critique of colonialism and lament the failures of post-independence Algeria. They recount casual trysts and longer-lasting friendships. Escaping the Orientalist clichés of earlier writers, they take the busy port and capital of Algiers in the 1950s and 1960s as a venue for sexual pleasures, political activism, and literary efforts.

Sénac is a special figure in French life for the openness of his homosexual sentiments mixed with ideological and personal dedication to anti-colonialism and a defence of the cultural and political rights of the Algerians among whom he lived, a commitment that went beyond literature to become fully personal. He was a Frenchman by culture (he never learned Arabic and did not take out Algerian citizenship) who identified with the colonized land of his birth and upbringing, the Maghrebins who composed the majority of its population, and their aspirations to independence. The links between literary vocation, political stance, and sexual desire are even clearer in his life and work than in the cases of Gide, Genet, or Augiéras.

HOMOSEXUALITY AND COLONIALISM

Traces of homosexuality in the colonies range from canonical literature to tacky anecdotes, classic novels to avant-garde poetry, and unknown troopers and colonists to such "greats" as Gide and Genet. Lyautey and de Lattre de Tassigny were establishment figures and heros of France's civilizing mission; on the other side stood rebels such as Herbart, Guérin, and Sénac. Their experiences range from anonymous encounters with youths in the Atlas mountains, Algerian oases, and metropolitan Algiers (and *boys* in Indochina) to the clearly abiding friendships between Rimbaud and Djami or Genet and Bentaga. Such a breadth of representation is hardly surprising. It confirms the gay lib slogan, "We are everywhere," but also suggests that in diverse cases, homosexuality was connected in some major way with the colonial venture, with the comfort of masculine military camaraderie for some, the seduction of handsome foreign youths for many, the opportunities overseas for sexual initiation and pleasures censured in Europe for all of them. Yet homosexuality might itself make foreign countries attractive, whether Muslim North Africa or Buddhist Indochina, and lead to a colonial vocation.

Homosexuality, as played out in the colonies, forms a key theme in works by authors as different as Gide, Genet, and Farrère, for whom the exoticism of foreign locations was linked to the seductions of sex. The transcendental experience of the North African desert is written about by Lyautey and Augiéras; the pleasures of sex, whether described discreetly or in detail, are recorded in the novels of Gide, the poems of Sénac and the fictionalized autobiographies of Augiéras (as well as the sexual travelogue of Jacobus X.). Homosexuality is a crucial aspect of the lives of these writers and others of their compatriots. The feeling of being considered a sexual pariah by right-minded people could stimulate a feeling of identification with victims of imperialism. When Gide damned colonial labor exploitation in equatorial Africa in the interwar years, when Sénac opted for an independent Algeria, and when Guérin and Genet were drawn to the gay and anti-colonial movements, a fight for sexual emancipation and colonial liberation went hand in hand. The sexual, and the homosexual, in the colonies as in Europe, was personal, cultural, and political.[35]

NOTES

1. The pioneering study is Ronald Hyam, *Empire and Sexuality: The British Experience* (Manchester, 1990).
2. Rudi C. Bleys, *The Geography of Perversion: Male-to-Male Sexual Behavior Outside the West and the Ethnographic Imagination, 1750-1918* (New York, 1995).
3. For an overview, see Robert Aldrich, "Homosexuality and Colonialism," *Thamyris* 3 (1996): 175-91.
4. Jacobus X., *L'Art d'aimer aux colonies* [1893] (Paris, 1927), 54-62, 67-78 (Cochinchina), 97-8 (Tonkin), 129 (Cambodia), 156, 163-7 (Guiana), 255-6 (Africa), 300-7 (New Caledonia), 384 (Tahiti).
5. Ibid., 55-65, 81, 87.
6. Ibid., 58. The words in italics were published in Latin.
7. Ibid., 299.
8. Ibid., 156.
9. Ibid., 167.
10. Ibid., 255.
11. Ibid., 311-2, 337.
12. Michael Sibalis, "Tardieu, Ambroise," in *Who's Who in Gay and Lesbian History: From Antiquity to the Mid-Twentieth Century*, ed. Robert Aldrich and Garry Wotherspoon (London, 2000), 432-3.
13. Bleys, *Geography of Perversion*, 149.
14. Gérard Zwang, *La Fonction érotique* (Paris, 1975), quoted in Christian Gury, *Lyautey-Charlus* (Paris, 1998), 67.
15. Quoted in ibid., 64.
16. Georges Saint-Paul, *Invertis et homosexuels*, 2nd ed. (Paris, 1930), 36. I am grateful to Michael Sibalis for this and the following two references.
17. René Jude, *Les Dégénéres dans les bataillons d'Afrique* (Vannes, 1907).
18. Paul Rebierre, *"Joyeux" et demi-fous* (Paris, 1909).

19. Dr. Tranchant and Lieutenant Desvignes, in *Les Condamnés militaires du pénitencier de Bossuet,* quoted in Gury, *Lyautey-Charlus*, 248.

20. "Médecine militaire: Déni de justice," *Le Bulletin médical* 6 (1892): 65-7.

21. See Michel Larivière, *Homosexuels et bisexuels célèbres: Le Dictionnaire* (Paris, 1997), passim.

22. Gury, *Lyautey-Charlus.*

23. Quoted in Larivière, *Homosexuels et bisexuels,* 230.

24. On Flaubert, see his letters to Maxime du Camp and the novel *Salammbô.* On Saint-Saëns, Brian Rees, *Camille Saint-Saëns: A Life* (London, 1999), 239. In *Somebody Else: Arthur Rimbaud in Africa, 1880-91* (London, 1997), chapter 15, Charles Nicholl goes to great (and unconvincing) lengths to prove that Djami Ouddei was not Rimbaud's lover. On Loti, Lesley Blanch, *Pierre Loti: Portrait of an Escapist* (London, 1983). On Dinet, François Pouillon, *Les Deux vies d'Etienne Dinet, peintre en Islam* (Paris, 1997), who admits the intimate relationship between the two men but denies that it was sexual. Paul Gauguin confesses to his temptation in *Noa Noa: Voyage to Tahiti*, ed. Jean Loize (Oxford, 1966), 23-5.

25. Claude Farrère, *Les Civilisés* [1905] (Paris, 1997). Another colonial novel with a homoerotic theme is *Malaisie* (Paris, 1930) by Henri Fauconnier, a pioneering rubber-planter in Malaya. The plot revolves around the friendship between two Frenchmen and their relationships with male Malay servants, and the novel is suffused with homosocial tension among the four male characters.

26. See, e.g., Alan Sheridan, *André Gide: A Life in the Present* (London, 1998).

27. Gert Hekma, "François Augiéras (1925-1971)," *Paidika* 3 (1991): 57-64; and Paul Placet, *François Augiéras: Un Barbare en Occident* (Périgueux, 1988).

28. Guy Dugas, "Les Oncles d'Algérie," in *François Augiéras, ou Le Théâtre des esprits* (Poitiers, 1998), 38-46.

29. François Augiéras, *Le Voyage des morts* [1959] (Paris, 1979), 75, 168, 186, 79, 185, 94, 125.

30. Details of Genet's involvement with the Arab world are taken from Edmund White, *Genet* (New York, 1993).

31. Pierre Herbart, *La Ligne de force* (Paris, 1958) details his travels to the Far East and opposition to colonialism. See also his *Souvenirs imaginaires* (Paris, 1968), and Philippe Berthier, *Pierre Herbart: Morale et style de la désinvolture* (Paris, 1998).

32. Daniel Guérin, *Autobiographie de jeunesse* (Paris, 1972), especially 208, 222-3.

33. Daniel Guérin, *Le Feu du sang: Autobiographie politique et charnelle* (Paris, 1977), 8, 10; and the special issue of *Alternative libertaire*, published (*hors-série*) in 1999. In English, see Peter Sedgwick, "Out of Hiding: The Comradeships of Daniel Guérin," *Salmagundi* 58-9 (1982-3): 197-220.

34. Jean Sénac, *Oeuvres poétiques* (Arles, 1999) and *Pour une terre possible . . . Poèmes et autres textes inédits* (Paris, 1999). On his life and work, see most recently, Jamel-Eddine Bencheikh and Christiane Chaulet-Achour, *Jean Sénac: Clandestin des deux rives* (Paris, 1999).

35. The formal end of the empire did not bring to an end French homosexual fascination with the former colonies, especially those of North Africa, as can be seen in novels by Dominique Fernandez, Michel Tournier, Rachid O., Eyet-Chékib Djaziri, and Gregory Bastien, as well as the memoirs of Roland Barthes.

Folles, Swells, Effeminates, and Homophiles in Saint-Germain-des-Prés of the 1950s: A New "Precious" Society?

Georges Sidéris

Editors' note: This is a translation of the original text.[1]

In *Giovanni's Room* the American novelist James Baldwin described the atmosphere in a homosexual bar in the Saint-Germain-des-Prés quarter of Paris during the 1950s. Among the bar's clients, Baldwin focused on "*les folles* [the effeminate queens], always dressed in the most improbable combinations, screaming like parrots the details of their latest love affairs . . . they always called each other 'she.' "[2] Saint-Germain-des-Prés at that time was the principal setting for male homosexual life in Paris. According to a 1954 article in the anarchist periodical *L'Unique*, "this quarter has become homosexuality's command post."[3] It was the site of what would today be called "gay visibility." But homosexual life was not confined to this one quarter. The rue du Colisée and the avenue Gabriel, the Champs-Élysées and the streets around the place de l'Étoile, the Montparnasse quarter (on the Left Bank) and Montmartre quarter (on the Right Bank), the rue des Martyrs, the Saint-Lazare railway station, the Montagne Sainte-Geneviève in the Latin Quarter (famous for its balls where "the men wear evening gowns, the women trousers"), place Pigalle, the

[Haworth co-indexing entry note]: "*Folles,* Swells, Effeminates, and Homophiles in Saint-Germain-des-Prés of the 1950s: A New 'Precious' Society?" Sidéris, Georges. Co-published simultaneously in *Journal of Homosexuality* (Harrington Park Press, an imprint of The Haworth Press, Inc.) Vol. 41, No. 3/4, 2001, pp. 219-231; and: *Homosexuality in French History and Culture* (ed: Jeffrey Merrick, and Michael Sibalis) Harrington Park Press, an imprint of The Haworth Press, Inc., 2001, pp. 219-231. Single or multiple copies of this article are available for a fee from The Haworth Document Delivery Service [1-800-342-9678, 9:00 a.m. - 5:00 p.m. (EST). E-mail address: getinfo@haworthpressinc.com].

rue de Lappe near the Bastille, and the *grands boulevards* in general were also heavily frequented by homosexuals.[4] This list should also include such traditional sites of homosexual cruising as the Bois de Boulogne and the Bois de Vincennes, the quays along the Seine, the Tuileries Gardens, the Champs de Mars, and the city's many bathhouses. Finally, there appeared in these years a number of homosexual venues, or rather venues regularly frequented by homosexuals, in the area around the rue Sainte-Anne.[5]

Saint-Germain-des-Prés, however, had a special place in the homosexual geography and sociability of the period. The air of freedom, merry-making, and non-conformity given it by existentialists such as Jean-Paul Sartre and Simone de Beauvoir, the presence of numerous artists and writers, the theatres that put on politically committed plays, in short the more open and tolerant attitude that prevailed there, probably explain in part this homosexual presence in Saint-Germain, where one might encounter, for example, open homosexuals like the writers Jean Genet and Jean Cocteau or the actor Jean Marais.[6] Homosexuals showed themselves openly in the cafés, particularly the Flore, the Reine Blanche, the Royal Saint-Germain, and the Pergola.[7] The Fiacre, a specifically homosexual bar and restaurant at 4 rue du Cherche-Midi, was world famous and much appreciated. It drew an international clientele like the British writer Christopher Isherwood in 1955, and in the summer the overflow of customers spilled out onto the street. There was homosexual cruising by men of all social classes in Saint-Germain, as almost everywhere else in Paris, in the street urinals. These structures, which punctuated the sidewalks of the boulevard Saint-Germain and indeed the entire neighbourhood, offered the unlucky visitor a second chance for a sexual encounter a little further along should he fail to make contact in the first urinal he tried.[8] The homosexual press of the period recognized and promoted the homosexual presence in Saint-Germain-des-Prés. *Futur*, a homosexual newspaper that appeared in the early 1950s, trumpeted in October 1952 that "Saint-Germain-des-Prés, capital of non-conformity, [is] the only place in Paris where you can amuse yourself according to your tastes."[9]

Thus, the post-war homosexual geography of Paris was very different from that of pre-war Paris, which had been dominated by the Montmartre, Pigalle, and Montparnasse quarters of the city.[10] Saint-Germain offered the daily spectacle of a free and open homosexual life, where different styles of homosexuality rubbed shoulders, but the quarter was famous above all for its *folles*, who were not specific to it but who stood out by their effeminate mannerisms, their swishing walk, their elegant clothes, sometimes their facial makeup, and especially their mannered way of speaking, often punctuated with piercing shrieks, which distinguished them from other homosexuals.[11] In writing of Saint-Germain's *folles*, Baldwin remarked significantly: "I always found it difficult to believe that they ever went to bed with anybody, for a man who wanted a woman would certainly have rather had a real one and a man who wanted a man would certainly not want one of *them*. Perhaps, indeed, that was why they screamed so loud."[12] Baldwin subscribed here to a "virile" vision of homosexuality and of human love in general, a vision that might today be qualified as "hetero-centric." He could not imagine that the *folles* could be attractive to other men, either heterosexual or homosexual.

Indeed, generally speaking, effeminacy has been condemned in Western culture since the second half of the eighteenth century as the opposite of the ideally virile man. Jews and homosexuals have been portrayed as effeminate beings, counter-types incapable of attaining that masculine ideal. In such representations, the homosexual threatened the male-centred order by blurring what ought to be a clear distinction between the sexes.[13] The question of the relation between homosexuality and femininity, examined in terms of the problem of "sexual inversion," can be found not only in the discourses hostile to homosexuals, but also, between about 1850 and 1950, in the reflections and preoccupations of homosexuals themselves.[14] As George Mosse has noted, the love stories published in German homosexual periodicals between 1929 and 1979 stressed the normative ideal of virility through the evocation of "beautiful young men."[15]

This homosexual effervescence in Saint-Germain-des-Prés was not to everybody's taste; it annoyed the political authorities and the forces of law and order. In a speech at a general assembly of Interpol in 1958, the director of criminal investigations at the Paris Prefecture of Police, after dealing with cases of prostitution, blackmail, and murder involving homosexuals, described the homosexual world as "a milieu favourable to delinquency" and a "breeding ground" for criminal viruses. His treatment of homosexuality as pathological served to justify the remainder of the talk, which constituted, in effect, the speech's real purpose. The director went on to say that "One can therefore easily imagine the danger presented by homosexual proselytism and publicity." This preoccupation with public manifestations of homosexuality seems to have been the central focus of the talk to the extent that it was repeated by the director.

> What draws our attention and leads us to believe that homosexuality has increased in France, is that for several years, it has been making itself more conspicuous. Its adepts meet in certain public places, cafés, bars, [and] cabarets, where they constitute almost the only clientele; they sometimes stand out by their distinctive behavior, notably their clothing, which, not to speak of transvestism, which is forbidden by the law, reveals to everybody's eyes, the morals of certain ephebes, by their bleached hair, [and] by their general affected bearing which leaves no doubt.[16]

It seems likely that Saint-Germain was included in this "description" of homosexual life, even if the wording remains rather vague. "Affectation" was one of the elements, indeed the characteristic sign that publicly "signified" homosexuality. Homosexual visibility at Saint-Germain and consequently homosexual sociability–particularly among the "effeminates," who were the most conspicuous there–posed a problem for the authorities. Moreover, their hostility toward homosexual effeminacy was widely shared even by "homophile" periodicals and by many homosexuals themselves.

The term "homophilia" covered several realities. Derived from the Greek roots *"homos" (the same) and "philein*" (to love), it meant "an emotional attraction to someone resembling oneself."[17] Homophilia defined the homosexual in terms not only of his sexuality, but of his entire being. As a natural phenomenon, the homophile both demanded respect and required study.[18] Homophilia also referred more broadly to the international homosexual movement, which was fighting to change public opinion, that is to say, challenging anti-homosexual prejudice and seeking to promote sexual equality in all fields and to repeal discriminatory legislation against homosexuals wherever it existed.[19] "Homophilia" has also been used to refer to the period of homosexual history that stretches from the end of World War II to the late 1960s, that is to say, until the appearance of revolutionary movements for homosexual liberation like the Gay Liberation Front in the United States after the Stonewall riots of June 1969 or the Homosexual Front for Revolutionary Action (FHAR) in France in 1971.[20] Homophile ideas were adopted and spread in France by the monthly periodical *Arcadie* and in other countries by the reviews *Der Kreis* in Switzerland, *Vriendschap* in the Netherlands, and *The Mattachine Review* and *One* in the United States.[21]

In 1960 *Der Kreis* declared, in a review of a Michael Nelson's 1958 novel, *A Room in Chelsea Square*:

> The worst thing in this book is the intentionally frivolous tone, the wholly feminine preciousness that is really the most nauseating thing among men. You will get an exact picture of the novel by taking a turn around Saint-Germain-des-Prés, whether at the Flore or the Fiacre. This tends to give the public the impression that the homosexual world is made up of frivolous and feminine creatures.[22]

The following year, Marc Daniel wrote in *Arcadie*, "You speak a great deal about a certain androphile world–one that moves between the bars of the Champs-Élysées and those of Saint-Germain-des-Prés–elegant and smart, refined and ridiculous. . . . This world doubtlessly exists . . . but I really believe that it exists only in those [particular] places, or, from June to September, on the Croisette [in Cannes]."[23] Again, in 1959, another article in the same periodical described Saint-Germain and its effeminates this way:

> It was 11 p.m. I was dawdling at the carrefour Saint-Germain-des-Prés, curious once again to regard 'their' appearance, 'their' silhouette, to observe . . . the crush of male prostitutes, the footsteps of the eager cruisers, of the playful, of the small groups of four or five friends triumphantly self-assured and defiant in their staccato paces, noisy, letting out high-pitched cries, hand in hand or arm on shoulder, rigged out in a combination of America and Saint-Germain-des-Prés. What a bedlam, what a display in front of every café![24]

It is pointless to accumulate such quotations. We will mention only one more by André Baudry, which is particularly significant because of Baudry's position as founder and director of *Arcadie*, which was both a homophile periodical published from 1954 and a private club established in 1957 as a SARL (private business with limited liability) under the name Literary and Scientific Club of the Latin Countries (CLESPALA).[25] In November 1961, Baudry, speaking of Saint-Germain, wrote in the review: "Homophiles do not want to be confused with these caricatures, these peddlers of love or embraces, these exhibitionists, these 'boys who bear no resemblance to a boy.' That is understood."[26] Thus, effeminacy and the homosexual lifestyle at Saint-Germain were called into question in *Arcadie* by a number of writers, including those in the top ranks of the editorial staff.[27]

These quotations suggest that *Der Kreis* and *Arcadie* had assimilated the social stigmatization of homosexuals into their own discourse. We must, however, nuance this conclusion. To be sure, *Arcadie* did not speak highly of effeminacy, but in the 1950s its tone was more usually one of disapproval and disparagement rather than outright hostility. It is true, of course, that effeminacy was contrary to *Arcadie*'s conception of the ideal homophile. For *Arcadie* homosexuality was natural, a variant form of sexuality. For that reason, *Arcadie* sought to educate its readers as to the physiological, psychological, and psychoanalytical causes of homosexuality. Baudry knew Kinsey's report, which he mentioned in the very first issue of *Arcadie*.[28] For *Arcadie*, the homophile was a man who happened to love men but who was otherwise like anyone else. As Baudry expressed it, "*Arcadie* at least has the merit of wanting to make things clear, of wanting homophiles to blend in with others, without singularities, without eccentricities."[29] By "singularities" and "eccentricities" Baudry undoubtedly meant effeminacy. Effeminacy was the opposite of the behavior expected of the homophile, whose discretion would permit him to integrate into the wider society so that "nothing distinguishes him."[30]

All of these various condemnations of effeminacy demonstrate the existence of an effeminate form of homosociability that was too recent to be truly understood by everyone in the 1950s. People interpreted what they saw as outlandish behavior in terms of an existing dichotomy between virility and effeminacy. But the effeminacy evident in post-war Saint-Germain no longer had the same significance as effeminacy before World War II. Saint-Germain was a quarter distinguished by social and cultural non-conformity, and homosexual effeminacy there was but one aspect of this broader non-conformity in the way that it called into question established gender norms. Indeed, for what was this homosexual sociability at Saint-Germain criticized: effeminacy, affectation, preciousness, silliness, and excessive (even extravagant) elegance in clothing, body, speech, bearing, and literary expression? The vocabulary used by critics evoked seventeenth-century "preciousness," both as it really existed and also in the form mocked by the playwright Molière: a society distinguished by its taste for a certain affectation, by its worldliness, by its extravagant language, by its desire to stand out, but also a society that can equally be seen as manifesting imagination and liberty.[31] One inevitably thinks, too, of the *incroyables* and *merveilleuses* under the Directory (1795-99) and of the nineteenth-century dandies, who similarly expressed their freedom through fashion and lifestyle.[32]

The presence of effeminates and *folles* in Paris and more generally in French homosexual life was nothing new, any more than the condemnations that they aroused. What changed the situation, however, was that an effeminate style and more generally an uninhibited homosexual lifestyle, distinguished by elegance to the point of affection, flourished in a district reputed for its social and cultural nonconformity. Saint-Germain was defying the established hetero-centric order, and that provoked opposition, sometimes very virulent indeed, both from the established authorities and even from certain homosexual militants and periodicals. It is understandable that in a France emerging from wartime restrictions and just entering into a new age of consumerism and leisure, this elegance could shock and appear provocative.[33] It nonetheless remains true that this urban sociability, which permitted homosexuals to establish and maintain relations with other homosexuals, was fundamental to their elaboration of a specific identity.[34] A lifestyle labelled outrageous by its detractors in fact reflected the will of a certain number of homosexuals to live free of the moral and material constraints within which the dominant social and moral order wanted to confine them. They mixed elegance, affectation, and worldly frivolity in word, body, and clothing, in the heart of a quarter where nonconformist men of letters and artists rubbed shoulders. They affirmed an identity that took the form of what might be called a "new homosexual preciousness."

It was the periodical *Futur* that most clearly voiced and celebrated this reality. *Futur*, published in the first half of the 1950s by Jean Thibault, affirmed its approval of the free homosexual life at Saint-Germain, "where everybody can appear as he is deep down."[35] *Futur* never stopped denouncing police surveillance, notably at Saint-Germain, and the moralizing attitude of France's Christian democratic party (MRP) and in particular of the parliamentary deputy Pierre-Henri Teitgen (president of the party from 1952 to 1956).[36] *Futur* put this slogan on its masthead: "Tartuffe [a religious hypocrite in Molière's play of that name] is despicable, but Tartuffe reigns over the public authorities." Even if *Futur* apparently did not appreciate pre-war Pigalle, where "so many homosexuals of all kinds used to show off, so many young men ostentatiously made up strolled about," it always took pleasure in the homosexual life that thrived in Saint-Germain.

On the other hand, *Arcadie* seems to have perceptibly shifted its position on effeminacy from the late 1950s. The tone became harsher, even blatantly hostile. In 1958, Baudry declared: "Homosexuality must no longer be . . . a synonym for neurosis, exhibitionism, or effeminacy."[37] In 1976, in an article referring to past years, he wrote:

> The homophile lives within society. Nothing distinguishes him. There was once a very sad time, let us hope long gone, when many homophiles sought to be conspicuous. We know all too well their eccentric get-ups, swaying walks, cackling voices, made-up faces, in other words that carnival that went on all year long. Let us rejoice to see that the new generation of homosexuals, as a whole, is adopting a behavior that is more virile, more dignified, more healthy, more human. . . . The homosexual who lives in society is a man, not a doll, a clown, a sexless being, or an imitation woman; any more than a lesbian is an imitation man.[38]

André Baudry here accepted the "virile" conception of men as formulated by dominant social norms. But in so doing, he crossed over a line and began treating effeminacy as pathological, as when he pronounced in favour of a "more virile, more dignified, more healthy" behavior for homophiles. But the effeminates, especially those at Saint-Germain, were the most visible part of the homosexual world. André Baudry and *Arcadie* did more than simply refuse to identify with their lifestyle; in condemning effeminacy in the terms that they did, they displayed what could be called today a form of "homophobia" directed against other homosexuals.[39]

Why did their thinking take this direction? The answer lies with the increased police surveillance and repression evident in the 1950s. *Futur* had already been complaining about police raids in Saint-Germain in the early and mid-1950s.[40] By the end of the decade, the public expression of homosexuality there and particularly the conspicuous effeminacy were frequently associated with male prostitution and this brought increased calls for stepped up police intervention in the press.[41] *Arcadie*, which claimed to represent all homophiles and which sought to educate the authorities about homophilia, feared above all the negative psychological impact of this identification of homosexuality with prostitution and effeminacy.[42] Here we touch on the heart of the question. The respective positions of *Futur* and *Arcadie* were ideological and political. In the first half of the 1950s, *Futur* repeatedly denounced puritanism and the reigning moral order in France, the symbol of which was, in its eyes, the MRP. For *Futur*, homosexuals had to denounce and fight against the anti-homosexual legislation linked to this moral order if they wanted to win equal rights. *Futur* wanted to change social attitudes in order to achieve true equality in the exercise of one's sexuality. For this reason, *Futur* rejoiced in the presence of homosexuals in Saint-Germain because they represented a free expression of homosexual desire.[43] The situation was quite different for *Arcadie*, which had no intention of challenging the fundamental moral order that governed society. *Arcadie* wanted the social integration of homophiles by having them accept social norms.[44] *Arcadie*'s strategy consequently stood in stark opposition to *Futur*'s stress on self-affirmation and visibility. Their respective treatment of effeminacy and of Saint-Germain is one of the points where the divergence between their conceptions can most easily be seen.

The facts that since 1791 France has had no legislation outlawing homosexual relations between consenting adults, that *Arcadie* continued to appear uncensored on the French newsstands, and that other homophile reviews like *One* were available abroad, were, for Baudry, all encouraging signs that homosexuals were winning the battle for social acceptance.[45] But the situation changed abruptly in 1960. On 18 July of that year, taking advantage of a debate in the National Assembly on the "social scourges" of alcoholism and prostitution, the deputy Paul Mirguet denounced "the seriousness of this scourge of homosexuality, a scourge against which we have the duty to protect our children." He persuaded parliament to adopt a sub-amendment to the Law of 30 July 1960, so that homosexuality was included among the social scourges. The law authorized the government to take "all measures necessary to fight against homosexuality."[46] As a result, an ordinance issued on 25 November 1960 added a line to Article 330 of the Penal Code, increasing the penalty for an offense against decency when it involved "an act against nature with an individual of the same sex."[47] A social scourge, homosexuality was henceforth a crime within the public sphere, and its manifestation had to remain strictly confined to the private sphere. From the moment that the amendment was voted, Baudry blamed prostitution and transvestism for its adoption. The new and harsher legislation confirmed, in his eyes, the need to struggle against prostitution and those excesses that had so discredited homophilia.[48] *Arcadie*, therefore, became even more critical of effeminates and consequently of the "precious" culture that flourished publicly in Saint-Germain-des-Prés. Nor was *Arcadie* alone in the homosexual movement in taking up this position against effeminacy at Saint-Germain in 1959-1960.

A new monthly revue, *Juventus*, published in 1959-60 (the first number appeared in May 1959) took up much the same position. Beginning in the second issue, the review clearly set out its views.

> You say that people reject you? Go then one evening to Saint-Germain-des-Prés and open your eyes and take a good look at your fellow creatures. Look at their bearing, their gestures, listen to their shrieks and consider their ways. If you are revolted, it's because you have understood. You have understood that a man, a real one, cannot stand that another man caricature a woman. . . . You will have understood that the ostracism of which you complain is a function of the provocation that you revel in.[49]

Juventus, whose motto was "Virility, Health, Truth," promoted a virile homosexuality that was (it thought) more likely to make homosexuals acceptable to society. Even if *Juventus* was an ephemeral periodical, its language and its photographs, which emphasized health, the body, nature, and youth, conformed to the spirit of the age, when France, invigorated by the baby boom, was modernizing and becoming a consumer society, and when the body was being uncovered and observed (think of Roger Vadim's 1956 film, *And God Created Woman*, in which Brigitte Bardot incarnated the new woman, free with her body and in her aspirations).[50] But at the same time, *Juventus* condemned the "precious" lifestyle that it perceived as the cause of social rejection. Once again, the effeminates of Saint-Germain were scapegoated for the harassment experienced by the homosexual world. But those homosexuals hostile to Saint-Germain failed to see that its artificial and affected culture represented a distinctive and authentic homosexual identity that challenged a normalizing society, which is what *Futur* was saying when it evoked Saint-Germain as the "only place in Paris where one can enjoy oneself according to one's tastes." Indeed, homosexual life in the 1960s continued to thrive at Saint-Germain, which still incarnated the world of the "third sex," with its *folles*, effeminates, and *précieux*, despite the criticism levelled against it.[51]

It was only in the 1970s that this world disappeared. Homosexual life in Paris changed and migrated toward other districts. Only then would there be regret for this society that had produced a genuine homosexual way of life, playful and festive, but which now developed elsewhere and took other forms.[52] Henceforth, in the words of someone nostalgic for the good old days, "There is no longer any appeal . . . to Saint-Germain-des-Prés."[53]

Saint-Germain des Prés in the 1950s was the site for the elaboration and the expression of what we can call a "new precious society" of homosexuals. This homosexual lifestyle that flourished in a district with a specific character–festive, light-hearted, and nonconformist–constituted a refusal of the social order and the dominant morality, which tried to limit the expression of homosexuality to the strictly private sphere, where homosexuals were expected to remain discreet. Effeminates in general and those of Saint-Germain in particular encountered disapproval, not only from the established authorities, but also from homophiles who did not accept their culture of effeminacy and preciousness, which they considered caricatural and likely to provoke an increased repression of homosexuality. The homophilic discourse on effeminacy and the homosexual life at Saint-Germain shifted in the course of the 1950s from disapproval and disparagement to frank and outright hostility. In the end, increased policing and a new political situation had encouraged the development among homosexuals themselves of a "homophobia" directed against effeminates. But it must be noted that a similar current of thought developed simultaneously among many homosexuals unaffiliated with *Arcadie* or *Juventus*. Its foundations, it seems, were generational rather than ideological. Younger homosexuals began disparaging the "precious" lifestyle as an outmoded expression of homosexual identity. Saint-Germain, however, still remained, well into the 1960s, a vibrant and privileged site of homosexual preciousness; it would be interesting to study this continuation in the French homosexual lifestyle and in French society in general.

NOTES

1. Translated by Michael Sibalis.
2. James Baldwin, *Giovanni's Room* (New York, 1956), 39.
3. Gaston Criel, "Lettre de Paris: Histoire et psychologie d'un mythe: Saint-Germain-des-Prés," *L'Unique* 89-90 (November-December 1954): 209.
4. See "Yvan Audouard vous présente le troisième sexe comme si vous en étiez," *France Dimanche* 120 (19 December 1948): 7 (quotation from this article); Rodney Garland, *Le Coeur en exil* (originally published as *The Heart in Exile* [London, 1953]) (Paris, 1959), 229; and the list of Parisian establishments in the German homosexual periodical *Der Neue Ring*, 12 December 1958, v.
5. Michael Sibalis, "Paris," in *Queer Sites: Gay Urban Histories since 1600*, ed. David Higgs (London, 1999), Pierre Servez, *Le Mal du siècle* (Paris, 1955), 30-6; and Frédéric Martel, *Le Rose et le noir: Les Homosexuels en France depuis 1968* (Paris, 1996), 89.

6. Pascal Ory and Jean-François Sirinelli, *Les Intellectuels en France, de l'affaire Dreyfus à nos jours* (Paris, 1992), 148-89. Jean-Paul Caracalla, *Saint-Germain-des-Prés* (Paris, 1993) reproduces photographs of Genet (168), Cocteau (59, 64-65, 123) and Marais (97).

7. "Saint-Germain-des-Prés, capitale du non-conformisme," *Futur* 1 (October 1952): 2. For these establishments, see Caracalla, *Saint-Germain*, 83, 87, 95; and "Le 3e sexe envahit Saint-Germain-des-Prés," *France Dimanche* 787 (21-7 September 1961), 8.

8. Sibalis, "Paris," 18-21, 29 -30; Martel, *Rose*, 83-4; and Daniel Garcia, *Les Années Palace* (Paris, 1999), 18-9.

9. "Saint-Germain-des-Prés, capitale," 2.

10. Florence Tamagne, *L'Histoire de l'homosexualité en Europe: Berlin, Londres, Paris, 1919-1939* (Paris, 2000), 79-91; and Sibalis, "Paris," 27-9.

11. Alexandre Raphael, "Les Lois de l'hospitalité," *Arcadie* (October 1959), 547; and "3e sexe," 8. On Paris's *folles*, see Jean Genet, *Notre-Dame-des-Fleurs* (Paris, 1988), especially 64, 96-8; and Roger Peyrefitte, *Des Français* (Paris, 1970), 229-30.

12. Baldwin, *Giovanni's Room*, 39.

13. See George L. Mosse, *The Image of Man: The Creation of Modern Masculinity* (New York, 1996), 3-16, 66-76.

14. See the discussion of Marcel Proust and Karl Heinrich Ulrichs in Didier Eribon, *Réflexions sur la question gay* (Paris, 1999), 120-8.

15. Mosse, *Image*, 149.

16. M. Fernet, "L'Homosexualité et son influence sur la délinquance," *Revue internationale de la police criminelle* 124 (January 1959): 17-20.

17. On the origins of the term, which was already employed in Germany before World War II, and its post-war development, see Hans Warmerdam and Pieter Koenders, *Cultuur En Ontspanning Het COC 1946-1966* (Utrecht, 1987), 76; and "Homophile," in *Encyclopedia of Homosexuality*, ed. Wayne R. Dynes, 2 vols. (New York, 1990), 1: 552. The definition quoted is from Marc Daniel and André Baudry, *Les Homosexuels* (Paris, 1973), 16.

18. Daniel and Baudry, *Homosexuels*, 16-7; and "Homosexualité ou Homophilie," *Arcadie* (November 1959), 591-5.

19. Daniel and Baudry, *Homosexuels*, 126-31; and Suzanne Daniel, "La Femme homophile dans la société actuelle," *Arcadie* (February 1954), 33.

20. "Homophile" and "Movement, Homosexual" in *Encyclopedia of Homosexuality*, 2: 839-44; and "Les Origines du f.h.a.r.," in FHAR, *Rapport contre la normalité* (Paris, 1971), 16-7.

21. For the presentation of *Arcadie* at the moment of its first appearance, see Baudry, "Nova et Vetera," *Arcadie* (January 1954), 15-7. For the other reviews, see "Mattachine Society," in *Encyclopedia of Homosexuality*, 2: 779-82; *Homophile Studies in Theory and Practice*, ed. W. Dorr Legg, et al. (San Francisco, 1994); and Warmerdam and Koenders, *Cultuur*, 33, 76.

22. Jylou, "Les Particuliers," *Der Kreis* (May 1960), 26.

23. Marc Daniel, "Lettre à Monsieur Paul Reboux," *Arcadie* (January 1955), 63.

24. Raphael, "Lois," 547.

25. The Club was registered at the Tribunal de Commerce de Paris on 28 February 1957.

26. Baudry, "Notre responsabilité," *Arcadie* (November 1961), 554. Baudry was here responding to an article in the popular press for which he gave no exact reference,

but which appears to have been "3e sexe," cited above. This article conflated homosexuality and male prostitution in the quarter and called for a law that "would permit a victorious struggle against this vice [homosexuality] that raises its head whenever a country is decadent."

27. See also Jacques Girard, *Le Mouvement homosexuel en France, 1945-1980* (Paris, 1981), 53-4.

28. Baudry, "Nova," 17. On the report's importance for homosexuality in this period, see Michel Dorais, "La Recherche des causes de l'homosexualité: Une Science-fiction?" in *La Peur de l'autre en soi: Du sexisme à l'homophobie*, ed. Daniel Welzer-Lang et al. (Montréal, 1994), 126-31; and Martel, *Rose*, 67-8.

29. Baudry, "La Faute," *Arcadie* (April 1959), 206.

30. Baudry, "Les Homophiles dans la société," *Arcadie* (December 1967), 544. See Girard, *Mouvement*, 53-5; and Eribon, *Réflexions*, 422, n. 1.

31. Jean-Michel Pelous, *Amour précieux, amour galant (1654-1675): Essai sur la représentation de l'amour dans la littérature et la société mondaines* (Paris, 1980), 305-22, 401-12.

32. On the *incroyables*, *merveilleuses*, and dandies, see Anette Höfer, "Petits-maîtres, Muscadins, Incroyables, Merveilleuses," in *Handbuch politisch-sozialer Grundbegriffe in Frankreich 1680-1820*, ed. Rolf Reichardt and Hans-Jürgen Lüsebrink, vol. 16-8 (Munich, 1996), 229-34.

33. On the beginnings of the consumer society in France and resistance to change, see Dominique Borne, *Histoire de la société française depuis 1945*, 2nd ed. (Paris, 1990), 30-1.

34. Eribon, *Réflexions*, 42-5.

35. Girard, *Mouvement*, 31-4; and "Saint-Germain-des-Prés, capitale," 2.

36. "Les Puritains veulent à tout prix nous délivrer du mal," *Futur* 1 (October 1952), 1, 4. On the "moral ideal" of the MRP, see Philip Williams, *La Vie politique sous la IVième République* (Paris, 1971), 181. On repression in this period, see Georges Sidéris, "Des folles de Saint-Germain-des-Prés au 'fléau social': Le Discours homophile contre l'efféminement dans les années 1950: Une Expression de la haine de soi?" in *La Haine de soi: Difficiles identités*, ed. E. Benbassa and J.-C. Attias (Brussels, 2000), 124-5, 139.

37. Baudry, "Appel" *Arcadie* (December 1958), 6.

38. Baudry, "Homophiles," 544.

39. See Daniel Borillo, *L'Homophobie* (Paris, 2000), 100-3; Eribon, *Réflexions*, 102-3, 130-2; Welzer-Lang, "L'Homophobie: La Face cachée du masculin," in *Peur*, 13-91; and Sidéris, "Folles," 127-8, 131-2.

40. Daniel Guérin, *Shakespeare et Gide en correctionnelle? Essais* (Paris, 1959), 94-106; and "Saint-Germain-des-Prés, capitale," 2.

41. "3e sexe," 8.

42. See Baudry, "Notre responsabilité," 553-7.

43. "Puritains," 4; "Saint-Germain-des Prés, capitale," 2; and "Chacun peut et doit lutter contre les tartuffes organisés," *Futur* (July 1954), 1.

44. Baudry, "Homophiles," 543-5.

45. Baudry, "Quatrième année," *Arcadie* (January 1957), 13-7.

46. *Journal Officiel*, 19 July 1960 (Assemblée Nationale, 2e séance du 18 juillet 1960), 1981-3.

47. Janine Mossuz-Lavau, *Les Lois de l'amour: Les Politiques de la sexualité en France (1950-1990)* (Paris, 1991), 239-40.

48. Baudry, "La Voix d'Arcadie," *Arcadie* (January 1961), 5-9; and letter from Baudry to Mirguet, 20 July 1960, published in "Lettre personnelle," (circular sent by *Arcadie* to its subscribers), March 1965, Bibliothèque du Saulchoir (Paris), Fonds Max Lyonnet, no. 115. The exchange between Mirguet and Baudry can be consulted in the section "Archives" on the website *Séminaire gai* (http://semgai.free.fr).

49. "Editorial," *Juventus* 2 (15 June 1959): 5.

50. For the photos, see, for example, the back of the cover of the second and third issues and page 30 of the fourth. On the profound changes in French society, see Borne, *Histoire,* 27-44, 164-6. On film, see Raymond Chirat, *La IVe République et ses films* (Paris, 1985), 86.

51. On this permanence, see "3e sexe," 8; Sibalis, "Paris," 29-30; and Sidéris, "Folles," 134, 136.

52. Sibalis, "Paris," 30-6.

53. P. Bonard, "Il n'y a plus d'attrait . . . à Saint-Germain-des Prés," *Adonis* 2 (10 December 1975): 11. The title of this article is an untranslatable pun on a line from a famous song recorded by Juliette Greco: "Il n'y a plus d'après à Saint-Germain-des-Prés."

The Birth of a French Homosexual Press in the 1950s

Olivier Jablonski

Editors' note: This is a translation of the original text.[1]

The 1950s saw the appearance of a significant number of homosexual periodicals in France. This was all the more remarkable in light of the conservative social and political forces that created an unfavorable climate for such ventures. Postwar France had embarked on a process of economic and social modernization and the development of a consumer society. Cultural life was also changing, as evidenced by the intellectual ferment centered on Saint-Germain-des-Prés. Sexuality and contraception were subjects of heated debate. Opposition to sexual freedom was embodied in the Popular Republican Movement (MRP), a political party of Christian democratic tendency that had emerged from the wartime Resistance.[2] The MRP was the party of Catholic morality and family values. It tried to control sexuality and morals, notably by regulating literature and the cinema. It also objected to the increasingly obvious presence of homosexuality in the public space, whether in the form of novels, scandals in the press, or street cruising and prostitution. This presence aroused public concern, sometimes a puritanical reaction or even a "moral panic," a fear of the social dangers of homosexuality, and an intensified combat against its practice. This context explains why public offenses against decency would be more firmly repressed in cases involving homosexuals than in those involving heterosexuals under Article 330, Line 2, of the Penal Code (as amended by the Ordinance of 25 November 1960).[3] The ordinance was a reaction to almost ten years of effort by French homosexuals to change social conditions.

[Haworth co-indexing entry note]: "The Birth of a French Homosexual Press in the 1950s." Jablonski, Olivier. Co-published simultaneously in *Journal of Homosexuality* (Harrington Park Press, an imprint of The Haworth Press, Inc.) Vol. 41, No. 3/4, 2001, pp. 233-248; and: *Homosexuality in French History and Culture* (ed: Jeffrey Merrick, and Michael Sibalis) Harrington Park Press, an imprint of The Haworth Press, Inc., 2001, pp. 233-248. Single or multiple copies of this article are available for a fee from The Haworth Document Delivery Service [1-800-342-9678, 9:00 a.m. - 5:00 p.m. (EST). E-mail address: getinfo@haworthpressinc.com].

The attitude of the authorities at the time was best expressed by the director of criminal investigations for Paris in a speech to the general assembly of Interpol in 1958: "What . . . leads us to believe in an increase in homosexuality in France is that for several years, it has been more conspicuous." The director pointed to the presence of "adepts" of homosexuality in certain public places, to homosexual soliciting, and to the existence of several private clubs, reviews, and newspapers. Indeed, he found it outrageous that "the editor of a newspaper for homosexuals" (he was referring to Jean Thibault, who edited *Futur*) had claimed "that this category of persons has the same right as anyone else to express their opinion."[4] It is true that for the last several years France had seen dynamic homosexual groups and an active homosexual press.

Developments in France must be understood within a broader international context, in which the German experience was particularly important. Germany's actively militant groups during the first part of the twentieth century, most notably Magnus Hirschfeld's Scientific Humanitarian Committee and the diversified homosexual press that existed under the Weimar Republic, had served as models for similar initiatives elsewhere in Europe. The coming to power of the Nazis dramatically put an end to the struggle for homosexual emancipation and the social integration of homosexuals. The rebirth of the homosexual movement across Europe after 1945 was facilitated by two factors. First of all, Swiss neutrality had permitted the survival of a link between the prewar and postwar movements in the form of a German-language review, the *Swiss Friendship Banner*, better known by the name that it took later, *Der Kreis*.[5] Heir to the German experience and published in a bilingual French and German edition from December 1941, *Der Kreis* provided essential encouragement in the early stages of the French postwar homosexual movement. Secondly, the International Committee for Sexual Equality, founded in Amsterdam following a meeting of European homosexual groups in 1951, resurrected the idea of a general struggle for homosexual emancipation. Inspired by the Universal Declaration of Human Rights adopted by the United Nations in 1948, the International Committee worked mainly with German groups for the repeal of Paragraph 175 of the German Penal Code, which outlawed homosexual acts in that country.

But the European context should not obscure French distinctiveness. First of all, the practice of homosexuality in France was strongly influenced by "sensual individualism" (to use Florence Tamagne's expression). She means that the French homosexual has always been fiercely individualistic as the result of both a more favorable social situation than in other countries (homosexuality has not been criminalized in France since 1791) and a certain political immaturity. At the same time, militant activity has been difficult, as demonstrated by the experience of *Inversions* in 1924.[6] When this homosexual review was condemned for offending morals in March 1926, homosexual intellectuals failed to rally to its defense.[7]

The French homosexual movement of the 1950s has been little studied, in large part because of the widely held opinion that the homophile militancy of the period was not radical enough and, therefore, not worth a detailed examination.[8] This attitude has been due largely to the influence of the revolutionary homosexual groups that developed in France after May 1968, which had nothing but contempt for their predecessors. Another reason is the relative lack of source material. Little is now remembered of the 1950s except for the association and periodical *Arcadie*, and, unfortunately, *Arcadie* had little to say about militant homosexual activities that it did not initiate. While it claimed to represent all homosexuals, it in fact represented only those who were loyal to it. Moreover, the dominant actor in its story, André Baudry, who is still alive, refuses to give interviews and continues to block access to his archives.

But *Arcadie* was only one of several periodicals intended primarily for male homosexuals to be published in the 1950s, although most of the others did not survive very long.[9] These periodicals were the product of a new generation that knew little of the prewar period. Jean Thibault was not quite twenty-three when he founded *Futur* in 1952; André Baudry, the future director of *Arcadie*, was thirty in that same year when he wrote his first articles for *Der Kreis*. Like their European counterparts, the French periodicals adopted very different styles. They were sometimes apolitical, like *Der Kreis* in Switzerland, sometimes more dynamic and militant, like the gay movement COC and its journal *Vriendschap* in the Netherlands. They usually took the form of what might be called a "group/review," which is to say that they were simultaneously both periodicals and social groupings of militants. The periodical sought to spread its progressive ideas on homosexuality while entertaining its readers and encouraging encounters through personal advertisements; the social group held regular meetings and occasional dances to encourage socializing and to raise money. Almost all the periodicals included inserts with photographs of nearly naked men (in order to increase sales and because readers demanded them).

Futur, which first came out in October 1952, was sold openly on newsstands. Its four folio pages resembled those of any other newspaper of the period, although it seemed inspired by one in particular: the weekly satirical newspaper *Le Canard Enchaîné*, which had made it its mission to unmask hypocrisy in society and government. *Futur* was a political newspaper with a virulently anticlerical tone that preached sexual equality and repeatedly attacked those whom it called "puritans" (advocates of family values and of the strict moral regulation of youth). But it also printed international news (the activities of foreign homosexual groups, the repression of homosexuals and racial injustice in the United States, homosexual scandals in Great Britain), as well as reviews of books and films, personal advertisements (for example, by people looking for work), and letters from its readers. From the very first, *Futur*'s main target was the MRP, which it dubbed the Movement of Repressed Churchgoers. In an article entitled "Termite Teitgen," *Futur* took on the party's president, Pierre-Henri Teitgen, a former lawyer and member of the Resistance, who, as Minister of Justice from May 1945 to December 1946, had supervised the reform of the Penal Code and maintained, as Article 331, Line 3, the ordinance issued by Marshal Pétain on 6 August 1942 that criminalized "unnatural" sexual acts with minors under twenty-one, whereas the heterosexual age of consent was fixed at fifteen.

This newspaper is interesting primarily for the uninhibited tone of its words and images. Its pages included photographs of beautiful young (sometimes extremely young) men in languorous poses, and its language was too free and provocative to remain unanswered by the government. The moral climate of the period caught up with *Futur*, and, after the very first issue, it could not be publicly displayed on the newsstands that sold it or be sold to minors.[10] Official intimidation and harassment, the ban on public display, and the prosecution of Thibault on a morals charge in July 1953 (he and a friend were found guilty of sexual relations with several teenage boys) meant that the journal appeared only very irregularly.[11] A total of nineteen known numbers came out between October 1952 and April 1956. A first series sold on newsstands until March 1953; a second series, with a considerably reduced press run, sold by subscription and at a single place in Paris from June to November 1954; then a third series was available at newsstands in the Paris region from February to November 1955. A final issue appeared in April 1956, just before the publishers were finally condemned on a charge of offending morals by publishing their newspaper. The authorities had launched an earlier prosecution against Thibault in April 1955 but dropped the charges "based essentially on the pledge that he made before the examining magistrate that his review would not reappear," a pledge that he failed to honor. The court's judgment in 1956 repeated the arguments already developed in a similar trial of the homosexual review *Inversions*. The periodical offended morals by its systematic justification of homosexuality, by its encouragement of homosexual relations, in particular by means of personal advertisements, and by the "unacceptable character" of its "virulent criticisms . . . of the ordinance of 8 February 1945 [which later became Article 331, Line 3 of the Penal Code] and the restrictions that it imposes on the free expression of homosexuality" and of the other laws intended to protect youth against sexual perversions. "*Futur* constitutes a danger to public morality and an offense against morals," the judges concluded.[12] Thibault reportedly left France to live in the colonies (and immediately vanished from public view). This was the end of the first postwar French newspaper with a marked homosexual content.

The content of *Futur*'s nineteen issues was repetitive, as if most of the articles were written by the same person, but readers appreciated it as a breath of freedom. The circulation was not negligible if one can believe the director, who claimed "several thousand readers."[13] Robert Lagarde, a young homosexual and founder of the homosexual group *Le Verseau* in 1953, who met the staff of *Futur*, recently recalled them this way: "Extremely nice people . . . they had a rather political approach. It did not displease me. But I think that this was what caused them the most difficulty. . . . I have the impression that they were two or three who put out this newspaper."[14] And Lagarde added:

> It must have been for the French the first time that such a journal appeared. [The readers] had the craziest ideas [to explain its existence]. People wondered how such a thing could exist. It was really a revolution. It was something extraordinary for France. . . . At the time, I had the impression that it was very difficult to change things. One had to blow things up! . . . That was the tragic side of this period. In the sense that there was a kind of blocked society.[15]

Another reader, Marcel P., has very similar memories of how he and other homosexuals reacted to *Futur*:

> I bought the first issue at a newsstand in Lyon, at the train station. Someone had told me of its existence. In the provinces [outside of Paris], it caused a stir in the homosexual world. . . . It's great, we have a newspaper! I went several times to several bookstores that answered that they did not know it. They wondered, because of the title, if it discussed industry! I took a lot of precautions! It was crazy![16]

Arcadie, whose first issue came out in January 1954, a little more than one year after *Futur* began publication, was very different in style and content. These differences were due to the personality of its founder, André Baudry. An amazing man who left nobody indifferent, he could be courageous and tenacious, but also arrogant and ambitious. Some remained steadfastly loyal to him over the years, while others were put off by his difficult personality, his domineering will, and his endless moralizing. He was so deeply impregnated with Roman Catholicism that he was soon nicknamed "the Pope."[17] Born in 1922 and educated at a Jesuit college, Baudry owed his entry into the homosexual milieu of Paris to count Jacques de Ricaumont, who had collaborated with several German homosexual reviews. Ricaumont introduced Baudry to *Der Kreis* and encouraged him to submit articles, which he did beginning in 1952 under the pen name André Romane. From the start, his writings promoted his personal ideas about what the ideal homosexual should be: "Every homosexual must resolve to present a perfect and irreproachable image of homosexuality every time that he has the great joy of meeting a young man," a typically homophile position.[18] He was particularly interested in the relationship between religion and homosexuality.

Ricaumont also put Baudry in touch with the International Committee for Sexual Equality. He became a member of its executive committee in 1953. Now part of an international movement that advocated improved conditions for homosexuals, Baudry thought of creating a movement and a press in France in the image of what already existed abroad.[19] He took charge of the meetings of the French subscribers to *Der Kreis*, a group of about forty people called Circle of France, which grew to two hundred members by 1953.[20] With this as his base of action, Baudry summoned French homosexuals to participate in an ambitious project: to facilitate the acceptance of homosexuality by the political and intellectual leaders of the country by improving the behavior of homosexuals themselves. This was the height of the international "homophile" movement with its notions of friendship, respectability, discretion, and dignity. For Baudry, dignity implied controlling sexual desire.

Believing that it was necessary to reach out to the general public, Baudry contributed to the third issue of *Futur* a review of Father Marc Oraison's *Christian Life and Sexual Problems* but very quickly relations between *Futur* and Baudry deteriorated.[21] He reproached the newspaper for its virulent and political tone and judged its articles to be "too thin, too sectarian."[22] "They [the staff of *Futur*] pursue their ridiculous goal, which will not advance our cause in the least. This mixture of politics and these sterile and violent criticisms only irritate people," he declared.[23] In January 1954 he launched his own monthly review, whose name, *Arcadie*, was proposed by the novelist Roger Peyrefitte. It appeared without interruption until the summer of 1982. In announcing the new review to the world, Baudry publicly distanced himself from *Futur*: "But at no price will we use the [same] terms as a journal that appeared last year and *believed* that it was defending us."[24] He preferred to seek inspiration from the very conventional but more literary and artistic (and more commercial) *Der Kreis*, a review with which he had not quarreled!

With the support of Peyrefitte and Jean Cocteau, Baudry did everything possible to publicize *Arcadie*, to get press and radio coverage, and to win the support of writers and intellectuals.[25] The homosexual writer Marcel Jouhandeau, in charge of the *Nouvelle Revue française* (founded by André Gide) not only refused his help but also openly attacked *Arcadie*, declaring that the review was "preparing the way for a terrible persecution that will soon strike [sexual] nonconformists" and expressing the hope that this "ridiculous boutique" would be shut down by the authorities.[26]

Comprising sixty pages, austere in tone, reflecting Baudry's desire for homosexual integrity and respectability, *Arcadie* showed all the characteristics common to homophile reviews in other countries, such as *The Mattachine Review*, *Vriendschap*, or *Vennen*. Like them, it offered readers articles about homosexuality and information on the situation for homosexuals in foreign countries, as well as poetry, short stories, reviews of films and plays, and even some advertisements. Its organizational structure was typical of most French literary reviews: closely identified with its director to the point that it would be unlikely to survive his departure and supported by a core group of individuals united in close friendship. *Arcadie* was in fact more than a periodical or even an association; it was a micro-society.

To encourage the emergence of a homophile community while rejecting homosexual separatism and the formation of a ghetto, to bring about the social integration of homosexuals without their having to give up their differences ("Beside others, with others," was Baudry's motto), to educate homosexuals so that they would accept themselves and get others to accept them better, these were *Arcadie*'s goals. The homophile would be a new kind of homosexual, courageous, temperate, and perseverant. His morality would be based on respect, solidarity, and moderation. It was a profoundly Catholic morality that Baudry expected of the homophile (who was in practice more likely to be a male homosexual than a lesbian), which was not true for other homophile groups in France and abroad. But the common denominator of all the movements of this period was their stress on respectability in order to curry favor with the authorities. *Arcadie* added dignity; for Baudry, it was essentially the comportment of homophiles themselves that explained the hostility and social exclusion of which they were the victims. Baudry's ultimately restrictive and reactionary morality was not accepted by everybody, and it caused conflict between him and other French homosexual groups, like Le Verseau, and other newspapers, like *Futur* and *Juventus*.

Arcadie, according to the wishes of its director, was not sold on newsstands but was available at a few sales points in France and abroad and distributed to subscribers by mail. It was very careful about what it published. The tone of its articles was serious and restrained, and its short stories were only discreetly erotic. Yet this did not protect it from a government ban on sale to minors and on public display, imposed on 26 May 1954 (and abrogated only on 22 May 1975), the same sentence already imposed on *Futur*. Although Baudry has always explicitly denied the fact (but public records belie his statements), the courts condemned him, like the publishers of *Futur*, for offending morals by means of the press. The judges ruled that *Arcadie* represented a "danger to youth" and singled out the review's alleged "proselytism." They ordered "the confiscation and the destruction of the seized proofs and of all objects that have served to commit the crime" and fined Baudry forty thousand francs.[27] The French authorities obviously did not want a homosexual press to exist in France. Because of the ban on its sale to minors, *Arcadie* was automatically denied the reduced postal rate given to most periodicals, and a few years later it also lost the right to be distributed by the national press distribution services.[28] As for the number of its subscribers, the information provided by *Arcadie* is subject to caution. We can estimate the print run at about three thousand copies in the 1950s, and it probably never exceeded ten thousand at any time in later years, which is, nevertheless, a considerable number given the review's limited financial resources and its austere contents.[29]

But if *Arcadie* wanted to present a respectable face to the world, it also had to attract readers who might be put off by its arid appearance. Subscribers who requested it also received a mimeographed circular, which provided more specific information: a letter from the director, warnings about police surveillance or gay-bashing in cruising places, announcements of the group's cultural activities, and so on. Also, faithful to its model, *Der Kreis*, the review offered a monthly insert: a "special sheet" comprising personal advertisements by men seeking to meet others and mildly erotic photographs of variable (and often mediocre) quality. The insert was discontinued as a precaution after the National Assembly in July 1960 voted a law that declared homosexuality (along with prostitution and alcoholism) to be a "social scourge" and after the government in November 1960 doubled the penalty in cases of public offenses against morals when homosexuals were involved. *Arcadie* did maintain its mimeographed circulars, however. Parallel to the review, the social meetings of homosexuals organized by Baudry continued to take place, and in 1957 he created a commercial society under the name CLESPALA (Literary and Scientific Club of the Latin Countries), often also called Arcadie because of its ties to the review. Indeed, membership in the club was automatic with the purchase of a subscription to the review. The "diocese" (the word was André Du Dognon's) had a cramped locale for headquarters, where members held weekend dances (under the stern surveillance of the director) and listened to his "word of the month," a speech that some derided as "the sermon."[30] Baudry invited the police to attend so they could observe the exemplary behavior of the members.

Homosexuals at the time (and since) have had very different opinions of Arcadie, ranging from unconditional support to pure and simple rejection. People afraid of having their homosexuality discovered and looking for no more than brief sexual encounters had no desire or need for Arcadie. But many others found moral comfort there. "Arcadie was an institution that served on the one hand as a safeguard against possible mistakes and on the other as a moral savior," Robert Francès, who contributed to the review, has recently remarked.[31] René B., who belongs today to an association of gay retirees, concurs: "Me, what I would like to say about Baudry, [is that] for him it was a mission, a ministry. He wanted to free us of our guilt [about being homosexual], to make us dignified. And I believe that he succeeded, because as for me, I never suffered from neurosis in my life, my homosexual life."[32] The main problem, and this was true of all homosexual groups and newspapers of the period, was the prevalent fear of being noted in police files, which certainly kept some people from subscribing to *Arcadie* or attending club gatherings. Marcel P. remembers today: "I did not want to get mixed up in it [Arcadie], because I believed, it's rather obvious, whatever Baudry might have said, in the risk of having my name taken down. I dreaded the police files."[33] He was referring here to the widespread belief that Baudry made his membership lists available to the police. Fernand P. felt much the same way: "Me, I refused to go to Arcadie until the 1980s, when I was 65-years-old and had retired. I was afraid because of the story that was circulating in Paris about the police files."[34] It has never been proved, however, that Baudry's famous list was ever consulted by the police, although he certainly did maintain good, even close, relations with the Paris prefecture of police.[35]

There was a place alongside *Futur* and *Arcadie* for other publishing initiatives, including the very sober *Prétexte*, which appeared in two distinct periods, in 1952 and 1958. Its directors were Jean-Jacques Thierry and Jean-Louis Ornequint. As indicated by the subtitle, *André Gide Notebook*, the review was almost entirely dedicated to the work of the great writer and to the pederasty that Gide promoted. It was supposed to be a trimestrial, but only two issues actually appeared in 1952, in February (one year after Gide's death) and November. It reappeared in January 1958, apparently for only two issues, and still focused only on homosexual literature.

Prétexte was a seed-bed for two other reviews: *Gioventù* and *Juventus*. Thierry went on from *Prétexte* to publish *Gioventù* (two issues known, in September and October 1956). With the same format and appearance as *Arcadie*, this literary and cultural review claimed to be elitist, in contrast to *Arcadie* and *Futur*, which Thierry judged too "corporative," too popular, and of an insufficiently high literary level: "our ambition is to show the intellectual and cerebral difference existing in our opinion between homosexuality and the uranism so dear to André Gide."[36] Ornequint, for his part, was soon writing for *Juventus*, the first new review since *Arcadie* to survive for more than a few issues. The first number came out on 15 May 1959, the last on 1 May 1960. Its publishers were Yves Baschey and Jean Basile (who may well have been using Ornequint as his pseudonym).[37] "This most refreshing periodical deserves a successful future, because it presents the voice of Juventus on homophile matters in a very critical and humorous way." So wrote (in English) the newsletter of the International Committee for Sexual Equality.[38] *Juventus* was sold by subscription and was apparently not available on newsstands, but several Parisian bookstores did sell it. At first sight, it resembled *Arcadie* in format, pagination, and general appearance, but the publishers had a very different take on homosexuality, telling their readers in the very first issue:

> If you are looking for something to excuse your errors, if you are looking for something to feed your torments, if you are looking for something to delight your senses, close these pages and do not read on. You can find all that elsewhere. If, on the contrary, you like gaiety, health, if you want to be a man with dignity, continue reading. . . . *Juventus* does not want to preach; it wants to please and entertain you, perhaps to help you. Virility, health, truth are your best weapons. . . . Turn the page, [and] you will understand that *Juventus* has just given its first and last sermon.[39]

The difference with *Arcadie* was thus made clear ("sermon" was an obvious reference to the ritual Friday evening speeches delivered by Baudry), and people recognized this very well at the time. The newsletter of the International Committee for Sexual Equality described it this way (in its usual awkward English) in late 1960:

> *Juventus*, as is clear from its articles, has chosen for a style of living, in which homophilism is consciously incorporated, but which never loses its respect for human dignity; all this appears to be possible without feelings of guilt or wickedness. . . . Therefore, the contents of *Juventus* has revealed an autobiographical candidness and subjective honesty, which are surprising, so far.[40]

If the above commentary was so flattering, it was because after its first issue, *Juventus* modernized its appearance, with a cover in two colors, a fresher and cleaner layout, high-quality paper, and photographs of beautiful men. In short, its presentation contrasted sharply with the drabness of *Arcadie*. There were about fifty pages in each issue, and the various rubrics were much less elitist than *Arcadie*'s, with little classical poetry and few scientific articles on homosexuality. *Juventus* felt neither shame nor guilt, and so it published instead short stories, brief news items, interviews, and book reviews, all written in a light and non-militant tone. The review's most interesting feature was the regular inclusion of letters from readers. In this way, it did not limit itself to expressing only the publishers' opinions, and the continual dialogue between the editors and the readers made for a livelier review.

If the outward appearance of *Juventus* was so modern compared to *Arcadie*, it had, nonetheless, not entirely broken free of the conservative attitudes of the period. It considered homosexuality a lifestyle as acceptable as any other, but it still thought that there was a homosexual problem for which homosexuals themselves were to blame, as an editorial in the second issue indicated:

> You say that people reject you? Go then one evening to Saint-Germain-des-Prés and open your eyes and take a good look at your fellow creatures. Look at their bearing, their gestures, listen to their shrieks and consider their ways. If you are revolted, it's because you have understood. You have understood that a man, a real one, cannot stand that another man caricature a woman; you have understood that whatever is not natural to your condition as a man is ridiculous. . . . Try to appear completely dignified, to behave like a man even if you feel like a woman and you will see that you will be accepted everywhere! You will have won your battle, the battle of all of us, the day when you have understood that the ostracism of which you complain is a function of the provocation that you revel in.[41]

Juventus thus continued to promote the homophile ideal of dignity. It may have represented a more modern phase of homophilia than *Arcadie*, but it still fell far short of the radical affirmations of homosexual identity that would be put forward by the Homosexual Front for Revolutionary Action and other gay liberation groups in the 1970s.

Juventus disappeared after one year and apparently only nine issues.[42] The reason is unknown, but several factors suggest an explanation. First of all, there was the government ban (November 1959) on its public display and its sale to minors.[43] Of course, *Arcadie* had managed to publish despite a similar ban, but even before the ban *Juventus*'s sales seem to have been insufficient. In a circular of 28 October 1959 addressed to subscribers, the editorial board indicated that there were only three hundred subscribers and that the review needed one thousand to survive. *Juventus* apparently lacked a hard core of subscribers, in part because it received no press coverage. Because the publishers did not or could not sell the review at newsstands, its distribution was limited. In addition, and this was a recurring theme in readers' letters, there was (as in the case of *Arcadie*) the worry, even the fear, of the consequences of taking out subscriptions. *Juventus* began to print personal advertisements in its last issues, but it was too late to attract new readers. Nor did it propose other activities and services the way *Arcadie* did. The publisher Jean Basile left France in 1960 and emigrated to Canada, where he continued his militant career.[44]

In all of the periodicals discussed so far photographic images were rare and usually of poor quality. This is all the more surprising in that the second half of the 1950s saw the development of homoerotic photography, under the guise of an esthetic admiration for bodybuilding, in both the United States and Europe.[45] But France was very different and had no domestically published photographic review intended for a specifically homosexual readership. And yet the demand was there, and it was apparently a very strong one, as Baudry regularly mentioned in the circulars he sent to the readers of *Arcadie* (of course, he disapproved of such photographs). There was, however, a highly-developed system for selling photographs by mail order. Several French photographic studios were active in the field. The best known belonged to Jean Ferrero (in Nice) and Gregor Arax (in Paris), but for the most part they distributed their production abroad. Ferrero has said that "the reviews did not pay [for the photographs that they printed in their inserts], [but] they provided a sort of publicity by circulating the photographs and the address of the studio." He found the sale of his photographs by mail to be a "very lucrative activity. There were as many as seven employees and a secretary who looked after distribution and shipment."[46]

Among the foreign bodybuilding magazines available on the newsstand, the most noteworthy was *Muscles*, a Belgian review sold after the Second World War, which published the famous sketches by Quintance and photographs from the Athletic Model Guild. From 1957, French readers could also find *Physique Pictorial*, *Body Beautiful*, and *Tomorrow's Man*. But by a decree of 10 November 1959 (in the same month that *Juventus* was banned from public display and sale to minors), the government delivered a severe blow to *Body Beautiful*, *Physique Artistry*, and *Physique Pictorial*: they could no longer be sold on French territory. Two months later, on 16 January 1960, it was the turn of *Adonis*. The authorities had seen through the pretense that these were publications for bodybuilders. The ban occurred under Article 14 of the Law on the Press of 1881 (modified by the decree of 6 May 1939) relative to the regulation of the foreign press. The intent of this clause was to keep subversive foreign propaganda out of France. It made no mention of morals, and it should be noted that foreign reviews featuring naked women were not banned, but merely forbidden for public display and sale to minors (under the law of 1949). The homoerotic press was thus subject to a special control, in the same way as certain foreign political periodicals, whether communist, anti-French, or in favor of Algerian independence. If this type of publication disappeared from the newsstands, the demand remained strong enough that a discreet distribution was most likely organized. French magazines carried advertisements for ordering the banned foreign reviews directly from abroad.

There was thus a great variety in the kinds of homosexual publications available in the 1950s. From the very political *Futur* through the stern and communitarian *Arcadie* to the entertaining *Juventus*, each of these publications reflected both the wider context and its own vision of homosexuality.

Principally concerned by the injustice that set the sexual majority for heterosexuals at fifteen and for homosexuals at twenty-one, *Futur* demanded emancipation in a militant and humanist tone similar to that of the press that had emerged from the French Resistance and that was shaped by the Universal Declaration of Human Rights of 1948. It denounced the status quo but did not propose any specific political alternative. *Arcadie* took a totally different position, under the influence of its founder's Catholicism and the intellectual milieu in which he moved. Although *Arcadie* claimed to militate for sexual equality, the review was oriented more toward the construction and support of a homophile community. More than defending their rights, the review concerned itself with the moralization of the "homophile people." There was also a social difference between the two publications, which was accentuated with the appearance of *Juventus*, an apolitical and recreational review, indicating the arrival of a mass consumer society and a new and freer homosexual man with a new spirit of health, virility, youth.

Even in French society, where homosexuality was not forbidden by law, there was strict regulation of its expression in accordance with bourgeois notions of morality. As we have seen, in the 1950s no homosexual periodical managed entirely to escape this repression, whether in the form of restrictions on its distribution or by direct censorship (as in the case of foreign reviews). The government commission that regulated publications intended for youth, instituted by the Law of 1949, had the right to ask the Minister of the Interior to forbid their public display and their sale to minors (as happened in the cases of *Arcadie*, *Futur*, and *Juventus*). But its role went even further, because it reported to the public prosecutor those publications that could be charged with offending morals. It most likely did so in the cases of *Arcadie* and *Futur*. Indeed, the commission went as far as to ask that "the appropriateness of a government bill repressing homosexual propaganda be examined."[47] Only *Arcadie* managed to survive for many years, probably because of its network of supporters and its discreet tone.

It is true that in this period there was increased repression of homosexual activity, but no increased repression against the homosexual press. What occurred was rather a continuation of repressive policies put in place before World War II and to which *Inversions*, the only homosexual review to appear in the interwar years, had already fallen victim. Of course, the degree of repression always depended on the vitality of the homosexual press, and, because this press was more dynamic in the 1950s, it consequently experienced a more intense reaction from the authorities. The public and governmental attitude toward the emergence of a homosexual press demonstrates the reluctance of French society in the 1950s and 1960s to accept the transition from a discreet homosexuality to a more conspicuous and outspoken homosexuality.

NOTES

1. Translated by Michael Sibalis.
2. See Philip Williams, *La Vie politique sous la IVème République* (Paris, 1971), 181.
3. "When the public offense against morals consists of an act against nature with an individual of the same sex, the penalty will be imprisonment for six months to three years and a fine of one thousand to fifteen thousand new francs."
4. M. Fernet, "L'Homosexualité et son influence sur la délinquance," *Revue internationale de la police criminelle* 124 (1959): 17-20.
5. Hubert Kennedy, *The Ideal Gay Man: The Story of Der Kreis* (New York, 1999).
6. Florence Tamagne, *Histoire de l'homosexualité en Europe: Berlin, Londres, Paris 1919-1939* (Paris, 2000), 158-60.
7. AP, Tribunal correctionnelle, 12e chambre, 20 March 1926, found the review "licentious" and sentenced the publishers to six months in prison. *Inversions* appealed, and the Cour d'Appel de Paris reduced the sentence to three months; the judges found that "each page is a shameless apology for pederasty, a systematic appeal to homosexual passions." *Sirey, recueil général des lois et arrêts* (Paris, 1927), 93-4. On 31 March 1927, the Cour de Cassation (Chambre Criminelle) rejected a further appeal. See the pages on *Inversions* in Gilles Barbedette and Michel Carassou, *Paris Gay 1925* (Paris, 1981), 151-301. Note that what they print as the judgement of the Cour de Cassation is in fact the text of the verdict of the Cour d'Appel.
8. The only book on the period is Jacques Girard, *Le Mouvement homosexuel en France, 1945-1980* (Paris, 1981), which focuses principally on the press. It provides an excellent description of the two principal publications: *Futur* and *Arcadie.*
9. For lesbian writing in this period, see Claudie Lesselier, "Formes de résistances et d'expression lesbiennes dans les années cinquante et soixante en France," in *Homosexualités: Expression/répression*, ed. Louis-Georges Tin (Paris, 2000), 105-16, available on the Internet at <http://semgai.free.fr/articles.html>.
10. Ban imposed by decree of the Minister of the Interior, 30 October 1952, under Article 14 of the Law of 16 July 1949 on publications intended for the young. *Futur* appealed to the Conseil d'Etat, which confirmed the ban on the grounds that the newspaper was contrary to morality, because it defended and exalted homosexuality, that it was a licentious publication ("Homosexuality is licentiousness. To justify this vice is to be licentious."), and that it presented a danger to the young. Arrêt Thibault, Conseil d'Etat, 5 December 1956 (2e et 4e sous-sections réunies), in *Recueil Dalloz* (Paris, 1957), 20.
11. AP, Audience de la 15e chambre correctionnelle, 18 July 1953. Thibault was sentenced to eighteen months in prison (suspended) and fifty thousand francs fine and his colleague to two years (suspended) and one hundred fifty thousand francs for "shameful acts with minors of the same sex under twenty-one."
12. AP, Audience de la 17e chambre correctionnelle, 26 April 1956.
13. Archif van het International Committee for Sexual Equality, Plaastsingslist van het Archief van de Nederlandse Vereniging van HomoFielen COC–1945-1970, Algemeen Rijksarchief, Den Haag [hereafter, AICSE], #2-19-038, letter by Jean Thibault, 20 May 1955.
14. Interview with the author, Amsterdam, July 1997.
15. Interview with the author, Amsterdam, July 1997.
16. Interview with the author, Vincennes, June 1997.
17. The first to use the nickname was *Futur*, September 1955.

18. André Romane, "Jeunesse de France et Homosexualité," *Der Kreis* 5 (1952), 20-5.
19. André Romane, "Perspectives françaises," *I.C.S.E. Newsletter* (January 1953), 44.
20. AICSE, #2-19-038, Box 161/2, letter by Baudry, 28 November 1953.
21. He signed the review "A.F.," in *Futur*, December 1952. Baudry indicated that he was the author in a letter to the I.C.S.E., 26 February 1953. AICSE, #2-19-038, Box 161/2.
22. AICSE, #2-19-038, Box 161/2, letter by André Baudry, 14 November 1952.
23. AICSE, #2-19-038, Box 161/2, letter by André Baudry, 26 February 1953.
24. *I.C.S.E. Newsletter*, November-December 1953, 162.
25. For the first issue of the review, Peyrefitte offered an unpublished short story and Cocteau a sketch and a message of support, the same message he had sent to the first congress of the I.C.S.E. in 1951!
26. Marcel Jouhandeau, "Correspondance," *La Nouvelle Revue Française* (March 1954), 533.
27. AP, Audience de la 17e chambre correctionnelle, 17 March 1956. For Baudry's denial, see an interview published as "André Baudry: Je milite pour les homosexuels," *Le Nouvel Accord* 6 (May 1964), 55: "I am nevertheless anxious to state that the trial . . . ended in an acquittal." Frédéric Martel, *Le Rose et le noir: Les Homosexuels en France depuis 1968* (Paris, 1996), 71, repeats the denial.
28. Under the ordinance of 23 December 1958 (article 40) modifying the legal status of distributors and the distribution of periodicals.
29. The most fanciful figures have been given over the years, usually by Baudry himself, who claimed fifty thousand subscribers in 1979. See "25 ans d'Arcadie: Entretien avec André Baudry," *Masques* 1 (May 1979): 114.
30. André Du Dognon, *Peyrefitte démaquillé* (Paris, 1976), 99; and two polemical articles in *Futur*: "Ne pas se couvrir de ridicule" (June 1955) and "Réponse au sermon d'un Pape abusif" (September 1955).
31. Interview with the author, Paris, April 1999.
32. Interview with the author, Paris, January 1999.
33. Interview with the author, Vincennes, June 1997.
34. Interview with the author, Paris, April 1997.
35. As proved by a letter by André Baudry to the writer Daniel Guérin, 10 January 1958. Guérin was supposed to participate in a conference and debate in Paris on "Psycho-analysis and Problems of Homosexuality," and Baudry indicated in his letter that "Arcadie will not participate after all. . . . And we would prefer that in this debate, Arcadie not be spoken of very much. . . . This is due . . . above all to friendly advice from the Prefecture [of police] which advises against Arcadie's participating in this debate." See Bibliothèque de Documentation Intercontemporaine, Université de Paris-Nanterre, Fonds Guérin, dossier FE 721/14/9.
36. AICSE, #2-19-038, Box 161/2, letter by Jean-Jacques Thierry, 11 February 1956.
37. The last issue of *Der Kreis* paid homage to Ornequint as the publisher of *Juventus*, who emigrated to Canada in 1960. But the publisher of *Juventus* was supposedly Jean Basile, who also went to Canada at about the same time. One can perhaps conclude that Ornequint and Basile were one and the same. Charles Welti, "En guise d'adieu," *Der Kreis* (December 1967), 26.
38. *I.C.S.E. Newsletter*, September 1960, 3. We know the name of the editors only from this presentation (they were never mentioned in the review itself).
39. "Éditorial," *Juventus*, 1 (15 May 1959): 3.

40. *I.C.S.E. Newsletter*, last issue 1960, 5.

41. "Éditorial," *Juventus* 2 (15 June 1959): 4.

42. It is difficult to figure out exactly when the review disappeared. The last known issue that I have found, dated May 1960, is in the archives of *Gai Pied*, which are now closed. There may in fact have been later issues. The only thing certain is that Jean-Louis Ornequint continued his *Juventus* column in *Der Kreis*, from November 1960.

43. Decree of 6 November 1959, *Journal Officiel*, 17 November 1959. The three principal homosexual reviews were thus all banned in the same way.

44. He founded the Quebec countercultural review *Mainmise* in 1970, then participated in the Quebec homosexual newspaper, *Berdache*.

45. See Thomas Waugh, *Hard to Imagine* (New York, 1996).

46. Interview with the author, Paris, May 1997.

47. *Compte rendu des travaux de la commission de surveillance et de contrôle des publications destinées à l'enfance et à l'adolescence, 1er janvier 1955* (Paris, 1955), 15-20.

The Construction of a Political and Media Presence: The Homosexual Liberation Groups in France Between 1975 and 1978

Jean Le Bitoux

I used to go to the famous general assemblies of the Homosexual Front for Revolutionary Action (FHAR) at the School of Fine Arts in Paris.[1] I was then a student at the Conservatory of Music in Nice, and I wrote from time to time for the gay press. At twenty-three, which is to say five years younger than the principal founders of FHAR, I was really just an inexperienced and dazzled observer venturing to take part in a movement that was only just getting started. In the following pages, I will rapidly sketch this homosexual revolution before going on to its sequel.

FHAR was the result of shame ripening into anger. It was able to emerge politically only in the aftermath of the student insurrection and labor strikes of May 1968. It was an unexpected and historic opportunity for the rebellious young homosexual that I then was, but it was spoiled for me when I observed that competing factions disagreed irremediably over both form and content, as much over the way we homosexuals should appear to others as over how we should express the social injustice of which we were victims. It was not surprising that once the first wave of social rebellion "against normality" had run out of steam, only the shrieks of the *gazolines* (a group of transvestite radicals within FHAR) could still be heard. As for the verbal injunctions in the amphitheatre at the School of Fine Arts or the strategic plans quickly forgotten

[Haworth co-indexing entry note]: "The Construction of a Political and Media Presence: The Homosexual Liberation Groups in France Between 1975 and 1978." Le Bitoux, Jean. Co-published simultaneously in *Journal of Homosexuality* (Harrington Park Press, an imprint of The Haworth Press, Inc.) Vol. 41, No. 3/4, 2001, pp. 249-264; and: *Homosexuality in French History and Culture* (ed: Jeffrey Merrick, and Michael Sibalis) Harrington Park Press, an imprint of The Haworth Press, Inc., 2001, pp. 249-264. Single or multiple copies of this article are available for a fee from The Haworth Document Delivery Service [1-800-342-9678, 9:00 a.m. - 5:00 p.m. (EST). E-mail address: getinfo@haworthpressinc.com].

amidst mocking laughter, they were soon followed by orgasms in the orgies that took place in the classrooms upstairs; the general assembly had turned into a fuckfest (*baisodrome*), which the police finally closed down in 1974.

These multiple expressions that emerged from the shadows certainly gave the movement a dynamism, but they also knocked the protest movement off course because of the profusion of directions. Moreover, as numerous founders of FHAR will acknowledge today, the collective leadership did not seem to care about the future, about welcoming anybody into the group, explaining anything, or even preserving traces of the movement. The archives of this period are still widely dispersed.[2]

I participated in the events of May 1968 in Bordeaux and not on the Boulevard Saint-Michel in the Latin Quarter. I was a co-founder of FHAR, but in Nice and not in Paris. I could not hope to influence the course of this primarily Parisian history. This history was very confusing because so many different fronts, not so much ideological as strategic, were opened at the same time. I finally managed to reach Paris to live out this political and social adventure at the very moment that FHAR fell apart. I had a terrible feeling of impotence and an animosity toward the movement's leaders that would last for a very long time.[3]

Some members of this generation of students, who did not have the money to enjoy Paris's homosexual nightlife, which, in any case, they denounced for being "bourgeois" and ashamed of itself, refused to accept a return to normality. As for the leaders of FHAR, almost all of them abandoned the homosexual movement, although they reemerged later, principally in the cultural, artistic, literary, and journalistic fields.

Certainly, I understand that one cannot indict an entire movement or, rather, a new socio-cultural phenomenon, even if it chose to sabotage itself in full flight. FHAR's political program, which denounced all authorities and all "micro-fascisms," as Félix Guattari put it, may have consisted of nothing more than declarations and denunciations. Nonetheless, FHAR existed as a movement only by its taking a position. Its collapse in 1973 left an entire generation forlorn and adrift, unable to do anything else but return to cruising in the dangerous Tuileries gardens, on the terrace of the Café de Flore, at Arcadie's Saturday evening dances, where one had to behave respectably, or in the expensive nightclubs of the rue Sainte-Anne. Two years without militancy followed, with cruel results: a return to solitude and nocturnal clandestinity, a few suicides, a recourse to prostitution, even some psychiatric hospitalizations.

The end of FHAR was good news for Arcadie. After numerous resignations by people like Françoise d'Eaubonne, Daniel Guérin, or Pierre Hahn at the moment of FHAR's birth, André Baudry, who ran the association, encouraged by the defeat of the May 1968 movement in France and the collapse of radicalism, thought that it was time to take back the initiative. He decided to impose his authority by expelling a group of young people who, it seemed to him, were becoming too political. He made a mistake: These exiles encountered a few survivors from FHAR.

As a result, meetings started up again in 1975 at the Jussieu campus of the University of Paris. I was pleased to observe that, thanks to a classified advertisement in the newspaper *Libération*, the GLH (Homosexual Liberation Group) had been founded. I was also happy to meet up again with Alain Huet, Audrey Coz, and Alain Burosse. In the days of FHAR, Audrey and I liked disrupting gay parties in the chic quarters after an evening at the cinémathèque du Trocadéro, where Hélène Hazera, a friend of its founder Henri Langlois, sold the tickets. Alain Burosse, for his part, had participated in a commando action that one night. At the entrance to the restaurant *La Frégate*, he emptied a garbage can over the heads of the actors Jean Poiret and Michel Serreau, who were then triumphing in the play *La Cage aux Folles*.

I felt more comfortable with this new wave of militancy. It was more structured because the "loudmouths" who had dominated FHAR had vanished into thin air. There was a biweekly general assembly, which alternated with a committee to welcome newcomers, and a news bulletin that communicated internal and external information, the minutes of the general assemblies, the executive board, working groups and neighborhood committees, excerpts from the press, and important translations, a valuable tool that later became *Libido Hebdo*, which I edited between 1976 and 1978.

I also supported from the start the plan to construct a national network by listening to and involving the provinces in this movement, something FHAR had neglected to do. Like FHAR, we recruited among university and high-school students, intellectuals, militants, teachers, and trade unionists, social groups then in ferment that were causing trouble for President Valéry Giscard-d'Estaing. It was also necessary to seek common ground among ourselves and to be less aggressive toward and communicate more openly with journalists and political parties. Finally, we had to build a strong homosexual community in Paris and in other large cities.

Alain Huet soon became president of the GLH. The former editor of FHAR's newspaper *L'Antinorm*, he was one of the few who had tried to keep the homosexual movement alive after the death of FHAR, notably during the presidential elections of 1975, with Guy Chevalier, one of the authors of the revolutionary homosexual placards put up in May 1968 in the occupied Sorbonne. In the GLH, Huet at first worked closely with Michel Heim, who was more interested in the social side of our association, and with me, who remained faithful to the revolutionary principles of FHAR and advocated entering into contact with the press and the political world. But it was more and more difficult for these three tendencies to coexist within a single association, and the GLH soon found it necessary to split apart, because at the time our positions seemed irreconcilable.

A trip to Great Britain in the autumn of 1975 precipitated the break between the three group leaders. We went to a congress organized in Sheffield by the Campaign for Homosexual Equality, Britain's equivalent of Arcadie. A more radical group, the Gay Liberation Front, had not died out in Britain as FHAR had in France; in London, we saw the work of its gay and lesbian centers, like the one in Brixton. In a nightclub, I met and became involved with a young man of twenty, who was, at the time, considered a legal minor, and I caused something of a scandal by bringing him along to the congress.

As I reported in the *Quotidien de Paris*, there were other incidents: "The welcoming speech at City Hall by the mayor of Sheffield was interrupted by a militant of the Gay Liberation Front who asked him why the waitresses were paid less than the waiters."[4] Alain, Michel, and I were soon in disagreement. Michel, impressed by the delegates, who were wearing ties, wanted to integrate homosexuality into society without making any "ideological" waves, while Alain told us that he rejected this entire bourgeois ritual but thought that we had nothing in common with the women's movement. For my part, allergic to a gathering that had no political or social program, I decided to abandon the *spontanéisme* (a radical Maoist tendency in France) that had killed off FHAR. I also decided to make the homosexual question the priority in my social and political activism. I decided this time to engage in praxis.

Three months later, on 14 December 1975, the GLH in Paris split into three factions. There emerged the GLH Base Groups (Groupes de Bases), led by Michel Heim and dedicated to conviviality; the GLH December 14th (14 Décembre), led by Alain Huet according to libertarian and anti-feminist principles; and the GLH Politics and Daily Life (Politique et Quotidien) or GLH-PQ, which I led for three years and which everybody agrees was the most productive of the three–and the only one to survive until 1978.

Certainly, FHAR was dead, but it was necessary to keep alive at least the best part of its political message, while adapting it to new times, which had seen not only several significant social gains, such as the right to abort and the lowering of the sexual majority from twenty-one to eighteen, but also the bloody end of extreme left-wing terrorism, from the Italian Red Brigades to the Baader-Meinhof gang in Germany. The public image of the homosexual was still mainly bourgeois, most homosexuals still felt ashamed of their orientation, and French intellectuals still grandly ignored the whole question, whereas they talk endlessly of it today. Moreover, Arcadie was still around. Our first priority was therefore to contest its stuffy strategy: "Let us be dignified, and we will be respected." We knew all too well the bankruptcy of this wait-and-see policy that had permitted the maintenance of Pétain's anti-homosexual law of 1942 and had failed to prevent the passage of a law in July 1960 that made homosexuality a "social scourge," along with prostitution and alcoholism that the French Republic was to fight against.

In the mid-1970s, notably through their appearance on the television program *Dossiers à l'Écran* in January 1975, the novelists Yves Navarre and Jean-Louis Bory had publicly criticized Arcadie at the risk of "dividing the homophile people," as André Baudry complained.[5] The GLH-PQ subsequently organized two attacks on Studio 101 at the Maison de la Radio (a broadcasting center in Paris) to interrupt two broadcasts on France Culture. The first, on 26 January 1976, featured two homophobic sexologists. We intervened by distributing three hundred tracts denouncing these sexologists as "dangerous charlatans," who had already been condemned by FHAR in its day, and who had "persevered in their odious confiscation of our sexuality. Their discourse mystifies reality and serves to camouflage traditional psychiatric practices toward those who do not conform to the criteria of Normality."[6] The second broadcast, taped on 4 February 1976 and programmed for 6 April, was with Arcadie. Arcadie was indignant and replied to us: "Arcadie did not need FHAR and its exhibition of transvestites to promote homophile visibility. . . . Arcadie will remain, today like yesterday, at the forefront of the combat to defend homosexuals. That is its duty. It will not fail!"[7]

There were other "commando" operations, like the one in November 1977 in response to a homophobic incident at a café on the boulevard Saint-Germain (the owner had kicked out two men for exchanging a kiss). Several dozen of us showed up at the café after one of our general assemblies at the Jussieu campus. We ordered our drinks, then explained to the owner why we refused to pay for them. Then the windows shattered. The waiters and the guard dogs were unable to catch us.[8] Other provocations were equally amusing. To put an end to tacky "leftist" tracts, we mimeographed ones with innovative layouts: a sketch by Tom of Finland to express our solidarity with soldiers' committees, or another by Egon Schiele for our solidarity with lesbians. We also formed discussion groups like the one that studied the works of Simone de Beauvoir, Luce Irigaray or Sheila Rowbotham–gays and lesbians together in an alliance that would later fall apart.

Once we had opened negotiations with journalists, we were able to place a large number of articles in French dailies and weeklies between 1976 and 1978, like those by Jacqueline Rémy in the magazine *L'Express*, which have chronicled twenty-five years of our chaotic history from FHAR to the PACS (the civil partnership opened to gays and lesbians by a new law in 1999). These articles were for us a proof that things were changing, in short a breath of fresh air for homosexuals everywhere.

This happened in no small part thanks to the newspaper *Libération*, created in 1973, which took (and maintains to this day) a position favorable to our social visibility. And for good reason: This position resulted from discussions in favor of solidarity with the homosexual movement that took place among its founders (Serge Victor, Philippe Gavi, and Jean-Paul Sartre), meetings sometimes held at Michel Foucault's apartment with Serge July, the editor, and which have been chronicled in a book entitled *We Are Right to Revolt*.[9] These historic discussions recapitulate the journalistic and political debate of the time, and the following excerpt reveals a great deal about us:

> Philippe Gavi: "Everybody can use the women's struggle, the Communist Party as much as the Socialist Party. But the homosexuals, because they are still a minority, no one will touch them." Jean-Paul Sartre: "You are raising a tricky question. Because the homosexual movement is not popular. If we print articles on homosexuality in the newspaper, we will get numerous letters from readers completely opposed, who will tell us: 'Homosexuality is horrible, it is contrary to the class struggle,' and on the other side one or two letters from FHAR. How do you expect to combine the two opinions? . . . It is not a matter of shouting 'Long live homosexuals.' Personally, I would not be able to shout it, because I am not homosexual. It is a matter of showing the newspaper's readers that homosexuals have the right to live and to be respected like anyone else." Philippe Gavi: "I agree. It will not be easy."

Thus, *Libération*, for years on end, would give national coverage to the homosexual question, especially during the dark years that we were then living through with the lack of press coverage, of social and political representation, and of night life, and thus also in terms of social and even familial relations. As for personal advertisements, after appearing in a watered-down version in the weekly *Le Nouvel Observateur*, they began to appear in large number in the Saturday supplement to *Libération* called *Sandwich*.

Other press coverage was not always as favorable. I remember, for instance, one article in a leftist newspaper entitled ironically, "Is It Enough to Be Sodomized to Be a Revolutionary?" In 1978, the Communist Revolutionary League (a Trotskyist political party) lost its homosexual commission, whose members resigned as the result of unfortunate articles in the party's daily newspaper, *Rouge*, and the party's repeated postponement of a promised debate on the homosexual question. They went on to found a homosexual cultural review, *Masques*. The extreme left-wing party Lutte Ouvrière in no way renounced its machismo and its homophobia and for a long time refused to accept a homosexual stand at its annual festival, although both the Socialist Party and the Communist Revolutionary League did at theirs. The League's position was that, first of all, everybody, heterosexual and homosexual, had to work together to make the revolution, and then we would see what happened; meanwhile, during this purportedly pre-revolutionary period (which we were in fact less and less persuaded to be living in), this influential organization railed against "secondary" fronts in the class struggle that were allegedly disrupting the ongoing revolution with petty bourgeois demands for a selfish improvement in daily life. As for the Communist Party, since the day when its general secretary Jacques Duclos told homosexuals to get psychiatric treatment in the early 1970s, Pierre Juquin, the party's spokesman, explained in the columns of *Le Nouvel Observateur* why homosexuals, who polluted the noble demonstrations of the Left, had nothing at all to do with the workers' movement.[10]

This effervescence was evidently not without consequences for our political negotiations. The Socialist Party took a long time getting off the mark. François Mitterrand, its leader (and future President of France), considered homosexuality only a secondary concern. Nonetheless, Robert Badinter, who would later become Mitterand's Minister of Justice, made a minimal promise on behalf of the socialists in his book *Liberty, Liberties*: the abrogation of Article 331, Line 3, of the Penal Code, based on a decree issued by Marshal Pétain in 1942 during the German occupation, which criminalized homosexual relations with a minor less than twenty-one years old.[11] Laurent Fabius, later Mitterrand's Prime Minister, confirmed the Socialist Party's position in a letter of 7 February 1978. But for promises to become acts, there had to be a veritable electric shock coming from the homosexuals themselves, mobilized by the GLH-PQ. Such was the first Gay Pride celebration in 1977. Such were the homosexual candidacies in the municipal elections at Aix-en-Provence in 1977, and especially the legislative elections in Paris in March 1978. Such, too, was the Pagoda Affair in January 1978, which involved the banning of a homosexual film festival, a fascist attack, the arrest of a delegation sent to the Ministry of Culture, petitions by prestigious personalities, and finally a riot on the rue Sainte-Anne. Within a few short weeks, a page in French homosexual history would be decisively turned.

The festival of gay and lesbian films at the Pagoda theatre had been preceded by one that we organized from 20 to 26 April 1977 with Frédéric Mitterrand, nephew of the future President, and then in charge of the Olympic movie theatre on the rue Francis-de-Pressensé. Five thousand people had attended. Along with the showings, we held debates on the ghetto, the lesbian movement, transvestism, pedophilia, or (a complex subject) latent homosexuality. For an entire week, *Libération* gave a page every day to the event. This cultural initiative emerged out of the GLH-PQ's wish to rid itself of its reputation for being a radical political group obsessed only with social struggle. By calling itself "Politics and Daily Life," this faction intended to indicate that its dynamic came not only from its ideological convictions, but also from community groups, from wherever a few dozen homosexuals lived, developed an energy, and formulated proposals that a few hundred militants would then discuss in collective meetings. The film festival was also intended to establish a link with the European-wide cultural dynamic of homosexuals, which was then extremely creative, as demonstrated especially by the films of Pier Paolo Pasolini in Italy and Rainer Werner Fassbinder in Germany.

This first Parisian festival of gay and lesbian films was followed in the summer by a series called "Fag Films, Lesbian Films, and Others" at the La Rochelle film festival, where many young homosexual directors presented their work. Heir to these cultural roots, then, the festival held at the Pagoda theatre, from 16 to 31 January 1978, took place in a relatively tense political context. The legislative elections of March 1978 were fast approaching, and the GLH-PQ had decided to run candidates in Paris. This was the straw that broke the camel's back.

The Minister of Culture, Michel d'Ornano, refused to authorize the showing of an important number of gay films, including Jean Genet's *Chant d'Amour*.[12] On Friday, 27 January 1978, suspecting that we would ignore the ban, out-of-uniform policemen stationed themselves in the projection booth. From there they watched passively that evening as an extreme right-wing commando group attacked the festival. Armed with iron bars, these militants of Jeune Nation, whom d'Ornano had often used as a security force at his political rallies, after robbing the cash register, surged into the darkened theater, where Fassbinder's *Fox and His Friends* was being shown. They released tear gas in the dark and spattered red ink, so that when the lights came on, the audience thought they were covered in blood. Panic ensued. Many people rushed out the exits and toward the gardens of the former Chinese embassy, where the commandos continued to club them. Some, like the filmmaker Guy Gilles, injured their hands climbing over the railings along the street.

A few hours later, the fascists issued a press release: it was unacceptable for homosexual candidates to run in the forthcoming legislative elections. If this happened, they would know how to take care of them. As one of the announced candidates for Paris along with Guy Hocquenghem, I got the message. I had to move secretly, indeed to give up campaigning in the last days. Already in 1975, the neo-Nazis of Ordre Nouveau had bombed the headquarters of the GLH on the rue du Faubourg Saint-Denis. As Luc Bernard wrote in the press, "It is as if homosexuality is accepted only as long as it stays hidden, as long as one can ignore it. And on the other hand, the candidacy of homosexuals in the legislative elections is provoking some unrest."[13]

On the very same evening as the fascist attack, despite my hasty visit to the police station of Paris's sixth district to report it and to ask for police protection, no additional policemen were sent to place Saint-Germain-des-Prés, where a large gay and lesbian dance was being held as part of the festival. At midnight, the street lights on the square suddenly went out for a time, causing us to fear that a massacre, or at least a general gay bashing, was about to occur.

The next day, on Saturday, 28 January, I placed an anonymous announcement in the columns of *Libération*, the young daily newspaper where I was then working as a journalist, that there would be a protest demonstration that midnight. Remembering Christopher Street some nine years earlier, we occupied the Rue Sainte-Anne with its chic nightclubs, its hustlers, its bathhouses, and its leather bars, in brief, the falsely gay and hypocritically fashionable showcase for Parisian homosexuality. When there were a hundred of us gathered on the sidewalk, we began by interrupting the traffic. We had noticed a construction site not far away, which provided us with paving stones to begin building one or two barricades in front of two clubs, Le Sept and Le Bronx. A police van appeared at the bottom of the rue Sainte-Anne and stopped before the demonstrators who were blocking traffic by distributing tracts against homophobic violence. The police asked who was responsible. Nobody answered. Then the police grabbed our banner and began making arbitrary arrests. The police van tried to leave with many of our arrested friends. Some of us lay on the ground under its wheels.

I was hoping for–we all were hoping for–a French "Christopher Street," but this nighttime riot could not go very far. It failed, despite the heroic gesture by the GLH-PQ militants, because for two hours, during the entire event, the security staff of all the chic nightclubs along the street prevented their customers from leaving. Those clients, who, informed by the latest arrivals of what was going on in the street, expressed solidarity with us and wanted to come out to fight by our side, were unable to join us. Conversely, certain homosexuals pursued by the police officers were kept by the doormen from taking refuge inside the establishments. The lack of solidarity was flagrant. The only thing we could do was to flee the scene, chased by the police reinforcements that arrived with sirens howling. The police van finally broke through the human chain that blocked it from advancing. One individual, who threw stones at the van, was arrested, convicted, and fined. The homosexual movement took up a collection to pay his fine. Michel Aribaud, for that was his name, would eventually become one of the biggest gay entrepreneurs of the 1980s.[14]

The following Wednesday, 1 February, at 2 p.m., a delegation of intellectuals and journalists presented itself at the Ministry of Culture on the rue de Valois to demand an explanation for what had happened at the Pagoda. They brought a petition signed by, among others, Michel Foucault, Simone de Beauvoir, Jean Elleinstein, Didier Motchane, Maurice Nadeau, and François Chatelet. The delegates were asked to wait, and then the police showed up, took everybody away (including André Glucksmann, René Schérer, the journalists from *Libération* and *Le Monde*, and even the correspondent of the *Manchester Guardian*) and held them for four hours for an identity check. The police simultaneously broke up a protest by GLH-PQ militants at the nearby Carrousel du Louvre. Several days later, Guy Hocquenghem and André Glucksmann signed a joint article in *Le Monde*, entitled "Queen Victoria Strikes Again," which dealt, above all, with ministerial censorship.[15]

A petition (somewhat "communitarian" in inspiration) was soon circulated, the text of which follows:

> In Paris in March 1978, five candidates will run in the legislative elections. In the name of their legitimacy, they are posing the problem of the repression of homosexuals by the Penal Code and by existing police and psychiatric practices. Whether they politically agree or disagree with the homosexual candidates, the undersigned intend, by means of the present petition, to protest against any attack on the right of these homosexuals to run as such in these elections, and in addition to declare that they support the right and the principle of homosexual candidacies in the face of arbitrary governmental action which forbids a cultural festival because it is homosexual and in the face of fascist aggression and of their threats to prevent by any means the existence of such candidacies.

It was signed by many well-known intellectuals, writers, actors, and directors: Fernando Arrabal, Jean-Louis Bory, Simone de Beauvoir, Marie Cardinale, Marcel Carné, Copi, Gilles and Fanny Deleuze, Marguerite Duras, Xavière Gauthier, André Glucksmann, Félix Guattari, Jean Edern-Hallier, Christian Hennion, Alain Krivine, Georges Lapassade, Annie Leclerc, Bernard Muldworf, Maurice Nadeau, Yves Navarre, Madeleine Renaud, and Christiane Rochefort.

I had launched my political campaign in the March 1978 legislative elections with Guy Hocquenghem. It was a unique event in the history of the French homosexual movement. I had first been obliged to reconcile with Guy. Several GLH-PQ militants, like Frank Arnal and Pablo Rouy, both of whom later participated with me in the magazine *Gai Pied*, had withdrawn their own proposed candidacies, one of them arguing that he had not yet come out to his parents and the other that the publicity would harm working relations with his fellow nurses. I found myself absolutely alone and, therefore, had to seek the support of a former heavyweight in the homosexual movement. A mutual friend arranged a meeting at the Closerie des Lilas. I did not very much like Guy for having sought personal fame in the early 1970s, when the press spoke of him as the leader of FHAR, a movement that in fact rejected the very principle of leadership. I had more recently reacted violently against one of those provocative articles that he regularly wrote. In November 1975, when Pier

Paolo Pasolini was murdered, Guy actually justified the crime in an article in *Libération* entitled "Not everybody can die in his bed." We answered his article with one entitled "Guy Hocquenghem confuses the taste of sperm with the taste of blood."[16] These disagreements had left their mark, but our meeting was polite. We reached agreement when Hocquenghem accepted the GLH-PQ's political program, which I proposed as our platform for the electoral campaign. This program, drawn up by a homosexual movement to which Guy no longer belonged, had as its first demand the abrogation of Article 331, Line 3, of the Penal Code. The cartoonist Copi offered us a poster that was placarded on all the electoral billboards along the boulevard Saint-Germain, where I was a candidate in the sixth district, and along the boulevard Barbès, where Guy was running in the eighteenth district. Our tally was worst than mediocre, because the campaign had not even managed to raise enough money to print its ballots (in France, political parties prepare ballots with the name of their candidates, which the voters then put in the ballot box).

Astonished by our militant determination and by the support that we received from the cultural world, certain politicians decided to exploit it for themselves. In the midst of the electoral campaign, Senator Henri Caillavet, a center-left candidate, told the press that he had tabled a bill to amend Article 331. A parliamentary struggle ensued between the Senate and the National Assembly, which lasted more than four years, at the end of which, under the presidency of François Mitterrand, parliament abrogated Line 3 of the article on 4 August 1982. By putting the amendment of Article 331 on the political agenda, the GLH-PQ had achieved in three years what Arcadie had failed to do in twenty-five.

We had several other reasons to be proud of ourselves. We did not register our association at the Prefecture of Police (a requirement for getting a post office box) under a misleading name (Arcadie officially called itself "The Literary and Scientific Club of the Latin Countries" and even FHAR had disguised itself as the "Humanitarian and Anti-Racist Front") but as the GLH, the Group for Homosexual Liberation. For the first time, an association had succeeded in using the word "homosexual" in its name, without having the police refuse to register it as "contrary to good morals."

Despite these "reformist" gains, our ultimate objectives remained very precise, as Jacques Girard ironically described them in 1981: "GLH-PQ continues to swing like a pendulum, spouting in turn a revolutionary discourse to homosexuals and a homosexual discourse to revolutionaries." Our discourse about the "gay ghetto" was even more precise. As Girard put it:

> The GLH-PQ cannot ask homosexuals to leave the ghetto any more than one can ask a worker to leave the factory. The point is rather to analyze it:

> Why does it exist? What is its purpose? Strictly speaking, there is no homosexual ghetto, but rather several sorts of enclosures that are not homogenous. We can distinguish, on the one hand, the clubs, bars, and bathhouses, which are more and more expensive, and, on the other, the public parks and urinals along the streets, which are free but dangerous. The GLH-PQ believes that police repression and gay bashing by thugs is driving homosexuals out of the "wild ghetto" toward the "commercial ghetto" dominated by a bourgeois ideology.[17]

In fact, the GLH-PQ wanted to redraw the map of homosexual Paris. The municipality's removal of hundreds of street urinals was well underway. The clubs of rue Sainte-Anne were in decline, and the legendary bar Le Fiacre at Saint-Germain-des-Prés was dying. Fabrice Emaer, owner of the chic club Le Sept on the rue Sainte-Anne, abandoned it in March 1978 to open his huge discotheque, Le Palace, on the rue du Faubourg Montmartre. The first gay establishment in the Marais quarter was Joël Leroux's bar, opened on the rue du Plâtre in December 1978, which sold beer at only ten francs a glass. Jean Nicolas, the theoretician of the GLH-PQ, wrote this prescient analysis of the new pseudo-popular "ghetto" that was beginning to appear parallel with and in opposition to the posh clubs of the rue Sainte-Anne:

> On entering one removes anything that might recall the individual's integration into normal social relations and keeps on only the markings that show that one is a fag. It is in this type of ghetto that the ideology of homosexual identity is most firmly rooted.[18]

It was clear to the GLH-PQ that it was necessary to denounce the rue Saint-Anne: the posh nightclub, the "understanding" hotel, male prostitution inside the clubs or on the sidewalk, the bathhouse, the leather bar, or the nearby restaurant filled with middle-class men ashamed of their homosexuality. Our attempt to spark a French Christopher Street riot on the rue Sainte-Anne at the time of the gay film festival should be understood within this context.

Christopher Street had been one of our points of reference; the American Gay Pride parade, the logical sequel to this riot, was another. Now, French homosexuals had never, even in the days of FHAR, found the courage to march alone, except for marching with the women's movement–with which we shared several objectives, notably concerning male chauvinism–at the tail end of the annual May Day demonstration, to the great displeasure of the General Confederation of Labor, the Communist Party, and the prudish extreme left. The very first homosexual march took place on Saturday, 25 June 1977, a sort of "soft" riot, so to speak. I had announced the demonstration–what would turn out to be France's first Gay Pride march, from the place de la République to the place des Fêtes, organized by the GLH-PQ–on the front page of *Libération* in an article entitled "Gay Anger."[19] The word "gay" was little used by French militants in those days. In another tip of the hat to our big American brothers, our march was dedicated to denouncing Anita Bryant, the heroine of American homophobes. Several hundred gays and lesbians showed up, surrounded by a hundred photographers. *Le Monde* chronicled this first collective coming out in an article subtitled: "I'm not ashamed, I'm afraid."[20]

Other of our ideas never got off the ground, such as a telephone help line, because we could not raise the necessary money, or such as a lesbian and gay center (we symbolically occupied an unused boutique near the Gaité metro station, but our efforts were insufficiently structured).[21] But at least we launched these ideas. It might be said that everything that marks the breadth of today's French homosexual movement was initiated between 1975 and 1978. The publicity given to our efforts by numerous newspapers, which was the result of patiently explaining ourselves, also brought fruits. Favorable articles on the homosexual question finally began to appear, and not in the extreme left-wing press.[22] I even published a work called *Press Dossier on Homosexuality*, which compiled all the newspaper reports of this period.[23]

It is perhaps surprising that the question of the martyrdom and deportation of homosexuals by the Nazis, a political subject if there ever was one, was not central to our demands. The witnesses, like Heinz Heger and Pierre Seel, had not yet spoken out, but the facts were known well enough.[24] We began the custom of laying wreaths for deportees on the occasion of France's annual remembrance day. On 27 April 1977, however, we were not even allowed to take part in the official ceremonies. The police stopped the homosexual delegation and confiscated the wreaths.[25]

It was equally important to assure a visibility in the media. Certain of our courageous elders had shown us the way. After the coming out of the writer and journalist Jean-Louis Bory in his book, *My Half of the Orange* (1973), Dominique Fernandez followed with his, *The Pink Star* (1978).[26] After I interviewed Fernandez for *Libération*, we became friends, and in the spring of 1978 a television network asked us to make a documentary report about the homosexual condition in France. Months of filming followed, notably in the communal apartment on the boulevard Voltaire where I was then living and where the magazine *Gai Pied* would be born a few months later. A number of friends from the GLH-PQ and the GLH in Marseille dared to be interviewed on camera. The program, repeatedly postponed on the orders of the French President's office, was not broadcast until 9 November 1979, but our ratings that evening were higher than either the interview with François Mitterrand on one of the competing networks or a film starring Alain Delon on the other. In the live debate that followed our report, in which the political right had refused to participate, Senator Caillavet and the socialist deputy Raymond Forni (now speaker of the National Assembly) spoke courageously in favor of respecting differences and decriminalizing homosexuality by modifying Article 331.

After three years of intense militant activity and the impossibility of having any private life, I was totally exhausted, and I was not the only one. Moreover, within the GLH-PQ, after the successive withdrawal of integrationist reformists, misogynist anarchists, and interventionist maoists, there no longer remained anyone but *spontanéiste* queens and militant Trotskyites. Irreconcilable quarrels between them brought about the death of the GLH-PQ. The political candidacies in favor of homosexual identity, including Patrick Cardon's in the municipal elections in Aix-en-Provence in 1977, caused the explosion, and the Trotskyites declared this initiative to be counterrevolutionary.

In the meantime, new volunteers were less committed to militancy than the old-timers, and for good reason. The distribution of tracts on the terrace of the Café de Flore had ceased, like the picnics on the Buttes Chaumont, at the Bois de Vincennes, or on the lawns surrounding the student residences at the Cité Universitaire. Commando actions were no more than a memory. No more graffiti in the metro or on the last of the public urinals. Our quarrels had turned our thoughts inward. Above all, we were being dominated by media stars, which was far from our initial ideas. The homosexual reality, however, was going to change very quickly as a result of our incessant agitation. The legislative elections in Paris had been only a final burst of solidarity. Meetings, sticking up posters, and interviews masked the approaching end of an exhausted group.

In the summer of 1978, I resigned from the GLH-PQ in an open letter published in *Libération* and entitled "On Misery in the Gay Militant Milieu," in which I lambasted the "leftist" tics in our way of functioning as well as the sterile and provocative eccentricities of certain queens.[27] It seemed to me that militancy of this sort had outlived its day and run out of arguments. In my resignation, which signed the death warrant of the GLH in Paris, I wished good luck to the CHA's, the District Homosexual Committees into which the GLH-PQ had split. I hoped that these committees, closer to life at the grass roots in the various city quarters, could restart the homosexual movement, along with the surviving GLH groups outside of Paris. The GLH of Marseilles, for example, founded a year later the first Homosexual Summer University, where the Emergency Committee against the Repression of Homosexuals (CUARH) would be established as a federation of homosexual associations with a nationwide mission. CUARH would keep up the pressure on France's elected representatives until the final amendment of Article 331 on 4 August 1982.

For my own part, confident after my two years' experience as a reporter at *Libération* and exhausted after seven years of militancy at the ground level, I went on to found the magazine *Gai Pied* with the support of Michel Foucault, whom I met in the summer of 1978 after reading the first volume of his *History of Sexuality*, which drastically changed certain of our strategies and our way of looking at the homosexual question. Moreover, in the space of a few months, the right-wing government of Giscard-d'Estaing banned a dozen homosexual periodicals, and we had to restock the empty newsstands.[28] That same summer, we met in a house in Haute-Provence, at Maazel, with a number of leaders who had resigned from the regional GLH. They became correspondents for this now famous magazine which, from the first issue in February 1979, declared itself a national periodical and not merely a Parisian one. We had embarked on a new adventure.

REFERENCES

1. At the beginning of gay prehistory in France, there was the association Arcadie, born in 1954 ten years after the Allies liberated France from the Germans. Then, in the aftermath of the events of May 1968, there was the Homosexual Front for Revolutionary Action in 1971. In 1975 it was the turn of the GLH (the Homosexual Liberation Group), which took over the struggle for homosexual visibility and equality, which had been going nowhere. This political and social movement of a new kind managed, after three years, to put the homosexual question on the political agenda. It is described here by one of its principal participants, the author of these pages. Translated by Michael Sibalis.

2. This was evident from the debate on FHAR held in Paris on the occasion of Gay Pride 1996, when veterans of FHAR, such as Anne-Marie Fauret, Gilles Chatelet, and Hélène Hazéra, spoke, and a film recalling this period was shown. It was directed by Philippe Genet and featured Michel Cressole, Bertrand Cordier, Robert and Jean-Michel Mandopoulos.

3. I nevertheless remained close to Pierre Hahn, Daniel Guérin, Françoise d'Eaubonne, and Marc Roy, who would join me when I founded *Gai Pied* in the spring of 1979.

4. *Le Quotidien de Paris*, 23 September 1975.

5. The text of the broadcast was published as *Les Homosexuels aux dossiers de l'écran* (Paris, 1975).

6. "Le Long passé de la sexologie" (Paris, n.d.), mimeographed tract in my private papers. See also *Le Quotidien de Paris*, 30 January 1976.

7. Pierre Fontanié, "Le Droit d'être homosexuel," *Arcadie* 269 (May 1976): 309-10.

8. *Libération*, 23 November 1977: "Really, the café owners lack a certain tolerance. The owner of the Apollinaire had thrown out two homosexuals because they kissed under his eyes. . . . The end result of the brawl: two seriously injured and two broken windows."

9. *On a raison de se révolter* (Paris, 1974), 115-7.

10. *Le Nouvel Observateur*, 15 May 1972.

11. Robert Badinter, *Liberté, libertés: Réflexions du comité pour une charte des libertés animé par Robert Badinter* (Paris, 1976).

12. "Un Week-end anti-pédé," *Libération*, 30 January 1978. The press coverage of the event was published in a dossier: *L'Affaire La Pagode* (Paris, n.d.). See also Olivier Jablonski, "Les Festivals gais et lesbiens de cinéma en France en question," *La Revue h* 5/6 (1998): 8-13.

13. Luc Bernard, "Des moeurs à la politique, l'itinéraire de l'intolérance," *Le Quotidien de Paris*, 30 January 1978.

14. Pierre Hahn, "Les Homosexuels aussi," *Politique Hebdo*, 22 January 1978.

15. "La Reine Victoria a encore frappé," *Le Monde*, 7 February 1978.

16. Guy Hocquenghem, "Tout le monde ne peut pas mourir dans son lit," *Libération*, 29 March 1976; and GLH-PQ, "Guy Hocquenghem confond le goût de sperme et celui du sang," *Libération*, 20 April 1976.

17. Jacques Girard, *Le Mouvement homosexuel en France, 1945-1980* (Paris, 1981), 129-31.

18. *Bulletin national des GLH*, February 1976, 14ff.

19. "La Colère gaie," *Libération*, 25 June 1977.

20. Bertrand Le Gendre, "Une Manifestation d'homosexuels à Paris," *Le Monde*, 28 June 1977.

21. Christian Colombani, "La Maison des homos," *Le Monde*, 16 June 1977.

22. See, for example, the collection of articles put together by Jacqueline Rémy in *L'Express*, 23 January 1978.

23. *Dossier de presse sur l'homosexualité* (Paris, 1978).

24. Heinz Heger, *Die Männer mit dem rosa Winkel* (Hamburg, [1972]); and Pierre Seel, *Moi, Pierre Seel, déporté homosexuel* (Paris, 1994).

25. Pierre Hahn, "Des illusions perdues aux réalités d'aujourd'hui," *Politique Hebdo*, 13 June 1977.

26. Jean-Louis Bory, *Ma moitié d'orange* (Paris, 1973); and Dominique Fernandez, *L'Étoile rose* (Paris, 1978).

27. Jean Le Bitoux, "De la misère en milieu mili-tante," *Libération*, 6 May 1977. The title contains an untranslatable pun on *militant* (militant) and *tante* (auntie).

28. Between 1976 and 1979, the Ministry of the Interior successively banned the following periodicals (of varying quality): *Homo*, *Dialogues Homophiles*, *Incognito Magazine*, *In*, *Dialogue Mens*, *Soft Men*, *Olympe*, *New Boys*, *Homo 2000*, and *Alter Ego*. The review *Gaie Presse*, close to GLH-PQ, in whose first issues I had participated, was similarly banned by a decree of 1 March 1978 (in the *Journal Officiel*, 11 March 1978). In contrast, a decree of 22 April 1975 (in the *Journal Officiel*, 28 May 1975) had lifted the ban on *Arcadie*.

Gay Mimesis and Misogyny: Two Aspects of the Same Refusal of the Other?

Marie-Jo Bonnet

Editors' note: This is a translation of the original text.[1]

For several years now French gays have been in the habit of saying "gays *and* lesbians" as if the "and" goes without saying and as if it were possible to claim sexual inclusiveness while simultaneously denying sexual difference. This contradiction nevertheless manages to work well enough in French society, because everybody pretends to believe that gay men also represent lesbians, while lesbians represent only themselves. If this problem is not a recent one, I want to analyze in this essay how the misogyny that is virtually inherent in the contemporary gay movement rests on a mechanism that, to my knowledge, historians of the homosexual movement have not yet studied: mimesis.[2] Whether in its relationship to women in the struggle for legal recognition of homosexual couples or during Gay Pride celebrations, the gay (male) movement has always used mimesis to get what it wants. And it is not only because the gay movement seeks "sexual indifference" (i.e., the right to be treated "indifferently," just like everyone else), as people used to say in the 1980s; it is because mimesis is a way for it to protect itself against homophobia while avoiding its own dissolution into the wider society.

The definition given by the Robert dictionary seems to me particularly illuminating in explaining this phenomenon, even if it situates mimesis within the realm of animal behavior: Mimesis–the ability of certain animal species, in order to as-

[Haworth co-indexing entry note]: "Gay Mimesis and Misogyny: Two Aspects of the Same Refusal of the Other?" Bonnet, Marie-Jo. Co-published simultaneously in *Journal of Homosexuality* (Harrington Park Press, an imprint of The Haworth Press, Inc.) Vol. 41, No. 3/4, 2001, pp. 265-280; and: *Homosexuality in French History and Culture* (ed: Jeffrey Merrick, and Michael Sibalis) Harrington Park Press, an imprint of The Haworth Press, Inc., 2001, pp. 265-280. Single or multiple copies of this article are available for a fee from The Haworth Document Delivery Service [1-800-342-9678, 9:00 a.m. - 5:00 p.m. (EST). E-mail address: getinfo@haworthpressinc.com].

sure their own protection, to give themselves an appearance similar to their environment, to another creature in this environment, or to a member of a species that is better protected or more feared." For example, a threatened species may take the same color or the same shape as another species. Although the definition says nothing of the same sex, most probably, the first theoreticians of homosexuality consciously used the mimetic mechanism in constructing their theories.

To resemble the heterosexuals around them, is that not what gays have been trying to do with the PACS (Pacte civil de solidarité, the legal partnership between couples of the same or opposite sex, instituted by parliament in 1999) or by displaying, during the so-called Lesbian and Gay Pride parade, a phallic representation that reflects the idols worshipped by our global society? But if mimesis is to some degree a protective reaction against homophobia, it has proved so successful a strategy of adapting to a hostile environment that gays have never hesitated to sacrifice lesbians to it, and with them the necessity of assuming their difference, so that adaptation has become integration into the dominant social models.

The history of the gay movement in the last thirty years, however, shows that in their use of mimesis gay men have shown a remarkable persistence not only in using the phallic model as the most efficient adaptive technique, but also in universalizing this model and applying it to other forms of homosexuality. This observation brings me to the following question: Is the 2000 model so different from the 1960 model, when André Baudry, the president of the homosexual association Arcadie, condemned "effeminates" on the grounds that they did not show the "respectable face of homosexuality"?[3] In 1963, homosexual respectability meant rejecting "effeminates"; today it triumphs by occulting lesbians and the difference between the sexes, reducing the question of the legal recognition of homosexuality to that of "sexual equality," which means today a mimetic rivalry between masculine models.[4]

One would think that the gay movement would be in a better position than other movements to establish a sexed but nonsexual link with women. But apparently the gay movement is not interested in equality between the sexes. Not only has the gay movement failed to find the political means to promote sexual equality, but it has so often "instrumentalized" lesbians that one wonders whether gay mimesis is not a new way to restructure and reinforce the masculine sexual order so brutally challenged by the women's revolt of the 1970s.

FEMINIST MIMESIS: FHAR'S ALLIANCE WITH THE MLF

It cannot be repeated often enough: feminists founded FHAR (Homosexual Front for Revolutionary Action). "It is a secret for no one that the women had a predominant role in the creation of FHAR.... The MLF [Women's Liberation Movement] was the inspiration for our movement at the start and perhaps there would never have been a beginning if the women had not themselves begun," Guy Hocquenghem acknowledged.[5] In February 1971, Anne-Marie Grélois, Maryse, and Françoise d'Eaubonne, who were members of both Arcadie (a relatively conservative homophile group founded in 1954 under the direction of André Baudry) and of the MLF, had the idea of calling a meeting of Arcadie's lesbian members. This initiative proved so successful that they broadened it to include the most progressive male homosexuals in Arcadie. This made possible a liberation movement that was as "explosive" as it was unexpected in the aftermath of May 1968.[6] The homosexual revolt took a form that had never been seen before.

First of all, it was unprecedented from a political point of view. The homosexual revolt attracted young people from the extreme left, many of whom believed that they were experiencing a sexual revolution. "Proletarians of the world, caress each other," they wrote on a banner for the annual May Day march in Paris, at the same time as they denounced "the dictatorship of the normals." Secondly, there was "the freshness and the spontaneity of the movement," as Guy Hocquenghem observed, which freed homosexuality of the clandestinity, shame, and guilt attached to what was officially considered a "social scourge" (in the terms of a law voted by parliament in July 1960). But above all, its involvement with the MLF made it a completely exceptional phenomenon in the history of homosexual liberation. For the first time, at least in France, men openly opposed "male chauvinist society." "The homosexual revolt opposed the patriarchal and capitalist family. From the very start it declared itself on the side of women," wrote Hocquenghem in 1972.[7] FHAR fought alongside women for the right to practice contraception and to abort at a time when the struggle was still a risky one.[8] FHAR participated in all of the MLF's demonstrations, and its members were the only men whom the founders of a women's only movement were willing to accept as "allies." FHAR's commitment was so total that it even formally disassociated itself from "fascist virility."

Indeed, FHAR's alliance with the MLF seemed so self-evident that the feminist movement became the counter-example that FHAR used to oppose the militaristic organizations prevalent on the extreme left. FHAR adopted feminist slogans, such as "our body belongs to us," which appeared on the first page of issue #12 of the newspaper *Tout*, in which lesbians and homosexuals spoke out publicly for the very first time.[9] FHAR organized itself along the same anarchist lines as the MLF, with a weekly general assembly held at the Paris School of Fine Arts "without structure or hierarchy," and which welcomed everybody: men, women, effeminates, transvestites, leather queens, family men, young, and old. With pleasure as their guiding principle, the general assemblies became a crucible of new ideas and new modes of behavior. Not only were old ways of thinking shattered along with the old taboos and prohibitions, but the hope of "changing one's life" no longer seemed a dream.

But very quickly the lesbians began to feel uncomfortable in the general assemblies, where the men did not listen to them and called them "romantic schoolgirls" whenever they talked of love. Misogyny reappeared with such force that the women, who were in the process of challenging the very foundations of male domination, found it intolerable. They decided to meet separately in a group they called the Red Dykes.[10] But the desire to pursue the experiment with mixing the sexes still survived, as a tract written at the time by Anne-Marie and Maryse demonstrates:

> In our women's only groups, we also analyze the sexist and male chauvinist attitudes of certain homosexuals. This contributes to the creation of new human relationships, a necessary precondition to acting to change life. As males, homosexual men participate in the oppression of women and the presence of lesbians can only encourage them to become aware of their role as oppressors, which is often unconscious.[11]

Soon the very goals of the sexual revolution would be the subject of a burning debate between men and women. The gay men wanted "to enjoy with no restrictions" (*jouir sans entraves*), whereas the lesbians were tackling the oppression of women, as indicated by a letter from Sylvie published in issue #12 of *Tout*: "The struggle for homosexual liberation is subordinate to the struggle for the liberation of woman and of the couple in general (on that day [when the battle is won], homosexual men will no longer have any complexes about femininity)." The conflict also centered on the contradiction between male sexuality and the women's reflections on love, as Anne-Marie Grélois explained in her article in *Report Against Normality*, published in the autumn of 1971: "We lesbians, we want to talk about our *love*, because we are fed up with hearing men talk about *sex* and nothing else. Our pleasure in itself does not refer to any image of power or oppression."[12]

When it came right down to it, there was no unanimous support among gay men for calling into question the couple, sexual roles, and the standard behavior of submitting to male desires. When the feminist militants of the MLF declared in *Tout* that "Your sexual revolution is not ours,"[13] a "member of FHAR" responded this way:

> We homosexual men cannot accept the "deconstruction of roles" unless we have the right to every role, not when certain roles (being the object of desire, for example) are forbidden to us. . . . The fact remains that as far as the ideology of FHAR is concerned, I have reached the conclusion

> that it is indeed rather different from that of the MLF, even if we are natural allies. Sexuality is central to the revolt of homosexuals. This is evidently especially true for the men; it is principally in this respect that we have been repressed. While physical relations between homosexual women are quite well tolerated by a society that oppresses them as women, sexual relations between men are still a major social taboo.[14]

One can see that with this text published in June 1971, which is to say after only four months of unprecedented political activism by men and women working together, the homosexual men had learned nothing from the lesbians. The men did not even try to get to know the women and accepted the women's collaboration only because they belonged to the MLF. In fact, FHAR felt closer to the (heterosexual) women of the MLF than to the lesbians. The homosexual men needed the women's strength and creativity to make their appearance on the public scene. Once the "major taboo" had been publicly broken, they no longer needed this alliance, and they would no longer even keep the lesbians as members when, fed up with being overshadowed by the gay men, most of them definitively rejoined the MLF in July 1971. The "Balance Sheet" drawn up by several members of FHAR in #16 of *Tout* was a telling refusal to call into question male domination:

> Of course we will have to fight hard against the misogyny among us, but be that as it may, it will probably also be necessary in September that FHAR be composed of two distinct movements, one of faggots, one of lesbians.

Thus FHAR broke with the women over the issue of misogyny and recognized its essentially "non-mixed" nature (i.e., that it did not and could not bring together both sexes). But if it accepted this so easily, it was because it did not really affect them; the only confrontation that truly concerned them was with other men, at least with other left-wingers. Anne-Marie Grélois understood this very well when she wrote the following in her "Reply from the lesbians to their homosexual brothers":

> Men,
>
> You whose name designates both the male and the species,
> you who ceaselessly reinvent power
> . . . is it necessary, because one is a man, to speak implicitly only to other men?
>
> It is because always and everywhere man has been the only point of reference, the only worthwhile interlocutor, the one whose power others se-

> cretly envy! The penis symbolizes both the sceptre and the truncheon. What interest does all that have for women? None.
>
> In bourgeois and patriarchal society, *the* sexual organ is the penis, that sword for which we [women] are the scabbard. Homosexuality? It's a male sexual practice–because we women do not have a sexual organ, only a hole![15]

Indeed! The women were really only of secondary importance to these men, who were more concerned with their mimetic rivalry with the left-wing political extremists than by their alliance with the MLF. Guy Hocquenghem was lucid enough to recognize this the following year in his "Farewell to the dykes": "I announced that we had finally found true love. . . . I am afraid that I have to observe today that it was more a friendly complicity, totally dependent on a system of relations (with left-wingers and with women) over which we had no influence. The pleasure derived from this situation came more from a desire for vengeance on other men than from a veritable love for the women."[16] Was not this confession, despite everything, an embryonic consciousness that held out more promise than the events that would follow? The "alliance" between the sexes would last no more than a springtime, but it provoked a genuine confrontation between the men and the women that left its mark on "the faggots of FHAR" for the remainder of their days.

EGALITARIAN MIMESIS: THE CAMPAIGN FOR THE LEGAL RECOGNITION OF HOMOSEXUAL COUPLES (1995-1999)

We can see the same mimetic phenomenon at work twenty years later, but this time in another field: legal protection for homosexual couples. The historical context here was completely different. First, after the Left came to power in the presidential and legislative elections of 1981, one of the first acts by the new Minister of Justice, Robert Badinter, was to decriminalize homosexuality completely by abrogating the articles of the Penal Code that forbade homosexuals to have sexual relations with anyone under the age of twenty-one. The age of sexual majority became the same for everyone: fifteen. After the tremendous hopes raised by the sexual liberation movements and by everybody's deeply felt desire "to change one's life," the socialist left responded favorably to its homosexual electorate by changing . . . the subject, in the way it did with women by creating a Ministry of Women's Rights under Yvette Roudy. The Left took back the political initiative by making the demand for legal recognition of homosexual couples the new mimetic referent in a way that was all the more effective because AIDS had raised the issue, which went well beyond mere medical protection for gays. The "machines for producing pleasure" that Hocquenghem had condemned in a premonitory article in 1972 had become "machines for dying" that nobody and nothing could save.[17]

It was in this context of disease, death, and mourning that a new gay militancy developed around the associations Aides and Act Up. Under the leadership of gay men–because AIDS was a virus that presumably attacked only homosexual men and drug addicts–these associations had only a few lesbian members (no more than ten percent), who held subordinate positions and were restricted to the traditional roles of nurse and compassionate female friend.[18] Moreover, these associations benefited from large budgets paid for by the government or from the funds raised in charity drives. The militants working for these associations earned full-time salaries and financed medical and juridical research, a press, and a media presence that far exceeded anything available to lesbians.

Unlike gay men, for whom the AIDS epidemic opened an entirely new era, lesbians continued along the road they had begun to travel in the 1970s. But now they did so alone, because the feminists in turn had dropped them in the hope (how illusory!) that they would be more easily accepted by the male power structure if they sacrificed the most radical and innovative elements of the women's revolt. It was, therefore, only in the early 1990s that lesbians began to react against their being swept under the rug. They progressively created a score of associations in the big cities, with the clearly stated goal of bringing lesbians together. A new cultural militancy developed around the monthly *Lesbia Magazine* and around Cinéfable, an association that organized an annual festival of lesbian films, which enjoyed considerable success, despite the criticism from gay men, who did not accept a women's only movement. If one also takes into account the creation in 1997 of the National Lesbian Coordinating Committee, which federated these associations in order "to promote lesbian visibility and culture, [and] to struggle against lesbophobia and for the rights of women," one can see that, within only a few years, lesbians had achieved a presence on the political scene that they had never had before.

The originality in this civic practice, and we shall see how it was different from the institutionalization of feminism, was that the lesbians organized according to the principles that had made the MLF so strong (autonomy, sexual separatism, rejection of hierarchy, self-financing, volunteer work, respect of initiatives from below, rotating presidency), while at the same time they engaged in modernity, as Cinéfable put it so well in its 1996 catalogue: "In opposition to the idea of centralizing and bureaucratic structures, Cinéfable promotes solidarity among women, the dynamic of networks and projects."

One can see here the profound difference between lesbian militancy and gay male militancy. The latter was no longer using feminist mimesis but was, nonetheless, claiming to represent both sexes in order to solidify its political legitimacy. Associations calling themselves "Gay *and* Lesbian Center," "Gay *and* Lesbian Studies," "Lesbian *and* Gay Pride" were formed, although the power within them was completely in the hands of men.

It was within this double context of a fundamental difference between the gay and the lesbian movements and a total lack of dialogue that the idea of a homosexual partnership first developed. The purpose was to get legal recognition and protection for homosexual couples who were experiencing difficulties because of sickness.[19] Gay men, having in a certain way paid a heavy blood tribute to society, believed in the legitimacy of this idea, which was unthinkable in the 1970s. But at no time was their project discussed with the women. In moving into the juridical sphere of legal rights, gay men inevitably argued in terms of universalism, something inherent to French law, which must be the same for all and must apply to everybody. But the institutionalization of the homosexual couple implicitly excluded women from the "universalist" debate whenever they did not agree with the approach taken.

A first proposed bill, elaborated in 1990 under the name of Contract of Civil Partnership, wavered between a status specific to homosexuals and a new status available to both homosexuals and heterosexuals, but different from heterosexual concubinage (the French equivalent of common-law marriage). It was quickly abandoned because it did not really confer any rights. Gay men preferred a legal status more closely resembling marriage, which ignored the position of the women, who preferred to reinforce individual rights rather than the rights of the couple.[20] The men prevented any consideration of other possible schemes for the legal recognition of homosexuality and reduced the debate to a series of proposed bills that promoted equality between homosexual couples and heterosexual couples without ever making reference to the tie of homosexual love.

It is understandable that the 1990 bill was still rather vague in formulation because militants were venturing into unknown terrain, but the bill for a Contract of Civil Union, drafted by Vincent Legret, Jan-Paul Pouliquen, and Gérard Bach-Ignasse and presented to the National Assembly in 1992 also evaded the fundamental question by stating, in article one, that "Any legally competent individual . . . can contract with any other, of whatever sex, a Contract of Civil Union." The statement of purpose clearly indicated that the intention was "to promote an egalitarian law, applicable in the largest number of situations and not to enact measures specific only to homosexual couples." Five years later, the Contract of Civil and Social Union (CUCS) was proposed "to take notice of the tie uniting two legally competent individuals . . . who wish to establish between themselves a project for a life together."[21] Although the statement of purpose spoke of creating "a new form of union outside of marriage," it also declared that "the essence of the CUCS is the solidarity uniting the contracting parties, and the mutual moral and material support that they pledge [each other]."

One can see how the texts repeatedly avoided defining the couple, which also made it possible to elude the question of the difference between the sexes and any reflection on the fundamental meaning of the couple itself. Indeed, as everybody knows, the bourgeois republican marriage instituted by Napoleon's Civil Code of 1804 reinforced a model based on the complementarity of the two sexes and legalized male domination and the sexual division of society.[22] To avoid defining the couple, therefore, avoids tackling the symbolic questions that are so important to women, especially when the freedom to control one's own body (notably the right to abort) is not even recognized in French law as a fundamental human right, but only as a right enjoyed in certain circumstances (*droit derivé*).[23] It is also a refusal to give the tie of homosexual love symbolic value by calling things by their name, and this refusal would go so far that the promoters of the Contract of Social Union (CUS), submitted to the National Assembly in 1997, would even say that the contract could apply to couples composed of lovers, brothers, sisters, and even the priest and his maid.

Finally, in October 1999, parliament adopted the PACS, the Civil Pact of Solidarity, defined as "a contract concluded between two individuals of legal age, of either different sexes or the same sex, in order to organize their life together." The same day, a new text on concubinage was also adopted, thanks to the joint efforts of the Collective for a Free Union, the jurist Irène Théry, and Senator Robert Badinter. Concubinage was clearly different from the PACS, because it was defined as "a de facto union, characterised by a stable and continuous life together, between two persons of different sexes or the same sex who live together as a couple."

"Union" and "couple" on the one hand, contrasting with "contract" and "organize" on the other–this is what differentiates personal law, which recognizes a sexual union between two individuals, and a legal contract (the PACS), which deals with property even though it is inscribed in the Civil Code in the section on personal law. In the case of concubinage, the law recognizes individuals who are subject to the legislation; in the PACS, the law recognizes them as property owners (and I will not even discuss here the problems with the terms of the PACS, which was passed in spite of numerous criticisms). Prime Minister Lionel Jospin's socialist government wanted to make a clear political statement in the face of the traditionally homophobic Right. It ended up giving the homosexual couple a shaky legal status that has created more problems than it has resolved.

Why did the gay movement lock itself into this parody, when it might have developed other strategies? For example, the Syndicate of Lawyers of France opposed the CUS and advocated instead legal recognition of free unions, which would "permit the holding of a wide-ranging debate on the image of a world based on the male/female couple, the purpose of marriage, the relevance of new legal models of life as a couple, the significance of the desire for children, and the role of step-parents." The National Lesbian Coordinating Committee saw its role reduced to supporting the PACS unconditionally, although it had originally adopted a more nuanced position by refusing to choose between "improved concubinage, the PACS, and a renovated marriage." It had, moreover, put at the top of its list of demands "freedom of sexual orientation," something never recognized insofar as women are concerned, as proved by the United Nations Conference at Beijing in 1995.[25] For the National Lesbian Coordinating Committee, "The possibility of choosing between different contracts that would be available to homosexual and heterosexual persons seems in the end to be the most widely shared wish, from the moment that the individual rights of non-contracting parties are preserved, indeed expanded."[26] But a year later, the Committee expressed its pleasure at having obtained both the PACS *and* concubinage, declaring: "Of course, the law is not all-powerful in bringing about a change in attitudes. We hope that the social recognition brought about by the vote on the PACS and on concubinage will allow for ties of love, solidarity, and responsibility within homosexual couples to be lived and expressed more serenely."[27]

Gay men did not have the same relationship to this law as lesbians, and it is, therefore, not surprising that, identified as they were with it, which is to say, rejecting any criticism as homophobic, they made it their principal demand. In an article on "the creative force of the law," Professor Rémy Libchaber has correctly pointed out:

> the bill for a contract of union between partners has been constantly promoted by a group composed mainly of associations of homosexual male partners. However, in the statement of purpose of the legal proposals, this category is concealed so that the proposal can pass for achieving a truly general interest. . . . Thus the legal proposals seek to erase any trace of political pressure in order to carry the banner of universalism; but in so doing, they end up with the exact opposite because the particular interest of the proposal is manifest: demanded exclusively by one group, it is obviously specifically adapted [to the interests of that group].[28]

One can see, then, how the egalitarian mimesis of gay men has enabled them to obtain a law giving them equality with heterosexuals without having to engage in any debate on equality between the sexes. They thus followed an institutional logic very different from a symbolic logic necessary for the recognition of homosexuals, because the latter implies a recognition of the other as Other, and not merely as an equal. Everything has occurred as if the sole purpose of the legal recognition of homosexual couples were to establish their equality with heterosexual couples, which implicitly posits heterosexuality as the model for the integration of homosexuality into the national community. The PACS is a victory for male mimesis because it achieves an illusory legal recognition, on the basis of property and not of a relationship between two individual subjects, who remain as exposed as ever to homophobia and social violence. Women are well placed to know that if there is no real equality between the sexes in the French republican system, it is not for lack of laws on equality. It is because we live in a system of symbolic representation in which the male has been universalized. The PACS has been imposed, and parliament will undoubtedly vote laws on parity (the equal political representation of men and women in government), but all this will be in vain as long as women and/or homosexuals are not recognized as universal subjects to the same extent as others. It is the articulation between the one *and* the other that is missing in these laws on equality, just as it is missing in the gay movement, which is not even conscious of its denying the existence of lesbians when it speaks of feminist demands. In a manifesto "For Sexual Equality" published on the eve of Gay Pride, under the signatures ("Act Up Paris, Aides Fédération and Aides Ile-de-France, Sida Info Service, SOS Homophobie, and ten other associations") the following sentences appeared:

> In the name of the difference between the sexes, even on the political left, we are too often asked to choose between women's rights and gay and lesbian rights. For our part, instead of pitting them against each other, we want to unite the demands of feminism with those of the homosexual movement.[29]

Is this not what feminist lesbians have been doing for the past thirty years? But not one person among the signatories seems to have noticed this, because they are so used to universalizing the male point of view and not listening to the women. What more needs to be said?

Egalitarian mimesis reinforces a male homosexual vision of the world in which the Other, in this case the woman, disappears as Other to be integrated into a so-called universal model. Recognition occurs at the cost of negating otherness or, more precisely, reducing otherness to the specific, bringing back "the differential valence of the sexes," as Françoise Héritier has put it.[30] Thus, inscribing homosexuality within a new legal framework does not in the least change the position of women in a symbolic order in which the masculine dominates.

Moreover, gay egalitarianism obliterates the women's dynamic of autonomy and emancipation. It brings about a return to normative male values, which give the impression of being for everybody and to everybody's benefit; whereas, in fact, they conceal all the more successfully the necessary differentiation of homosexuals.

GAY MIMESIS AND SEXUAL CONSUMERISM

The annual "Gay and Lesbian Pride" marches organized in Paris and other large French cities are examples of demonstrations that claim to include both sexes but which in fact hide women from view. These marches, begun in 1977 and since 1995 bringing more than one hundred thousand people together every year, resemble mimetic parades visually structured around a phallic idol and its commercial avatars. The male sex is omnipresent, whether in its iconic form as a giant phallus composed of pink and white balloons, which the members of Aides set up on a float behind which they sang and danced, or in its organic form exhibited in frenzy and domineering aggressiveness. The female sex is grotesquely caricatured by drag queens, perched on fifty-centimetre high-heels, outrageously made up, and flaunting their naked buttocks, who, by reflecting the image that society has of homosexual men, demonstrate only their own tragic mindlessness. The gay men do not think about what they are showing nor the way that they show it. Thus, one can even see a float, advertising one particular gay business, featuring an entirely naked Black man in a cage, his penis rolled up in the rainbow flag, which is the height of stupidity for a movement that claims to stand for sexual freedom.

Homosexual pride has been turned into a carnival in the service of sexual consumerism which values (in the strict monetary sense of the term) one thing alone: the virile image exhibited by young, well-fed, tanned gay men, their heads shaved like soldiers, their muscles bulging, flaunting their genitals as if to reassure society as to their sexual identity by giving it proof of their masculinity. But these are derisory images, decoys waved by sham warriors who thrill to the sound of deafening music, like the Indians preparing themselves for battle in Hollywood films. They think that they are being shocking, whereas they are simply doing what society expects of them, in a tragic conformism that derives from either apolitical consensus or the most primitive male terrorism (it is hard to know which).

Mono-sexual pride, as the philosopher Alain Giry once called it, resembles the ithyphallic rites in which the ancient Romans paraded an enormous Phallus through the city streets. Gay men have transformed the phallic organ into a pagan idol that they can worship and consume. It would be an understatement to say that there is no place in Gay Pride for either women or femininity. Their invisibility has been so carefully programmed that they cannot even respond to it, because everyone comes there only to have fun. And why reflect on what is seen or on how the march might otherwise have been used to present a new image of homosexuality? Gays have invaded the streets and occupied all the space, creating a terrorism of visibility that transforms the object looked upon into an idol stripped of any transcendence.

The society of sexual consumption created by gay men has become blind and deaf to what the women have to say. In 1999, one lesbian group, the *Dé/générées* of Lille, distributed a tract during the Parisian march which said: "We do not recognize ourselves in the organization of the (Lesbian?) and Gay Pride, showcase for a homosexuality that is integrated, politically correct, commercial and trendy, masculine and misogynous. We lay claim to our diversity and to the critical view that we take on society."[31] No one took up the message, and the media continued to ignore the women in a purportedly "sexually mixed" march. Have we returned to the days of FHAR?

In Marseille in 1996, the city's three lesbian associations decided to march on the other side of the city from the Lesbian and Gay Pride parade in order to protest against the male minority who had registered statutes for an association to organize the demonstration that were "pretentious and designed to muffle dissenting opinion."[32] In Paris the situation is even more serious, because the march is organized by a public company, the Sogifred, created to eradicate the debt of 1.7 million francs run up by Gay Pride in 1996.[33] The success of the Gay and Lesbian Pride parade now depends on the financial participation of the National Syndicate of Gay Businesses, which continues to flourish and which uses its money to impose a tone, an image, and a sound. Politics has been taken hostage by business interests, which deliberately sacrifice the gay and lesbian associations, as Jacques Ars has pointed out, to a carnival atmosphere which does not even hide its commercial orientation (most of the floats advertise bars and clubs).[34] To resist the dictatorship of the media image, the lesbian associations have chosen a completely different way to demonstrate. They organize, on the evening of the march, a Lesbian Pride in the Salle Wagram in Paris. This forum brings together lesbian and feminist associations, book signings, video projections, and poetry readings, followed by the actual festivities themselves: more than three thousand women dancing to music chosen to please women of all ages.

Instead of challenging phallic visibility, the lesbians have chosen to create a gathering place, a space for meetings and exchanges, where nothing is ostentatious enough or noisy enough to draw media attention. And it is perhaps by this choice that they have won their victory over male voyeurism, in their wish to meet together in an autonomous space, where female desire can simply *be* without having to assure others of its legitimacy. There is no need to wear a mask there. It is enough to be oneself in order to come together with others. It is enough to dare to hide from the "outside" gaze in an apparent withdrawal into oneself in order to affirm proudly that lesbians exist even if a male chauvinist society does not see them. It is the home of the Amazons, where women learn the autonomous gaze of a subject in relation with others.

Lesbians are not more invisible than gays. They are here, present, alive, creative. But if the media do not see them, if gay men hide them from view, and if politicians do not listen to them, is it not because the media, the gay men, and the politicians fail to recognize the possibility that women desire something else besides the phallus?

Will gay men one day openly assume their feminine side (their *anima*, as Jung would say) without caricaturing it or projecting it on women or male prostitutes? This is the hope that I formulate here, because one can see that by identifying with the dominant masculine model, gay mimesis in the last thirty years has gone from being a simple defense strategy in the face of a hostile environment to becoming a veritable political offensive which has permitted gays to conquer more sexual freedom, more rights, more visibility, and perhaps more paternity, without ever calling the phallic order itself into question. Can they continue in this way, regardless of the women and of the truth peculiar to homosexuality? For if this mimesis functions so well, it is not only because it eroticizes the mimetic rivalry between masculine models: it is also because it rests on a constructivist conception of homosexuality according to which sexes, genders, and sexual preferences are social "constructions" that nobody can escape. Is this true as far as homosexuality is concerned? On the contrary, I believe that homosexuality is one of the sexual orientations that is the least constructed by education, even if it can be explained by an individual's personal history. Why can it not be the vector of an unprecedented human truth and of that part of personal liberty by which individuals free themselves from biological and social constraints in order to incarnate other cultural choices? But it seems that the gay movement is not taking this path. This is probably out of its attachment to its belief system, because the male model is an object of inexhaustible hedonistic worship and still self-sufficient, indeed even more so, in our global societies . . . which remain patriarchal.

NOTES

1. Translated by Michael Sibalis.

2. I am referring in particular to Frédéric Martel, *Le Rose et le noir: Les Homosexuels en France depuis 1968* (Paris, 1996); and Didier Eribon, *Réflexions sur la question gay* (Paris, 1998).

3. Georges Sidéris, "Des folles de Saint-Germain-des-Prés au 'Fléau social': Le Discours homophile contre l'efféminement dans les années 1950: Une Expression de la haine de soi," in *La Haine de soi*, ed. Esther Benbassa and Jean-Christophe Attias (Brussels, 2000), 121-42.

4. René Girard, *Des choses cachées depuis la fondation du monde* (Paris, 1978).

5. Guy Hocquenghem, Aux pédérastes incompréhensibles," *Partisans* 66-7 (1972): 155-6.

6. Françoise d'Eaubonne, "Le FHAR, origines et illustrations," and Alain Prique, L'Herbe folle de mai 68," *La Revue h* 2 (1966): 18-33.

7. Hocquenghem, "Aux pédérastes,"151.

8. "Partisans et adversaires de l'avortement se sont affrontés lors de la réunion du mouvement 'Laissez-les vivre,' " *Le Monde*, 8 March 1971.

9. *Tout*, 23 April 1971. A biweekly produced by the Maoist group "Long Live the Revolution," to which many militants of the MLF and FHAR (including Guy Hocquenghem) belonged, *Tout* played an important role in the origins of FHAR, especially with its twelfth issue, which sold fifty thousand copies and was seized by the authorities for "offending good morals and public morality."

10. Marie-Jo Bonnet, "De l'émancipation amoureuse des femmes dans la Cité: Lesbiennes et féministes au XXe siècle," *Les Temps Modernes* 598 (1998): 85-112.

11. *Des lesbiennes du F.H.A.R.* (mimeographed tract, 1971), from my personal archives.

12. "Réponse des lesbiennes à leurs frères homosexuels," FHAR, *Rapport contre la normalité* (Paris, 1971), 81.

13. "Pleasure cannot be a value in itself given that it is the expression of economic, social, and cultural structures. There can perfectly well be pleasure in completely sado-masochistic relations. This is essentially the sort of pleasure that women have experienced until now. Men and women, being alienated, have at the present only an alienated conception of pleasure. We have to find new forms of pleasure." "Votre révolution sexuelle n'est pas la nôtre," *Tout* 15 (30 June 1971).

14. "Réponse au texte des femmes," *Tout* 16 (July 1971). The latter text was written by Guy Hocquenghem. The practice of publishing anonymous texts at this time came from the MLF; it was not a refusal to take responsibility for one's words. As a historian, I indicate whenever possible the authors of anonymous texts.

15. "Réponse des lesbiennes," 80.

16. Hocquenghem, "Aux pédérastes," 156.

17. Ibid., 157: "If there exists an anti-humanist movement, it is this one, in which the sex machine, the plugged-in [sexual] organs occupy almost all the expressed desire. We are machines for producing pleasure."

18. Bonnet, "De l'émancipation," 104.

19. Marianne Schulz, "Chronologie du débat en France," *Esprit* 236 (1997): 97.

20. *En avant toutes: Les Assises nationales pour les Droits des Femmes* (Paris, 1998).

21. *Assemblée nationale: Contrat d'Union Civile et Sociale (CUCS), projet de loi No. 88, déposé le 23 juillet 1997; Assemblée nationale: Contrat d'Union Sociale (CUS), projet de loi No. 94, déposé le 5 septembre 1997.*

22. Elisabeth Badinter, *L'Un est l'autre* (Paris, 1986), 11.

23. Schulz, "Reconnaissance juridique de l'homosexualité: Quels enjeux pour les femmes?" in *Lien sexuel, lien social: Sexualité et reconnaissance juridique, supplement to Bulletin de l'ANEF* 29 (1999): 9-26.

24. Press communiqué, 8 September 1998.

25. Bonnet, "La Liberté sexuelle des femmes en question à Pékin," in *En avant toutes*, 263; and Florence Beaugé, "L'ONU et la cause des femmes," *Le Monde*, 23 June 2000, 17.

26. Press communiqué, May 1998.

27. Press communiqué, April 1999.

28. Rémy Libchaber, "Les Forces créatrices du droit . . . à propos des projets de contrats d'union entre concubins," *Revue trimestrielle de droit civil* 1 (1998): 226.

29. *Le Monde*, 26 June 1999.

30. Françoise Héritier, *Masculin, féminin* (Paris, 1996), 28.

31. See also Anne-Françoise Lefebvre and Nathalie Rubel, "Une Lesbian and Gay Pride peut-elle être lesbienne," *Ex-Aequo*, 10 (September 1997): 35.

32. Nicole Sirejean, "La Fierté homosexuelle à Marseille, ou petite chronique sur la classe des femmes et la classe des hommes," *Lesbia Magazine* 162 (1997): 10.

33. By way of comparison, the National Foundation for the Rights of Women, which brought together more than two thousand women and several men at Saint-Denis on 15-16 March 1997, was organized with a total budget of 451,500 francs without the least subsidy, and the organizers made a profit of 65,000 francs: two evolving worlds, two ways of managing money and human resources.

34. Jacques Ars, *Petits réflexions d'une vieille militante historique sur l'évolution des Lesbian and Gay Pride* (Rennes, 1997).

Contributors

Robert Aldrich, Professor of Economic History at the University of Sydney, has published many books about modern French economic and imperial history. He is the author of *The Seduction of the Mediterranean: Writing, Art, and Homosexual Fantasy* and coeditor (with Garry Wotherspoon) of two collections of articles about Australian gay culture.

Olivier Blanc, independent scholar, has published many books about eighteenth-century French history, including, most recently, *Les Libertines: Plaisir et liberté au temps des lumières*. His next book, *L'Amour au temps des lumières*, is forthcoming from Perrin in 2001.

Marie-Jo Bonnet, independent scholar, received her doctorate in history from the University of Paris-VII. She has published *Les Relations amoureuses entre les femmes du XVIe au XXe siècle* and *Les Deux amies: Essais sur le couple de femmes dans l'art*. Her guide to female artists in French museums will appear in 2001.

Leslie Choquette, L'Institut français Professor of Francophone Cultures and Director of the French Institute at Assumption College, is the author of *Frenchmen into Peasants: Modernity and Tradition in the Peopling of French Canada*, published by Harvard University Press.

Nicholas Dobelbower is a doctoral candidate at Duke University, where he is writing his dissertation on "The Criminal Type: The Articulation of Criminality and Sexuality in Nineteenth-Century France." He has published articles on the Dreyfus affair and on nineteenth-century French medical case histories and autobiographical texts addressing homosexuality.

Leonard Hinds, Assistant Professor of French Literature at Indiana University, received his BA from the University of Michigan and his PhD from Emory University. He has published articles on the early modern French novel and on libertine poetry. He is currently working on a critical edition of the experimental novel *Le Parasite Mormon.*

Olivier Jablonski, independent scholar, wrote his DEA (Diplôme d'études approfondies) thesis on criticism of the homosexual cinema in the review *Arcadie* and has published several articles on the European gay press.

Susan Lanser is Professor of Comparative Literature and English and Affiliate Professor of Women's Studies and of French at the University of Maryland. She is the author of *The Narrative Act* and *Fictions of Authority* and coeditor of *Women Critics, 1660-1820* and Helen Maria Williams's *Letters Written in France.* She is currently working on a book on "Sapphic Subjects and the Engendering of the Enlightenment."

Jean Le Bitoux, journalist and gay militant since 1971, has two books forthcoming: *Les Oubliés de la mémoire: De la persécution des homosexuels en Europe au temps du nazisme* (2001) and *Des citoyens de seconde zone: Trente ans d'émancipation homosexuelle en France* (2002).

Jeffrey Merrick, Professor of History at the University of Wisconsin-Milwaukee, is the author of *The Desacralization of the French Monarchy in the Eighteenth Century* and coeditor (with Bryant T. Ragan, Jr.) of *Homosexuality in Modern France* and *Homosexuality in Early Modern France,* both published by Oxford University Press.

William A. Peniston, Librarian at the Newark Museum, received his PhD in French History from the University of Rochester and has written several essays and articles on the male homosexual subculture of nineteenth-century Paris.

David Michael Robinson, Assistant Professor of English at the University of Arizona, teaches eighteenth-century literature and gay and lesbian studies. He has published articles on male friendship in Samuel Richardson's novels, seventeenth-century dramatizations of the Ovidian story of Iphis and Ianthe, and both real and fictional early eighteenth-century lesbians.

Marc D. Schachter received his doctorate in the Department of Literature at the University of California-Santa Cruz. He has published on Montaigne, Ariosto, and Spenser and is currently working on a book on the concept of voluntary servitude in classical antiquity and the Renaissance.

Lewis C. Seifert, Associate Professor of French Studies at Brown University, is the author of *Fairy Tales, Sexuality, and Gender in France, 1690-1715: Nostalgic Utopias* and is currently working on a study of masculinity and civility in early modern France.

Michael Sibalis, Associate Professor of History at Wilfrid Laurier University, has published numerous essays and articles on the nineteenth-century French labor movement, the police state of Napoleon I, and the history of homosexuality in France.

Georges Sidéris currently holds a two-year position with the CRNS (Conseil national de la recherche scientifique) and is working on his doctoral dissertation in history on Eunuchs and Power in Byzantium.

Michael L. Wilson, Associate Professor of History and Humanities and Associate Dean for Graduate Studies at the University of Texas-Dallas, has published articles on Henry James, French bohemianism, and the Paris World's Fair of 1900.

Index

The Pursuit of Sodomy: Male Homosexuality in Renaissance and Enlightenment Europe, edited by Kent Gerard, PhD, and Gert Hekma, PhD (Vol. 16, No. 1/2, 1989). *"Presenting a wealth of information in a compact form, this book should be welcomed by anyone with an interest in this period in European history or in the precursors to modern concepts of homosexuality." (The Canadian Journal of Human Sexuality)*

Psychopathology and Psychotherapy in Homosexuality, edited by Michael W. Ross, PhD (Vol. 15, No. 1/2, 1988). *"One of the more objective, scientific collections of articles concerning the mental health of gays and lesbians. . . . Extraordinarily thoughtful. . . . New thoughts about treatments. Vital viewpoints." (The Book Reader)*

Psychotherapy with Homosexual Men and Women: Integrated Identity Approaches for Clinical Practice, edited by Eli Coleman, PhD (Vol. 14, No. 1/2, 1987). *"An invaluable tool. . . . This is an extremely useful book for the clinician seeking better ways to understand gay and lesbian patients." (Hospital and Community Psychiatry)*

Interdisciplinary Research on Homosexuality in The Netherlands, edited by A. X. van Naerssen, PhD (Vol. 13, No. 2/3, 1987). *"Valuable not just for its insightful analysis of the evolution of gay rights in The Netherlands, but also for the lessons that can be extracted by our own society from the Dutch tradition of tolerance for homosexuals." (The San Francisco Chronicle)*

Historical, Literary, and Erotic Aspects of Lesbianism, edited by Monica Kehoe, PhD (Vol. 12, No. 3/4, 1986). *"Fascinating . . . Even though this entire volume is serious scholarship penned by degreed writers, most of it is vital, accessible, and thoroughly readable even to the casual student of lesbian history." (Lambda Rising)*

Anthropology and Homosexual Behavior, edited by Evelyn Blackwood, PhD (cand.) (Vol. 11, No. 3/4, 1986). *"A fascinating account of homosexuality during various historical periods and in non-Western cultures." (SIECUS Report)*

Bisexualities: Theory and Research, edited by Fritz Klein, MD, and Timothy J. Wolf, PhD (Vol. 11, No. 1/2, 1985). *"The editors have brought together a formidable array of new data challenging old stereotypes about a very important human phenomenon . . . A milestone in furthering our knowledge about sexual orientation." (David P. McWhirter, Co-author, The Male Couple)*

Homophobia: An Overview, edited by John P. De Cecco, PhD (Vol. 10, No. 1/2, 1984). *"Breaks ground in helping to make the study of homophobia a science." (Contemporary Psychiatry)*

Bisexual and Homosexual Identities: Critical Clinical Issues, edited by John P. De Cecco, PhD (Vol. 9, No. 4, 1985). *Leading experts provide valuable insights into sexual identity within a clinical context-broadly defined to include depth psychology, diagnostic classification, therapy, and psychomedical research on the hormonal basis of homosexuality.*

Bisexual and Homosexual Identities: Critical Theoretical Issues, edited by John P. De Cecco, PhD, and Michael G. Shively, MA (Vol. 9, No. 2/3, 1984). *"A valuable book . . . The careful scholarship, analytic rigor, and lucid exposition of virtually all of these essays make them thought-provoking and worth more than one reading." (Sex Roles, A Journal of Research)*

Homosexuality and Social Sex Roles, edited by Michael W. Ross, PhD (Vol. 9, No. 1, 1983). *"For a comprehensive review of the literature in this domain, exposure to some interesting methodological models, and a glance at 'older' theories undergoing contemporary scrutiny, I recommend this book." (Journal of Sex Education & Therapy)*

Literary Visions of Homosexuality, edited by Stuart Kellogg, PhD (Vol. 8, No. 3/4, 1985). *"An important book. Gay sensibility has never been given such a boost." (The Advocate)*

Alcoholism and Homosexuality, edited by Thomas O. Ziebold, PhD, and John E. Mongeon (Vol. 7, No. 4, 1985). *"A landmark in the fields of both alcoholism and homosexuality . . . a very lush work of high caliber." (The Journal of Sex Research)*

Homosexuality and Psychotherapy: A Practitioner's Handbook of Affirmative Models, edited by John C. Gonsiorek, PhD (Vol. 7, No. 2/3, 1985). *"A book that seeks to create affirmative psychotherapeutic models. . . . To say this book is needed by all doing therapy with gay or lesbian clients is an understatement." (The Advocate)*

Nature and Causes of Homosexuality: A Philosophic and Scientific Inquiry, edited by Noretta Koertge, PhD (Vol. 6, No. 4, 1982). *"An interesting, thought-provoking book, well worth reading as a corrective to much of the research literature on homosexuality." (Australian Journal of Sex, Marriage & Family)*

Historical Perspectives on Homosexuality, edited by Salvatore J. Licata, PhD, and Robert P. Petersen, PhD (cand.) (Vol. 6, No. 1/2, 1986). *"Scholarly and excellent. Its authority is impeccable, and its treatment of this neglected area exemplary." (Choice)*

Homosexuality and the Law, edited by Donald C. Knutson, PhD (Vol. 5, No. 1/2, 1979). *A comprehensive analysis of current legal issues and court decisions relevant to male and female homosexuality.*